The Mother–Infant Interaction Picture Book

The Mother–Infant Interaction Picture Book

Origins of Attachment

Beatrice Beebe, PhD

Phyllis Cohen, PhD

Frank Lachmann, PhD

With Illustrations by Dillon Yothers

W. W. Norton
Independent Publishers since 1923
New York • London

Printed in the United States of America
First Edition

For information about special discounts for bulk purchases, please contact
W. W. Norton Special Sales at specialsales@wwnorton.com or 800-233-4830

Manufacturing by RR Donnelley Willard
Book design by Bytheway Publishing Services
Production manager: Chris Critelli

Library of Congress Cataloging-in-Publication Data

Names: Beebe,
Beatrice, 1946- author. | Cohen, Phyllis (Psychotherapy trainer), author. | Lachmann, Frank M.,
author. Title: The mother-infant interaction picture book : origins of attachment / Beatrice Beebe,
Phyllis Cohen, Frank Lachmann.
Description: First edition. | New York : W.W. Norton & Company, 2016. | Series: A Norton professional book |
Includes bibliographical references and index.
Identifiers: LCCN 2015049559 |
ISBN 9780393707922 (hardcover)
Subjects: LCSH: Attachment behavior in children. | Infants—Care—Psychological aspects. |
Mother and infant—Psychological aspects. | Nonverbal communication in infants.
Classification: LCC RJ507.A77 B4327 2016 | DDC 155.42/2241—dc23 LC
record available at http://lccn.loc.gov/2015049559

W. W. Norton & Company, Inc., 500 Fifth Avenue, New York, N.Y. 10110
www.wwnorton.com
W. W. Norton & Company Ltd., Castle House, 75/76 Wells Street, London W1T 3QT

1 2 3 4 5 6 7 8 9 0

This book is dedicated to

Edward McCrorie

Ted Cohen

Annette Lachmann

Contents

Authors' Note

In this book we illustrate mother–infant face-to-face interactions filmed when the infants were four months old. The illustrations are taken from our research in which mother–infant interaction patterns at four months predicted subsequent infant attachment patterns at twelve months. Four months is an important moment to study because patterns of mother–infant interaction have already consolidated sufficiently that they predict developmental outcomes. We present ten illustrative sequences of interactions at four months, which predicted secure infant attachment at twelve months, as well as insecure attachment. Our research uses video microanalysis, which captures moment-to-moment sequences of interactions. This process is like a *social microscope,* enabling us to see subtle details of interactions that are too rapid and complex to grasp in real time with the naked eye. These moment-to-moment sequences teach us to see how both infant and mother affect each other. We see that infants at four months are already extraordinarily communicative and responsive to the movements and emotions of the partner. We want to preserve the confidentiality of the families who participated in this research. We asked an artist, Dillon Yothers, to draw the interaction sequences, based on the actual video frames. The drawings reveal the emotions, but conceal the identities of the mothers and infants. In this book we describe the moment-to-moment sequences of mother and infant behaviors. We translate the infant's nonverbal language, as well as that of the mother, into words. Although the research was based on infants interacting with their mothers, everything in this book is just as relevant to fathers, as well as any primary caregiver.

Acknowledgments

We have many people to thank. First we are grateful to the mothers and infants who so generously participated in this research. Beatrice Beebe thanks New York State Psychiatric Institute, where the research was conducted and the statistical team there who made our research possible: Patricia Cohen, Karen Buck, Henian Chen, Howard Andrews, and Sanghan Lee. We thank Christina Hoven, George Musa, Michael Myers, Martha Welch, and Brad Peterson for their generous contributions to the research. We thank Julie Herbstman, Amy Margolis, Frances Champagne, and Virginia Rauh for their support of our research.

We thank Dillon Yothers, our illustrator, who worked so patiently in the many revisions of the drawings that were necessary to create adequate disguises of the mothers and infants. We thank Jeffrey Cohn, our "facial expression expert," who helped us create and evaluate the disguises for all our drawings.

We thank the psychoanalytic communities who have encouraged our work over many decades: the New York University Postdoctoral Program in Psychotherapy and Psychoanalysis (Lachmann, Cohen, Beebe), the Institute for the Psychoanalytic Study of Subjectivity (Lachmann, Beebe), the Columbia Psychoanalytic Center (Beebe), the Postgraduate Center (Lachmann), and the New York Institute for Psychotherapy Training in Infancy, Childhood, and Adolescence (Cohen).

The work of many people informed this book. In particular, we wish to acknowledge the contributions of Daniel Stern and Joseph Jaffe, in memoriam; Stanley Feldstein, Cynthia Crown, and Michael Jasnow who contributed to the optimal midrange model of vocal rhythm coordination; Edward Tronick and his disruption (mismatch) and repair model; Miriam and Howard Steele, collaborators of Beatrice Beebe; and Karlen Lyons-Ruth, Jude Cassidy, Mary Sue Moore, and Marinus van IJzendoorn who have helped us understand the origins of attachment, particularly disorganized attachment.

We thank our in-house video team who assembled the video materials for this book and worked on the layouts: Annee Ackerman, Tina Lee, Molly Rappaport, Kristen Kim, Mirella Brussani, Daniel Friedman, and Danny Sims. We thank Kari Gray and Jennifer Lyne, former filmmakers turning psychologists, for creating the original frame-by-frame illustrations that informed these drawings.

We thank the editors of the text: Miriam Steele, Adrianne Lange, Lin Reicher, Sarah Hahn-Burke, Sohye Kim, Andrea Remez, Hope Igleheart, Priscilla Lincoln, Francoise Jaffe, Elizabeth Cramer, Lisa Piazza, and Sara Markese. We thank everyone who helped us to critique the disguises of the drawings and to interpret the emotions in the drawings: Beatrice Beebe's PhD dissertation seminar and psychoanalytic seminars: 8-Lecture A, 8-Lecture B, 8-Lecture C, and the Monday afternoon study group.

As this book goes to press, we thank the current research assistants in the Beebe lab who make everything possible. We thank Molly Rappaport, the in-house editor of the text. We thank Hope Igleheart, Sarah Berkson, Natalie Buchinsky, Dhru Desai, Allison Dorf, Annie Egleson, Julie Ewing, Anielle Fredman, Josef Kala, Sarah Kalmenson-Pinson, Killian Folse, Kristen Kim, Tina Lee, Christhin Monte, Mariam Rahman, Ann Rakoff, Nataliya Rubinchik, Steph Scrofani, Conor Shanahan, Anna-Lee Stafford, Andrea Tocci, Danruo Zhong, and Dafne Milne, our postdoctoral fellow. We thank John Burke and William Hohauser of ESPY TV for their video expertise and their dedication to our lab and our research over the past three decades.

This work was partially supported by grants from National Institute of Mental Health RO1 MH56130, the Bernard and Esther Besner Infant Research Fund, the Fund for Psychoanalytic Research of the American Psychoanalytic Association, the Kohler Stiftung, the Edward Aldwell Fund, and the Los Angeles Fund for Infant Research and Psychoanalysis.

We thank Annee Ackerman for allowing us to use her video material in the DVD in the back jacket of the book, and on the front cover. We thank Karen Dougherty, the filmmaker who created this DVD, for her outstanding work; and Dorothy Engelman, Richard Quinlan, and Q Media Solutions, for their generous contributions to the DVD. We thank Keren Amiran for her generous help in getting this DVD started.

We thank Deborah Malmud of W. W. Norton and her staff for their outstanding editorship of this book.

Introduction: The Role of Mother–Infant Face-to-Face Communication in the Development of Infant Secure and Insecure Attachment Patterns

We all enjoy watching infants and mothers as they play together. But what do we see? This book illustrates in drawings various patterns of communication between mothers and infants when the infants are four months old. These patterns were revealed by our research on the origins of infant attachment at one year. You see mother–infant communication patterns at four months that predicted secure as well as insecure infant attachment patterns at one year.

In our research, we study videotaped mother–infant interactions. We examine the videotapes moment to moment, a *microanalysis*. Microanalysis allows us to see details of parent–infant communication patterns that are too rapid and complex to grasp with the naked eye in real time. Microanalysis thus acts like a *social microscope.* It enables us to see how both the infant and parent affect each other, from moment to moment.

Although current research has many descriptions of mother–infant interaction, this book shows a different level of detail regarding how infants and parents respond to each other. As we study the drawings of second-by-second sequences of interactions in Part II of this book, you see this level of minute detail.

You see how the infants' and parents' faces open and widen into the most glorious smiles. But you also see how the infants' and parents' faces become sober, sad, distressed, averted, or withdrawn. You see sharp bodily aversions, a sudden cry face, or the reaction of going limp. You see how each partner affects the other, from one moment to the next. This book takes you on a journey in which you will be amazed at what you see.

Much of our communication occurs out of our awareness. It is difficult for anyone to be aware of his or her own nonverbal communication. But when we can observe it, for example with the help of a video, we can see in more detail the ways that we communicate. By studying the moment-to-moment video sequences of mothers and infants as they interact face-to-face, the subtleties of communication become visible. The split-second rapidity of these exchanges becomes immediately apparent. Much of this is missed in real time.

Infants begin life as social creatures. By four months, the age of the infants in this book, infants are extraordinarily communicative. They perceive and respond to every little shift in the parent's facial and vocal emotion, touch quality, and orientation. Parents intuitively know this, and they also respond to these infant behaviors, out of awareness. In the last half century, science has documented enormous subtlety and complexity in the communication patterns between infants and parents.

Moreover, these parent–infant communication patterns predict infant attachment patterns at one year, a key milestone in the infant's development. In our laboratory, mothers and infants first come when the infants are four months old. They are videotaped during face-to-face play. Then, at 12 months, mothers and infants take part in the Ainsworth separation-reunion paradigm (Ainsworth, Blehar, Waters, & Wall, 1978). In this attachment assessment, mother and infant go through periods of free play, separations, and reunions. Based on the extent to which the infant uses the parent as a secure base from which to explore, and as a safe haven when distressed, infants can be classified as having secure or insecure attachment patterns. An infant's attachment pattern at one year predicts many aspects of the child's development, including school achievement, social engagement, and emotional well-being (Sroufe, Egeland, Carlson, & Collins, 2005a). Remarkably, an infant's attachment status at one year also predicts young adult attachment status (Lyons-Ruth & Jacobvitz, 2008; Main, Hesse, & Kaplan, 2005; Sroufe, Egeland, Carlson, & Collins, 2005b)

WHY FOUR MONTHS

The research we describe examines mother–infant communication when infants are four months old. By three to four months, the infant's social capacity flowers. Although infants begin to make facial expressions before they are born, the full display of facial expression emerges only gradually from two to four months. When the infants are four months old, we invite mothers and infants to our laboratory to play together. We film them as they interact face-to-face. The infant is in an infant seat, and the mother is seated opposite. The mother is instructed to play with her infant as she would at home, but without toys. One camera is focused on the mother's face and hands, and one camera on the infant's face and hands. The two cameras generate a split-screen view, so that both partners can be seen at the same time. The mother and the infant are left alone in the filming chamber to play for five to ten minutes.

WHY FACE-TO-FACE COMMUNICATION

Why is face-to-face communication so important? Face-to-face communication in the early months of life sets the trajectory for patterns of relatedness and intimacy over the lifetime. Face-to-face communication elicits the infant's most advanced communication capacities. Its importance for social and cognitive development is widely recognized (Beebe & Lachmann, 2002, 2013; Cohn, Campbell, Matias, & Hopkins, 1990; Feldman, 2007; Field, 1995; Fogel, 1992; Jaffe, Beebe, Feldstein, Crown, & Jasnow, 2001; Lester, Hoffman, & Brazelton, 1985; Lewis & Feiring, 1989; Leyendecker, Lamb, Fracasso, Scholmerich, & Larson, 1997; Malatesta, Culver, Tesman, & Shepard, 1989; Martin, 1981; Messinger, 2002; Stern, 1985, 1995; Tronick, 1989, 2007).

THE KEY ROLE OF THE FACE-TO-FACE INTERACTION

An ongoing program of research in the lab of one of us (Beatrice Beebe) has examined maternal self-report depression and anxiety at six weeks and four months, mother–infant face-to-face interaction at four months, and infant attachment at twelve months, in a large community sample of families (Beebe et al., 2008, 2010, 2011). Maternal depression and anxiety at infant age six weeks or four months did robustly affect patterns of mother–infant self-regulation and interactive regulation at four months. But maternal depression at infant age six weeks or four months did not predict infant attachment outcomes at one year. Instead, it was the quality of the four-month mother–infant face-to-face interaction itself that predicted infant attachment outcomes (Beebe et al., 2010).

The implication is that, in a community sample, distressed maternal states of mind at six weeks or four months do not necessarily lead to insecure infant attachment outcomes, unless there is also difficulty in the patterns of face-to-face interaction itself. This work provides a further rationale for providing therapeutic support for mothers and infants when mothers are distressed. This support may then prevent later insecure infant attachment outcomes. An example of such therapeutic support can be found in a project for mothers who were pregnant and widowed on September 11 and their infants and young children (Beebe, Cohen, Sossin, & Markese, 2012).

In this book, our goal is to use drawings of film frames of mother–infant face-to-face interaction as a way of learning to see the subtlety and complexity of each partner's nonverbal language. We carefully selected brief, meaningful sequences between mothers and their infants. The drawings move slowly, moment-by-moment, through the stories of the interactions. This method allows the viewer to see and make conscious sense of nonverbal information that is typically out of awareness, and too rapid and subtle to observe in real time.

WHY MICROANALYSIS

Microanalysis reveals subtle, split-second events that are often too subtle to see with the naked eye in real time. It is this subterranean level of communication that our research reveals. We call it a social microscope. By investigating this level of detail, we were able to generate new ways of understanding communication patterns in infancy that predict secure and insecure attachment patterns at one year.

These moment-to-moment processes are rapid, subtle, co-created by both mother and infant, and generally out of awareness. Nevertheless, they continue to have an important effect on how we act and feel, from infancy to adulthood (Beebe & Lachmann, 2013; Grossman, Grossman, Winter, & Zimmerman, 2002).

THE POWER OF BRIEF SEGMENTS OF COMMUNICATION BEHAVIOR

We predicted infant attachment at one year from a very brief segment of mother–infant interaction (two and a half minutes; Beebe et al., 2010). How was this possible? Such a small segment of mother–infant interaction can reveal a relatively consistent pattern that is repeated in subsequent mother–infant interactions. Research has shown that patterns of face-to-face mother–infant interaction remain consistent (predictable) across weeks and months (Cohn & Tronick, 1989; Moore, Cohn, & Campbell, 2001; Weinberg & Tronick, 1998; Zelner, Beebe, & Jaffe, 1982).

Moreover, other research on adults compared many studies with varying lengths of videotaped material to determine the accuracy of predictions from brief observations of behavior (Ambady & Rosenthal, 1992). Judgments from very brief segments of behavior (under one half minute) were found to be as accurate as judgments from longer segments (up to five minutes), and longer segments did not increase accuracy. For example, a three-minute segment of videotaped conversation between a married couple is sufficient to predict the success of the marriage 15 years later (Carrere & Gottman, 1999).

LEARNING TO LOOK, LEARNING TO SEE

Our research informs the way we look. It provides an essential guide with which to view the videotaped interactions. We identified particular mother–infant pairs who illustrated specific findings. For example, we located pairs who illustrated *facial mirroring,* a process in which each partner becomes more and more positive in facial affect, culminating in huge open-mouth smiles. This pattern predicted secure infant attachment. And we located pairs who illustrated patterns of infant distress and maternal emotional withdrawal. In this pattern, as the infant becomes more and more distressed, the mother has more and more difficulty joining the infant's distress through empathic faces and sounds. This pattern predicted insecure-disorganized infant attachment.

By creating moment-to-moment analyses of the videotapes, we were able to study the various patterns to see how they unfolded. This visual grounding gives our work a visceral, intuitive, and immediate form of comprehension. Based on this research, we selected ten patterns of mother–infant communication for this book. For each pattern that we illustrate, we know the attachment outcome at 12 months, secure or various patterns of insecure attachment.

CONTINUITY AND TRANSFORMATION IN DEVELOPMENT

We offer a caveat. Although four-month interactions do predict social and cognitive outcomes, many transformations along the way are also possible. Development is a progressive and dynamic process that is not set in stone at any point in time. Research has documented both continuities and transformations in development. Moreover, most of the research is designed to predict outcomes across a group, rather than within the individual. Any one individual may not conform to the findings of the group (see Beebe & Lachmann, 2013).

WATCH OUR DVD FIRST

We want to prepare you to be able to look through our eyes and see what we see as we view the drawings. The best way to understand the drawings in this book is from a hands-on perspective. In this spirit, we invite you to join us in watching an original film, which can be found on the DVD located in a sleeve at the back of this book. The film shows a mother and infant at three and a half months playing face-to-face, while the infant is in an infant seat. This mother has given us permission to show the original film; it is not disguised. The mother was instructed to play with the infant as she would at home, but without toys. Two cameras were used: one filmed the mother, and one the infant. As you look at the film, you see mother and infant side-by-side, in a split-screen view; but they are actually positioned sitting face-to-face.

After you view the film in real time, we also show in the DVD how we look at this film moment to moment. Here you see that we are always looking for movement from one moment to the next. The DVD illustrates this way of looking. When you study the drawings in this book, it is important to continue this method of looking across two seconds, that is, across two drawings. Because the drawings are still, movement is lost. But you can train your eye to recreate the movement seen in the film version by always examining a sequence of two drawings at a time, looking back and forth between them, and trying to see what changes from one drawing to the next. For example, you may notice a change in the direction of looking, at or away from the partner; in the head orientation, vis-à-vis the partner or averted; or in the facial expression of either or both partners.

ALL OUR DRAWINGS ARE DISGUISED

We want to protect the confidentiality of all the families in our research. We enlisted a digital illustrator to draw each frame. He had the important and difficult task of disguising the identities of the mothers and infants while preserving their emotions, as reflected in their eyes, facial expressions, head orientations, and hands.

Each chapter contains a sequence of drawings illustrating a particular mother–infant interaction pattern, such as for example facial mirroring. Each drawing is labeled with a frame number. Under each drawing, we describe in words what we see, so that you can see what we see. We also provide an "Illustrated Glossary of Terms" at the end of Chapter 3.

SO, LET'S BEGIN BY WATCHING THE DVD

The DVD is located in the back of book.

PART I

How Does Mother–Infant Face-To-Face Communication Work?

This book illustrates research findings on the ways that mother–infant interactions at four months set the stage for secure and insecure attachment patterns at one year. Our 84 mother–infant pairs from a low-risk community sample of healthy firstborn infants (Beebe et al., 2010). The mother–infant interaction patterns that illustrate the research findings are presented as drawings of video frames.

This research integrated two different research methods. The first is mother–infant face-to-face interaction at four months. Mother–infant face-to-face interaction is organized around play, with no other goal than mutual enjoyment (Stern, 1985). The second is the assessment of secure and insecure infant attachment patterns at one year using the strange situation paradigm (Ainsworth et al., 1978). This paradigm examines how infants and mothers reunite following a brief separation.

For this book, we selected ten patterns of mother–infant interaction at four months to illustrate with drawings. The drawings are presented in Part II of the book. For each pattern, we know from the research whether that infant turned out to be securely or insecurely attached at one year. Roughly half the drawings illustrate secure infant attachment outcomes, and half insecure attachment outcomes. Thus for each set of drawings, we identify the four-month interaction pattern as one that predicts secure attachment, *future secure,* or one that predicts insecure attachment, *future insecure.*

The following three chapters help you to understand how mother–infant face-to-face communication works.

In Chapter 1, we introduce you to mother–infant face-to-face communication. In Chapter 2, we take you into our laboratory to show you how we study mothers and infants and how we code their nonverbal, *action-dialogue language.* Examples of our coding are provided with several illustrations. In Chapter 3, we discuss ways in which the action-dialogue language is used to create patterns of communication that shape development. At the end of the chapter, we provide a glossary of our terms, each illustrated with a drawing. In the following pages, for ease of comprehension, we refer to the mother as "she" and the infant as "he."

CHAPTER 1

Mother–Infant Face-to-Face Communication at Infant Age Four Months

FOUR-MONTH FACE-TO-FACE COMMUNICATION

Face-to-face communication in the early months of life sets the trajectory for patterns of relatedness as the infant develops over the lifetime (Beebe, Igleheart et al., 2015; Grossman et al., 2002; Lyons-Ruth, 2008; Lyons-Ruth & Jacobvitz, 2008; Main et al., 2005; Sroufe et al., 2005a, 2005b). Face-to-face communication elicits the infant's most advanced communication capacities. Its importance for social and cognitive development is widely recognized (Beebe & Lachmann, 2002; Feldman, 2007; Field, 1995; Fogel, 1992; Jaffe et al., 2001; Malatesta et al., 1989; Messinger, 2002; Stern, 1985, 1995; Tronick 1989, 2007). We invite mothers and infants to participate in the research when infants are four months old, when social development is flowering. We film them as they interact face-to-face. The mother and the infant are left alone in the filming chamber to play for five to ten minutes.

Before the filming, we make sure the infant and mother are comfortable. The infant is fed, diapered, and napped if necessary. We bring the mother and infant into the filming chamber only when the mother feels the infant is ready. If the infant is sick, we request the mother and infant to return another day.

ATTACHMENT ASSESSED AT ONE YEAR

The security or insecurity of infant attachment at one year is a key milestone in the infant's development, and it is also centrally important in the formation of the person (Sroufe, 2005). It is associated with many critical aspects of development across the life span, such as social relatedness, arousal modulation, emotional regulation, and curiosity, as well as attachment patterns and social adjustment in adulthood (Sroufe, 2005; Sroufe et al., 2005a, 2005b).

Secure attachment sets a trajectory in development that is likely to be protective. Sroufe (1983, 2005) and colleagues (Sroufe et al., 2005a, 2005b) suggest that secure attachment in infancy generates more positive expectations concerning self and others and more successful close relationships. It sets a path toward more flexibility and resilience and less vulnerability to life's challenges and stresses.

Infant attachment can be assessed once the infant is one year of age and able to walk or at least to crawl. It is assessed using the strange situation paradigm. In this assessment, mothers and infants are led through sequences of play, separation, and reunion (Ainsworth et al., 1978). Separations and reunions between infant and mother are a common occurrence in everyday life once the infant is this age. The assessment taps into how the infant manages the separation from his mother and the process of reunion between mother and infant (Cassidy, 1994; Sroufe et al. 2005a, 2005b; Steele & Steele, 2008).

Infants can be classified as having either secure or insecure patterns of attachment, using the coding criteria of the strange situation paradigm. Insecure patterns vary and are labeled avoidant, resistant, and disorganized. The attachment classification is based on the extent to which the infant uses the parent as a safe haven or touchpoint after the distress of the separation. For example, does the infant cuddle into the mother's body? The attachment classification is also based on the degree to which the infant can use the mother as a secure base from which to return to playing and exploring.

In the reunion episodes, the *secure* infant can easily be comforted. He uses the mother as a secure base and then returns to play. The *avoidant* infant shows little distress at separation, avoids the mother at reunion, and continues to play on his own. The *resistant* infant is very distressed at separation, but cannot be comforted by the mother's return and does not easily return to play. In the general population, approximately 55 percent to 65 percent of infants are classified as secure attachment, 15 percent as avoidant attachment, and 10 percent as resistant attachment (van IJzendoorn, Goldberg, Kroonenberg, & Frenkel, 1992; van IJzendoorn, Schuengel, & Bakermans-Kranenburg, 1999).

In the reunion episodes, the *disorganized* infant simultaneously approaches and avoids the mother. For example the infant may open the door for her but then sharply ignore her. Disorganized infants may show confusion, apprehension, or momentary freezing. For example, some of these infants may reach their hands out toward the mother as she enters, but at the same time back up. Or the infant may cling to the mother, but cry with his face averted. The mother herself may act frightened or frightening, and typically these mothers have a history of unresolved loss, mourning, or abuse (Lyons-Ruth, Bronfman, & Parsons, 1999; Main & Hesse, 1990). Approximately 15 percent of the general population is classified as disorganized attachment.

Mothers of secure infants have been described as more responsive and sensitive, more consistent and prompt in response to infant distress, more likely to hold their infants, less intrusive, and less tense and irritable. Secure (compared with insecure) infants have been described as more responsive in face-to-face play, better able to elicit responsive caretaking, more positive, more able to express distress, more able to communicate in a variety of ways, and more likely to quiet readily when picked up (Ainsworth et al., 1978; Antonucci & Levitt, 1984; Bates, Maslin, & Frankel, 1985; Belsky,

Rovine, & Taylor, 1984; Blehar, Lieberman, & Ainsworth, 1977; Crockenberg, 1983; De Wolff & van IJzendoorn, 1997; Egeland & Farber, 1984; Grossman, Grossman, Spangler, Suess, & Unzner, 1985; Isabella & Belsky, 1991; Mikaye, Chen, & Campos, 1985; Stayton, Ainsworth, & Main, 1973).

Secure attachment at one year is associated with better peer relations, school performance, and capacity to regulate emotions, as well as fewer adjustment problems in childhood and adolescence (Sroufe, 1983). Disorganized attachment is associated in childhood with oppositional, hostile-aggressive, fearful behavior, low self-esteem, and cognitive difficulties (Jacobsen, Edelstein, & Hofmann, 1994; Lyons-Ruth et al., 1999; Sroufe, 1983). Disorganized attachment at 12 to 18 months predicts more serious psychological problems in childhood and young adulthood (Grossman et al., 2002; Shi, Bureau, Easterbrooks, Zhao, & Lyons-Ruth, 2012; Sroufe et al., 2005a, 2005b). In this book, we have chosen to present four drawing illustrations of the disorganized type because disorganized attachment is the type of insecure attachment that predicts psychological difficulties.

Hesse and Main (2006) suggest that when the infant is developing toward a secure attachment, he does not have to worry about or be preoccupied by the mother's psychology. If the infant is developing toward an insecure attachment, he has to attend to the mother's psychology. Infants who are developing toward insecure-resistant attachment are likely to amp up and clamor for attention. Infants who are developing toward insecure-avoidant attachment are likely to dampen down and not ask for attention. But infants who are developing toward insecure-disorganized attachment are frightened and have no solution. Amping up or dampening down does not work, and the infant has no place to land (Hesse & Main, 2006).

Over 50 studies have shown that the security of the child's attachment to the parent at one year is dependent on the emotional availability and sensitivity of the parent (see De Wolff & van IJzendoorn, 1997 for a review). But few studies have been able to predict disorganized attachment from early mother–infant interactions. Our work is an exception (Beebe et al., 2010; Jaffe et al., 2001).

Based on the research, which is the foundation of this book, we were able to illustrate the details of the four-month origins of disorganized, resistant, and secure attachment (Beebe et al., 2010). Fewer than a dozen studies have used microanalysis of videotape to predict attachment outcomes. It is microanalysis, which operates like a social microscope, that allows us to identify the details of the origins of secure and insecure, especially disorganized, attachment.

A common question about our research concerns our ability to predict attachment outcomes at one year from just two and a half minutes of interaction at four months. Perhaps the infant had a bad day? Perhaps the mother's behavior on that day was not representative of her usual style?

The answer is that, by four to six months, patterns of behavior in mother–infant interaction are becoming organized and predictable. Weinberg (1991) examined the stability of behavior across two play sessions at six and six and a half months for 80 infants. Infant interactive behavior (infant looking at his mother, looking at object, scanning the room, signaling to his mother with vocalization and gesture) and the infant's facial affect (joy, interest, sadness, anger) were coded on a second-by-second basis. Significant session-to-session correlation was found. These findings corroborate session-to-session consistencies reported by other researchers for infants four to six months (Cohn & Tronick, 1989; Tronick, 1989; Zelner, 1982). Session-to-session consistency can be understood as an index of the degree to which behavior is being organized, or the degree to which a way of doing things is emerging that is relatively stable. These findings point to a strong, early organizing process in mother–infant communication.

OUR DRAWINGS ILLUSTRATE THE MOTHER–INFANT ACTION-DIALOGUE LANGUAGE

We want to orient you to our drawings, which are fascinating and complex. It takes keen eyes and lots of patience to identify the subtleties of these rapid, often split-second exchanges. In this chapter, we describe ways of looking at the infants' and mothers' action-dialogue language. How do infants at four months let us know what they feel, what they like and do not like? How do infants show us that they need a break from interacting? How do infants tell us they are sad, surprised, or wary? As mothers interact with their faces and vocalizations, as they lean in or touch, how do infants feel and respond? And reciprocally how do mothers feel and respond?

Usually language refers to words. In a broader understanding of language, it can refer to any systematic means of expression, such as the language of music or dance. We call the infant's communication a language in the same way that we might refer to the language of music. In this process, we introduce descriptions of looking and looking away from the partner, facial expressions, vocalizations, maternal spatial orientation and infant head orientation movements, and varieties of touch, with terms that are likely unfamiliar. We show drawings to illustrate these terms in Chapters 2 and 3, and we provide a glossary of these terms at the end of this chapter.

INFANTS BEGIN LIFE AS SOCIAL CREATURES

Contrary to a popular belief, infants are inherently social from birth. Early social experience is organized in an interactive framework (Beebe & Lachmann, 1988). The infants' perceptual abilities ensure this capacity for seeking out, perceiving, and interacting with social partners from birth (Berlyne, 1966; Brazelton, Koslowski, & Main, 1974; Haith, Hazan, & Goodman, 1988). From birth, infants are capable of coordinating their behaviors with those of the partner (Peery, 1980; Trevarthen, 1979). Thus, all interactions occur in a process of reciprocal, bidirectional adjustments in which each partner coordinates with the other. What emerges is a dyadic process that cannot be described on the basis of either partner alone.

Our view is very different from some current, still prevailing views that the parent's response to the infant organizes the infant's experience. That view emphasizes the parent's influence on the infant, a one-way direction of influence, to the relative exclusion of the child's influence on the parent (Bell, 1968; Lewis & Rosenblum, 1974). Instead, in our view, both infant and parent co-create the nature of the infant's experience, although the parent has the greater range, flexibility, and capacity. Our view is consistent with much current infant research (for example, Feldman, 2007; Messinger, 2002; Tronick, 1989, 2007). Moreover, as we soon discuss, we conceptualize each individual's own contribution to the dyadic cocreation as well. We think of the reciprocal, bidirectional regulation between partners as existing in dynamic relation to the self-regulation of each partner of the dyad (Beebe, Jaffe, & Lachmann, 1992; Beebe & Lachmann, 1994, 2002). We use the term mother–infant *dyad* and mother–infant *pair* interchangeably.

Psychological development occurs through an interaction between the unfolding biological predispositions of the infant and the patterns of interaction between the infant and the parents. But even the unfolding biological predispositions of the infant are interactively shaped by what happens in utero, such as the presence of maternal depression or anxiety, or conditions of stress (Monk, 2001).

What role does the infant play in the reciprocal, bidirectional exchange? In the late 1960s/early 1970s, a body of empirical research emerged that showed us that the social capacities of infants had been greatly underestimated (Ainsworth, 1969; Als, 1977; Brazelton et al., 1974; Fantz, Fagan, & Miranda, 1975; Kessen, Haith, & Salapatek 1970; Lewis & Brooks, 1975; Oster, 1978; Stechler & Carpenter, 1967; Stern, 1974). Stone, Smith, and Murphy (1973) summarized this work as portraying "The competent infant." Until this time, views of early interaction focused on feeding and the management of tension states. This new research emphasized a more active infant who initiates social interaction and play and who has an influential role in the nature of early interactions. The work in this book uses this view of infant capacities. From birth, the infant is inherently organized for active and stimulus-seeking behavior. Newborns show rooting, sucking, molding, and orienting behavior; the ability to scan visually, focus on, and track a moving object, such as the parent's face; the capacity to respond to visual stimuli by widening and brightening their eyes, changes in respiration, and fine nuances of facial expression. Newborns not only seek and initiate social interaction but can also modulate or regulate social stimulation in the face of aversive conditions with self-quieting measures, inhibiting their responsiveness or habituating to a disturbing stimulus. These inherently organized patterns of behavior equip the infant to engage in a primary relatedness with the social partner (Beebe, 1986; Tronick, 1989).

This work on early infant social capacities of the 1960s/1970s set the stage for a burgeoning interest in mother–infant face-to-face communication that continues to the present day. A large body of research has built on this understanding of infant capacities in an effort to identify how these capacities are used in the mother–infant face-to-face exchange by three to four months, when infants' social capacities flower.

INFANTS PERCEIVE CORRESPONDENCES AT BIRTH

As early as 42 minutes after birth, infants can imitate gestures of the experimenter (Meltzoff, 1990). They perceive similarities (correspondences) between their own behaviors and the behaviors they see the experimenter perform, like a mouth opening gesture, or a tongue thrust. The infant watches the experimenter perform a gesture for a minute, while the infant has a pacifier in his mouth. Then the pacifier is removed. The experimenter assumes a neutral pose. Slowly, the infant's own face matches more and more closely the facial movement of the experimenter, a gradual imitation of what he saw. Because it is not possible to imitate with the pacifier in his mouth, the infant could only do this by remembering the experimenter's gesture, a rudimentary form of representation.

How is this possible? The mechanism is cross-modal matching: the infant translates between what he sees (for example, the mouth opening gesture) and what he feels proprioceptively with his facial musculature. The infant is able to sense the degree of correspondence as he makes facial movements that are progressively similar to what he saw.

The infant can thus translate between environmental stimuli (such as the facial expressions and gestures of the partner) and inner states (proprioceptive feedback from facial muscles), detecting matches or correspondences, from the beginning of life. Through the perception of cross-modal correspondences, both infant and partner sense the state of the other, and sense whether the state is shared. Infant capacity to recognize cross-modal correspondences is a central means by which infants can capture the quality of the partner's inner feeling state (Meltzoff, 1990; Stern, 1985; Trevarthen, 1998). Far earlier than we thought, there is a rudimentary capacity to represent, and to match, the behavior of another person. These experiments show that infants begin life aware of the partner, and able to detect correspondences with the partner.

INFANTS PERCEIVE CONTINGENCIES AT BIRTH

Infants have intrinsic motivation to detect pattern, order, and sequence as events occur over time (DeCasper & Carstens, 1980; Papousek, 1992). They are *contingency detectors* from birth. That is, they do not have to be taught to detect if-then patterns and sequences.

For example, a particular infant behavior, such as mouth opening, may be followed by a maternal behavior, such as a smile. When this sequence is repeated a few times, it becomes predictable to the infant. Once it becomes predictable, it is termed *contingent.* The infant can detect this predictable sequence, or contingency, and come to expect it.

When the adult partner does provide, on average, predictable responses to infant behaviors, then the infant develops a form of interactive *agency.* That is, the infant comes to be able to expect that his own behavior generates predictable consequences in the partner's behavior. Providing contingent coordination with infant behavior is an essential function of the adult partner, which is intuitive and out of awareness (Papousek & Papousek, 1979). Moreover, the infant also coordinates contingently with the adult partner. The nature of each partner's contingent coordination with the other affects each partner's sense of interactive agency. The infant's ability to attend, process information, and modulate behavior and emotional state is affected by the nature of the moment-by-moment contingent coordination between the partners (Hay, 1997; Lewis & Goldberg, 1969; Stern, 1985, 1995; Tronick, 1989).

INFANTS DIFFER AT BIRTH

Infant temperament patterns, including sleep, feeding, arousal patterns, or special sensitivities to sound, smell, or touch, are important ways that infants may differ (DeGangi, Di Pietro, Greenspan, & Porges, 1991; Korner & Grobstein, 1977; Van den Boom, 1995). Neonates differ in their ability to regulate state and arousal (Brazelton, 1994). One aspect of the infant's management of arousal is the ability to dampen arousal in the face of overstimulation, and the capacity to inhibit behavior. For example, the fetus in the last trimester has the capacity to put itself to sleep in the face of repeated light flashes or sounds aimed at the fetus (Brazelton, 1973, 1992). Differences in these capacities contribute to emerging differences in infant capacities for self-regulation.

By the time infants are assessed in face-to-face interaction at four months, infant regulation of state and arousal has stabilized. Nevertheless, these infant differences at birth, and the ways they have been responded to by caretakers, may affect how infants and parents relate by four months.

THE POWER OF BRIEF MOMENTS OF INTERACTION

The human face is extraordinarily expressive. Throughout life, our expressive behaviors—such as an eyebrow raise or biting the lip—are rapid and usually unintended. Moreover, neither the sender nor the receiver is likely to be aware of them. Adults can choose their words carefully, but they are less able to monitor and control their facial and vocal expressions, head and hand gestures, rhythms of talking and listening, or patterns of looking and looking away (Ekman & Friesen, 1969).

Fleeting expressive behaviors have remarkable communicative power. Immediate affective reactions occur before conscious perception and cognition in both infant and adult face-to-face communication. In contexts of novelty, ambiguity, or threat, this process is amplified (Porges, 2003; Zajonc, 1985). Our evolutionary adaptation enables us to evaluate stimuli rapidly along the dimensions of pleasant-unpleasant, engaged-disengaged, and safety-threat, and to be prepared for rapid action. Thus much of our interpersonal understanding of each other is automatic and outside of conscious awareness (Iacoboni, 2009; Keysers & Gazzola, 2006; Pally, 2002). Also out of awareness, each partner communicates expectancies of the other's next move through these rapid, subtle processes.

People are fairly accurate in identifying emotions from an exposure to nonverbal behavior that lasts only a moment, about one third of a second (Ambady & Rosenthal, 1992; Rosenthal, Hall, DiMatteo, Rogers, & Archer, 1979). Thus, even a glimpse of a fleeting expression can be as powerful as viewing a longer expression. Instead of "only" a moment, it might be more accurate to say "such a powerful moment."

Many of the mother–infant interactions we study are extremely rapid and fleeting. For example, in the illustrations of this book, to capture an interactive sequence, we often need to present four drawings that encompass only a second or two of real time. Individual behaviors, such as a shift of gaze, a head turn, a mouth opening, last on the average one fourth to one third of a second. The duration of time between the onset of one individual's behavior and the onset of the partner's behavior is generally within one half second (Beebe, 1982; Cohn & Beebe, 1990; Stern, 1971). Examination of the beginnings and endings of these movements of the two partners reveals a semi-synchronous system in which one partner frequently begins adjusting or responding before the other's action is complete. Each person's action is continuously modified by the changing action of the partner (Beebe & Stern, 1977; Beebe, Stern, & Jaffe, 1979; Fogel, 1992; Stern, 1971).

Thus many aspects of these interactions occur out of awareness, often below the threshold of conscious perception, so rapid that they cannot be seen by the naked eye. They are considered *nonconscious,* and out of awareness. But they can usually be brought into awareness by focusing attention on them. We distinguish nonconscious from *unconscious.* What is unconscious is unavailable to consciousness for a reason such as conflict or trauma.

FLEETING NEGATIVE MOMENTS

In the drawings that we present in this book, some of the most unsettling and difficult moments are ones in which maternal expressions do not convey recognition of the infant's distress. For example, the mother may show a smile or a surprised facial expression that is very discrepant from the infant's expressions of distress. Sometimes mothers attempt to distract their infants from their distress, or jolly them out of it. These attempts tend not to work unless the mother can at first acknowledge the infant's distress.

In other moments, the mother might show a fleeting disgust expression, or eyebrows arched in searing disapproval, at those moments in which her infant is distressed. These maternal expressions are brief, momentary, usually well under a second. In real time we see distress in both partners, but we cannot quite grasp the exact expression. The mother is most likely unaware of her expression; yet, as the films show, the infants respond powerfully, usually with increased distress. Infants might respond through increased facial expressions or vocalizations of distress, sudden arching away, or agitated foot kicks. Infants perceive and respond to all the subtle changes in their mothers' expressions.

Overall, most mutual social interactions are experienced as rewarding. However, in some contexts, social interaction can become threatening. Porges (2003, 2011) proposed a dynamic between social approach and social aversion in human social communication. The social approach system promotes a sense of safety and security through close social interactions. It is sustained by reward-related brain activity. The social aversion system promotes survival in conditions of threat. It operates through the sympathetic nervous system, which activates flight or fight (Porges, 2003; Vrticka,

2012). We see this aversion system activated when infants perceive momentary threatening faces or gestures. Infants show versions of fight and flight, as we discuss below.

How do we understand these fleeting moments of maternal discrepant emotions, negative emotions, or threatening expressions? Although every mother could feel this way sometimes, these fleeting expressions tend to occur more frequently in mothers with infants who later are classified as disorganized attachment (Beebe et al., 2010; Beebe & Lachmann, 2013; Hesse & Main, 2006). These infants who will be classified disorganized attachment show far more vocal distress at four months than infants who will be classified as secure. Thus, the mother's response to infant distress is particularly important for these infants.

There is a strong concordance between the infant's attachment classification at one year, and the mother's own attachment classification in pregnancy (Fonagy, Steele, & Steele, 1991; Steele, Steele, & Fonagy, 1996). Thus, there is a high likelihood that infants with disorganized attachment have mothers with a disorganized attachment history themselves (Raby, Steele, Carlson, & Sroufe, 2015). If so, the mothers are also likely to have experienced abuse, or to be suffering from unresolved loss and mourning (Main & Solomon, 1990). Thus, it is important to recognize the struggle of these mothers. They have the complicated job of dealing with their own distress as they deal with the distress of their infants.

When traumatic early experiences are unresolved, they are like open wounds. We propose that, because mothers of disorganized attachment infants likely have unbearable distress in their own histories, when their infants become very upset, this upset may trigger aspects of the mothers' own dormant distressed experiences that had remained active out of awareness. At these moments, the infant's distress literally threatens the mother with reexperiencing her own distress. Thus, we argue, the mothers may out of awareness show fleeting discrepant emotions, negative emotions, or threatening expressions because they themselves feel threatened by the infant's distress (Beebe & Lachmann, 2013).

This way of understanding the mother's experience allows us to retain empathy for her when we see these fleeting negative faces in response to infant distress. It tends to be easier for everyone viewing our drawings to empathize with the infants rather than the mothers. But it is essential to be able to empathize with both partners, and not to blame the mother.

CHAPTER 2

Microanalysis Teaches Us to Observe: How We Code the Mother–Infant Action-Dialogue Language

The research on which this book is based is far from simple. Our research method of microanalysis identifies many nuances of behavior that would otherwise remain unexamined at a global, macro level. This level of detail is hard to analyze, but it is possible to obtain reliable assessments, to analyze the behaviors statistically, and to figure out how infants and mothers communicate. In this book, we invite you to look over our shoulder and see the many details that are often missed in real time. You will learn how we code interactions across the communication modalities of attention, emotion, orientation, and touch. You will see many ways in which these different modalities are all in play at the same time in these early interactions.

HOW DO WE CODE MOTHER–INFANT INTERACTIONS?

In our research, we meticulously coded the first two and a half minutes of each filmed mother–infant play session, a second-by-second microanalysis. This coding provides the basic elements of the nonverbal language that mothers and infants use. It took ten years to obtain the data we used to predict attachment outcomes. Many devoted doctoral students coded the films during this period (see Acknowledgments). The drawings in this book are selected from this large body of work to best illustrate our research findings.

We now describe the different communication modalities, how mothers and infants use them, and how we code them. Our coding is based on what mothers and infants actually do in face-to-face play. The camera captures the head, upper torso, and hands of both partners.

Many modalities operate at once during face-to-face communication. The meaning of each modality, such as maternal orientation (sitting upright, leaning forward, or looming in), depends on what is happening in the other modalities, such as gaze and facial expression. For example, when a mother looms directly in, close to her infant's face, if she is smiling, her infant is less likely to become upset. But if she looms in close when her face is neutral, and thus hard to interpret, her infant is likely to put his hands up to protect his face.

Gaze and facial affect are central modalities of communication. The infant's vocal affect is an important means of communication of emotion, particularly of distress. Infant-initiated touch is also an important behavior, which nevertheless often goes unnoticed. Affectionate to intrusive patterns of maternal touch are also central. The infant's head orientation sets the stage for looking and looking away. Maternal spatial orientation measures how the mother moves her body in space forward toward the infant or moves back and upright.

Some of the behaviors are completely symmetrical, in the sense that both partners have a similar repertoire of behaviors. For example, each partner can look at and away from the other's face; each partner has the full possible range of positive to negative facial expressions. But the mother's range of movement of her bodily orientation, from sitting upright, to moving forward, to looming in, is different from that of the infant, who is loosely strapped into the seat. However, the infant has a large range of head movements, from oriented vis-à-vis, to minor and major head aversions, to a full 90-degree head aversion in which his head is tucked into his shoulder, to arching his torso back and partially turning away from his mother. Touch behavior is also not symmetrical. The mother has a far greater repertoire of different kinds of touches than does the infant.

We code each communication modality one at a time, irrespective of the others. For example, when we code gaze, looking at or away from the partner's face, we ignore head orientation. When we code head orientation, we ignore gaze. In this way, we can see how the different communication modalities may operate together. And we can identify moments when two modalities become discrepant from one another. For example, in the origins of disorganized attachment, we were able to detect moments in which infants both smiled and whimpered in the same second (Beebe et al., 2010). We were able to detect this phenomenon because we had coded facial affect and vocal affect separately.

In what follows, and in our drawings in Part II of the book, you see that the infant is continually getting experience with a continuum of engagement and disengagement moments with his partner. Engagement and disengagement are being organized in rapid succession, and both partners contribute. These are forms of "being with" (Stern, 1985), such as direct mutual gaze, with gradations of positive affect, building up to the apex of positive affect, the open-mouth *gape smile*. But the infant is also getting experience with forms and degrees of disengagement, such as looking away, degrees of orienting the head and body away—from slight angles away from vis-à-vis, to increasing angles away, to 90-degree aversion, arching, or turning all the way around to the environment.

We code mother and infant during the face-to-face interaction in the following ways:

- *Attention:* Gazing at and away from the partner's face
- *Orientation*: Infant's head orientation from vis-à-vis to arch away, and mother's spatial orientation from sitting upright to leaning forward to looming in
- *Emotion*: Infant facial affect: degrees of positive to negative facial expressions; infant vocal affect: degrees of positive to negative vocal tones; mother facial affect: degrees of positive to negative facial expressions
- *Touch:* Infant touching self (own skin), object (chair, strap, clothing), or mother; mother touching infant, from affectionate to intrusive forms of touch

ATTENTION: GAZE

We begin by observing gaze. First recall that mother and infant are seated face-to-face, opposite each other in the same plane. The two views are combined into one split-screen view. When you look at the drawings, notice the black line that separates the two views.

Figure 1a depicts *mutual gaze*; both partners are gazing at the other's face. In Figure 1b, the infant breaks the gaze and looks down. The mother also looks down but continues to look at her infant.

Sometimes it is hard to see from one isolated frame where the partners are looking. When coding gaze at or away from the partner's face, the coder watches the video in real time. The coder can then examine all the frames second-by-second in sequence. So the coder has access to much more information than we can present here. Moreover, we always have two coders who have to agree on what constitutes a gaze at the partner, or a gaze away. Sometimes, it is hard to discern the exact direction of gaze because of the poor quality of the video.

Mothers tend to look at the infant's face most of the time, and it is the infant who typically makes and breaks the mutual gaze. The infant engages in cycles of looking at the mother's face for a period of time, looking away, and then looking back (Stern,

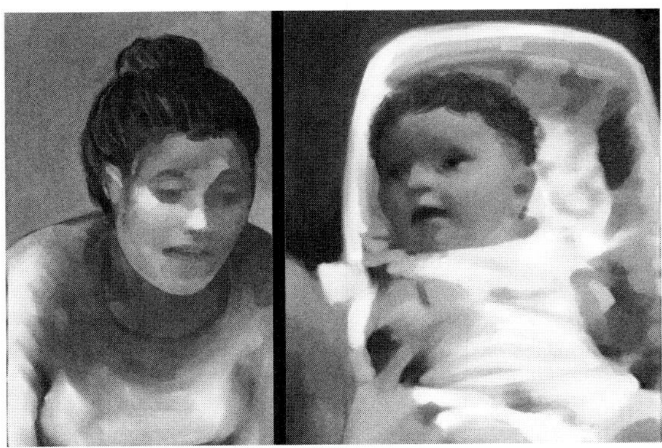

Figure 1a. Mutual gaze, both oriented vis-à-vis.

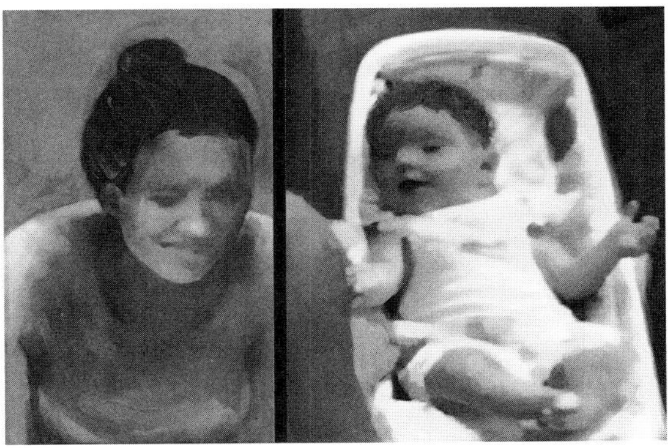

Figure 1b. Infant breaks gaze and looks down; mother looks down but continues to look at her infant.

1971, 1974). Thus, infant looking away is part of the infant's typical behavior. Infants tend to look away a little more than they look at their mothers. Looking into the face of a partner can be very stimulating; in fact most animals do not sustain long periods of such looking unless they are about to fight or make love (Chance & Larsen, 1996; Eibl-Eibesfeldt, 1970).

Infants as well as adults look away to reregulate their arousal. During mother–infant play, infant heart rate was studied to examine the levels of arousal that occur just before, and just after, infants look away (Field, 1981). The moment that the infant looks away is preceded by a burst of increasing arousal in the previous five seconds. Following the infant's looking away, infant heart rate decreases back down to baseline within the next five seconds, and during this period, the infant then returns to looking at the mother's face (Field, 1981). Thus, infant *gaze aversion* is an important aspect of infant self-regulation.

Mothers typically pace the amount of stimulation according to this infant look/look-away cycle, stimulating more as the infant looks, and decreasing stimulation as the infant looks away (Brazelton et al., 1974). This facilitates infant ability to dampen down his arousal when he looks away, a key infant mode of coping. However, as we discuss below in the *chase and dodge* pattern, if the mother increases her stimulation when the infant looks away, it interferes with the infant's ability to dampen his arousal.

Although these are typical patterns of mother–infant gaze, we have also noted a pattern of mutual *eye love* (Beebe, 1973; Beebe & Stern, 1977) in which mothers and infants can sustain prolonged mutual gaze for up to 100 seconds during periods of positive affect. These are the moments, of course, that every parent loves.

ORIENTATION

Infant Head Orientation

We next observe infant head orientation to the mother. Head orientation is an important aspect of infant communication that often goes unrecognized.

Is the infant's head oriented directly vis-à-vis the mother? This vis-à-vis orientation is illustrated above in Figure 1a. Of the two and a half minutes of the play session that we coded, infants typically tend to spend about one and a half minutes in vis-à-vis orientation. Infant gaze at mother's face is most likely from this vis-à-vis orientation.

Or is the infant's head averted at approximately 30, 60, or 90 degrees away from the vis-à-vis orientation? Infants spend at least a quarter of their time in orientations 30 degrees to 60 degrees away from vis-à-vis. These head positions are illustrated below in Figure 2a, 2b, and 2c, respectively.

In the 90-degree infant head aversion (Stern, 1971), which is rare, the infant's head is turned all the way away to the shoulder, which takes considerable energy. When head aversion movements of 30 degrees, 60 degrees, or 90 degrees are accompanied by oblique angles of the head down (or up), they communicate the infant's still further aversion. Infant arch, a whole body movement of head and back arching away from vis-à-vis, is the most extreme aversion posture and is also rare.

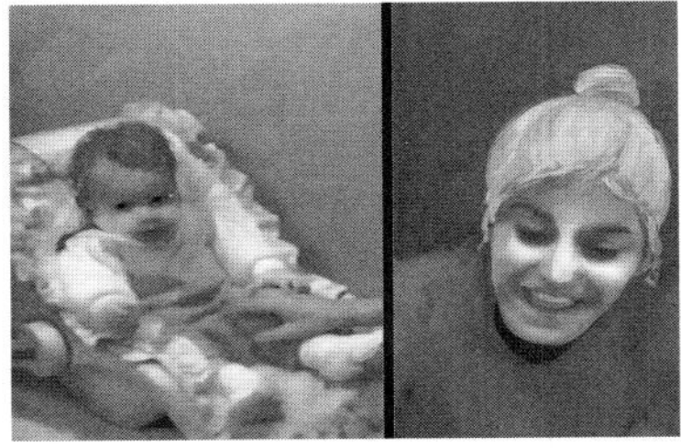

Figure 2a. Infant 30-degree aversion.

Figure 2b. Infant 60-degree aversion.

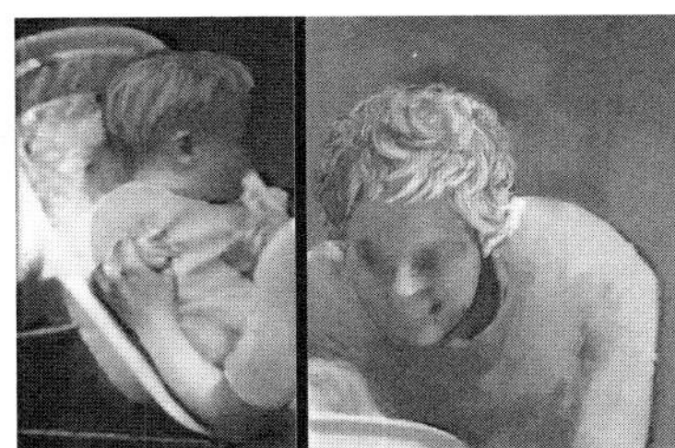

Figure 2c. Infant 90-degree aversion.

These increasing degrees of head aversion are described as degrees of severity of "cutoff" acts (Chance, 1962; McGrew, 1972). They are read by the mother as an active initiation of disengagement by her infant. As the infant turns away up to about 60 degrees, he can still monitor his mother with his peripheral vision, through which he can track the presence, direction, and intensity of her movements. By the time the infant is 90 degrees away, or arching back and away, however, he loses peripheral visual monitoring of his mother's movements. Usually when infants avert their gaze, they retain head orientation within an approximate 30- to 45-degree angle from the vis-à-vis. From this angle, they retain rapid access to visual reengagement with minimal effort (Koulomzin et al., 2002).

When we see 90-degree aversions, or arch, we infer that infants are struggling with the interaction. As we discuss below, 90-degree aversions often occur when mothers chase infants by moving toward the infant as the infant continues to move away. Other severe cutoff acts include *freezing,* that is becoming completely motionless (Fraiberg, 1982), or *going limp* and losing tonus (the body or the face becomes slack, without any muscle tension). These more extreme cutoff behaviors occur as part of the human equipment to protect in the face of potential threat.

The brain is phylogenetically equipped, prepared, and vigilant for forms of threat (Porges, 2003, 2011). A more evolutionarily modern part of the brain, the myelinated vagus nerve, usually allows us to quiet down any worries of threat and still to be able to socially engage. But if threat goes over certain thresholds or occurs in certain contexts, fear results, and the sympathetic nervous system kicks in to enable fight or flight.

While the infant's nervous system is not yet fully developed and the sympathetic nervous system is still under construction, we can still see infant versions of the fight, flight, or freeze responses. For example, we see infant versions of the flight response as the infants turn all the way around in the chair away from the mother toward the environment. We see infant versions of the fight response as they vocalize with angry/protest sounds, kick violently, show cry faces, and turn away from the mother with an intense body movement.

A very old part of the brain, the unmyelinated vagus nerve, can take over when threat is prolonged, or intense, generating forms of freeze and collapse. We see the infant version of the freeze response in the severe cutoff behavior of collapse of tonus, in which infants go motionless or limp. Moments of infant collapse of tonus are illustrated in our drawings in Part II (chase and dodge, collapse). We see moments of infant freeze, or a momentary facial collapse of tonus in the context of maternal threatening faces or maternal looming (see Beebe & Lachmann, 2013).

Mother Spatial Orientation

Unlike infants, mothers do not tend to move their heads from side to side, orienting toward and away. Instead, mothers tend to stay oriented vis-à-vis and visually focused on their infants. But mothers do move their upper bodies. They move from sitting upright, to leaning forward, to looming in close to the infant's face. These are the maternal spatial positions that we code. Mothers tend to spend about half their time in sitting upright, somewhat less than half the time in leaning forward, and they loom in only occasionally.

In moments when her infant looks away, it can be hard for a mother to pause, to wait, in order to give the infant time to calm down and to reregulate his arousal. Once the infant calms down, if the mother waits, he will usually look back, as we described earlier. Difficulty tolerating moments of infant gaze aversion is common when a mother experiences difficulty with her infant, or worries that her infant is not sufficiently interested in her.

Chase and dodge.

If a mother interprets her infant's gaze aversion with the idea that her infant does not love her or is not interested in her, she may pursue her infant by chasing him, moving toward him as he moves away. This pursuit increases the amount of stimulation the infant has to deal with as he looks away. This increased stimulation interferes with the infant's ability to dampen his arousal down sufficiently to be able to look back. In her pursuit or chase, a mother may call her infant's name, pull her infant's hand, loom forward close into her infant's face, or in rare instances, attempt to force her infant's head to get her infant to look at her. In our drawings, we describe this pattern of *chase and dodge* (see Figure 3a to 3c). Our research showed that the chase and dodge pattern is co-created: mother chase elicits infant dodge, and infant dodge elicits mother chase (see Beebe & Lachmann, 2002; Beebe & Stern, 1977). This pattern at four months predicted infant insecure (resistant) attachment at one year (Beebe et al., 2010).

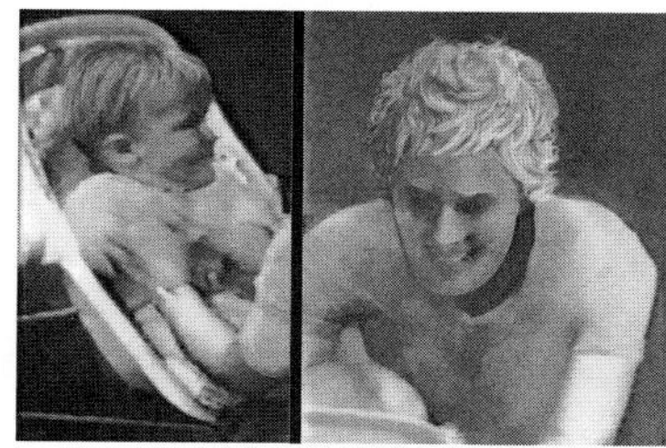

Figure 3a. Mother just begins to loom. Infant begins to turn away.

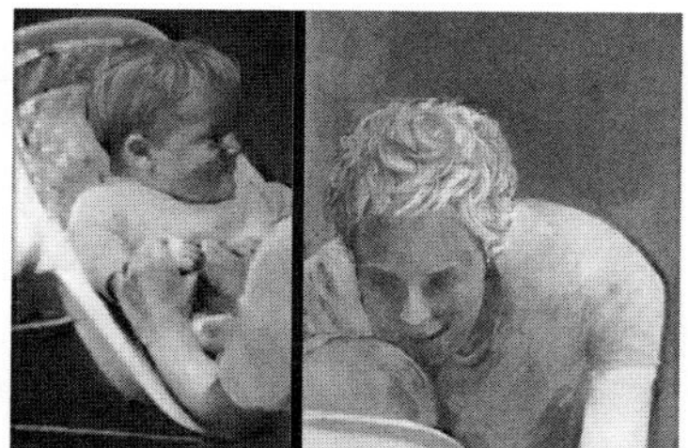

Figure 3b. Mother completes her loom.

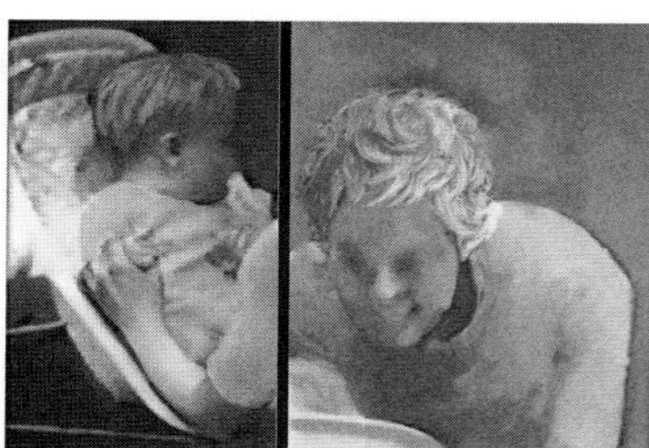

Figure 3c. Infant dodges (turns head away).

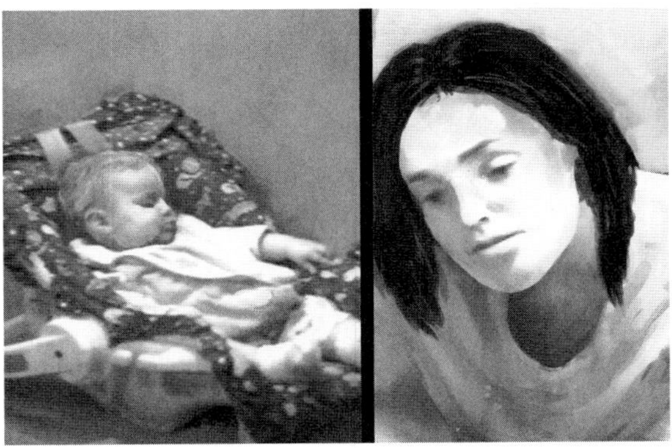

Figure 4a. Infant remains oriented away to his left, not looking; mother waits, remains upright, tilting her head in the direction of the infant's head tilt.

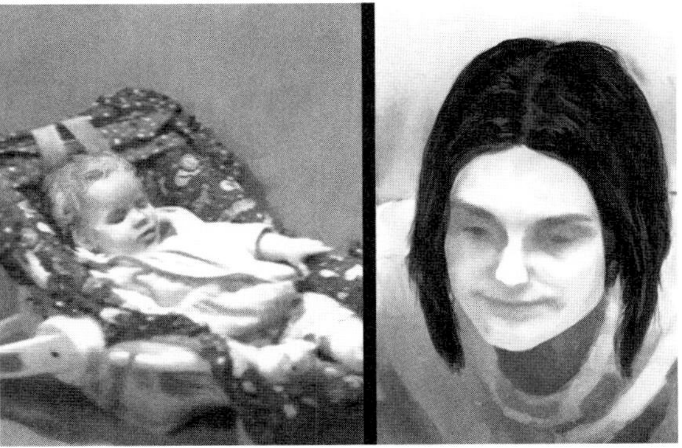

Figure 4b. Infant reorients his head vis-à-vis and remains looking down; mother follows infant's head movement and reorients vis-à-vis as she waits.

Secure Look-Away

The mother's loom or chase behavior is counterproductive; the infant then requires more time to reregulate his arousal down sufficiently to be able to return to gazing at his mother. Instead, if a mother can wait patiently to give her baby a time-out to reregulate, and trust her infant to return to her, the infant will rapidly reengage. In one of our sequences of drawings, secure look-away, briefly illustrated in Figure 4a and 4b, a mother patiently and calmly waits when her infant looks away, and this infant soon looks back. They reengage and smile.

In the secure look-away pattern illustrated in Figure 4a and 4b, both mother and infant seem able to tolerate the moment of infant looking away. The mother waits patiently with ease, rather than with disappointment and worry. She seems to feel secure that her infant will return to her. The infant does return to looking at her by the end of the sequence, as we illustrate later in the drawings. If mother and infant together manage the infant's look-look away cycle so that the infant can comfortably regulate his arousal, then they can enjoy periods of sustained mutual gaze with infant vis-à-vis orientation. During these periods, enjoyable facial and vocal communication usually take center stage.

EMOTION

Infant Facial Affect

We code infant facial expressions, which occur about 80 percent of the time during the face-to-face play session. Interest expressions may have the slightest hint of mouth opening or widening, but no actual smile (see Figure 5a). The infant's opening and closing of the mouth is a powerful and continuous form of communication (Beebe, 1973). An excited but less common variant of interest is a *neutral gape*, a fully opened

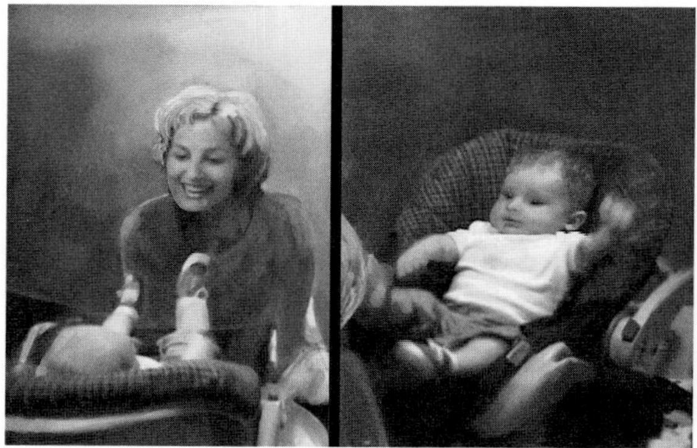

Figure 5a. Infant neutral interest expression.

Figure 5b. Infant low smile.

Figure 5c. Infant high smile with infant self touch.

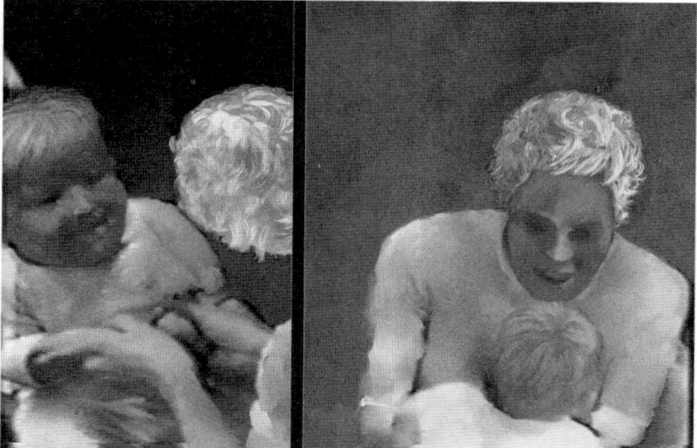

Figure 5d. Infant compressed lips.

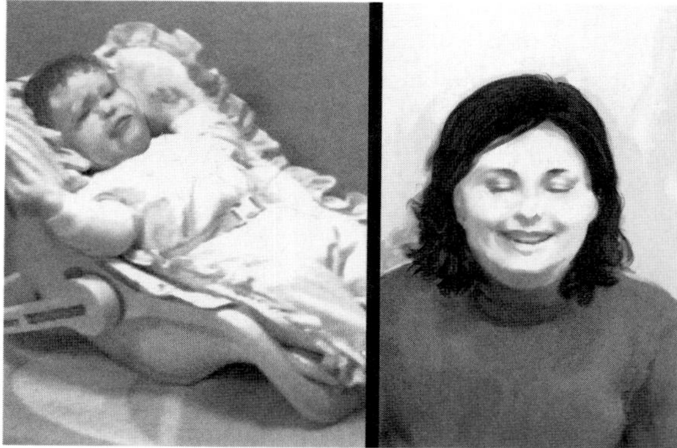

Figure 5e. Infant frown.

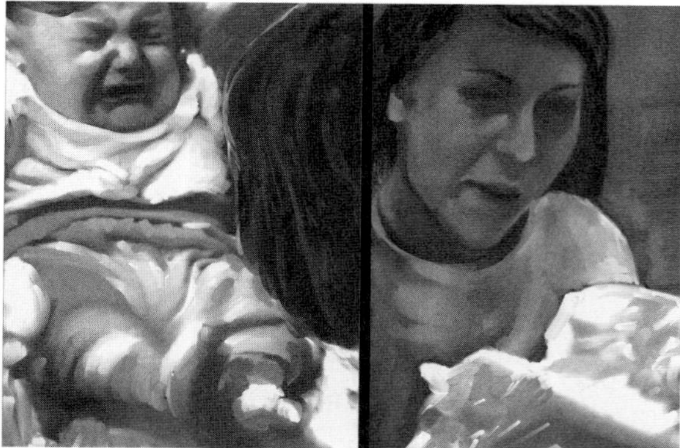

Figure 5f. Infant cry face.

mouth without any hint of widening or smiling, which is highly evocative (Beebe, 1973; Bennett, 1971; see Figure 6b). It is part of our evolutionary heritage: Monkeys and apes use this expression (Van Hooff, 1967).

We code two degrees of infant smiles, *low smile* and *high smile* (see Figure 5b and 5c). Together, low and high smiles occur less than 20 percent of the play session. Low smile has little or no mouth opening, but it does have upturned corners of the mouth (Figure 5b). High smile has medium to large mouth opening as well as upturned corners (Figure 5c). In our coding, the highest smile, *gape smile* (Figure 6b) is included in high smiles. Negative infant expressions (also coded as lower and higher) are more rare than positive expressions. Negative expressions include grimace, compressed lips (Figure 5d; coded as low-negative); frown (Figure 5e); and pre-cry face and cry face (Figure 5f; coded as high-negative).

Infant Vocal Affect

Vocal emotion—or vocal affect—we use these terms interchangeably, refers to the contours or shape of the sound, often termed "prosody." Across cultures, maternal sounds with a sinusoidal shape, moving up and down shaped like a bell, indicate approval; sounds that rapidly fall to the right, the right half of the bell, indicate maternal disapproval (Fernald, 1993). Infants apprehend vocal contours and are specifically responsive to approval and disapproval contours.

We code infant vocalizations as high positive, neutral/low positive, no-vocalization, fuss-whimper, angry-protest, and cry. Mothers often approximately match and elaborate the infants' vocal contours. This is a powerful mode of emotional communication between mothers and infants. Of course, because our book is based on visual drawings, we do not illustrate vocal interactions. Infant vocal affect and maternal vocal responses can be heard on our enclosed DVD.

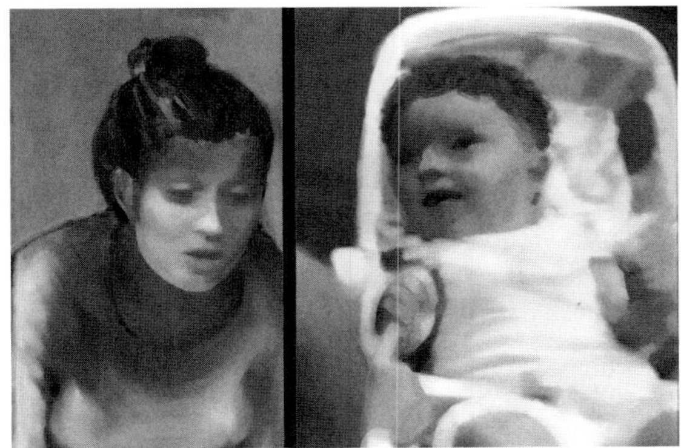

Figure 6a. Infant low smile with slight open mouth.

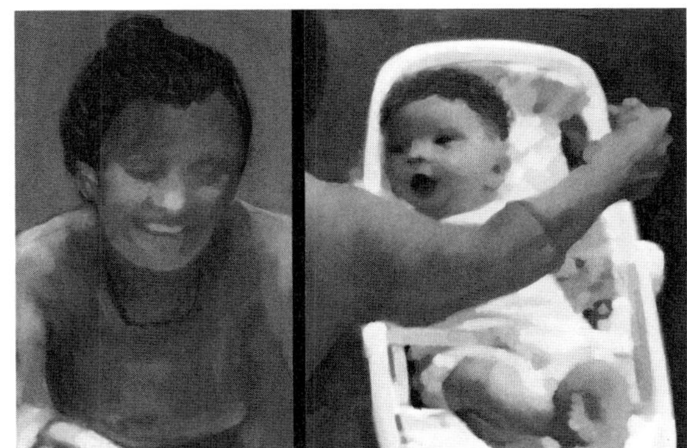

Figure 6b. Infant gape smile.

Figure 7a. Mother neutral interest expression, mouth slightly opened and widened; infant looks with neutral face.

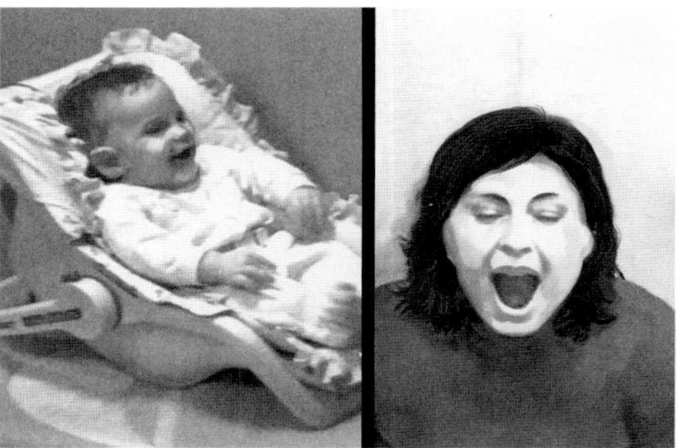

Figure 7b. Mother gape smile, infant full smile (not gape smile).

Mother Facial Affect

Mothers tend to spend almost half the time in neutral/interest facial expressions when interacting face-to-face with their infants (see Figure 7a). They spend a little less than half the time in low and medium smiles. Other expressions, such as the maternal gape smile (Figure 7b), mock surprise (Figure 7c), sympathetic woe face (Figure 7d and 7e), and negative faces, are more rare.

A fully widened smile by itself, with closed lips, is only moderately positive. As increasing degrees of mouth opening are added to a smile, positive affect increases up and up into the fully opened gape smile (Figure 7b), hugely exciting for both partners. Often both partners move their heads up toward each other, and excitedly vocalize at such moments, further increasing the intensity of positive affect (see Beebe, 1973; Beebe & Lachmann, 2002; Beebe et al., 2010; Messinger, Fogel, & Dickson, 2001; Stern, 1985; Tronick, 1989).

We do not code mother vocal affect; instead we use an automated system of analyzing mother and infant vocal rhythms, which is not presented here (see Jaffe et al., 2001).

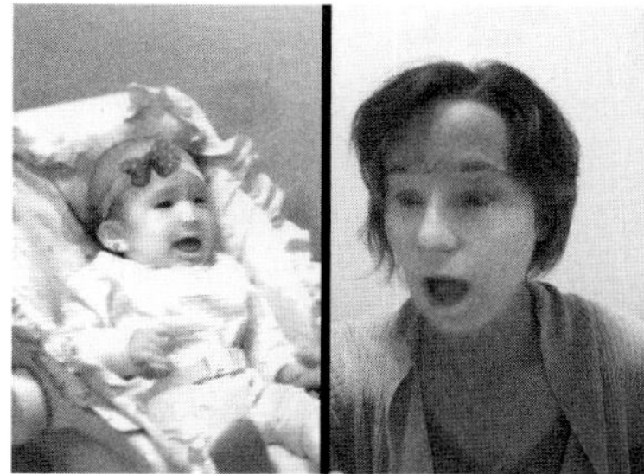

Figure 7c. Maternal mock surprise.

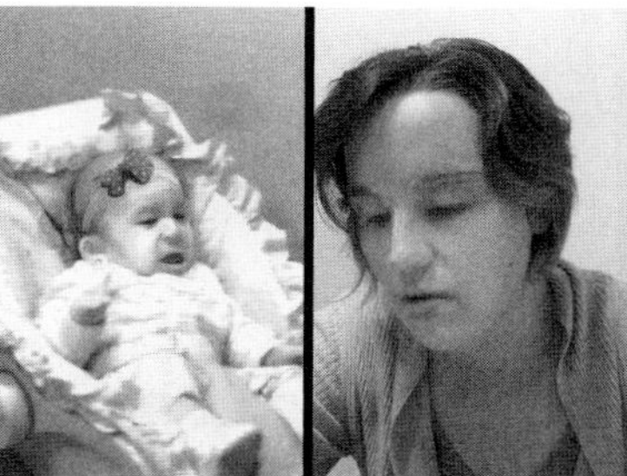

Figure 7d. Maternal partial woe face.

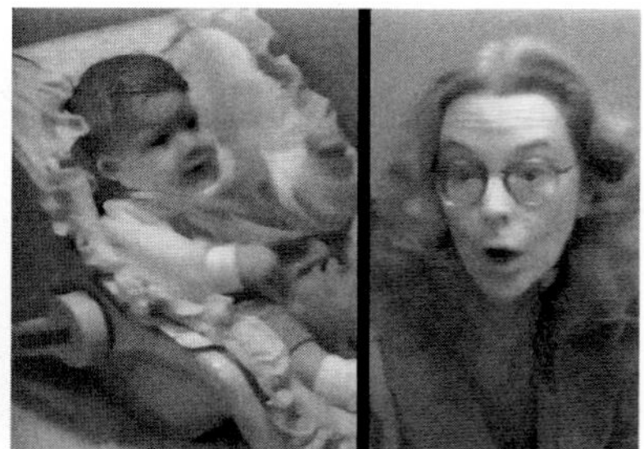

Figure 7e. Stranger woe face with surprise.

Facial mirroring.

In general, mothers and infants tend to match the direction of the other's positive-to-negative affective changes, increasing and decreasing together, often termed facial mirroring (Beebe, 2005; Beebe & Lachmann, 2013). This is an approximate and flexible form of matching; rarely is there an exact match of expressions. This process is more accurately described as elaboration (Fogel, 1993), echo, correspondence, or complementing (Trevarthen, 1977), rather than matching or imitation (Stern, 1985).

Moreover, as we describe below, matching is embedded in a process of match, mismatch, and rematch, which we term *disruption and repair* (see Tronick, 1989). In this process, the mutual engagement between mother and infant flexibly moves among more and less matched states.

TOUCH

Infant Touch

For the infant, we code touch in the following way: touch one's own skin (including mouthing), touch an object (such as strap, clothing, chair), touch one's mother (see Figure 8a), or no-touch. Infant touch patterns provide a layer of contact when infants are not communicating through gaze, facial expression, or vocalization. For example, in Figure 8a below, as the infant is looking at his mother, she is looking at the camera and we observed tiny movements of the infant reaching for the mother's hand and fingering her skin.

Mother Touch

For the mother, we code 21 different types of touch in an effort to capture nuances and qualities of maternal touch (Beebe et al., 2010; Stepakoff, Beebe, & Jaffe, 2000). We then place these different qualities of touch into an ordered scale, from affection-

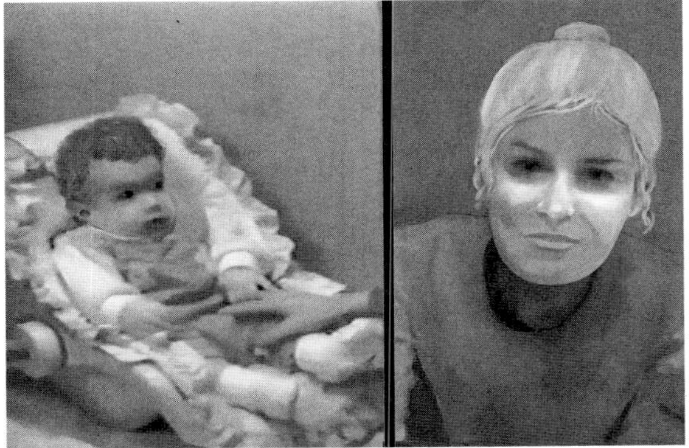

Figure 8a. Infant holds mother's finger.

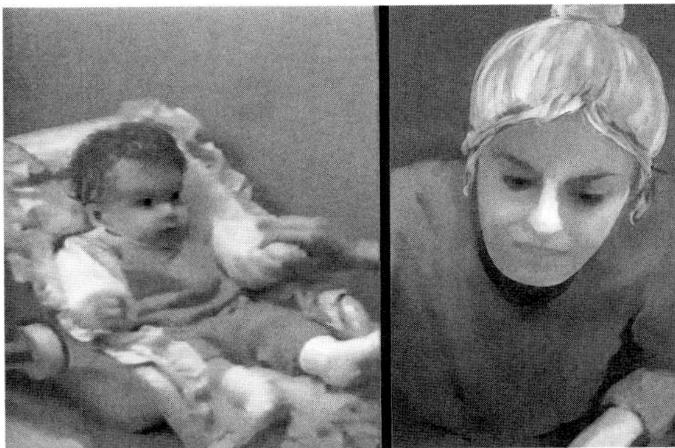

Figure 8b. Maternal static touch.

ate to intrusive. These touch qualities range from *affectionate,* such as stroke or caress; *static,* such as hold hand or finger (see Figure 8b); *playful,* such as tap, tickle, rub; *caretake,* such as adjust infant's clothing; *jiggle-bounce*; *touch* the infant *through an object*, such as piece of the infant's clothing; and *rough, intrusive* touch. In addition to its pleasurable, playful aspect, touch can be an important way of making contact when the interaction is not going well.

CHAPTER 3

Patterns of Communication Become Expected and Shape Infant Development

Now that we have described how we code mother and infant behaviors, we return to the ways in which mothers and infants use this action language to create corresponding or matched moments, how they may deal with infant distress, and how they may disrupt and repair their communication. In this process, different patterns of self- and interactive regulation are created. These different patterns become expected and remembered by both partners, and begin to shape the infant's development. Specifically, as we previously noted, these patterns shape the emerging security or insecurity of the infant's attachment.

HOW DO INFANTS AND PARENTS SENSE THE STATE OF THE OTHER? BEHAVIORAL CORRESPONDENCES CREATE RAPPORT

Correspondences provide each partner with ways of knowing whether one's feelings are shared and thereby acknowledged by the other. We learn that some feelings are shareable, and some are not (Stern, 1985). The joint ability of mother and infant to co-create patterns of correspondence is so important because these correspondences contribute to attachment security and the capacity for intimacy.

Many rapid processes of correspondence or matching of behaviors occur outside of our awareness (Chartrand & Bargh, 1999; Dimberg, Thunberg, & Elmehed, 2000; Kendon, 1970). In Figure 9 below, we see mother and infant with similar gape smiles, an example of a correspondence at the apex of positive facial affect. In this example, it is the similarity of the form of behavior, the actual facial expressions, with mutual gaze and vis-à-vis orientation, which create the correspondence.

Matching the infant's vocal contours (the shapes of the sounds) and vocal rhythms (the durations of sounds and silences) provides another form of correspondence and can also be an effective way to engage the infant. Because the infant does not have to orient or to look, approximately matching the infant's vocal rhythms or vocal contours is a nonintrusive way of helping the infant feel sensed: Someone is on his wavelength.

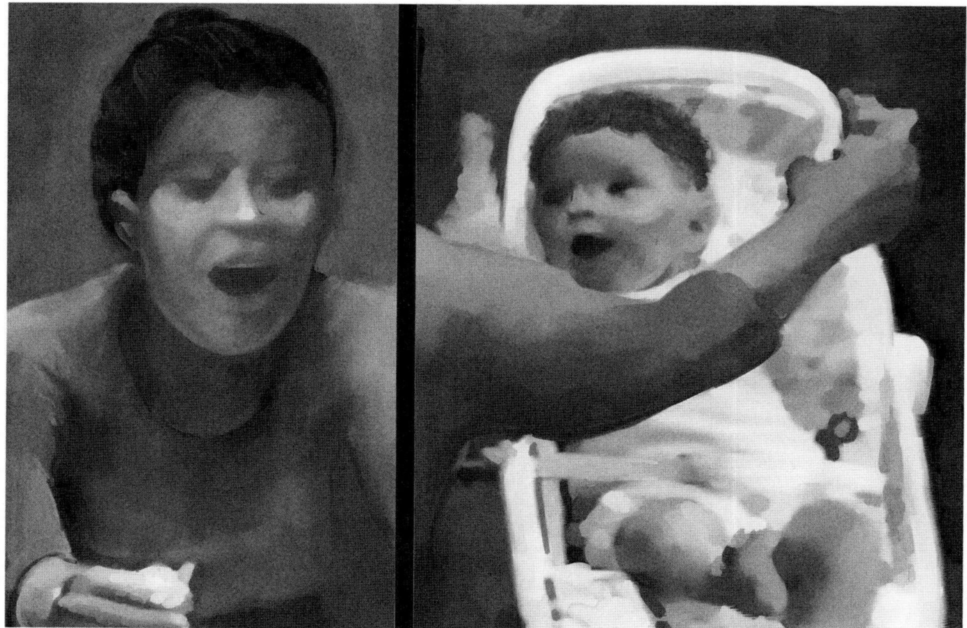

Figure 9. Mother and infant corresponding gape smiles.

Mother and infant both contribute to correspondences of behavior during face-to-face play. There are potential sources of correspondence in any behavioral modality (gaze, facial affect, vocal affect, vocal rhythm, and so on). Moreover, correspondences do not have to be within the same communication modality, such as maternal facial expression with infant facial expression, or maternal vocal rhythm with infant vocal rhythm. Instead, correspondences can be *cross-modal*; that is, partners can correspond with each other across different modalities. An example of cross-modal correspondence is maternal positive vocal contour with infant positive facial expression, or the reverse. We return here to the *how* of behavior, that is, the dynamic, shifting patterns of rhythms, shapes, and activations (Stern, 1985). Correspondences can occur through any of these dynamic patterns, through any combination of communication modalities.

Stern and colleagues explained correspondences in this way: "Dynamic micro-momentary shifts in intensity over time that are perceived as patterned changes within ourselves and others" allow us, rather automatically and without awareness, to "change with" the other, to "feel-what-has-been-perceived-in-the-other" (Stern, Hofer, Haft, & Dore, 1985, p. 263). Each partner potentially changes with the slight shifts of the other. Although we illustrated correspondences of facial affect above, some correspondences are harder to convey through our drawings, such as correspondences of rhythms.

The infant perceives the feeling state of the partner based on the form (shape) of the partner's behavior (looking or looking away, positive or negative facial expressions), the intensity, and the timing (Stern, 1985; Trevarthen, 1998). Critically, the infant perceives whether the partner's behavior corresponds to his own. The infant's capacity to recognize correspondences enables the infant to capture the quality of another's inner feeling and to discriminate whether it is shared (Stern, 1985). This process is automatic and implicit for the infant. For the mother, it is largely out of awareness. It is an aspect of procedural (action-sequence) knowing. However, when these patterns are brought into the mother's awareness, she can reflect on her infant's feeling state, especially if she is empathically supported in this process.

Another study of behavioral correspondences sheds light on a further way in which mothers may participate in the infant's emotional state. Dimberg and colleagues exposed adult subjects to 30 milliseconds (30/1,000 of a second) of happy, angry, and neutral target faces through a masking technique. In this technique, the subject is exposed for five seconds to a neutral pose of a face, for thirty milliseconds to an angry (or happy) pose of the same face, and again for five seconds to the neutral pose of the face. The angry (or happy) face was too fast for subjects to perceive it in awareness. The subjects wore miniature electrodes on their faces. Facial electromyographic activity revealed that the subjects displayed distinct facial muscle reactions, which corresponded to the happy and angry target faces (Dimberg et al., 2000). Thus, positive and negative facial reactions were evoked in the subjects out of their awareness. This research reveals another way of participating in the state of the other.

Most of the literature on correspondences describes shared positive states between mother and infant. But maternal empathic sharing of infant negative states turns out to be extremely important as well. As we come to see, when mothers can share their infants' states of distress with corresponding empathic woe faces of their own, their infants are more likely to become securely attached (Beebe et al., 2010). When infants learn that their distress is not shared, acknowledged, and empathized with by the mother, insecure attachment outcomes are more likely.

We add one caveat, whereas most forms of behavioral correspondence accrue to experiences of being known, or on the same wavelength, some forms of correspondence are not optimal. One striking example of a nonoptimal form of correspondence is the pattern of mutually escalating overarousal (Beebe, 2005). In this pattern, each partner escalates, as the infant builds to a frantic distress, and the mother makes increasingly frantic efforts to engage the infant. In this process, a four-month-old infant became so frantic that he actually vomited. At one year, this infant was classified as disorganized attachment (Beebe, 2005). While one moment alone does not determine an infant's later attachment status, it is likely that this pattern of mutually escalating overarousal was typical for this dyad.

HOW DO INFANTS AND PARENTS SENSE THE STATE OF THE OTHER? MATCHING OF FACIAL EXPRESSIONS AND PHYSIOLOGICAL AROUSAL

Ekman and colleagues found that a particular facial expression is associated with a particular pattern of physiological arousal (Ekman, Levenson, & Friesen, 1983; Levenson, Ekman, & Friesen, 1990). Matching the expression of the partner therefore produces a similar physiological state in the onlooker. As partners match each other's facial expressions, each recreates a psychophysiological state in him- or herself similar to that of the partner. Thus, each can participate in the subjective state of the other (Beebe & Lachmann, 1988, 2002). The individual's pattern of arousal provides an additional avenue of knowledge about the partner's emotional state (Levenson & Ruef, 1997). This process typically goes on outside of awareness.

HOW DO INFANTS AND PARENTS SENSE THE STATE OF THE OTHER? MIRROR NEURONS

Mirror neurons provide another way in which mother and infant can sense the state of the other. One day as the researcher Rizzolatti began to lick an ice-cream cone, a monkey was watching. Electrodes had already been implanted in the monkey's brain. As the monkey watched Rizzolatti lick the ice cream, the monkey's premotor cortex became active. Rizzolatti found that the same neurons activated as a monkey reaches for an ice-cream cone are also active when the monkey simply observes this action in the researcher. Mirror neurons operate similarly in humans. They provide an *action-recognition* mechanism: The actor's actions are reproduced in the premotor cortex of the observer (Iacoboni et al., 2005; Rizzolatti, Fadiga, Fogassi, & Gallese, 1996). Through mirror neurons, the observer has an enhanced capacity to recognize the intention of the actor (Wolf, Gales, Shane, & Shane, 2001) Pally (2000) suggested that mirror neurons can be seen this way: I understand your intention by understanding (in a procedural format) what my own intention would be, if I were doing what you are doing.

HOW DO INFANTS AND PARENTS SENSE THE STATE OF THE OTHER? EMBODIED SIMULATION

A new area of research termed *embodied simulation* builds on Ekman's findings (Ekman et al., 1983) and mirror neuron research to address how emotions are communicated during social interactions. As we have noted above, during social interactions, usually out of awareness, people tend to roughly match the behavior of others, creating correspondences of gestures, body postures, and facial expressions. Sometimes this process of creating correspondences is so rapid between two partners that it is not visible, such as facial mimicry which may occur within one half a second (Niedenthal, Mermillod, Maringer, & Hess, 2010). Thus, observing an action in the partner can elicit the performance of that action in the individual.

Embodied simulation research shows the reciprocal effect: Performing the action of the partner influences the individual's perception of the partner's action and facilitates recognition of the partner's action. This effect may operate consciously or nonconsciously. The effect is greatest in contexts of subtle nuances of emotion. Theories of embodied simulation suggest that this matching process reflects an internal simulation of the perceived expression (gesture, posture) of the partner, which then facilitates an understanding of its meaning. This area of research has shown that the observation of action, the execution of action, and the recognition of action all share the same neural substrates, including the brain's reward, motor, somatosensory, and affective systems (Niedenthal et al., 2010; Oberman, Winkielman, & Ramachandran, 2007).

VOCAL RHYTHM COORDINATION AND THE PREDICTION OF ATTACHMENT: THE OPTIMAL MIDRANGE MODEL

In common parlance, as well as in many prominent research paradigms, the notion of "more is better" prevails. In this view, more attunement, more contingency, more matching, or more correspondence would be considered better, and would be expected to result in optimal outcomes. However, an important group of studies have demonstrated that a midrange model of coordination is optimal for attachment (Belsky et al., 1984; Cohn & Elmore, 1988; Jaffe et al., 2001; Lewis & Feiring, 1989; Leyendecker et al., 1997; Malatesta et al., 1989; Roe, Roe, Drivas, & Bronstein, 1990; Sander, 1995). This work shows that more is not necessarily better. Why? In the midrange, we have more flexibility to move around and find the partner, more flexibility for disruption and repair.

One example of these studies (Beebe, 2000; Jaffe et al., 2001) predicted attachment at one year from mother–infant and stranger–infant vocal rhythm coordination at four months. The stranger is a novel partner (one of the authors, or a trained graduate student). Vocal rhythm refers to the pattern of durations of sounds and silences within one person's vocal stream. Coordination refers to an interactive process in which each individual alters his or her behavior, based on what the partner just did. Coordination of vocal rhythms is assessed in the following way: as each person shortens or elongates the durations of sounds and silences, how tightly or loosely does the partner coordinate by similarly shortening or elongating his or her own sound and silence durations? Midrange degrees of mother–infant and stranger–infant coordination at four months predicted secure attachment at one year; very high and very low degrees of coordination predicted insecure attachment classifications.

This research led us to conceptualize coordination on a continuum, with an optimal midrange, and two poles defined by very high (excessive) or very low (withdrawn) coordination with the partner. We dubbed high coordination as over-tracking, trying too hard, or vigilance. High coordination increases the predictability of the interaction, construed as a coping strategy in the context of insecure attachment. The very low pole of coordination is interpreted as a withdrawal: Both partners are behaving relatively independently of the other; neither is adjusting much to the partner's behavior.

This research challenges our very common concept that more is better. In this view, more attunement, more coordination, more synchrony are all positive. But sometimes, less is more. Finding the midrange is often optimal. This finding can help parents feel less pressure to be exactly in sync with their infants. Many times, slowing down, sitting back, and waiting to see what the infant will do next, can provide a moment for both partners to readjust.

THE REGULATION OF DISTRESS IS CO-CREATED

How do we identify moments of infant facial or vocal distress as we code mother–infant face-to-face interactions? As noted above, we code infant expressions of facial distress, such as grimace, frown, and compressed lips. We code distressed infant vocalizations as fuss/whimper, angry-protest, and cry.

Infants differ in their ability to manage moments of heightened distress, and mothers differ in their ability to respond to infant distress. Both partners bring their own capacities to soothe and dampen their own distress. But the mother in addition has the capacity to help the infant with his distress through methods of empathic joining.

Joining the Cry Rhythm

An effective way that a mother can help to facilitate her infant in distress is by loosely joining or matching the infant's fuss rhythm or cry rhythm. This rhythmic joining is accompanied by empathic vocal *woe* contours (prosody). In this process, the *rhythm and prosody* (vocal affect) of the distress is approximately matched, but not the volume or intensity. Joining the volume or intensity of the infant's distress risks overstimulating the infant.

When the mother joins the cry rhythm, the infant can recognize the correspondence of the mother's rhythm and prosody to his own. The infant can feel sensed and known in his distress. Once the infant's distress has been joined in this way, the infant can also contribute to the regulation of his distress. Both mother and infant can gradually slow down their rhythms, and the infant can gradually calm down. This is a mutually created process, in which each person's slight adjustment influences the other to make a similar slight adjustment (Beebe, 2000; Beebe et al., 2010; Gergely & Watson, 1997; Stern, 1985).

Maternal Woe-Face

As we show in our drawings in Part II, whether or not mothers can share infant states of distress with corresponding empathic woe faces (and woe voices) of their own will be critical in the development of attachment security or insecurity. An example of maternal woe face is shown above in Figures 7d and 7e. Moreover, if the infant can continue to look at the mother while distressed, mothers are far more likely to be able to empathize with their infants by showing a woe face (Beebe, Bigelow et al., 2015). This is one way in which the infant helps to shape the mother's response and contributes to the cocreation of distress regulation.

DISRUPTION AND REPAIR

Instead of the more romanticized notion that mothers and infants exactly match, or are mostly in sync, or mostly behave in corresponding ways (see Cohn & Tronick,

1989), the optimal midrange model of coordination we described provides a more flexible model than exact matching. But it does not specifically address infant distress.

There is a second flexible model developed by Tronick and colleagues (Cohn & Tronick, 1989; Gianino & Tronick, 1988; Tronick, 1989; see also Beebe & Lachmann, 1994) that specifically addresses infant distress: disruption and repair (also known as mismatch and repair). In this model, interactions proceed in sequences of match, mismatch, and rematch of facial-visual engagement. We note that infants have the capacity to notice if the partner matches or mismatches his behavior, as we discussed earlier. Moreover, the infant has the capacity to notice if the mismatch is repaired into a more matched state.

ILLUSTRATION OF DISRUPTION AND REPAIR

Mismatched states between mother and infant are very common (Cohn & Tronick, 1989; Tronick, 1989). These mismatched states, *interactive errors,* occur approximately two thirds of the time in face-to-face interaction. Transitions back and forth between matched (corresponding) and mismatched states occur once every three to five seconds. Thus mismatched states are frequent and part of normal interactions (see Tronick, 1989, 2007).

Research has shown that a greater likelihood of a rapid rematch between partners within two seconds after disruption predicts secure attachment at one year (Cohn, Campbell, & Ross, 1991). Thus, the concepts of matching of states of facial-visual engagement and correspondences of affect and rhythms are important, but they constitute too limited a model of mother–infant face-to-face communication. Mismatched states, and the repair of mismatched states, are just as important.

One example of repair occurs when a mother notices the mismatch, either consciously or nonconsciously, slows down for a moment, and waits for her infant to rejoin her. In Figure 10a–10c, we see an illustration of a mother–infant interaction

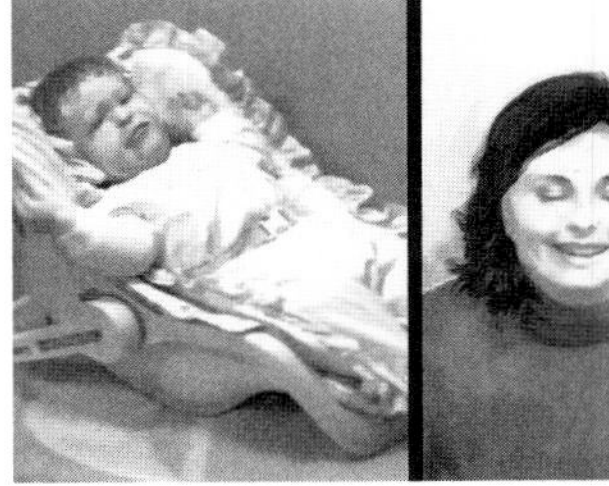

Figure 10a. Infant turns his head away, pulls his arms away in a "don't touch me" gesture, frowns, and grimaces slightly. The mother has dampened her smile, but she still has a hint of it, which is not matched with the infant's distress.

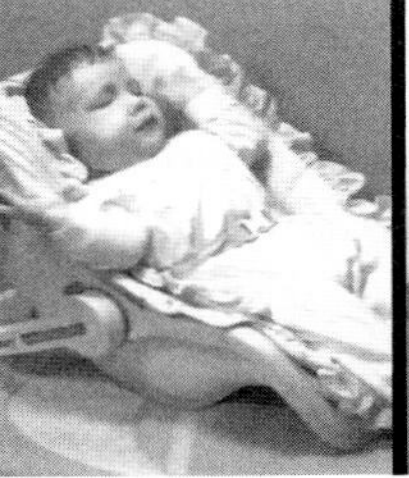

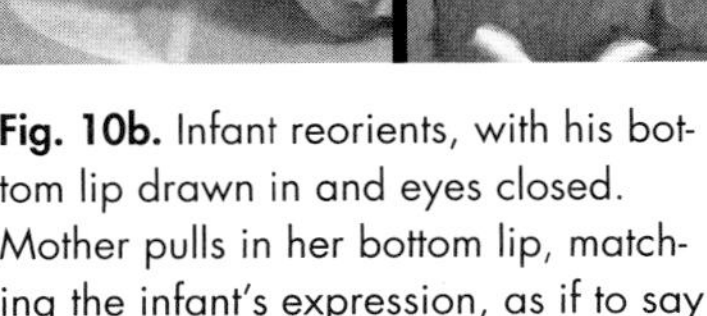

Fig. 10b. Infant reorients, with his bottom lip drawn in and eyes closed. Mother pulls in her bottom lip, matching the infant's expression, as if to say "uh-oh." She senses his state.

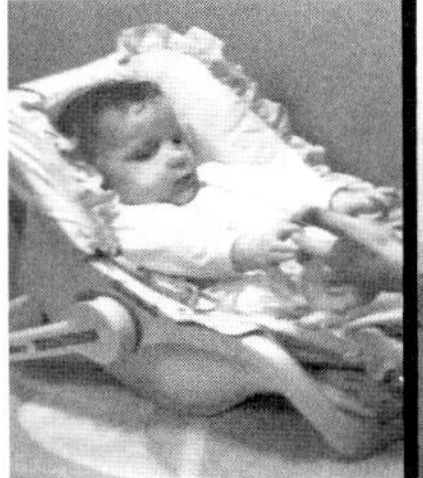

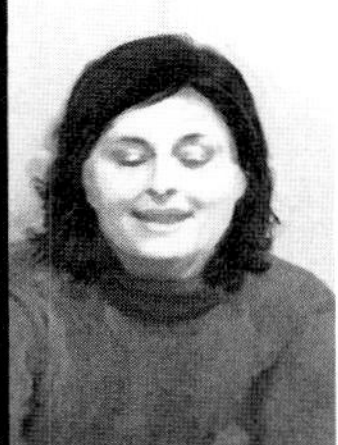

Figure 10c. Infant reaches for mother, and mother joins, reaching for the infant's hands. This begins the repair.

that is slightly disrupted and then repaired. In Figure 10a, as her infant turns his head away and arches back, the mother has a slight smile. In Figure 10b, the infant then reorients his head with his eyes closed, but his bottom lip is drawn in. The mother also pulls in her bottom lip, exactly matching the infant's expression, as if to say "uh-oh." She senses his state. This moment lasts one second. In Figure 10c, we see the repair as the infant reaches for his mother as the mother reaches for the infant's hands.

THE STRANGER AS PARTNER

In our research, mother and infant first play face-to-face, followed by infant and stranger playing face-to-face. The role of the stranger might be played by one of us, but more often by a trained graduate student or research assistant. The stranger–infant interaction has been shown to be a sensitive predictor of infant attachment patterns at one year (Jaffe et al., 2001). Moreover, stranger–infant vocal turn-taking in infancy predicts aspects of attachment in young adulthood (Beebe, Igleheart et al., 2015).

By the end of the first year, some infants develop *stranger anxiety.* But in the middle of the first year, and particularly at four months when we assess infants, the stranger is both a novel challenge, and at the same time, an intensely interesting new partner. Most four-month infants are very sociable with the stranger, to the point where often the stranger has an initial advantage over the mother. On the other hand, some infants are wary with the stranger (see Weinberg & Tronick, 1998). We assess the infant's capacity to engage with the stranger. Moreover, if the interaction is stressful with the mother, sometimes the infant can repair and reengage with the stranger.

SELF- AND INTERACTIVE REGULATION IN THE ACTION-DIALOGUE LANGUAGE

As we reviewed the infant and mother's action-dialogue language, we described many ways in which this language is used by the partners as they coordinate their behaviors. For example, we described forms of correspondence, particularly facial mirroring. We also described chase and dodge, secure look-away, distress regulation, and disruption and repair. These processes of coordination involve different modes of self- and interactive regulation. They are out-of-awareness but nevertheless highly organized. In fact, mothers and infants, as well as adults, learn to expect and anticipate these out-of-awareness forms of self- and interactive organization. These processes provide the foundation of nonverbal communication, and they operate throughout life.

INTERACTIVE REGULATION

Mother–infant interaction is co-created moment-to-moment by both partners. It unfolds as a reciprocal, bidirectional dyadic process across time. That is, each partner is changing with the other (Stern, 1985), and each partner is affecting the behavior of the other, often within split seconds (Beebe, 1982; Beebe et al., 2010; Beebe & Stern, 1977; Stern, 1971; Tronick, 1989, 2007). We term this process interactive regulation or coordination. It is a continuous, reciprocally coordinated process. Each affects, and is affected by, the partner's changing behavior, moment-by-moment. And each partner detects the process of affecting, and being affected by, the other. Interactive regulation occurs through all the modalities of communication that we have illustrated: attention, affect, orientation, and touch.

But mother and infant are not equal partners. They do not necessarily coordinate in similar, symmetrical, or equal ways. The infant is an active contributor, having a remarkable range of engagement as well as disengagement behaviors (Beebe & Stern, 1977; Brazelton et al., 1974; Murray & Trevarthen, 1985; Stern, 1971, 1985). But the mother has the greater flexibility and range. For example, in the chase and dodge illustration, the infant has veto power over the mother's efforts to engage him. But the mother can continue to loom and chase. All the infant can do is to say "no," by orienting his head away, protesting vocally, arching back, going limp, or freezing. Sometimes these infant behaviors can influence the mother to stop chasing, but sometimes she keeps going, even so.

Although the term *mutual influence* is often used interchangeably with interactive regulation or coconstructed interaction, we no longer use mutual influence because neither mutuality nor influence in their usual meanings is accurate. Mutuality usually has a desirable implication, but aversive interactions such as "chase and dodge" are also coconstructed, in the sense that each partner affects the other's behavior, but in an adverse way (Beebe & Stern, 1977). The term *influence* can also be misleading because no conscious intention to influence the behavior of the partner is implied in the documentations of interactive regulation (although obviously the parent has many conscious intentions to influence the infant). It is not a causal process, in the sense that one person's behavior *causes* the other's behavior. Rather, it is a probabilistic process: one person's behavior now, in the current moment, is predictable from what the partner just did, in the prior moment. Thus, we prefer the more neutral terms interactive regulation or coordination.

SELF-REGULATION

Self-regulation is just as important as interactive regulation. Processes of self-regulation and interactive regulation go on simultaneously within each partner. Each person monitors and coordinates with the partner, and at the same time regulates his or her own state, such as state of attention, emotion, and arousal. In this view, all interactions are a simultaneous product of self- and interactive processes (Gianino & Tronick, 1988; Sander, 1977; Thomas & Martin, 1976; Tronick, 1989).

The ability to respond and be socially engaged depends not only on the nature of the partner's input, and on one's own responsivity, but also on the regulation of the state of both participants (Beebe & Lachmann, 1994). Both infant and parent bring unique proclivities such as temperamental dispositions and arousal regulation styles that affect self-regulation. Each partner's self-regulation capacity and style affects the nature of the interactive regulation, and vice versa.

Self-regulation has many meanings. Its meaning also differs as development proceeds. A very general definition of self-regulation is the management of arousal. This refers to the level of activation of one's bodily states. It includes variations in the readiness to respond to the social partner (Kopp, 1989, 2002), and in the clarity of social cues, such as how clearly a baby conveys hunger, sleepiness, or approach and withdrawal (Als & Brazelton, 1981; Gianino & Tronick, 1988; Korner & Grobstein, 1976; Sander, 1977). It also includes the ability to dampen down distress. Self-touching, looking away, and restricting the range of facial expressiveness are examples of self-regulation strategies that dampen arousal (Field, 1981; Koulomzin et al., 2002). From infancy onward, people differ in crucial self-regulation capacities, which affect one's state: modulating arousal, shifting states, tolerating stimulation at different intensities, and using stimulation to organize behavior in predictable ways.

In our drawings, examples of self-regulation can be found in moments of looking away (Figure 2a and 2b), self-touching (Figure 5c), or fingering the partner's hand (Figures 8a and 10c). However, it is important to remember that these same behaviors also communicate to the partner, and therefore are part of the interactive process as well.

PATTERNS OF SELF- AND INTERACTIVE REGULATION BECOME EXPECTED: EXPECTANCIES AND PROCEDURAL MEMORY

In the interactive process, each partner develops expectancies of "how I affect you," and "how you affect me." Each also develops expectancies of how one's own self-regulation patterns unfold. Thus, both partners come to expect particular interactive patterns, associated with particular self-regulation processes. Infant expectancies of different patterns of self- and interactive regulation provide one process that contributes in fundamental ways to the trajectory of development.

The mother–infant preverbal action-dialogue generates *expectancies* in both partners of how action and interaction sequences unfold, from moment-to-moment. These actions include all the behaviors we have described above: looking and looking away from one's partner, facial and vocal emotion (such as prosody, intensity, pitch), spatial orientation toward and away from the partner, and different qualities of touch.

HOW DO INFANTS CREATE EXPECTANCIES OF THEIR DYADIC ACTION-DIALOGUE WORLD?

As we have already discussed, infants are contingency detectors from birth. They detect predictable consequences of their own actions, and of the partner's actions, by estimating probabilities of if-then sequences (Saffran, Aslin, & Newport, 1996; Tarabulsy, Tessier, & Kappas, 1996). For example, *if* I move my head up and smile at you, *then* you are very likely to move your head up and smile as well. When repeated over and over, this process generates an expectancy: The infant comes to expect this sequence. As we noted, the partner's provision of predictable coordination with the infant's behavior creates the foundation of the infant's experience of interactive agency.

For an event to be perceived as contingent by the infant, the sequence of behaviors (for example, infant behavior followed by partner behavior) must be predictable, that is, occurring with greater than chance probability. It must occur rather rapidly as well. In fact, contingencies tend to be extremely rapid. Stern (1977, 1985) coined the phrase the "split-second world" in characterizing the ways in which mothers and infants respond to each other during face-to-face interaction. We see this split-second world dramatically illustrated in the drawings in Part II. Infant learning of contingencies involves cognitive processes of expectation and anticipation (Tarabulsy et al., 1996). This process of anticipation helps explain why the world of action sequences is split-second.

ANTICIPATORY EXPECTANCIES

What is the evidence that infants anticipate events? Infants aged three and a half months were shown two series of slides of checkerboards, bull's-eyes, and schematic drawings of faces (Haith et al., 1988). One series regularly alternated to the left and the right of visual center in a steady rhythm, as the images moved up and down. Based on the regularity of the pattern, can the infant anticipate where the image will appear? The other series appeared randomly in left or right position. It was a control condition, and the infants could not possibly detect any pattern. Meanwhile, the researchers videotaped one of the infant's eyes. They found that the infants detected the spatial-temporal pattern that governed the regularly alternating series. In fact, the infants showed anticipatory eye movements. Their eyes focused on the slide a fraction of a second before it appeared. This ability to detect sequences of actions, to generate expectancies, and to anticipate events, gives the infant a way of maintaining continuity in an ever-changing world (Haith et al., 1988).

The drawings that we show in Part II illustrate how strikingly different patterns of action sequences are created in dyads on the way to secure infant attachment at one year, compared with dyads on the way to insecure attachment. As these patterns repeat over and over, both partners form generalized *anticipatory expectancies* of these action sequences.

These expectancies, imagined from the point of view of the infant (the mother's expectancies are comparable), are based on:

(a) Predictable processes within *oneself,* that is, "As *I* do this, then *I* do that." To illustrate, in the mother–infant facial mirroring interaction, the infant might come to expect, "As I look at you (mother) and begin to smile, I open my mouth and raise my head more and more until I am bursting with my biggest smile."
(b) Predictable sequences within one's partner, the mother, that is, "As *you* do this, then *you* do that." To illustrate, continuing with mother–infant facial mirroring example, the infant might come to expect, "Mother, as your smile widens, your mouth opens more, and your head goes up and up."
(c) Predictable interactive sequences between partners, from infant to mother, that is, "As *I* do this, then *you* do that." To illustrate, continuing with facial

mirroring, "As I (infant) open my mouth in bigger and bigger smiles, you, mother, smile at me and open your mouth and raise your head up until we are both reaching our smiles up and up toward each other."

(d) Predictable interactive sequences between partners, from mother to infant, that is, "As *you* do that, then *I* do this." To illustrate, continuing with mother–infant facial mirroring, "As you, mother, open your mouth and smile at me, I return your smile and open my own mouth more and more."

The particular patterns formed by the dyad guide the actions of each, are learned, and are remembered. These generalized expectancies of the interaction patterns of the action-dialogue are learned by mother and infant with an action sequence form of knowledge, rather than through verbal language. Earlier we termed this form of learning *procedural memory*. These procedural memories become quasi-automatic with repetition. Moreover, they influence future behavior (Emde, Birengen, Clyman, & Oppenheim, 1991; Grigsby & Hartlaub, 1994; Squire & Cohen, 1984). These expectancies involve anticipation of what will happen, as well as memories of what has generally happened in the past (Haith et al., 1988). However, this entire process remains mostly out of awareness.

As adults, we are used to making sense of our own actions, and the actions of others through symbolized mental states (desires, thoughts, memories, feelings) of self and other. This can be termed a language-based *theory of mind* (Fonagy, Gergely, Jurist, & Target, 2002). Infants make sense of actions of self and other through the procedural expectancies we have just described, the action-dialogue language. These expectancies define an early presymbolic *theory of mind* available before language (Beebe et al., 2013).

Stern (1995) considered an infant's expectancies to be central in the relationship with his or her parents. Infant expectancies are the infant's guide to how he will feel, how he will perceive, how he will act, and how he will interpret his relationship with his parents. Infant expectancies set the trajectory in development for everything the infant will come to think and feel about his parents in relation to himself. These expectancies form the basis for generalized expectancies, which are carried into other relationships (Beebe et al., 2009; Field et al., 1988).

The drawings in the next chapter provide a window into the process by which infants at four months develop expectancies of themselves and their parents during face-to-face interactions. Reciprocally, the drawings depict the process by which parents develop expectancies about their infants and themselves. In our descriptions of the drawings, we attempt to translate the action-dialogue language into words in an effort to facilitate our understanding of these action sequences and what each partner might be feeling or trying to do. However, we do not mean to imply that infants reflect on their expectancies. We do not imply that as infants develop, these patterns are actually translated into a linguistic format. Nor do parents usually translate their action-dialogue into words. Rather, we assume that for both mother and infant, these expectancies of early interactions are encoded in nonverbal, procedural, imagistic, acoustic, visceral, and temporal modes of information, and they continue to guide behavior in this procedural format (see Bucci, 1985, 1997).

Although we have introduced you to many examples of behavior in this chapter, we now provide a glossary of terms from our four domains of attention, orientation, emotion, and touch. Each term has an accompanying example from a film frame drawn by the artist.

In Part II of the book, we turn to drawings of ten examples of interactions. We look at the drawings together. We study the second-by-second sequences of interactions, and try to see what the mother and infant may be doing and feeling from frame to frame.

Illustrated Glossary of Terms

Infant attention: gazing at and away from the mother's face

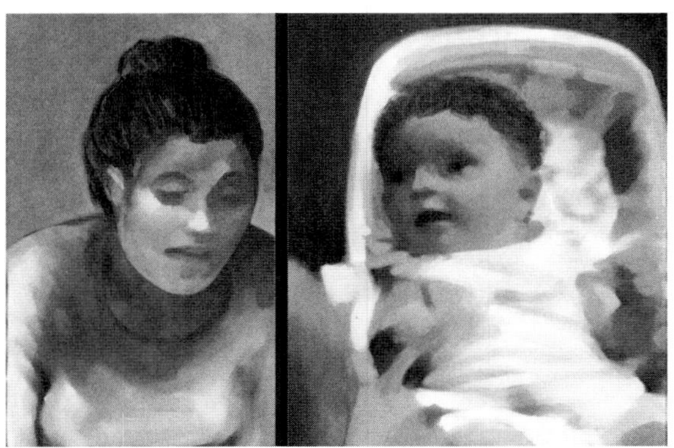

Infant gazes at mother

Infant gazes away

Mother attention: gazing at and away from the infant's face

Mother gazes at infant

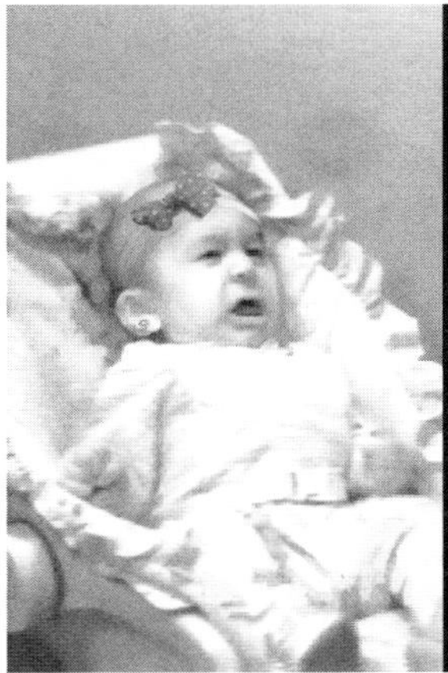

Mother gazes away, looks down

Infant head orientation: from vis-à-vis to arch away

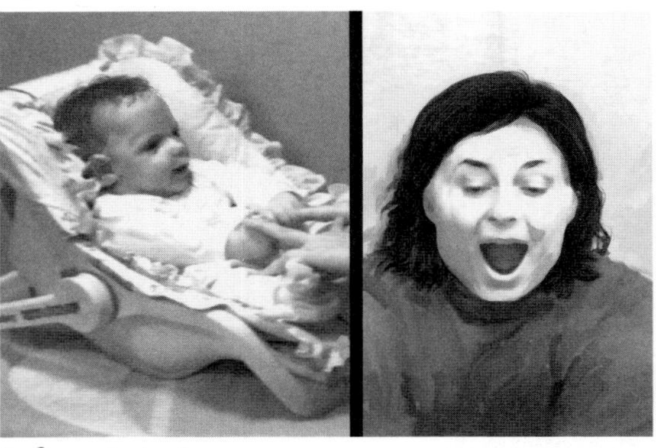

Infant vis-à-vis

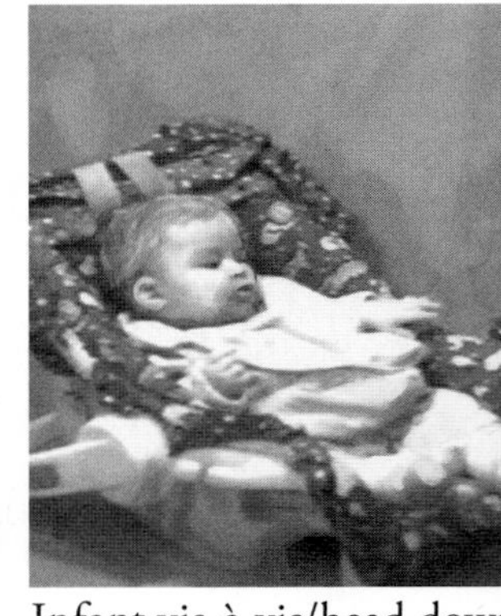

Infant vis-à-vis/head down

Infant 30- to 60-degree minor head aversion

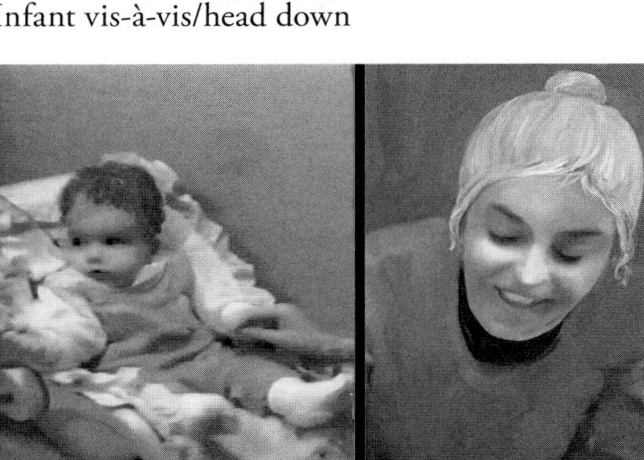

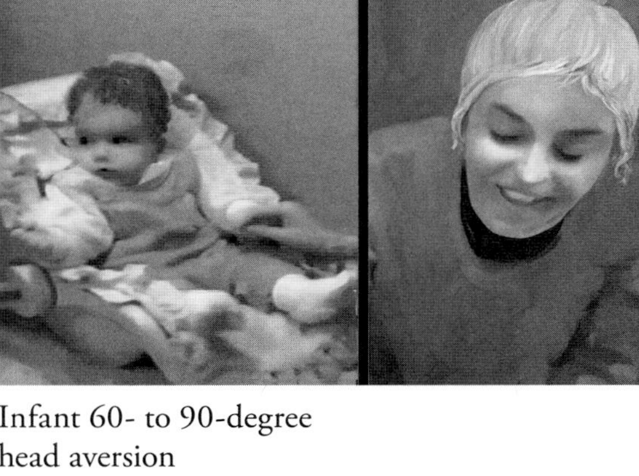

Infant 60- to 90-degree head aversion

Infant 90-degree head aversion

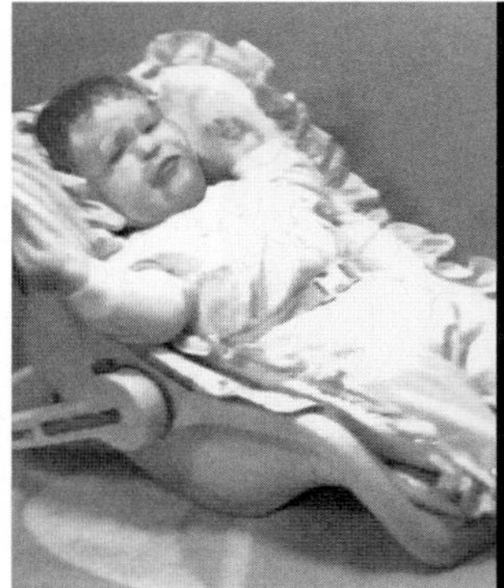

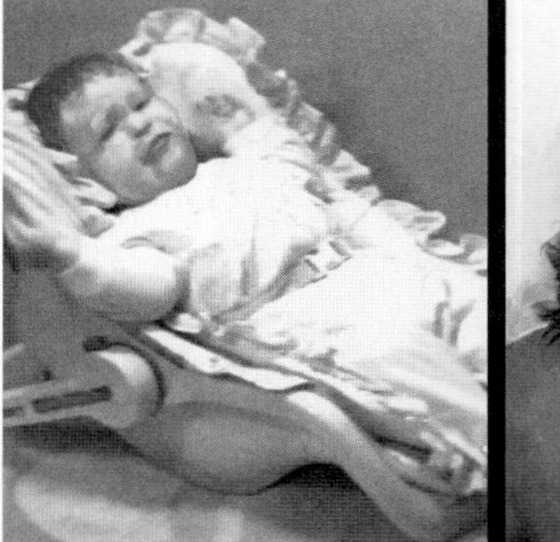

Infant arch

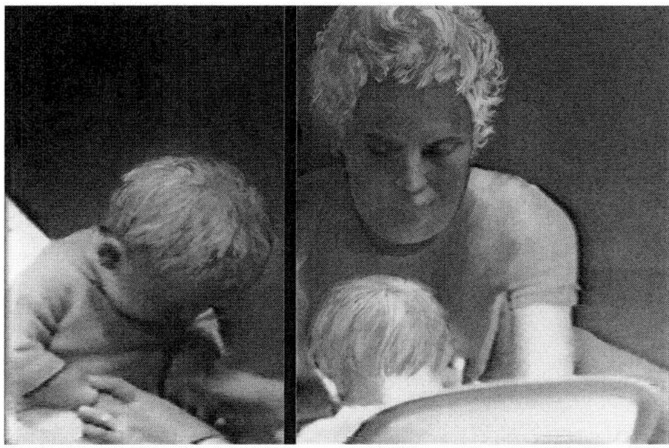

Infant loss of body tonus

Mother spatial orientation: from sitting upright to leaning forward to looming in

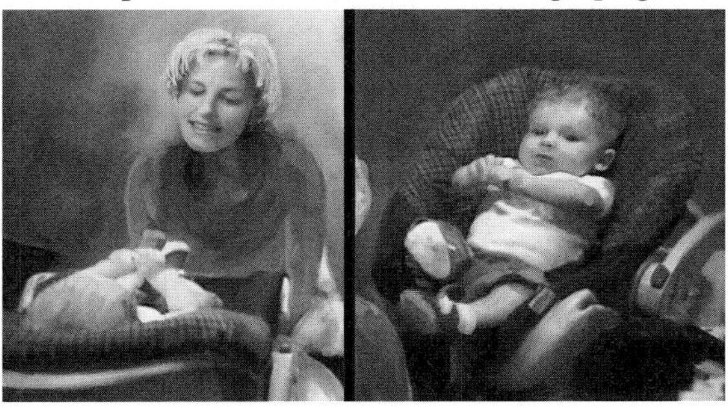

Mother upright

Mother forward

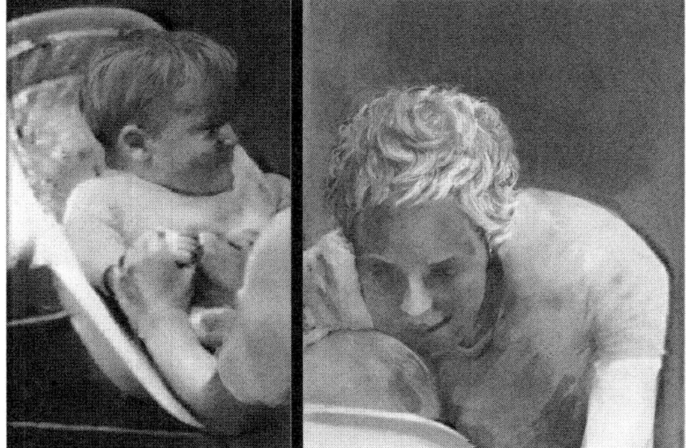

Mother loom

Infant emotion: Degrees of positive to negative facial expressions

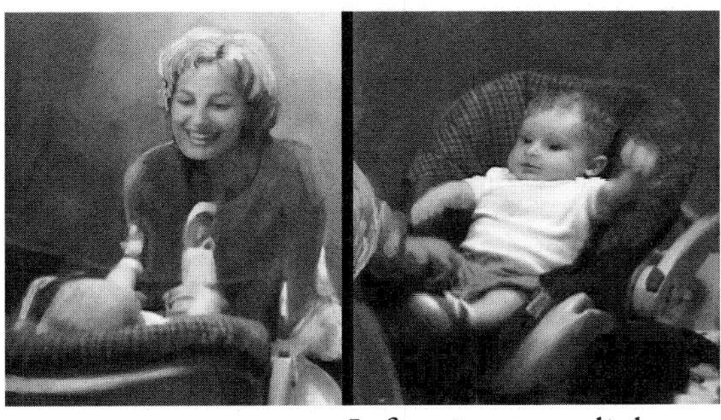

Infant interest: slight mouth opening and widening

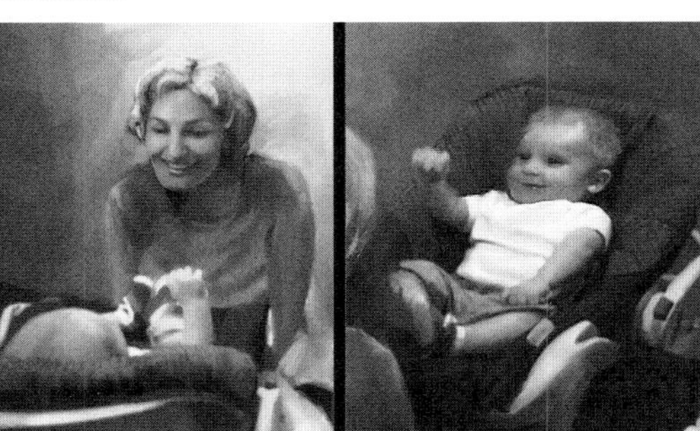

Infant low smile

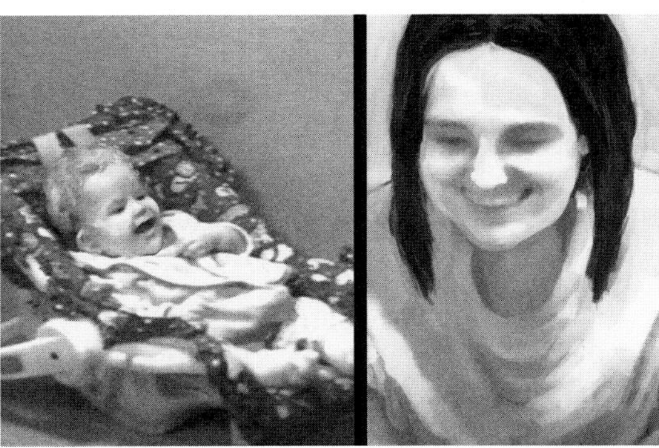

Infant full smile

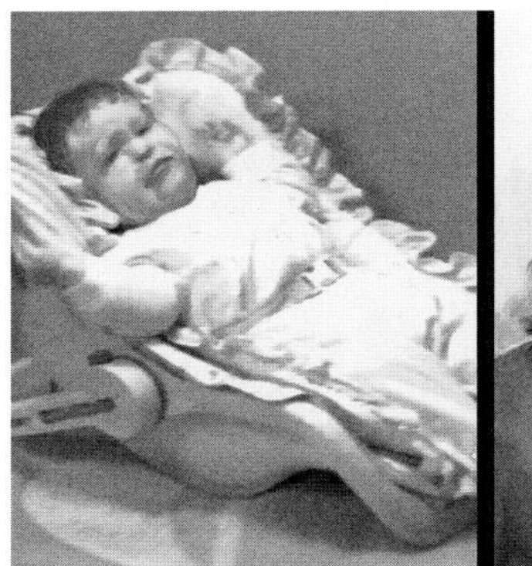

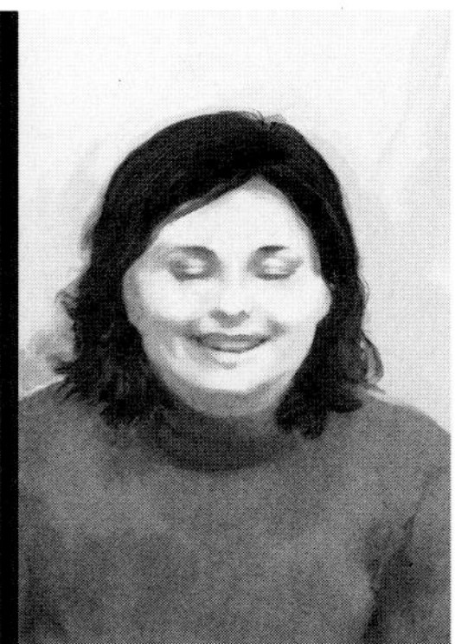

Infant negative, frown/grimace

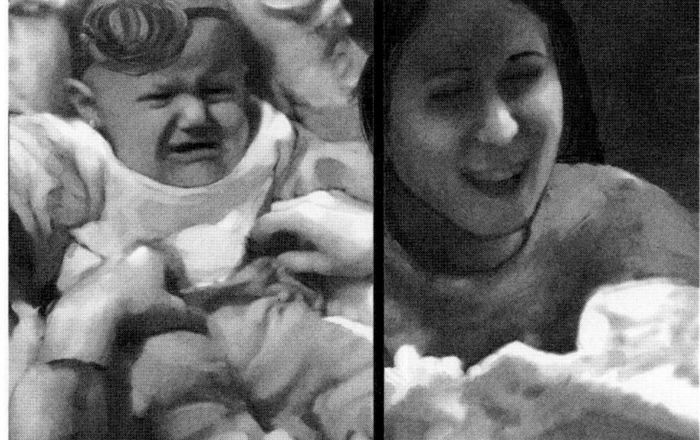

Infant negative pre-cry face

Mother emotion: Degrees of positive to negative facial expressions

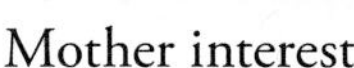

Mother interest

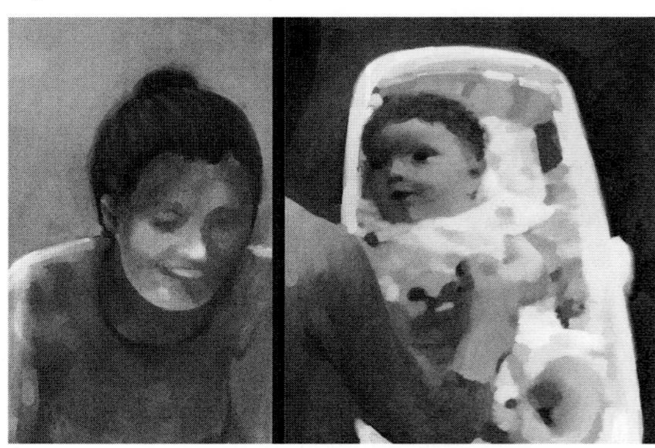

Mother smile

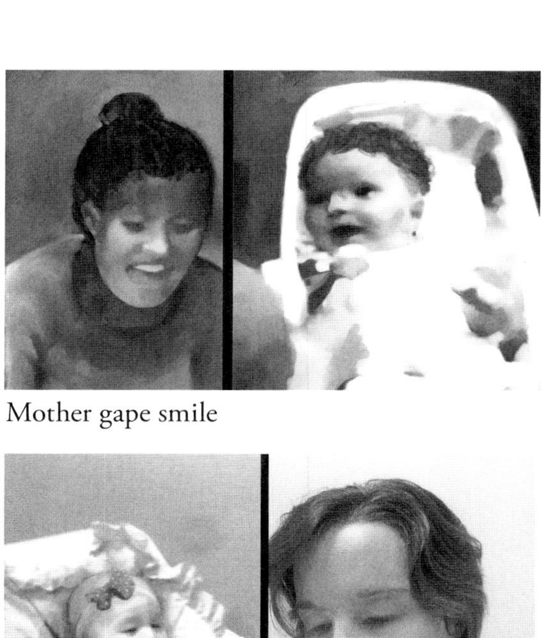

Mother gape smile

Mother mock surprise

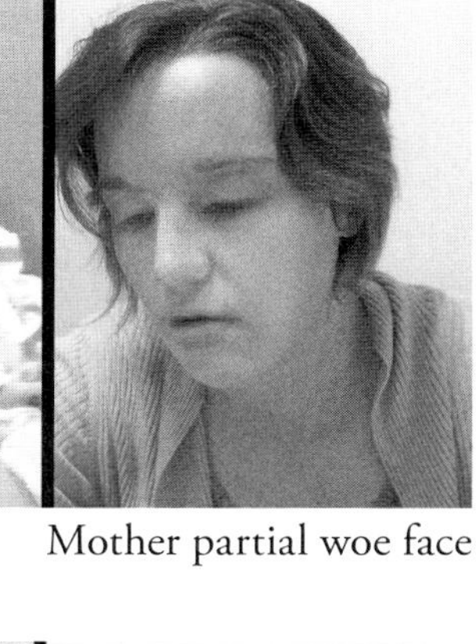

Mother partial woe face

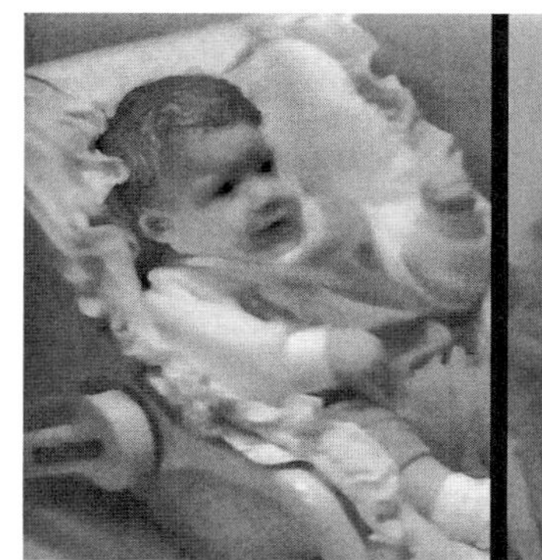

Stranger woe face
with surprise

Mother disgust face with
bared teeth

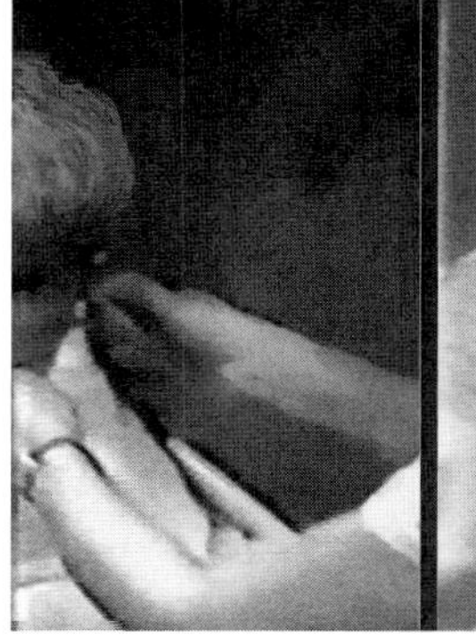

Mother grimace

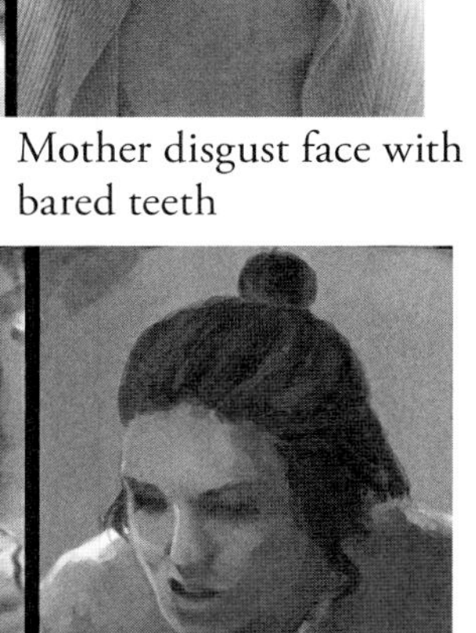

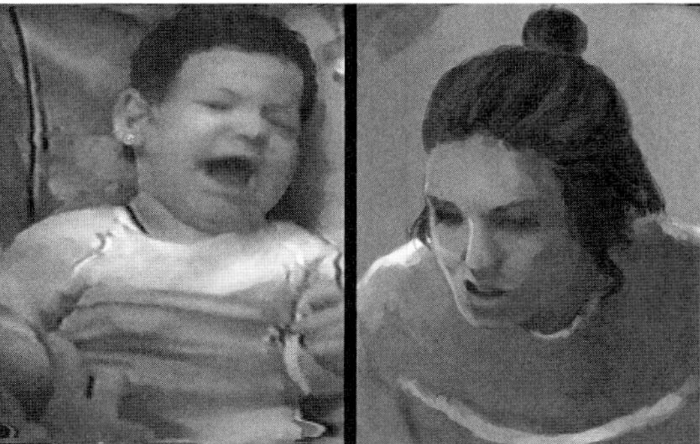

Mother sneer (nasolabial fold
right corner of mouth)

Sequence in which mother dampens her smile

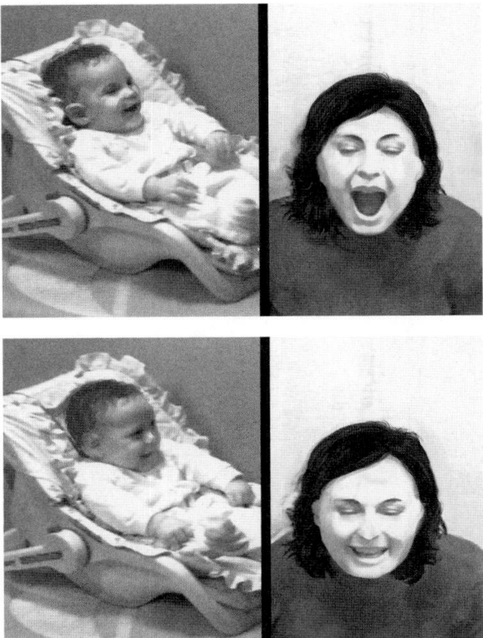

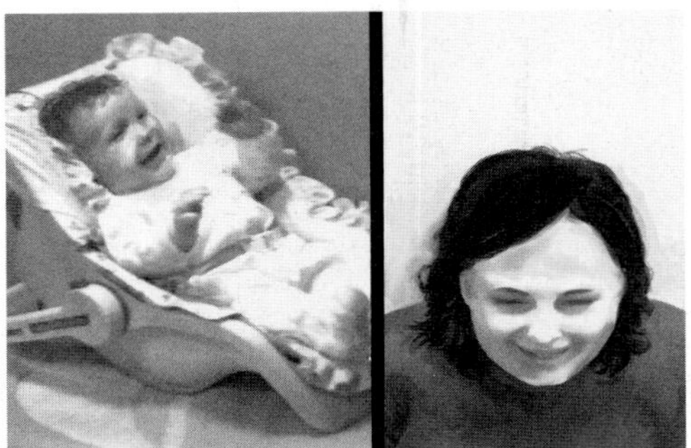

Infant touch: Touch self, object, or mother.

Infant touches self

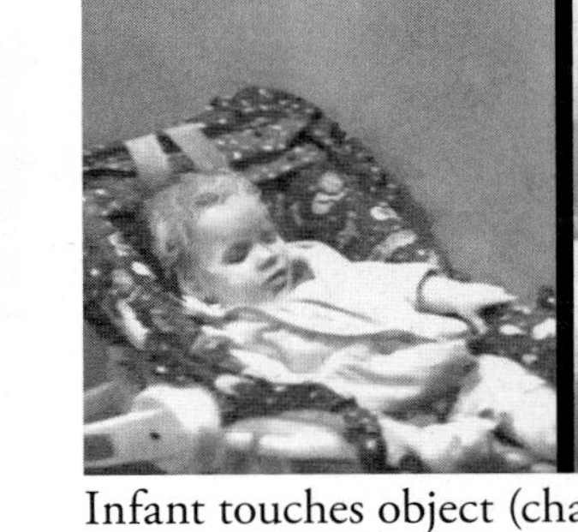

Infant touches object (chair)

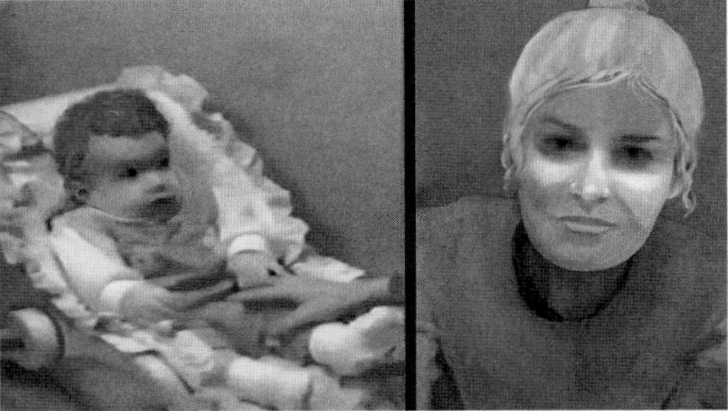

Infant touches mother

PART II

Drawings of Mother–Infant Patterns of Communication and Commentaries

Introduction to Part II

Part II, Drawings of Mother–Infant Patterns of Communication and Commentaries, is organized in the following way: The first four sets of drawings in Chapters 4 to 7 illustrate mother–infant interaction patterns at four months where infants were on the way to secure attachment at one year. Chapters 8 and 9 illustrate mother–infant interaction patterns where infants were on the way to insecure attachment, resistant and avoidant, respectively. The final four, Chapters 10 to 13 illustrate mother–infant patterns where infants were on the way to disorganized attachment at one year.

We begin with a Guide to the Drawings. This guide will facilitate an understanding of all our drawings.

Guide to the Drawings

Looking at these drawings can be done in layers. At a more global layer, look at the "Storyline" and then follow this story in the drawings. This is a good way to begin. However, you can also look at the detailed descriptions that accompany each drawing. This process requires patience. The central goal is to look from one drawing to the next, to see if you can identify movement. It requires some study for you to identify the movements that we describe. Note that the drawings are taken from film frames of split-screen videotaped mother–infant (or stranger–infant) face-to-face interactions. There are two cameras, one each on mother and on the infant. The two views are separated by a thick, black vertical line.

We have organized the drawings in the following ways:

- The ten patterns of drawings are presented in Chapters 4 to 13.
- Our goal is to use these drawings to illustrate different patterns of mother–infant interaction that predicted secure or insecure infant attachment patterns at one year.

- Recall that mother and infant are seated face-to-face opposite each other in the same plane. The two views are combined into one split-screen view. When you look at the drawings, notice the black line that separates the two views.
- Within each pattern of communication, each drawing of the sequence is labeled with a frame number. Each frame is labeled with "minute:second" (e.g., 01:10). These minute:second labels indicate the time sequence of the frames chosen to illustrate each particular interaction.
- A letter after a minute:second, for example, 01:10a, or 01:10b indicates a change within that same second, that is, second 10.
- We indicate sections where two separate segments of film were chosen from a particular interaction (e.g., "four seconds later").
- In each drawing, we have decided whether mother or infant behavior should be described first, based on the specific context.
- Microanalysis is performed by shifting back and forth across two sequential frames of film. Thus, it becomes possible to see the movement and change from one second (or fraction of a second) to the next. We label the frames, for example, as "from Frame 2 to Frame 3," to indicate that we are describing a change that began in Frame 2 that is now visible in Frame 3.
- The reader needs to infer the movement by running the eye back and forth between the two drawings.
- Each drawing has a brief description with it. We have attempted to describe the behaviors and feelings of the mothers and infants and strangers and infants in these drawings. We have tried to capture subtle shifts (many of which are only visible by running the eye back and forth between two drawings).
- There may be some instances in which a particular sequence could be read and interpreted differently. In these instances, we hope you take a leap of faith and try to see what we see. The reader has the disadvantage of only being able to view the drawings and not the original film frames. In addition, we are presenting a small number of frames from the full two and one half-minute sequence that was analyzed in the research study. Patterns that we describe in these drawings are representative of many similar sequences.

Introduction to Drawings Illustrating the Origins of Secure Attachment

Bowlby (1958, 1969) proposed that infant attachment behaviors are used to maintain proximity and contact with the primary caretaker, contributing to a bond that ties infant and caregiver, and which continues throughout life. Attachment is a construct that describes a *relationship* rather than an individual. Ainsworth and her colleagues (1978) further developed Bowlby's theory, suggesting that the developing quality of attachment is highly dependent upon maternal behaviors that are sensitive to the infant's signals and moods. Such sensitivity tends to promote a secure relationship in which the infant can use the mother as a base both for protection and nurturance as well as for exploration of the environment. The insecurely attached infant, on the other hand, spends either too much or too little time in proximity to the mother or exploring the environment, upsetting an attachment-exploration balance. The recurrent nature of the infant's experiences leads to the development of expectancies of self and others that influence the infant's emotional experiences and expectations throughout development (Erickson, Sroufe, & Egeland, 1983; Main, Kaplan, & Cassidy, 1985; van IJzendoorn, 1995; Waters, Merrick, Treboux, Crowell, & Albersheim, 2000).

Infant attachment is "vital in the formation of the person" (Sroufe, 2005, p. 365) because it affects so many critical developmental functions, such as social relatedness, arousal modulation, emotional regulation, and curiosity. However, secure attachment does not guarantee healthy functioning. Instead, it can be seen as a protective factor because it sets a trajectory in development for successful intimate relationships and flexible patterns of coping with stress (Sroufe, 2005).

As we noted in the Introduction, in the Ainsworth strange situation attachment assessment, mother and infant go through periods of free play, separations, and reunions (Ainsworth et al., 1978). Based on the extent to which the infant uses the parent as a secure base from which to explore, and as a safe haven when distressed, infants can be classified as having secure or insecure attachment patterns.

During the brief periods of separation from the mother, securely attached infants may show distress. However, during the reunion episodes, they seek contact from the mother, are easily comforted, and quickly return to play. These infants are able to express their distress openly. Because the mother (caregiver) is responsive to the infant's distress, the infant learns that negative emotions are acceptable, and that the parent will be available for comfort (Bell & Ainsworth, 1972; Cassidy, 1994). As a result, the experience of distress may be less threatening for a secure (vs. insecure) infant. A key aspect of security is the infant's ability to tolerate distress temporarily because he is confident that help is available, and that he can achieve mastery over threatening or frustrating situations (Kobak & Sceery, 1988). When there is no threat from the environment, secure infants use the caregiver as a secure base from which to explore. When a threat arises, secure infants view the caregiver as a safe haven (Ainsworth et al., 1978; Main & Solomon, 1986). This strategy is optimal because it allows the infant to fully explore the possibilities of the environment while maintaining access to the caregiver when needed (Cassidy, 1994).

An infant's attachment pattern at one year predicts many aspects of the child's development, including school achievement, social engagement, and emotional well-being (Sroufe et al., 2005a, 2005b). Secure attachment at one year is associated with better peer relations, school performance, and capacity to regulate emotions (Sroufe, 1983). Children with a secure attachment history and who functioned well in middle childhood had higher competence ratings and lower pathology ratings in adolescence than all other groups (Sroufe, Carlson, Levy, & Egeland, 1999).

How does secure infant attachment develop? During the infant's first year, repeated daily experiences between the parent and the infant, and the ways that each affects the other, generate expectancies of how the relationship will go. These expectancies organize infant attachment patterns (Beebe et al., 2010). Securely attached infants develop an expectation that their communicative gestures and emotions will usually be responded to in sensitive ways. This is similar to the "good-enough" mother described by Winnicott (1965). The drawings below illustrate some of the kinds of interactions in which infants can develop such expectations. Infants whose mothers respond sensitively to the full range of their emotions are more likely to be securely attached (Ainsworth et al., 1978; Belsky et al., 1984; Egeland & Farber, 1984).

MATERNAL SENSITIVITY

Maternal sensitivity is one of the central constructs of attachment theory and research (Beebe & Steele, 2013; Bretherton, 2013). Ainsworth's sensitivity construct derives from observations of 26 mother–infant dyads who were visited at home for four hours every three weeks over the first year. Observers took detailed notes of the infants' interactions with their mothers, and the notes were subsequently audio-recorded and transcribed. Based on the nine- to twelve-month narrative records, Ainsworth developed a Maternal Sensitivity Scale with four essential components: awareness of infant signals, accurate interpretation, appropriate response, and prompt response. For example, awareness of infant signals during play and social interaction is described as responding appropriately and not overstimulating the infant by interacting in ways that are too intense, vigorous, prolonged, or exciting. The mother (caregiver) can accurately interpret the infant's signs of overexcitement, undue tension, or incipient distress. She knows to shift the tempo or intensity before things have gone too far. She is unlikely to understimulate the infant because she picks up and responds to signals of boredom, or of wanting more interaction (Ainsworth, Bell, & Stayton, 1974).

Blehar, Lieberman, and Ainsworth (1977) also used the narrative transcripts described above to analyze early face-to-face interactions. At twelve months, infants identified as securely (vs. insecurely) attached to their mothers in the strange situation had been more responsive in early face-to-face encounters, and their mothers had been more contingently responsive and encouraging of interaction. Contingent responsivity was judged, coding from the narrative records. Infants later identified as anxiously (vs. securely) attached were more unresponsive, and their mothers were more likely to be impassive or abrupt. Securely (vs. insecurely) attached infants were more positively responsive to their mothers than to unfamiliar figures (strangers) in face-to-face interactions (see Beebe & Steele, 2013).

A comparison of many studies found that maternal sensitivity and infant–mother attachment were associated (De Wolff & van IJzendoorn, 1997). However, the modest size of the association led to the conclusion that maternal sensitivity is important in the origins of attachment security, but there are likely other contributors, such as the ones we have noted in Chapter 1 and research findings that we note in the following chapters.

THE ADULT ATTACHMENT INTERVIEW

What about the mothers (fathers) of securely attached infants? When mothers are interviewed about their own attachment histories in the last trimester of the pregnancy, the infant's attachment at one year can be predicted, even before the infant is born (Fonagy et al., 1991; Steele et al., 1996). Thus, attachment patterns can be transmitted from one generation to the next. The type of attachment that a person forms early in life influences how that person interacts with his or her own children (Kovan, Chung, & Sroufe, 2009; Main et al., 1985; Raby et al., 2015; Sroufe & Fleeson, 1986).

The Adult Attachment Interview (AAI; Hesse, 2008; Main, Hesse, & Goldwyn, 2008), is an hour-long, semistructured interview. It assesses an adult's current state of mind with respect to attachment experiences. Individuals are asked about childhood attachment experiences with their parents and are asked to describe specific memories of separation and rejection. They are also asked to describe the ways they were affected by these early experiences, and to reflect on their current relationship with their parents (Groh et al., 2014; Riem, Bakermans-Kranenburg, van IJzendoorn, Out, & Rombouts, 2012). It is the coherence of discourse rather than the content of the autobiographical account that determines the attachment classification (Hesse, 2008).

The flexibility and openness to a range of emotion seen in secure infants is also seen in the AAIs of their parents, most of whom are classified as secure (Cassidy, 1994). These adults tend to value attachment relationships, to describe their attachment experiences (whether positive or negative) coherently, and to consider them important in the development of their personality (Riem et al., 2012). Secure adults are also skilled at regulating their own emotions. Therefore, when faced with another's distress, they are free to focus on the needs of the other; they do not become overly emotionally aroused as they vicariously experience the others' distress (Eisenberg & Fabes, 1992; Peck, 2003).

THE CONTRIBUTION OF MICROANALYSIS

In the drawings to follow, illustrating the origins of secure infant attachment in mother–infant interactions at four months, you see many moments in which the mothers are able to attend to a wide range of infant expressions and emotions. You see moments in which the mothers can accurately interpret the infant's signs of overexcitement, undue tension, or incipient distress, and shift the tempo or intensity. These moments illustrate the concept of maternal sensitivity. As you see below, they also illustrate the concept of disruption and repair.

However, the microanalysis approach offers the possibility of identifying aspects of maternal sensitivity and the origins of attachment with a more detailed lens (Beebe & Steele, 2013). Our microanalysis study of the origins of attachment (Beebe et al., 2010) documented new communication patterns between mothers and infants at four months that have not been previously identified with the maternal sensitivity approach (Beebe & Steele, 2013). As we noted in the Introduction and Chapters 1 and 2, face-to-face communication is extremely rapid and often not quite perceptible in real time. Much of it is out of awareness. Moreover, in real time, it is often extremely difficult to discern the exact sequence of behaviors. Microanalysis operates like a *social microscope,* identifying the exact sequences of these subterranean, rapid communications.

Relatively few studies have predicted one-year attachment using detailed microanalytic coding of videotaped mother–infant interaction and assessments of mother and infant moment-by-moment contingent coordination. Summarizing half a dozen microanalysis studies, the following aspects of mother and infant behavior emerge in relation to infant attachment outcomes (see Beebe et al., 2010; Beebe & Steele, 2013):

(1) Mothers who engage and stimulate their infants while infants are looking at their mothers' faces, and who hold back on stimulating while infants look away, facilitate their infants' ability to use looking away as a coping mechanism to down-regulate arousal (Brazelton et al., 1974; Field, 1981). These maternal patterns are associated with secure infant attachment (Langhorst & Fogel, 1982).
(2) Mothers who tend to increase their stimulation right after the infant has become distressed are more likely to have infants who will be classified as insecurely attached (Langhorst & Fogel, 1982).
(3) Infants who look away extensively and who show patterns of postural avoidance are more likely to be classified as insecurely attached (Langhorst & Fogel, 1982).
(4) Mothers who coordinate with infant behavior on a midrange degree of contingency, neither very high nor very low, are more likely to have infants who will be classified as securely attached.

(a) For example, maternal contingent facial coordination with infant facial affect is defined as maternal changes contingent on infant positive-to-negative facial changes, within one second of the infant's changes. This concept can be described as the mother following the infant's direction of affective change. Midrange (moderate) maternal facial coordination predicted secure infant attachment; high levels of maternal facial coordination predicted avoidant infant attachment (Malatesta et al., 1989). This finding is an early example of the optimal midrange model: The highest coordination is not necessarily optimal for secure attachment.
(b) In a second example, mothers were given the AAI in the last trimester of pregnancy. Mothers who were secure/autonomous on the AAI showed moderate degrees of contingent coordination of social engagement when interacting face-to-face with their infants at four months. In contrast, mothers classified as preoccupied/entangled (analogous to the infant classification of resistant attachment) showed higher degrees of coordination (Slade et al., 1995; Tobias, 1995). Strikingly, the infants' level of coordination matched that of their mothers.
(c) In a third example, Jaffe et al. (2001) predicted twelve-month disorganized, resistant, and avoidant attachment, compared with secure, from degree of four-month mother–infant and stranger–infant vocal turn taking coordination. Vocal turn-taking coordination measures the degree to which each partner may match the duration of the switching pause as partners switch vocal turns. A midrange degree of interactive coordination (by mother with infant, infant with mother, stranger with infant, or infant with stranger) predicted secure attachment: a moderate degree of correspondence with the partner's rhythms of turn taking. Higher and lower degrees of coordination predicted disorganized and resistant attachment, and avoidant attachment, respectively.

Why is midrange coordination optimal? Higher coordination increases the predictability of the interaction and can be seen as excessive monitoring, trying too hard or vigilance. It is a coping strategy elicited by novelty, interactive challenge, or threat. Lower coordination can be seen as an inhibition of monitoring the partner, or a withdrawal. Midrange coordination may leave more space, more room for uncertainty, initiative, and flexibility within the experience of correspondence and contingency, optimal for secure attachment.

(5) In one study of four-month, mother–infant face-to-face interaction, secure vs. avoidant attachment at one year was predicted by the infant's behavior alone (the mother's behavior was not coded; Koulomzin et al., 2002). Future secure (vs. avoidant) infants at four months (a) looked at their mothers more, with a more sustained gaze pattern; (b) showed a greater range of positive and negative facial signaling; and (c) showed more coordinated gaze and head orientation patterns (yielding a stable focus of attention to the mother's face). Future avoidant infants

at four months showed (a) more frequent and variable touch behaviors, (b) more looking away, and (c) a greater likelihood of looking at the mother with a *wandering* head (the head does not remain vis-à-vis and instead drifts to averted head positions). Future avoidant infants showed a level of sustained looking at mother equal to that of future secure infants only if they were involved in self-touch or mouthing. Although the mother's behavior was not coded, this study suggests some of the ways in which the infant's own behavior is associated with attachment patterns. This study confirms the concept in attachment research that secure infants have access to a wider range of positive and negative emotions. It also shows that more stable patterns of looking at the mother's face, and more stable head orientation patterns, are associated with secure attachment. Moreover, the finding for avoidant infants suggests an infant self-regulation strategy, that of self-touch and mouthing, which helps avoidant infants sustain looking at their mothers. Clinically, we have noted that maternal interruption of infant touch patterns disturbs the infant's ability to self-regulate (Beebe, 2003, 2005; Cohen & Beebe, 2002).

(6) Maternal facilitation of repair following disruptions predicts attachment security. The still-face paradigm (Tronick, 1989) introduces a brief interruption into mother–infant face-to-face play. Following regular play, the mother is instructed to hold a completely still face for two minutes. Thereafter, the play resumes normally. Tronick (1989) found that infants who experienced more repairs of mismatches in an ongoing interaction, and who used more adaptive methods of coping with the still-face experiment (such as continuing to signal the mother), were more likely to become securely attached. Using the still-face paradigm, another study showed that six-month future secure, but not avoidant, infants displayed positive signaling and eliciting behaviors (such as reaching toward the mother, or vocalizing to her) while their mothers maintained a still face. Infants who continued to signal their still-faced mothers, in a positive fashion, were more likely to become securely attached (Cohn et al., 1991). Remarkably, an infant of six months will try to repair a nonresponsive mother.

TWO PRINCIPLES: ONGOING REGULATIONS AND DISRUPTION AND REPAIR

Beebe and Lachmann (1994) suggested several principles that organize infant experiences of face-to-face relating. Two of these are ongoing regulations and disruption and repair. On the one hand, there is an ongoing organizing process, based on the infant's creation of expectancies of characteristic interaction patterns. In the ongoing regulations principle, it is the very availability of the mother, her sensitivity, consistency, and predictability, and the ways that the infant reciprocally responds, that constitute the organizing process. On the other hand, disruptions and efforts to resolve them also generate infant expectancies and provide powerful opportunities for organizing experience.

The two principles, ongoing regulations and disruption and repair, organize different chunks of time and different aspects of experience. To the degree that the ongoing regulations are in the positive range, such as various matching interactions, experience is organized by what is predictable, expectable, coherent, and coordinated. In this view, the goal of the system is optimal coordination. In contrast, the principle of disruption and repair points toward experience as organized by contrast, disjunction, and difference. The gap between what is expected and what is happening can also be repaired. In this view, the goal of the system is optimal disjunction and repair. These counterpoints are simultaneously constituted (Beebe & Lachmann, 1994, 2002, 2013).

Disruption and repair organize experiences of coping, effectance, rerighting, and hope (Tronick, 1989). Interactions are represented as reparable. The expectation develops that it is possible to maintain engagement with the partner in the face of strains and mismatches. In contrast, optimally coordinated ongoing regulations organize experiences of coherence, predictability, fitting together with the partner, and being well-related. The expectation develops that it is possible for the coordination to be sustained. The firmer the expectation that coordination can be sustained, the more likely the infant will be able to tolerate and benefit from experiences of disruption and repair (Beebe & Lachmann, 1994).

In the drawings that follow, illustrating the origins of secure attachment, there are moments in which the infant becomes slightly distressed. The mother quickly recognizes the infant's experience and proceeds to try to help the infant reregulate. These moments illustrate minor disruptions and rapid repairs. You also see glorious moments in which both mother and infant together rise into the highest positive affect. These hugely positive moments are largely missing from the illustrations of interactions of dyads on the way to insecure attachment, or disorganized attachment.

Notice how the infant responds to everything the mother does, even the tiniest movements. And reciprocally, notice how the mother is aware, at the procedural, action-sequence level (but not necessarily consciously), of everything the infant does. This extraordinary moment-by-moment reciprocal coordination of mother and infant actions is what the microanalysis approach offers. As we progress from the origins of secure attachment to the later chapters on the origins of insecure attachment, you see that this extraordinary reciprocal coordination is the basis of all interactions, whether they are optimal or nonoptimal, whether they contain distress or joy, and whether they lead to secure or insecure attachment outcomes.

The patterns of moment-by-moment mother–infant interaction at four months in the chapters below illustrate the details of the process by which mothers and infants co-create procedural expectancies of intimate relating, which lead to attachment security or insecurity at twelve months.

CHAPTER 4

Facial Mirroring in the Origins of Secure Attachment

DRAWINGS: FACIAL MIRRORING

This sequence depicts a mother and infant at four months where the infant was classified as secure attachment at one year (Beebe et al., 2010).

This sequence of drawings presents 19 frames, over 26 seconds. The mother and infant begin in a mutual gaze with a positive engagement. After a 13-second gap, as the infant looks down and dampens, the mother begins to gently poke her infant's belly as if to say "come back." When the infant opens his eyes, there is a slight mismatch and repair. The mother at first greets the infant with a level of excitement much higher than that of the infant. But the mother immediately repairs by staying closer to the infant's state. Then they gradually build back up to a peak level of mutual positive excitement.

Because it is hard to see exactly what is happening with the hands, we note that the infant's hand is wrapped around the mother's finger as she swings her finger back and forth, until she takes both his hands and moves them out wide (Frames 10–12).

Note: Because of the split screen and the angle of the cameras, it is often hard to know whether mother and infant are directly looking, particularly from one frame. For example, in sequence 4.1, Frame 1 below, from the video in real time, it is clear that the mother and the infant are looking at each other at that moment. We ask the reader to take a leap of faith as we describe the gaze patterns in the drawings that follow.

4.1 MINUTE:SECOND 01:33–01:35

Storyline: The mother and infant rise into mutual delight. They respond to the other's slight head and mouth movements as they increase their positive facial affect with mutual gaze.

Frame 1. Minute:Second 01:33a
The mother and the infant are directly oriented to each other vis-à-vis and gazing at each other. Their faces have slightly positive interest expressions. The infant holds his mother's finger with his right hand.

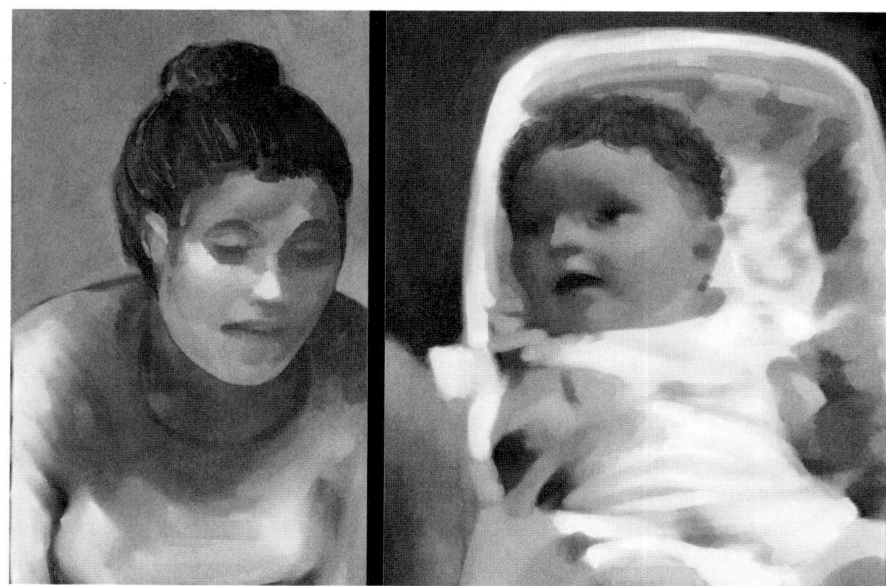

Frame 2. Minute:Second 01:33b
From Frame 1 to 2, within the same second, the infant's interest expression becomes more positive, and there is a hint of a smile. The mother partially closes her mouth (from the film we know that she is singing).

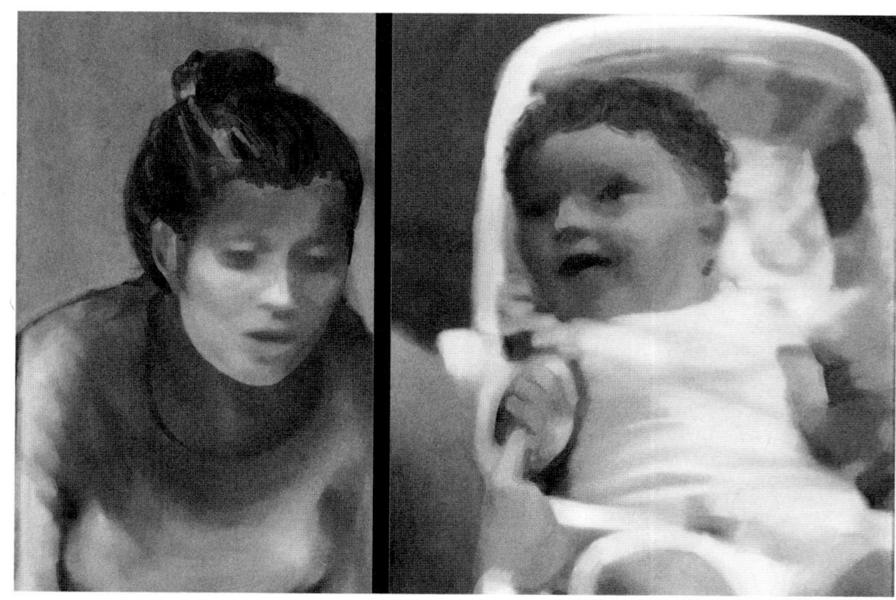

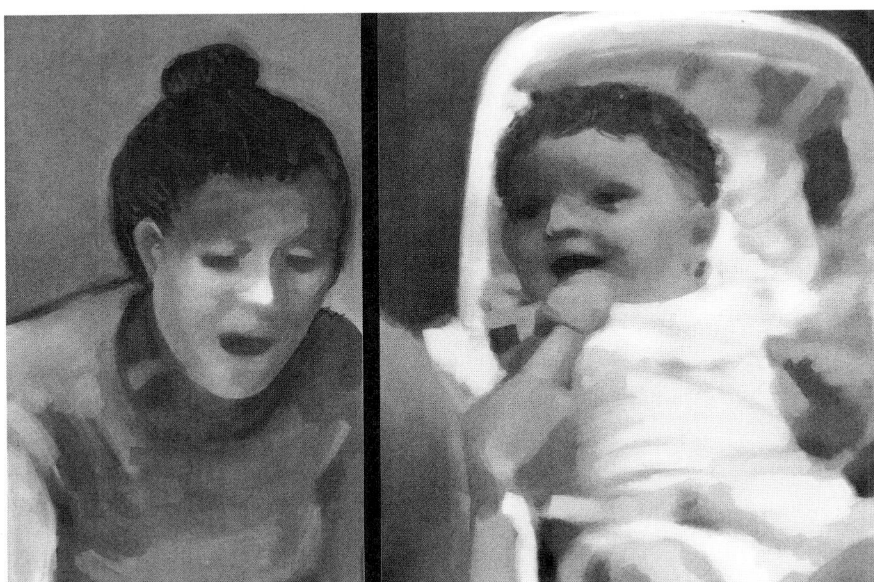

Frame 3. Minute:Second 01:34
From Frame 2 to 3, in the next second, both continue in mutual gaze and become more positive. The mother has a partial gape smile, while the infant has a full smile. The mother and infant again match the other's facial expressions. The infant continues to hold the mother's finger with his right hand.

Frame 4. Minute:Second 01:35
From Frame 3 to 4, one second later, both the mother and infant heighten their smiles. The mother reaches a full gape smile.

4.2 THIRTEEN SECONDS LATER: MINUTE:SECOND 01:48–01:52A

Storyline: As the infant begins to look down, to move his head down, and to close his mouth, the mother's smile tenses. She moves forward and gently pokes his tummy. We do not know exactly why the infant looks away here. Likely, he needs a moment of reregulation of his arousal, a time-out.

Frame 5. Minute:Second 01:48
After a break of 13 seconds, as this sequence opens, both are looking at the other with a hint of a positive expression. The mother is leaning in. The infant opens the fingers of his left hand. This finger opening movement continues across these four frames. With his right hand, the infant continues to hold the mother's finger, which she is swinging back and forth.

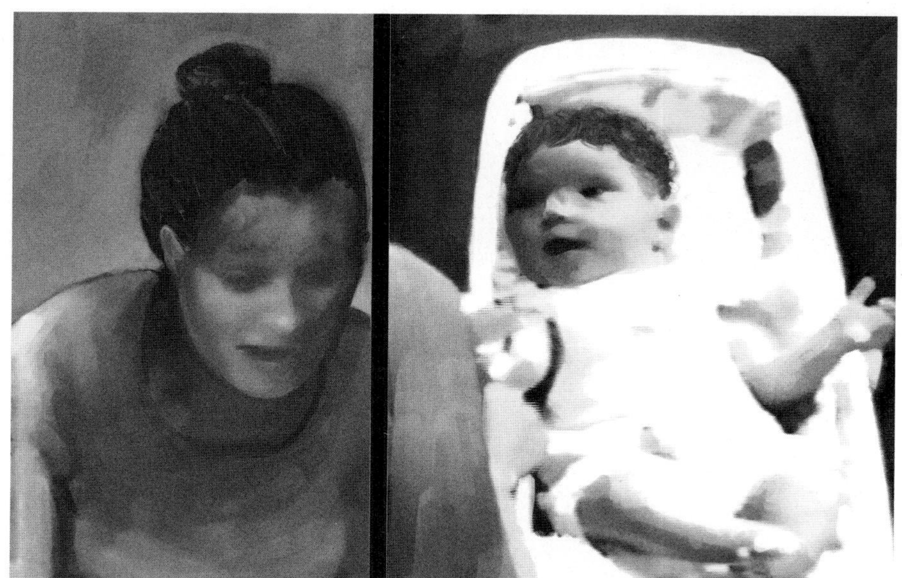

Frame 6. Minute:Second 01:49
From Frame 5 to 6, in the next second, the infant looks down, breaking eye contact, and his head moves slightly down. The mother moves back slightly, and her mouth tenses slightly.

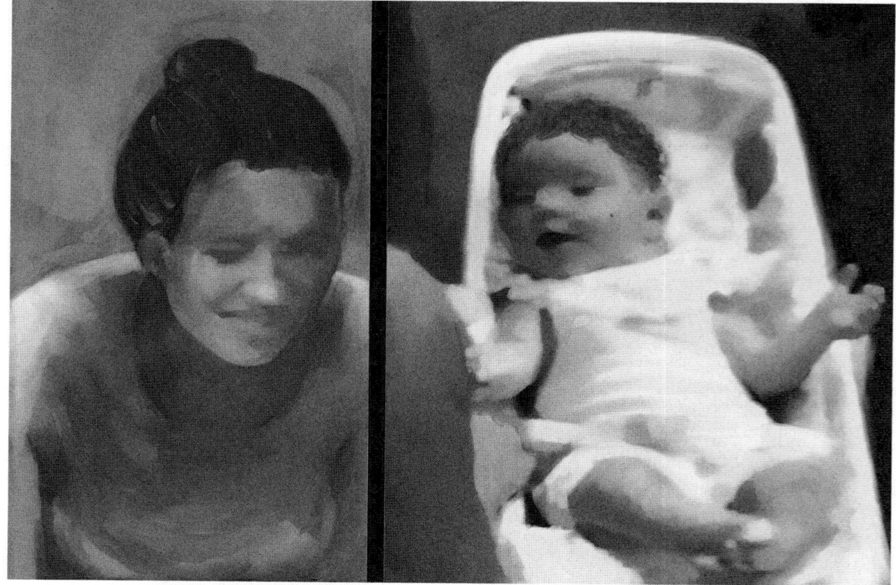

4.3 MINUTE:SECOND 01:52–01:53

Storyline: As the infant returns to look, a slight mismatch and repair occurs. The mother greets him with an excited smile (Frame 10), but the infant briefly looks down again (Frame 11). When he returns to look, this time the mother greets him with a more moderate smile (Frame 12), closer to his state, and the infant maintains her gaze. As the mother notices very carefully what her infant does, she reregulates herself.

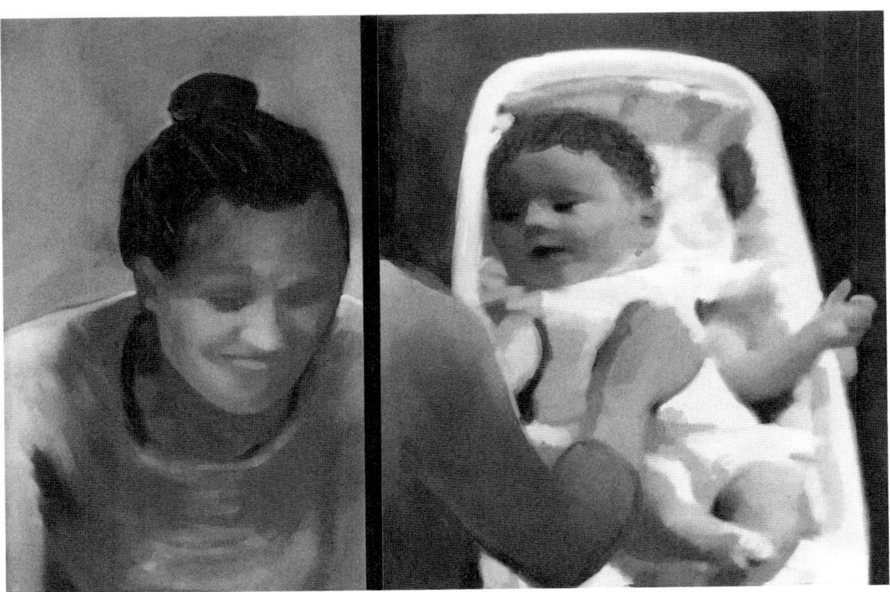

Frame 7. Minute:Second 01:50
From Frame 6 to 7, one second later, the infant's head moves down slightly as his mouth begins to close. The mother moves her right hand in to poke the infant gently on his belly. She continues to look at the infant with a slightly tense smile.

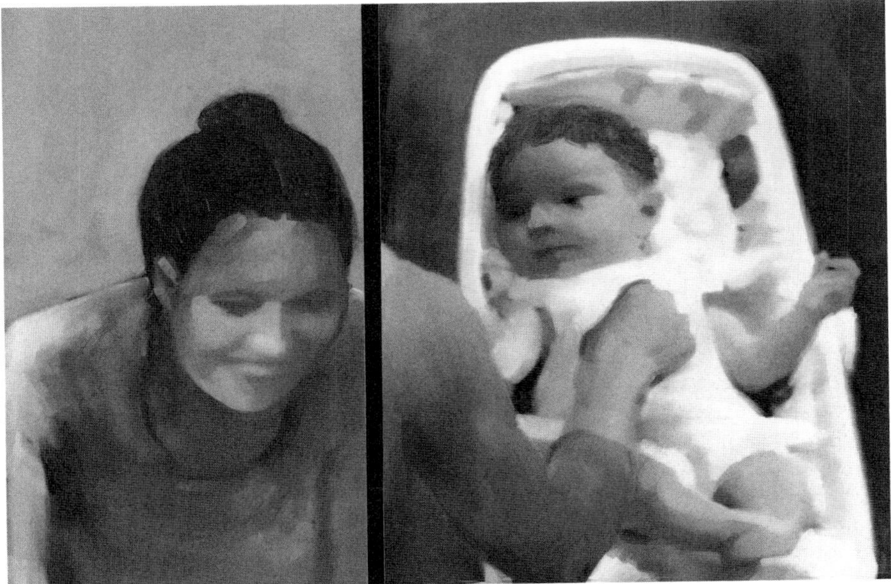

Frame 8. Minute:Second 01:52a
From Frame 7 to 8, approximately two and a half seconds later, the mother continues to poke the infant's belly, and she continues to look with a slightly tense smile. The infant's head moves further down as his eyes and mouth close. His left hand begins to close.

Frame 9. Minute:Second 01:52b
From Frame 8 to 9, within the same second, the infant opens his eyes and begins to look at his mother. His mouth continues to be fully closed. He has an attentive, interest expression. His left hand is now fully closed. The mother's smile becomes muted, still slightly tensed.

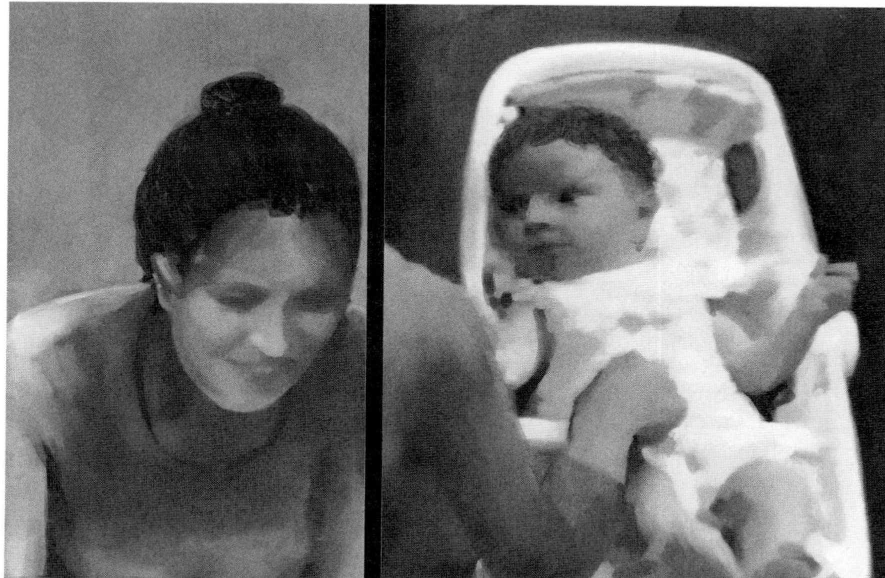

Frame 10. Minute:Second 01:53a
From Frame 9 to 10, a fraction of a second later, the infant looks directly at his mother with a slightly more positive interest expression. The mother smiles, opening her mouth, much more excited than the infant. She begins to reach her right hand toward his left hand.

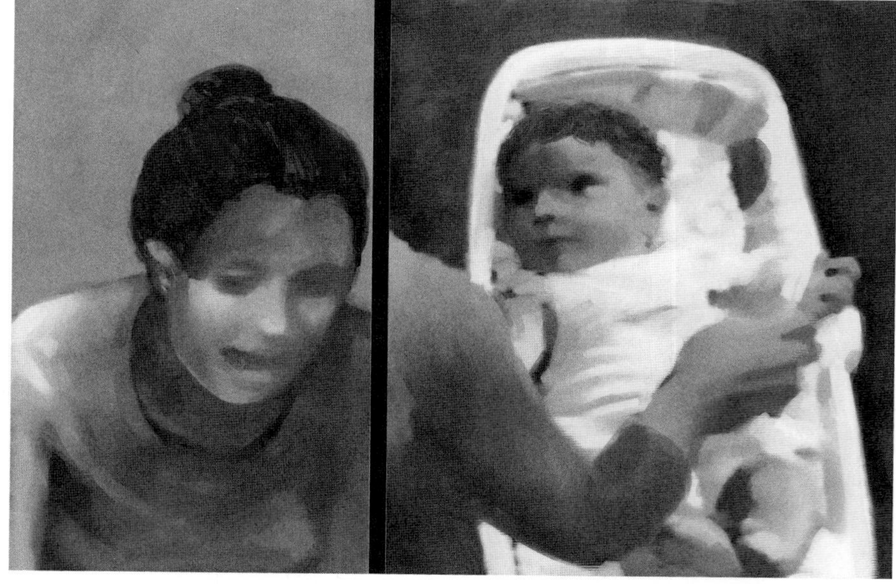

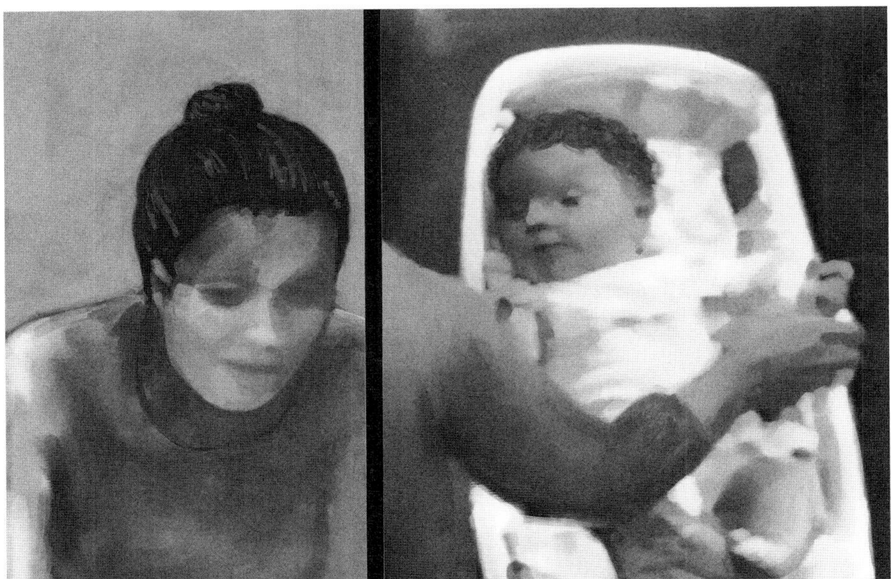

Frame 11. Minute:Second 01:53b
From Frame 10 to 11, within the same second, the infant closes his eyes again. The mother sobers, closing her mouth. Here, she matches his state more closely. This happens very quickly, within less than a half a second. She continues to reach for the infant's left hand.

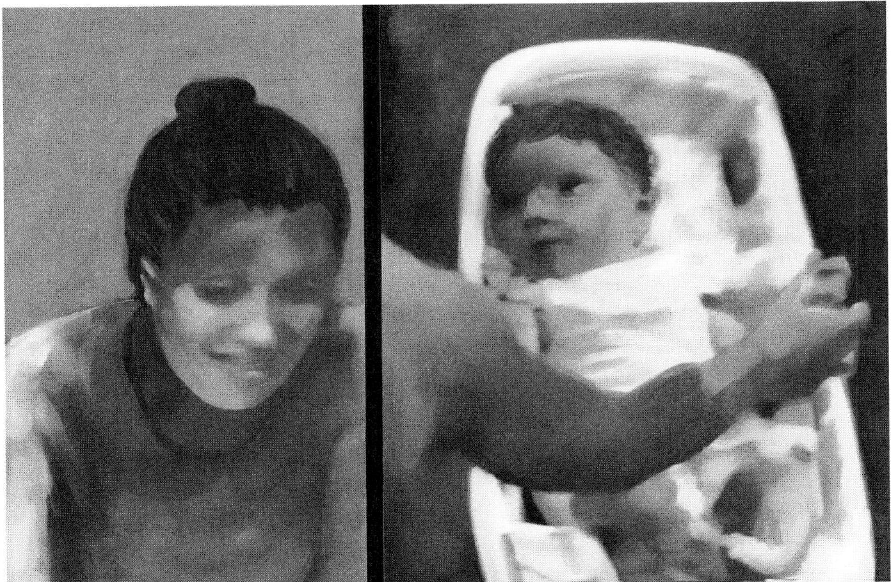

Frame 12. Minute:Second 01:53c
From Frame 11 to 12, within a fraction of a second, the infant opens his eyes and looks with an interest face with a hint of widening, slightly more positive. The mother's smile is more moderate than in Frame 10. She stays close to the infant's lower level of excitement. She is still reaching for the infant's left hand.

4.4 MINUTE:SECOND 01:54–01:56B

Storyline: Mother and infant rebuild their mutually positive engagement. Each responds to the other with bigger and bigger smiles and mouth openings.

Frame 13. Minute:Second 01:54
From Frame 12 to 13, in the next second, each has become slightly more positive. The mother has a slightly more open smile, and the infant has a more positive interest expression. The mother makes full contact with infant's left hand.

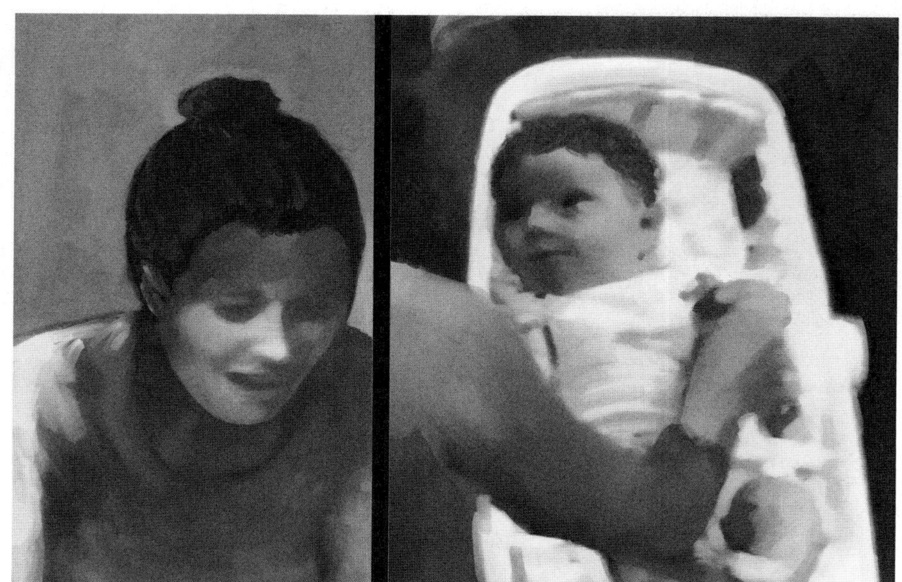

Frame 14. Minute:Second 01:55
From Frame 13 to 14, one second later, each continues to become slightly more positive. The mother has a bigger smile, and the infant has a slightly more open-mouth, positive interest expression. The mother moves the infant's left hand inward with her right hand.

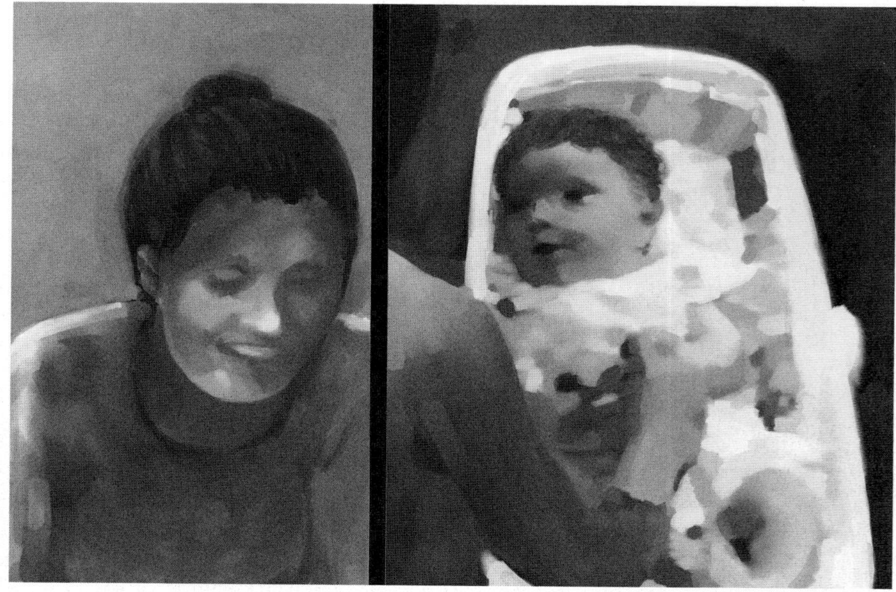

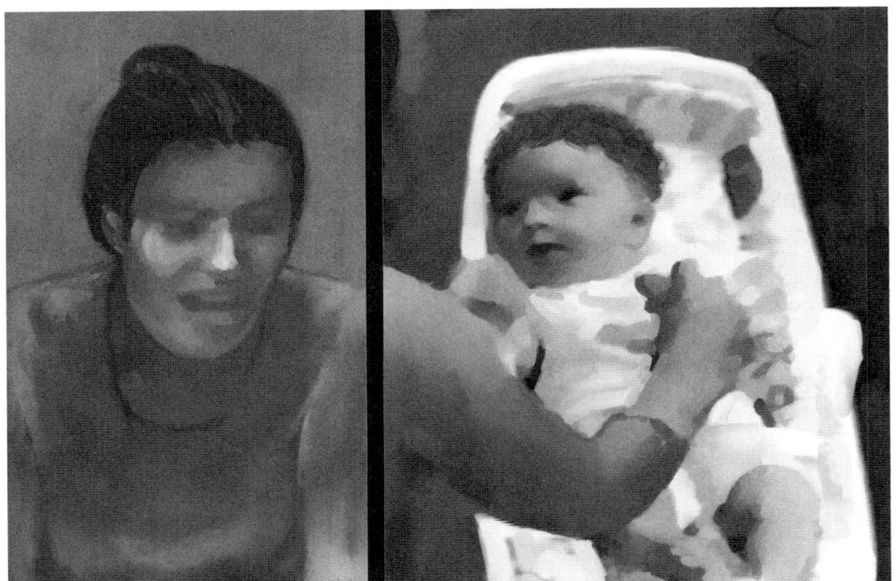

Frame 15. Minute:Second 01:56a
From Frame 14 to 15, approximately a half of a second later, both the mother and infant slightly increase their positive engagement by opening their mouths more. The mother's head moves back, and she shifts the infant's left hand again.

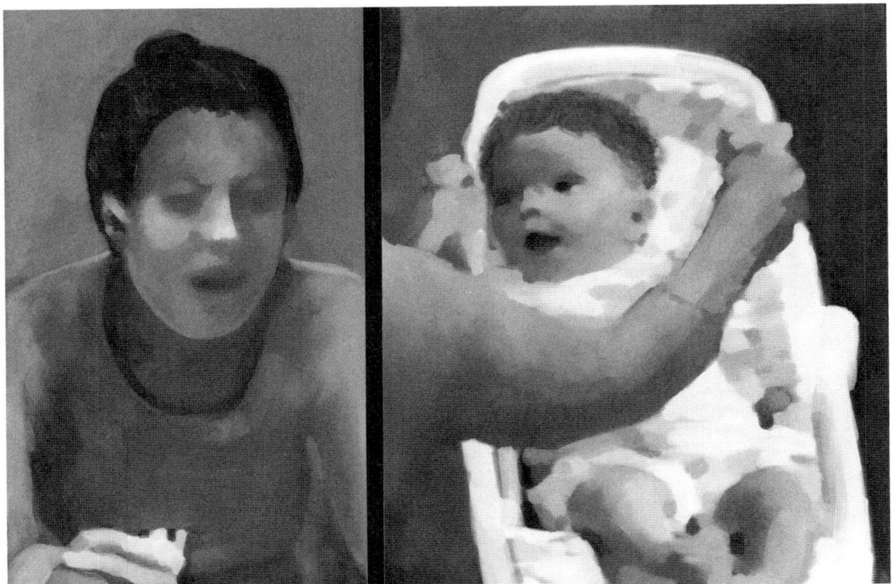

Frame 16. Minute:Second 01:56b
From Frame 15 to 16, within the same second, both continue to increase their positive engagement by moving their heads up and opening their mouths more. Mother raises infant's hands up. Both look excited.

4.5 MINUTE:SECOND 01:57–01:59

Storyline: Mother and infant each respond to the other's slight shifts as they reach the apex of mutual positive affect. These are the moments that parents and infants love.

Frame 17. Minute:Second 01:57
From Frame 16 to 17, in the next second, the mother and infant continue in mutual gaze, and both display the apex of positive affect, full gape smiles. Their heads rise in unison. As the mother raises the infant's left arm up a bit more, the infant lifts his right foot and his toes go up.

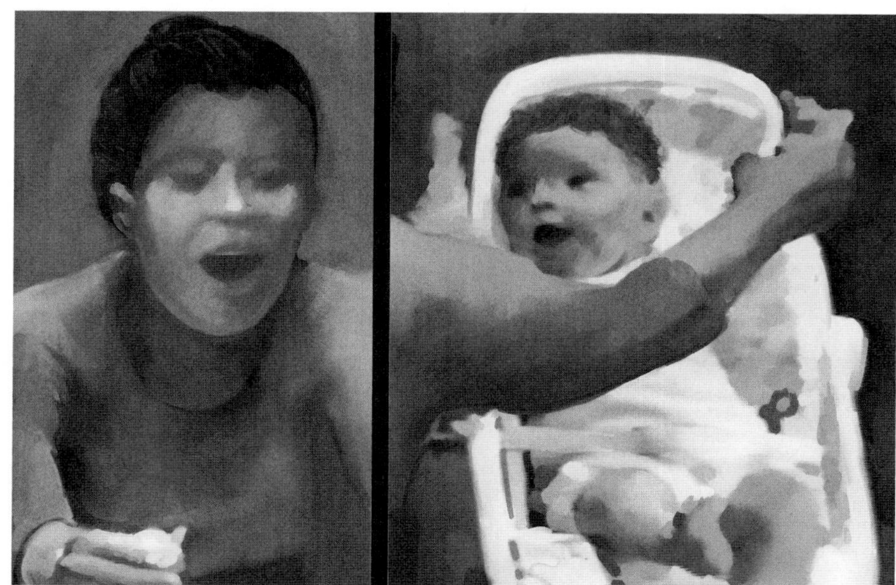

Frame 18. Minute:Second 01:58
From Frame 17 to 18, one second later, the mother and infant continue to look and smile at each other in a very positive engagement. The mother shifts to a moderate smile, closing her mouth a bit. The infant's gape smile continues.

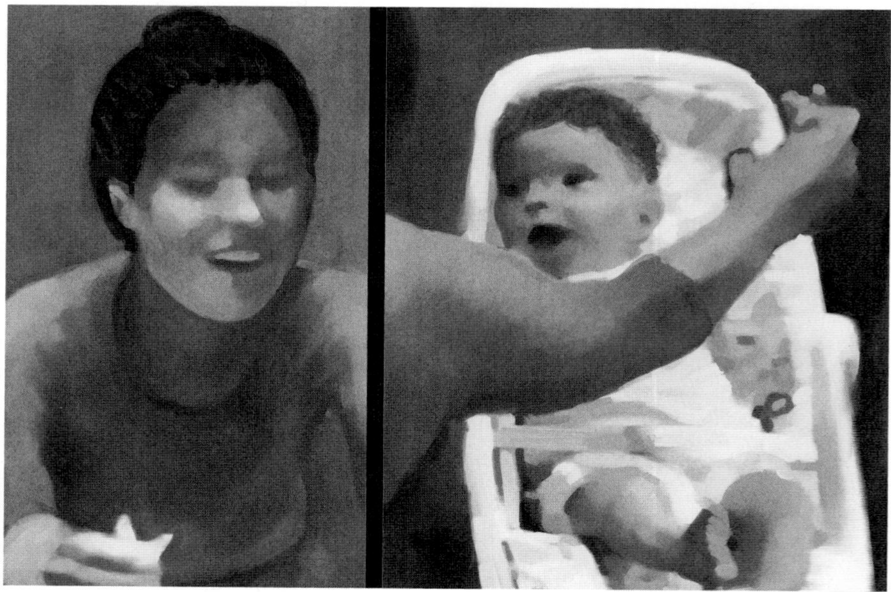

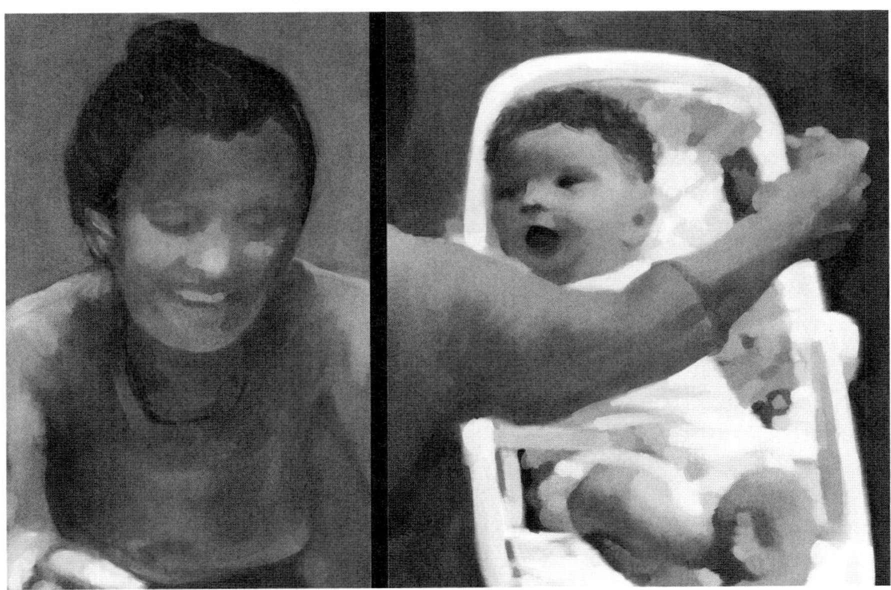

Frame 19. Minute:Second 01:59
From Frame 18 to 19, in the next second, their positive engagement continues; the mother has a joyous look; the infant continues his full gape smile.

COMMENTARY ON FACIAL MIRRORING

Facial affect carries unique information with an enormous degree of modulation and subtlety. How each partner's face attracts and responds to the other's face is one of the foundations of intimacy throughout life.

We chose the sequence "Facial Mirroring in the Origins of Secure Attachment" because it illustrates moments in which mother and infant move bit by bit up into peak positive heights of delight together. Portions of the following description are adapted from Beebe and Lachmann (2013).

By now you realize that the level of detail revealed by the frame-by-frame drawings is very different from what we can all see in real time. Mother and infant both move their heads up and increasingly open their mouths as they move incrementally into increasing levels of display of positive facial affect. The extraordinary synchronization of movements is visible only in the microanalysis. The combination of head up and mouth opening has a reaching quality. Similarly, the pair closes down together, moving their heads down and closing their mouths roughly in unison.

The complex interaction that occurs around the moment in which the infant breaks eye contact and looks down also cannot be discerned in real time. Watching in real time, my students often insist that the infant looked down because the mother moved her finger in toward the infant's belly, about to gently poke. But the microanalysis reveals the opposite order: the infant looked down first, the mother reacted with some facial tensing, and then she gently poked the infant's belly.

There is a slight misstep as the infant looks back and seems to be ready to return to the mutual gaze engagement, and the mother is poised to go back up. The mother gives the infant a big open smile. But the infant is dampened (Frame 10). The infant looks down very quickly one more time (Frame 11). The mother reacts by closing and slightly tensing her mouth. As the infant looks back for the second time, the mother now stays very close to the infant's state. She has a more moderate smile (Frame 12). She does not move ahead of him by beginning to rise into smiles before he is quite ready. This is an important moment as she gives him time to readjust, and she follows his lead. This moment illustrates a very slight disruption and its repair.

They then both move incrementally back up to peak positive shared gape smiles (Frames 16–19). In this process, they are both learning the sequences that lead to intense moments of positive mutual engagement. They are also learning how to gently increment down and disengage from such heights, allowing the infant a moment of reregulation, a visual time-out, as he looks down for a moment. Infants use such moments of looking away to reregulate their arousal, dampening their heart rate down into a more comfortable range, and then they can look back (Field, 1981). Mother and infant then both rejoin in mutual gaze and build back up to the height of positive affect, with fully opened gape smiles. Expectancies of comfortably matching the direction of affective change, moment-by-moment, are thus created in both partners. This expectancy includes room for moments of looking away and reregulation of arousal. This expectancy also includes the possibility of both reaching a marvelous height of fully positive open smiles.

Illustrations of Expectancies

We now turn to the question of what the infant comes to expect from his or her interactive encounters. How are infant expectancies of social interactions created? We use the descriptions of the drawings to illustrate in more detail how the action sequences of the exchange develop into expectancies. For each pattern, we attempt to translate the action-dialogue into language, as if the infant or mother could put the experience into words.

In the facial mirroring sequence, in a dyad on the way to secure infant attachment, if the action dialogue could be translated into language, we infer that mother and infant create the following expectancies of their interaction: "We follow each other's moves as we look at each other and look away. We follow each other's faces up and down, as we become more and less positive. We can go bit by bit all the way up to the top together, to sunbursts of joyous open smiles. We each can anticipate how the other's gaze, face, and engagement will go. What we feel, and what we do, shows up in the other in a resonant way: We do not have to be vigilant; we do not have to withdraw." The infant might feel, "I feel secure because I am with you. I feel sensed and joined by you. I feel known by you." The mother might feel, "I feel secure with you. I feel I know you. I can anticipate how you will feel. I know you love me. I am so happy that you are my baby."

Relevant Research

The research findings that underlie this book identified patterns of interaction at four months leading to secure and insecure attachment patterns at one year. Secure attachment at one year is associated in childhood with better peer relations, school performance, and capacity to regulate emotions, as well as less psychopathology (Sroufe, 1983). Here we describe the four-month patterns that predicted secure infant attachment, adapted from Beebe et al. (2010).

In *future secure* dyads at four months, where infants will be classified as secure at one year, mothers and infants followed the other's direction of attention as each looked and looked away from the partner's face. Thus, each can predict the other's likelihood of looking and looking away. Mothers facially followed the direction of infant facial and vocal affect as the infant became more and less positive and negative. Infants reciprocally followed the direction of maternal facial affect with their own facial and vocal affect.

This is a bidirectional facial/vocal mirroring process: Each can predict the other's affective behavior, and each can anticipate that the partner will follow his or her own direction of affective change. As this process repeats, over and over, both mother and infant come to expect matching and being matched, that is, changing in the same affective direction. This is a rough similarity but does not imply any exact matching of facial expression. Each comes to expect the experience of seeing the other's face continuously changing to become roughly more similar to his or her own; each comes to expect the experience of his or her own face continuously changing to become roughly more similar to that of the partner. Both come to expect a split-second, moment-by-moment, contingent interactive process of matching and being matched in the direction of affective change. This matching provides each with a behavioral basis for entering into the other's feeling state. This process operates largely out of awareness for the mother. It is based on procedural, action-sequence knowledge.

Similarity of behavior implies a congruence of feeling, a relationship between matching and empathy. How might this work? The work of Ekman et al. (1983) and Zajonc (1985) showed that matching the expression of the partner is highly correlated with matching the physiological arousal pattern of the partner. Ekman et al. (1983) showed that a particular facial expression is associated with a particular pattern of autonomic activity. Reproducing the expression of another person produces a similar physiological state in the onlooker. This mechanism of empathy is an approximate facial matching, which is correlated with an approximate physiological matching. This mechanism of empathy is equally relevant to parent–infant and adult–adult interactions.

If the research findings could be translated into language, we infer that mothers and infants in future secure dyads come to expect, "I can anticipate when you will look and look away; I know your rhythms of looking at me; I feel seen by you. As you feel happy or distressed, I follow your feelings up and down with my own feelings of happiness or distress. As I feel happy or distressed, I can count on you to follow my feelings as well. What I feel and what I do resonates in you. I can count on you to share my feelings, to get what I feel; I feel known by you. I know how your face goes, I know you" (Beebe et al., 2010).

CHAPTER 5

Disruption and Repair in the Origins of Secure Attachment

DRAWINGS: DISRUPTION AND REPAIR

This sequence depicts a mother and infant at four months where the infant was classified as secure attachment at one year (Beebe et al., 2010).

In this sequence of 12 frames over 23 seconds, we see the mother and infant begin with a high positive mutual gaze and open-mouthed smiles. As the infant disengages and becomes distressed, the mother sobers and follows him down. She helps him reconnect by moving back, matching him, and using her hands. In the end, they repair in a strong mutual gaze, with gape smiles and a sense of joyful delight.

5.1 MINUTE:SECOND 16:02–16:06A

Storyline: Across four seconds, mother and infant begin smiling, but the infant then starts to withdraw, and the mother dampens her smile; they lose their enjoyment.

Frame 1. Minute:Second 16:02
As we enter this sequence, the mother and infant are both smiling with mutual gaze. The mother has a fully open-mouth, joyful gape smile. Both are enjoying the other.

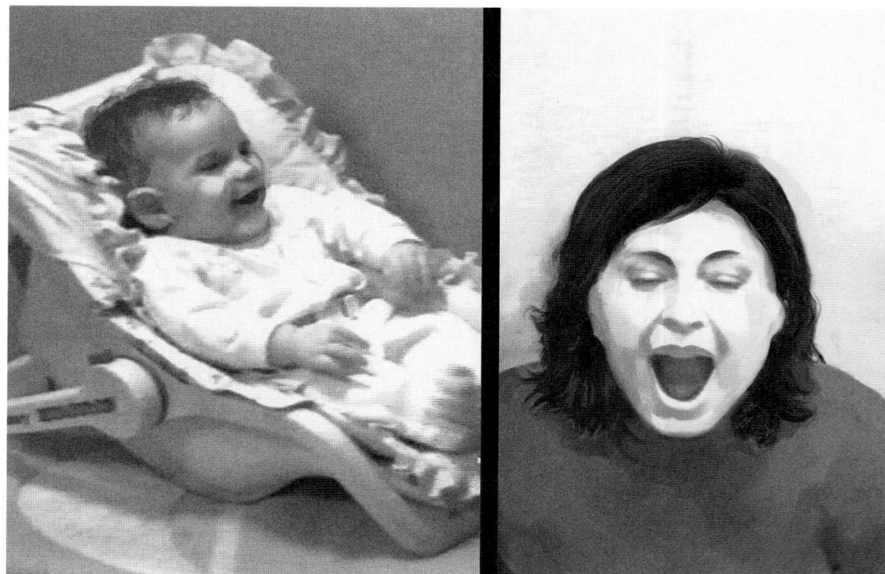

Frame 2. Minute:Second 16:03
From Frame 1 to 2, in the next second, both infant and mother dampen their engagement. Both move their heads down and dampen their smiles.

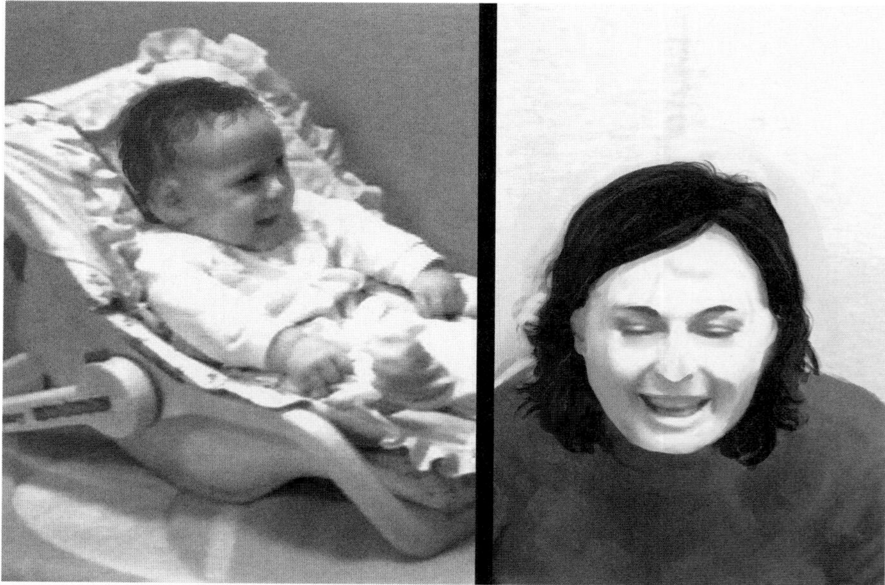

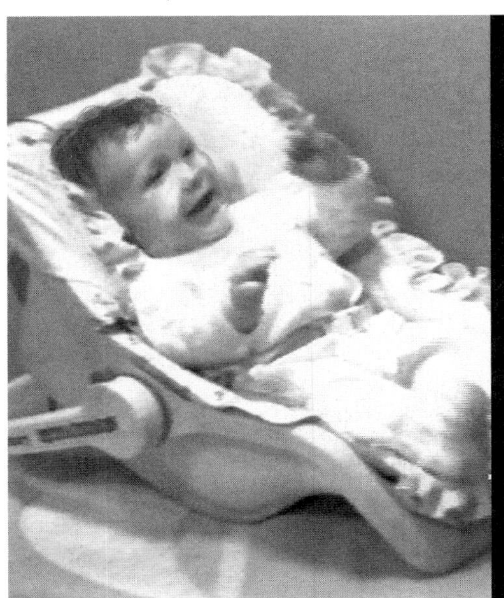

Frame 3. Minute:Second 16:05
From Frame 2 to 3, two seconds later, the infant's head, body, and hands begin to pull back, but he is still looking and partially smiling. The mother leans her head in closer to her infant, and her smile dampens further.

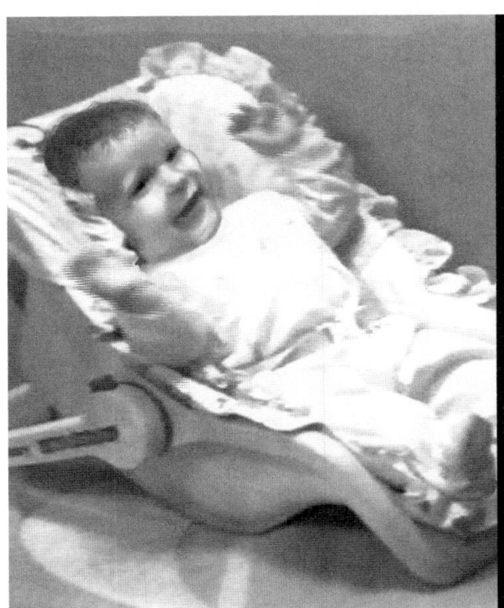
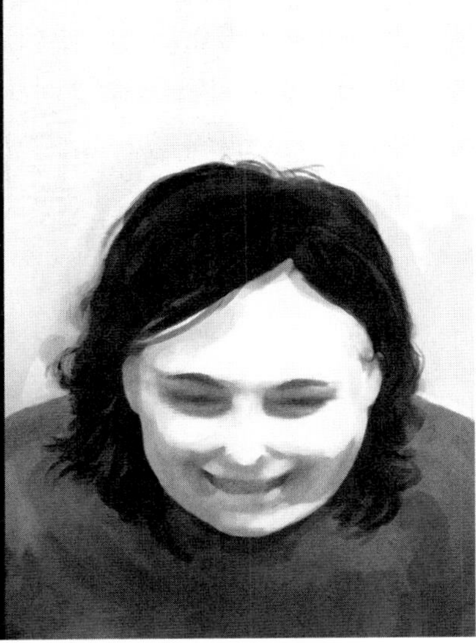

Frame 4. Minute:Second 16:06a
From Frame 3 to 4, less than one second later, the infant breaks eye contact, turns his head away slightly to his right, and moves his hands further back in a "don't touch me" gesture. His smile dampens further. The mother's dampened smile remains.

5.2 MINUTE:SECOND 16:06B–16:07

Storyline: As the infant becomes distressed, the mother moves back and joins the infant's distressed state by exactly matching his expression.

Frame 5. Minute:Second 16:06b
From Frame 4 to 5, roughly a half second later, the infant looks distressed. He frowns, arches back, turns his head away further to his right, and continues to look away. His hands are now fully in a "don't touch me" gesture. The mother leans back and looks down. Her dampened smile remains.

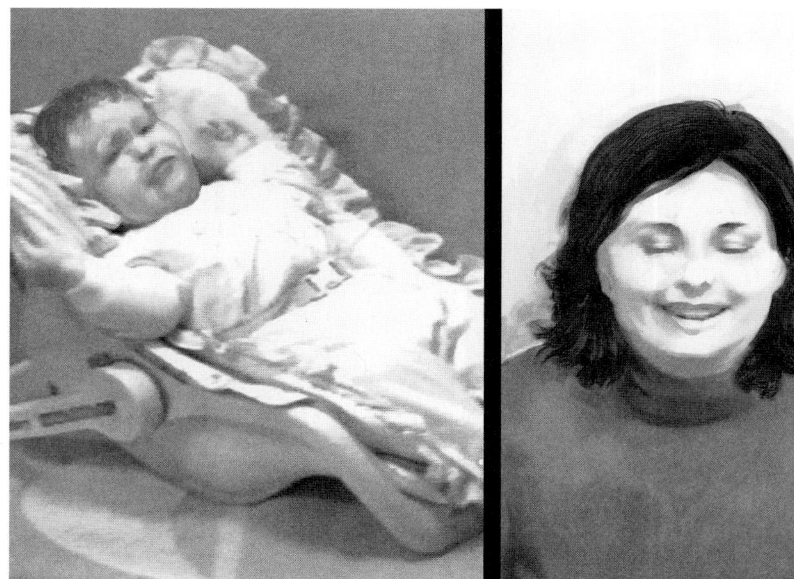

Frame 6. Minute:Second 16:07
From Frame 5 to 6, about a half second later, we see an extraordinary moment in which the mother precisely matches the infant's distressed state. As the infant reorients back to vis-à-vis with his eyes closed, he pulls in his bottom lip, in an "uh-oh" expression. This expression may indicate a way of managing an upset state, an effort to hold in distress. The mother matches the infant's pulled-in bottom lip expression. However, at this point, the infant does not see his mother matching his state. His hands are still fully pulled back.

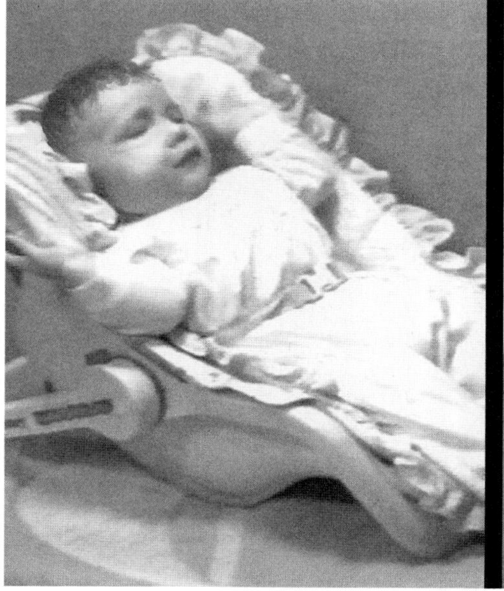

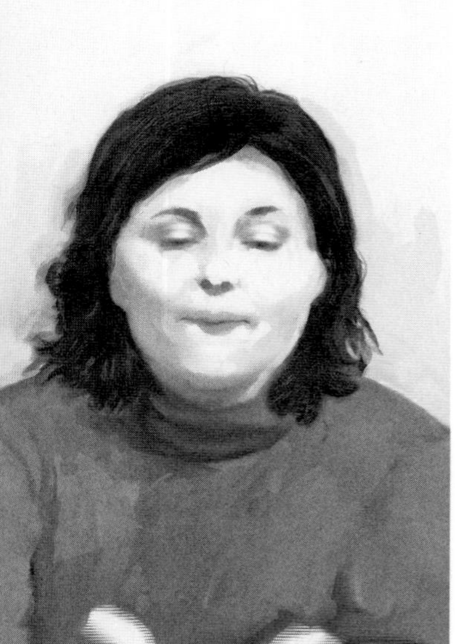

5.3 MINUTE:SECOND 16:08–16:24

Storyline: Over 17 seconds, the mother and infant reconnect with their hands. They go back up into a mutually delighted engagement.

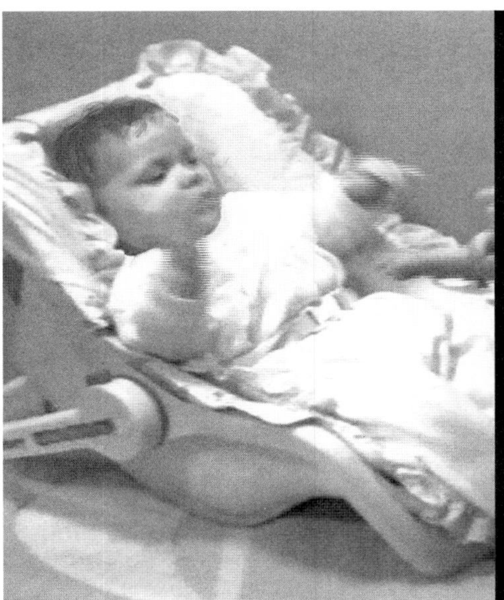
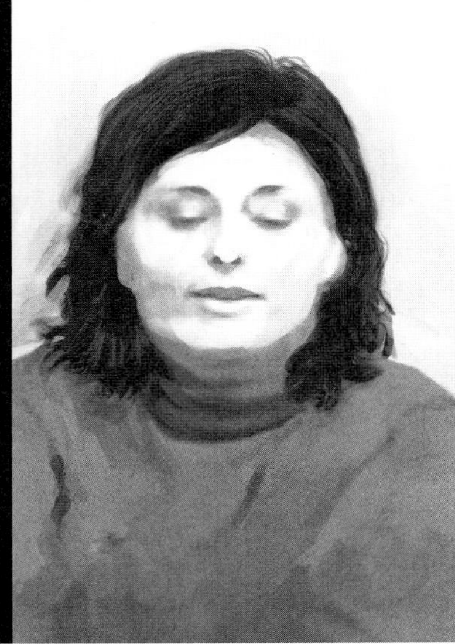

Frame 7. Minute:Second 16:08
From Frame 6 to 7, in the next second, the mother and infant both begin to reach for each other with their hands. The mother's finger (visible in the infant's frame) moves toward the infant. The infant looks down at his mother's hands; his arms are coming down. The mother's face looks sobered.

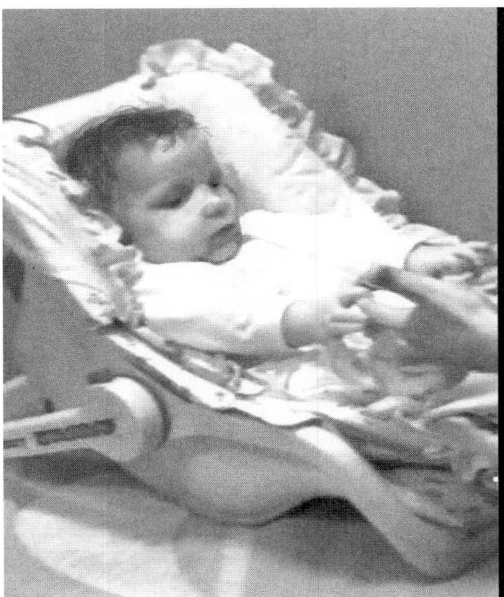
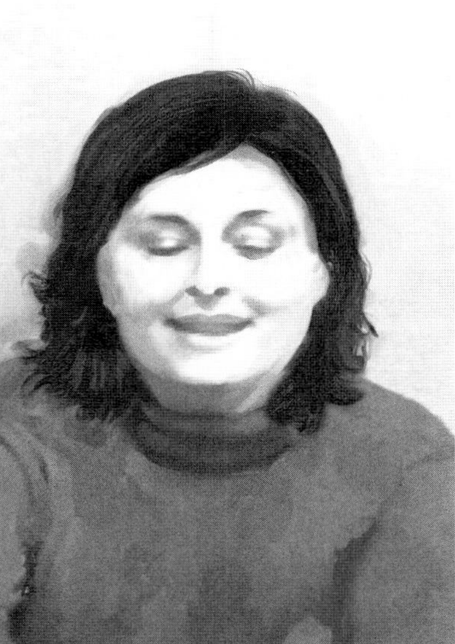

Frame 8. Minute:Second 16:10
From Frame 7 to 8, two seconds later, the mother and infant begin to reconnect through their hands. Their hands touch, the infant grasps the mother's left hand with his right hand, and he looks intently at their hands. The mother begins to smile slightly.

Frame 9. Minute:Second 16:13

From Frame 8 to 9, three seconds later, the infant's face has shifted into a positive interest expression, with a slightly open and widened mouth. He continues to look at their hands and to grasp his mother's fingers, but he does not yet look at his mother. The mother raises her hands as her mouth opens wider.

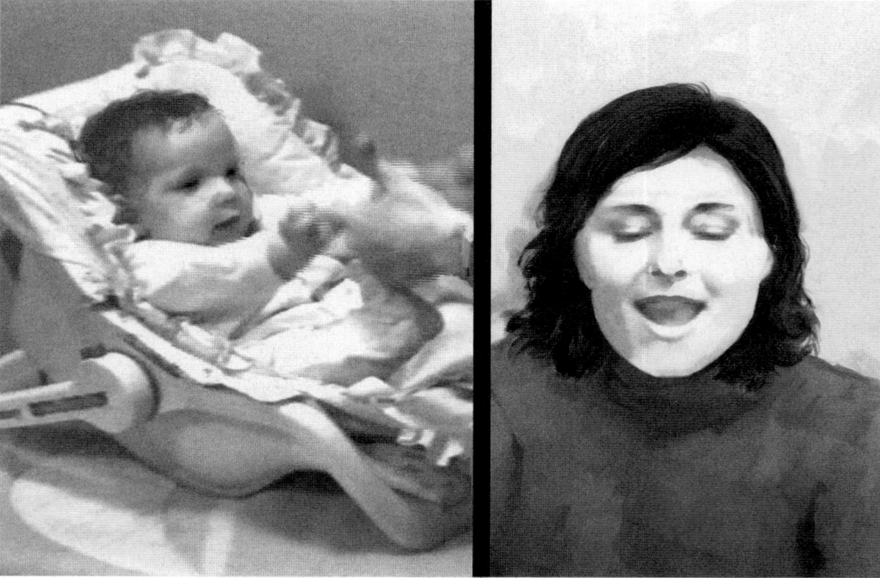

Frame 10. Minute:Second 16:15

From Frame 9 to 10, two seconds later, the infant now looks at his mother with a positive interest face, with a hint of a beginning smile. The mother greets him with a slight smile. They are now back together. The mother raises her hands further up, and the infant holds onto the fingers of both of her hands.

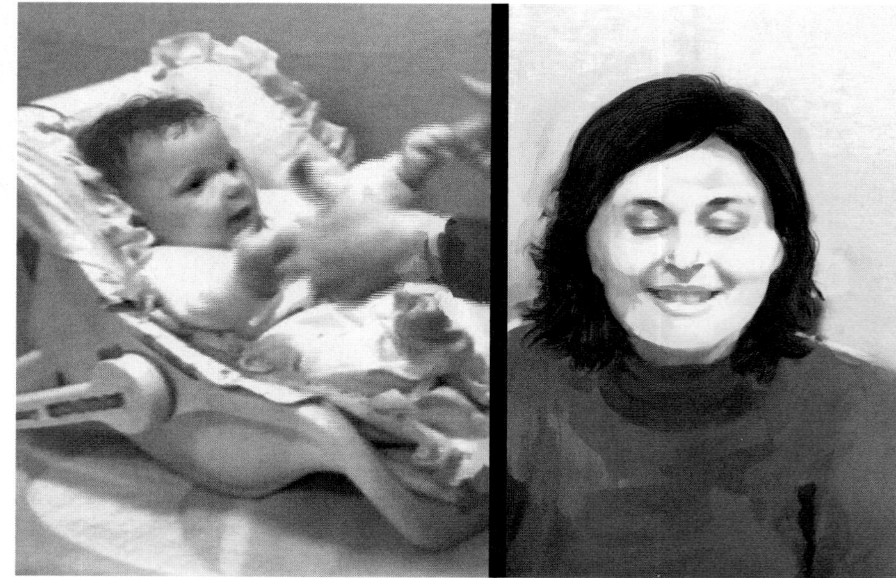

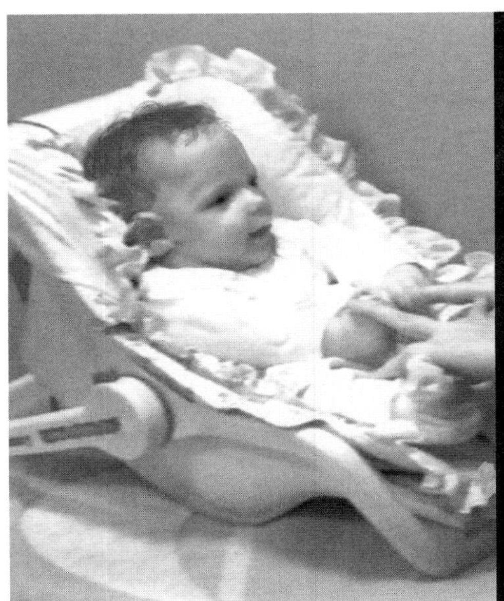
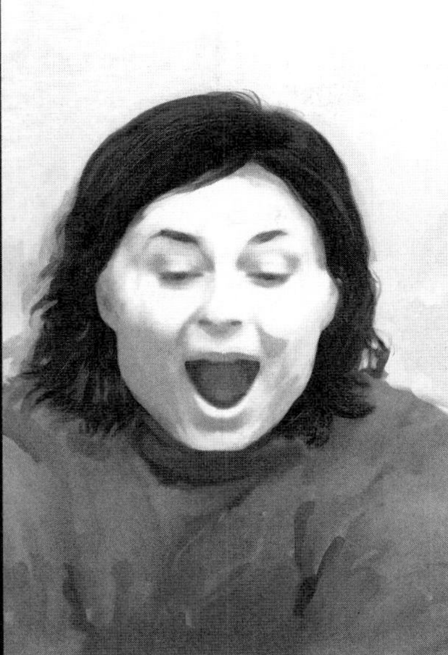

Frame 11. Minute:Second 16:20
From Frame 10 to 11, five seconds later, the infant continues to look at his mother with an interest expression. The mother greets her infant with a mock surprise expression, a fully open mouth and raised eyebrows. Their hands shift down; the mother offers her fingers, and the fingers of the infant's left hand curl around her fingers.

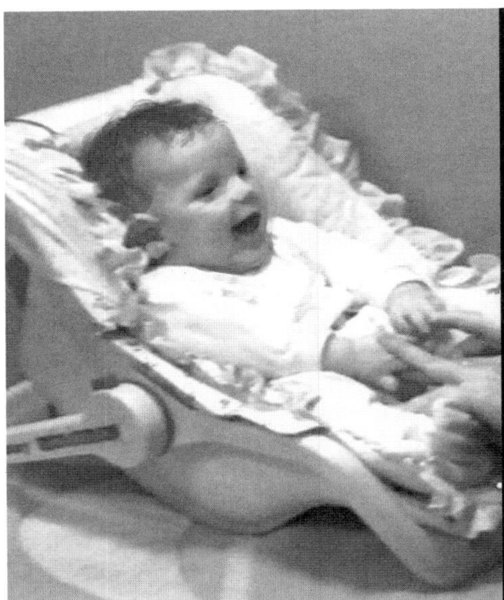

Frame 12. Minute:Second 16:24
From Frame 11 to 12, four seconds later, the mother and infant achieve a full repair and together rise back up into mutual delight. Both have joyful gape smiles. They remain in contact through their fingers.

COMMENTARY ON DISRUPTION AND REPAIR

We chose this sequence because it illustrates a positive interaction in which the infant suddenly became distressed, and the ways in which the mother and infant rapidly repaired and resumed their positive interaction. Portions of the following descriptions are adapted from Beebe et al. (2010), Beebe and Lachmann (1994, 2002, 2013), and Beebe, Lachmann, and Jaffe (1997).

All mothers and infants (and all people) have missteps in their communication and must learn to repair them. Usually this process occurs seamlessly, out of awareness. But sometimes we have to bring this process into awareness to repair it. Whereas the previous interaction, facial mirroring, had a tiny misstep in the dance, the dyad illustrating disruption and repair has a slightly larger misstep.

From watching the real-time video of this sequence, we learn that, in the course of a very positive interaction, the mother leans in slightly toward the infant, and then leans in further with a partial loom movement in which her head and face move in close to the infant's face. The infant quickly becomes distressed, frowns, and moves his head back as he raises his arms. He seems to be reacting to the loom. He looks away from his mother and whimpers. Thus, the mother's loom seems to have precipitated the disruption in this sequence. As we discuss in the later drawings on the interactions of dyads where the infant is later classified as disorganized attachment, maternal loom movements occur more frequently in disorganized attachment than secure attachment. However, in this dyad, the mother catches it quickly and immediately responds by repairing it. By the time we join them in the frame-by-frame analysis in the drawings, this loom has already occurred. The drawings were chosen to illustrate the process of repair.

Comment on Disruption and Repair

This sequence illustrates maternal management of infant distress by joining the infant's distress. The mother exactly matches her infant's "uh-oh" expression of the bottom lip pulled in (Frame 6). The infant's eyes are closed during this moment. But we can see that the mother joins the exact quality of the infant's distress, exquisitely sensing the infant's state. This moment is not visible in the real-time video, but it is the key to understanding this interaction. Then both participate in the repair, reaching for each other. From the real-time video, it is not easy to see that they reach their hands out to each other in the exact same moment (Frames 6–7). They then gradually build back up to the original positive engagement.

Illustrations of Expectancies

We now turn to the question of what the infant comes to expect from his or her interactive encounters. How are infant expectancies of social interactions created? We use the descriptions of the drawings to illustrate how the action sequences of the exchange develop into expectancies. We attempt to translate the action-dialogue into language, as if the infant or mother could put the experience into words.

In the disruption and repair illustration of a dyad on the way to secure infant attachment, if the action dialogue could be translated into language, we infer that the infant creates the following expectancies of their interaction: "You sense how I feel. If I become distressed, I can expect you to recognize my distress, to join me in my moment of hesitation or worry. I know that you will wait for a moment while I reregulate myself at my own pace. You are right there, ready to join me bit by bit, as I gradually come back to engage with you. Then I can anticipate that we will together find each other's faces, and move bit by bit back up into mutually joyous smiles."

We infer that the mother comes to expect: "If you look away, and become distressed, I know how to help you. I can slow down, and wait for you to come back. I can find you again by reaching for your hands, making contact through our hands. I can trust that gradually you will come back to me. We can find each other's faces again, and we can return to our mutually joyous smiles."

Relevant Research

In sequences of disruption and repair, interactions are organized by some difficulty in the interaction, and ensuing efforts to resolve the difficulty. Infants notice a disruption of an ongoing sequence and notice if the disruption is repaired (Stern et al., 1985).

Although matching interactions, such as our facial mirroring illustration above, are very important, matching provides too limited a model for facial-visual communication, as we noted above in Chapter 3 (see Cohn & Tronick, 1989; Tronick, 1989).

In facial mirroring interactions, mother and infant do not exactly match exact affective expression or visual engagement. Instead, they roughly match the direction of facial-visual engagement change, becoming more or less positive together.

In successful face-to-face play interactions, mothers and infants do not necessarily match their states of engagement (Kronen, 1982; Malatesta & Haviland, 1983; Tronick, 1989). For example, mothers and infants match only approximately one third of the time; the rest of the time they may be slightly mismatched (for example, a smiling mother and a neutral-faced baby; Cohn & Tronick, 1989; Malatesta & Haviland, 1983). In Tronick and Cohn's research, when mother–infant pairs entered a mismatched state, they returned to a matched state within two seconds, an *interactive repair* (Cohn & Tronick, 1989; Tronick, 1989). Their work suggests that ordinary successful interactions should be described as continuously shifting back and forth between relatively matched states and minor disruptions or mismatches, with the flexibility to move back and forth very quickly. This is Tronick and colleagues' disruption and repair model, also known as mismatch and repair.

Furthermore, the capacity for interactive repair predicts attachment at one year. The better the pair is able to repair mismatches at four to six months, the more likely the infant is to be securely attached at one year (Cohn et al., 1991). Both mother and infant come to expect the possibility of repair. Moreover, repairs are mutually regulated: Both mother and infant contributed to repairs (Cohn & Tronick, 1989; Tronick, 1989). Thus, the reparative function is a mutual achievement, a competence of the dyad, rather than of the individual.

Experiences of repair increase the infant's effectance, elaborates his coping capacity, and contributes to an expectation of being able to repair, which he can take to other partners (Beebe & Lachmann, 1994; Beebe, Lachmann, & Jaffe, 1997); Gianino & Tronick, 1988). The experience of repair is also very important for the mother. It increases her confidence in her ability to help her infant, and in their mutual capacity to refind each other after a misstep. Her self-esteem as a mother is thereby reinforced. Repair organizes expectancies of coping, effectiveness, rerighting, and hope, in both partners. Interactions are reparable. The expectation is developed that it is possible to maintain engagement in the face of strains and mismatches. These capacities provide one definition of what is being organized in the infants' and mothers' expectancies of interaction patterns of disruption and repair (Beebe & Lachmann, 1994).

What is at stake is the dyad's capacity to co-create repair, a critical dimension of intimate relatedness. The expectation of the possibility of repair facilitates the development of secure attachment.

CHAPTER 6

Infant Look Away in the Origins of Secure Attachment

DRAWINGS: INFANT LOOK AWAY/SECURE PATTERN

This sequence depicts a mother and infant at four months where the infant was classified as secure attachment at one year (Beebe et al., 2010).

This sequence of drawings depicts 14 frames, over 19 seconds. This pair begins in a mutually positive engagement. Then the infant gradually sobers and looks away. The mother patiently waits, and stays closely connected to her infant. At one moment, she offers her hands, but the infant shows that he does not want them by turning away. The mother immediately retracts her hands and waits again. Her face is calm, and her expression conveys a confidence that her infant will return. When he does look at her again, she greets him with a smile. They gradually regain a mutually positive engagement.

6.1 MINUTE:SECOND 22:13–22:17

Storyline: They begin in a mutually positive engagement. As the infant sobers and looks away, the mother moves in.

Frame 1. Minute:Second 22:13
The infant and mother look at each other, both fully smiling, in a mutually positive engagement.

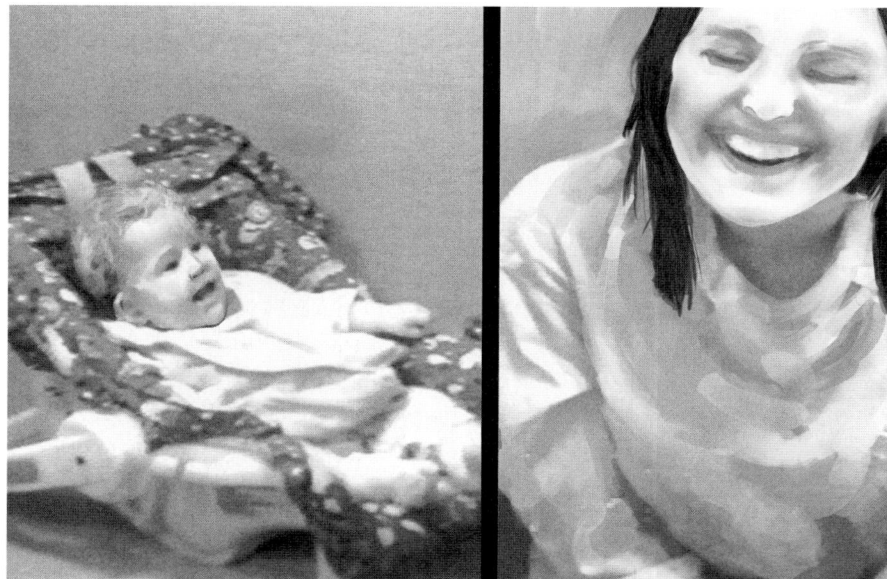

Frame 2. Minute:Second 22:17
From Frame 1 to 2, four seconds later, the mother moves forward, still smiling, with slightly less animation. The infant begins to look down and to sober.

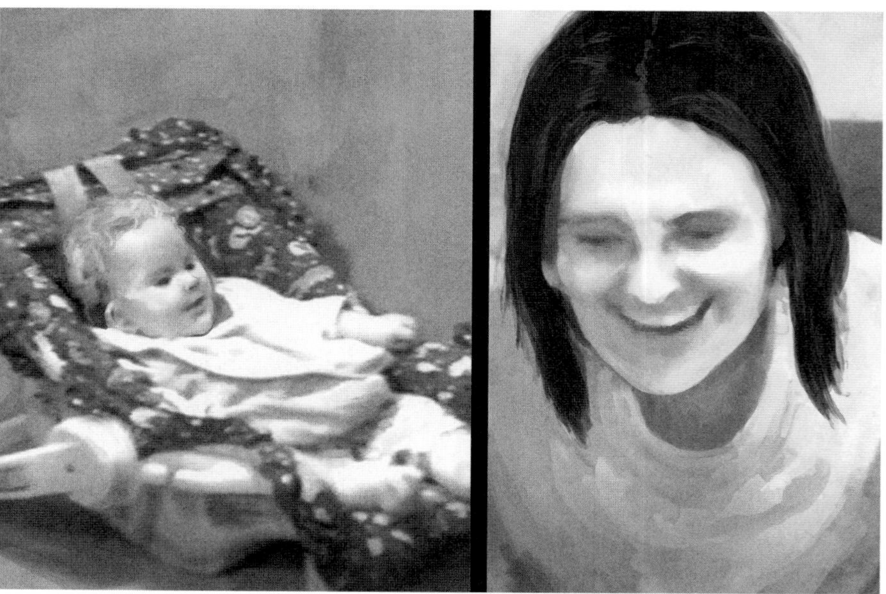

6.2 MINUTE:SECOND 22:20–22:32

Storyline: The mother sobers and waits while the infant looks down and away. When the mother offers her hands, the infant refuses them; the mother waits.

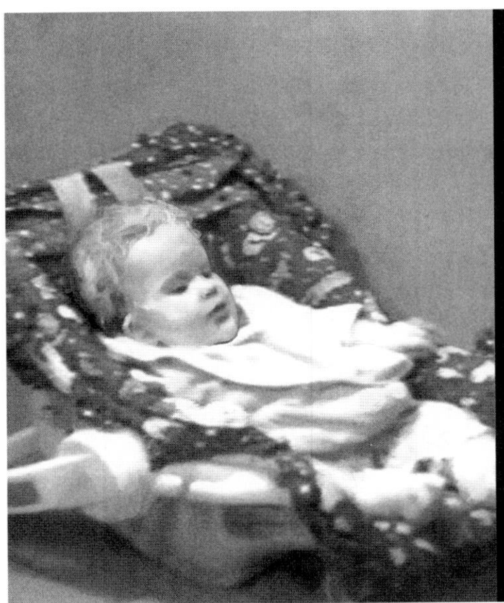

Frame 3. Minute:Second 22:20
From Frame 2 to 3, three seconds later, the infant is looking down. The mother's face sobers to a partially open mouth, "positive attention," with a less animated expression that matches the infant's state.

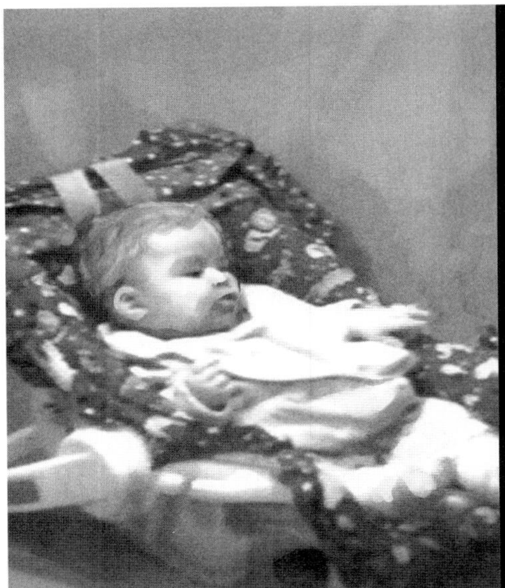

Frame 4. Minute:Second 22:21
From Frame 3 to 4, in the next second, the infant moves his head to the left; both hands begin to shift. The mother sobers further and closes her mouth, which slightly tightens.

Frame 5. Minute:Second 22:24

From Frame 4 to 5, three seconds later, the infant moves his head down and to his right, through the vis-à-vis, without looking at his mother. He is looking down, with his eyes just barely open. His face is sober. The mother moves her head slightly back and offers her hands to the infant, smiling with a partially open mouth.

Frame 6. Minute:Second 22:27

From Frame 5 to 6, three seconds later, the infant rejects the mother's offer of her hands by turning further away and arching back. His entire face is slightly tightened inward. He pulls his hands up and back in a "don't touch me" gesture. The mother simultaneously curls her fingers back, and her smile fades.

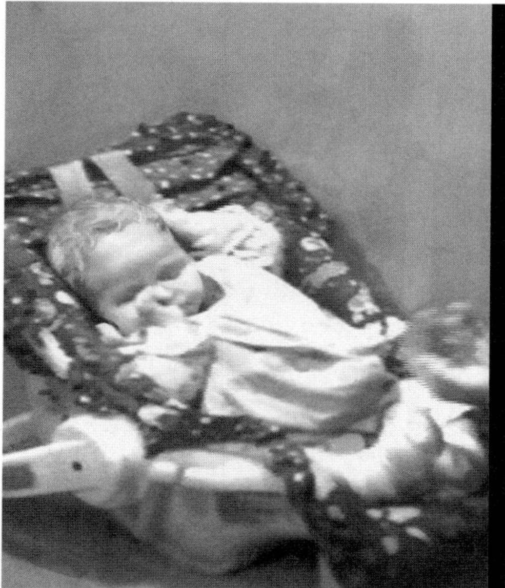

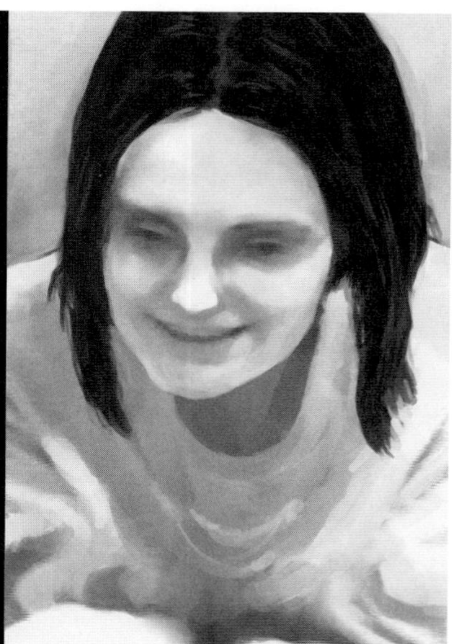

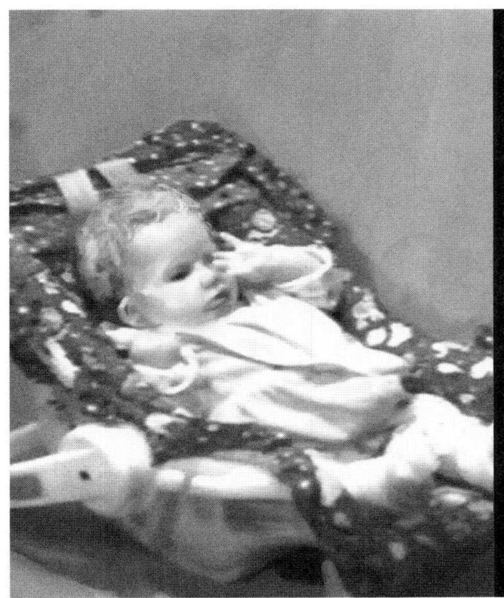

Frame 7. Minute:Second 22:30
From Frame 6 to 7, three seconds later, the infant reorients vis-à-vis and peeks at his mother through his left hand and right eye. The mother leans slightly forward with a concerned expression. She has a furrowed brow, with parted lips.

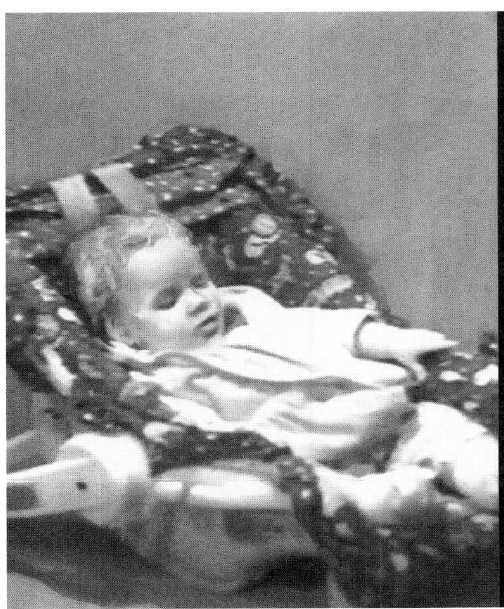
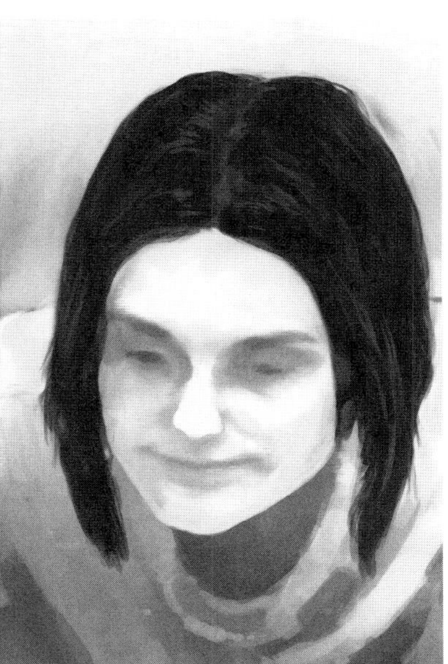

Frame 8. Minute:Second 22:32
From Frame 7 to 8, three seconds later, the infant closes his eyes and rests his left hand on the chair, as the mother leans in closer with a calm, interest expression.

6.3 MINUTE:SECOND 22:33–22:37

Storyline: The mother waits patiently while the infant looks away; when the infant returns, the mother greets.

Frame 9. Minute:Second 22:33
From Frame 8 to 9, in the next second, the infant tilts his head to his left away from his mother and looks down at his own hand, fingering the chair. The mother's head tilts to her right, matching the direction of the infant's head tilt. Her face is calm as she waits patiently.

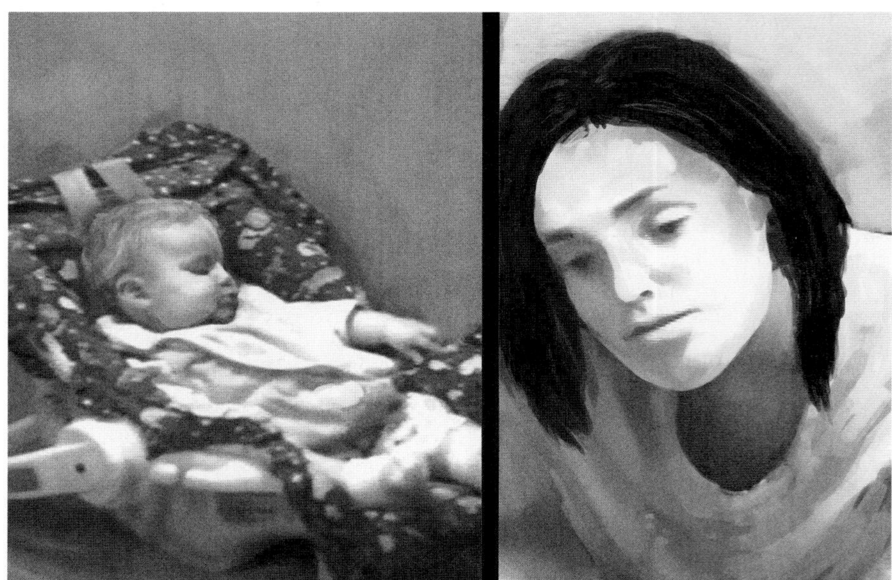

Frame 10. Minute:Second 22:35a
From Frame 9 to 10, less than two seconds later, the infant turns his head back to the vis-à-vis, looks at his mother, lifts his left hand, and reaches toward her. The mother greets him with an open face interest expression with a partially open mouth. Her head is slightly more upright, matching the infant's orientation.

Frame 11. Minute:Second 22:35b
From Frame 10 to 11, within the same second, while continuing to look, the infant lifts his head, opens his mouth slightly, and his left arm crosses his chest. The mother leans forward and greets him with an open mouth, a hint of a smile, and a hint of surprise in her eyebrows.

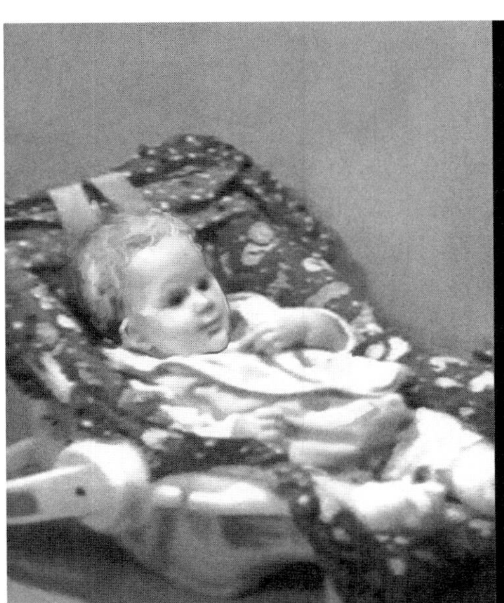

Frame 12. Minute:Second 22:37
From Frame 11 to 12, approximately a second and a half later, the infant opens his eyes fully, lowers his head, and lowers his left hand to his chest. He has a positive attention expression, a hint of mouth widening. The mother moves slightly back, and she smiles widely with an open mouth.

6.4 MINUTE:SECOND 22:38–22:41

Storyline: The infant rebuilds his joyful connection, and they enjoy mutual smiles.

Frame 13. Minute:Second 22:38
From Frame 12 to 13, in the next second, the infant begins to smile, continuing to look at his mother. The mother moves back further, with a more moderate smile, and slightly raised eyebrows.

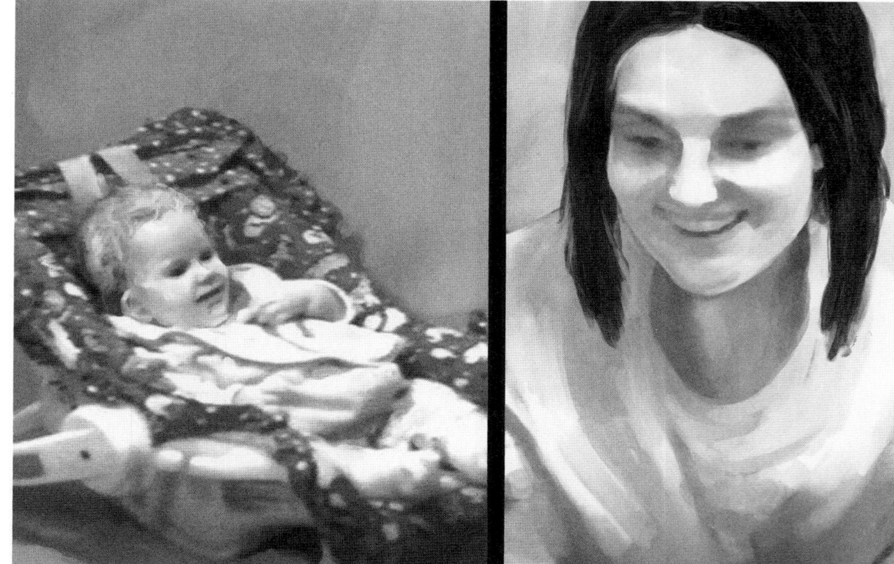

Frame 14. Minute:Second 22:41
From Frame 13 to 14, three seconds later, infant smiles widely, opening his mouth and moving his head up. The mother moves slightly forward and smiles fully. They achieve a full mutually positive engagement.

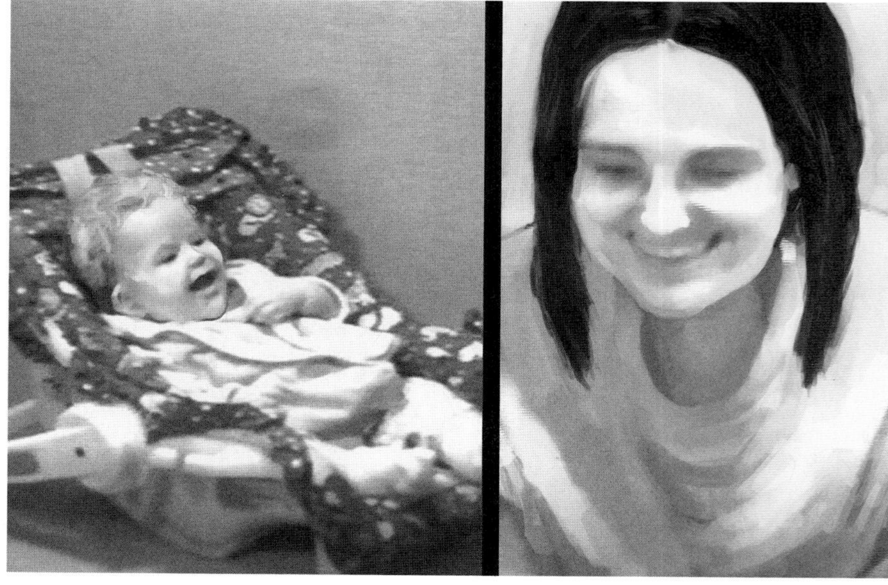

COMMENTARY ON INFANT LOOK AWAY/SECURE PATTERN

Looking into the face of a partner can be very stimulating. Most animals do not sustain long periods of such looking unless they are about to fight or make love, as the ethologists note (Chance & Larsen, 1996; Eibl-Eibesfeldt, 1970). Infants look away to manage this arousal. It is a critical infant coping capacity. Looking and looking away give the infant moment-by-moment control over the amount of visual contact that is comfortable to manage (Stern, 1971, 1985).

Most mothers intuitively understand the infant's need to reregulate in a moment of infant looking away. They try to engage their infants while the infant is looking, and they tend to cool it when the infant looks away (Brazelton et al., 1974). But it can be hard for mothers to tolerate the moments when infants look away. If the mother feels that her infant does not like her or is not interested in her, she may pursue her infant, increasing rather than decreasing the amount of stimulation. We saw an example of maternal pursuit or chase in the brief example of a chase and dodge sequence illustrated in Chapter 2, and we see the full sequence in Chapter 8. Maternal chase behavior is counterproductive; the infant then requires more time to regulate arousal down sufficiently to return to gazing at the mother. Instead, if the mother can be helped to give the baby a time-out to reregulate, cooling it when the infant looks away, trusting her infant to return to her, the infant will rapidly reengage. As we noted in the Introduction to Drawings Illustrating the Origins of Secure Attachment, this maternal pattern, giving the infant a time-out to reregulate when the infant looks away, predicts secure attachment (Langhorst & Fogel, 1982).

When a four-month infant looks away from the mother's face, he does not completely stop visually monitoring his mother, unless he turns all the way away from her toward the environment, a 90-degree to 180-degree turn. More usually, looking away with a less severe head turn away, less than 90 degrees, infants can continue to use peripheral visual monitoring. Thus, the infant looking away does not necessarily mean that the infant is completely away.

We chose the sequence infant look away in the origins of secure infant attachment because it beautifully illustrates the mother's capacity to wait, calmly, with no other agenda, as her infant looks away from her (see for example Frame 9). This mother shows us what it can be like to trust in the infant's eventual return to a mutual gaze. At the end of the sequence, the infant does return, and they regain a mutually positive engagement (Frames 14–15). Portions of the following descriptions are adapted from Beebe (2005, 2014), Beebe et al. (2010), Cohen and Beebe (2002), and Stern (1971, 1974).

Illustrations of Expectancies

We now turn to the question of what the infant comes to expect from his or her interactive encounters. We attempt to translate the action-dialogue into language, as if the infant or mother could put the experience into words.

In the secure look away sequence of a dyad on the way to secure infant attachment, if the action-dialogue could be translated into language, we imagine that the infant may create the following expectancies of their interaction:

"When I look away, you sense that I need space. You quickly calm down, and you match my mood. If I need to turn away more, and take more time calming down myself, I know you will wait for me. You will not try to shift me before I am ready. If you offer me your hands, and I don't want them, you can quickly readjust. When I am ready to look back, you are right there to greet me. And I know we can refind our smiles."

We imagine that the mother may create the following expectancies of their interaction: "When we are having such a good time playing, I know that sometimes you need to take a break. I try to give you space. If I offer you my hands, and you don't want them, it's ok. I can wait. I feel calm as I wait for you. I know that you will be coming back to me just as soon as you can. And then we will refind our smiles."

Relevant Research

By three to four months, infants have very developed visual systems. By this age, the infant's ability to focus is approximately equivalent to that of adults (Kaye & Fogel, 1980; Stern, 1971; Tronick, 1989; White, Castle, & Held, 1964). Thus, the infant has control over the level of visual contact that is similar to that of adults. As Stern (1971) notes, this is the first action system in which infants have a level of control over the contact similar to that of adults.

Field (1981) verified that infants organize their cycles of looking and looking away to regulate their degree of arousal. She monitored infant heart rate during face-to-face play. She showed that the moment that the infant looks away is preceded by a burst of arousal in the previous five seconds. Following the infant's gaze aversion, heart rate decreases back down to baseline within the next five seconds, and then the infant returns to looking at mother's face. Thus, Field demonstrated that infant gaze aversion is an important aspect of infant self-regulation.

Brazelton et al. (1974) first showed that mothers typically pace their amount of stimulation according to the infant's cycles of looking and looking away, stimulating more as the infant looks, and stimulating less as the infant looks away. Although these are typical patterns, we have also noted a pattern of mutual *eye love* in which mothers and infants can sustain prolonged mutual gaze for up to 100 seconds during periods of positive affect (Beebe, 1973; Beebe & Stern, 1977). Although rare, these are the moments, of course, that every parent loves.

Beebe, Bigelow et al. (2015) found that infants' looking away affected how mothers and infants coordinate with each other in every communication modality examined. The infant looking at the mother was associated with higher interpersonal coordination of facial and vocal affect and lower coordination of touch. Only when infants were looking in the prior second did they coordinate their facial affect with maternal facial affect. Mothers coordinated their facial affect with infant facial and vocal affect more strongly when infants were looking in the prior second. Only when infants were looking in the prior second were mothers likely to respond to infant vocal and facial distress with an empathic woe face. This finding points to an important contribution of the infant, that is, the infant's ability to seek the partner's face in a moment of distress. Thus moment-by-moment, the cycles of infant looking and looking away function as a powerful ongoing context of the mother–infant interaction.

What is at stake in moments of infant looking and looking away is the dyad's ability to negotiate a moment of temporary infant visual disengagement. And usually this visual engagement is only partial, with infant peripheral visual monitoring remaining intact. The mother's confidence in her own ability to engage her infant, and her confidence in her infant's attachment to her, are critical in her ability to tolerate the moment of her infant looking away.

In this set of drawings, the mother conveyed a peaceful confidence in her infant's involvement with her. She was able to calm herself down as her infant began to look away. She was able to wait. When her infant rejected her offer of her hands, she did not become miffed or feel rejected. At each moment, she was sensitive to whether her infant needed her to be more engaged or less engaged, to be sitting more forward or moving slightly back, to be more openly facially expressive, or to be more facially dampened and waiting.

For the infant's part, he was able to reregulate himself and return to looking at his mother rather quickly. When he came back to her, he gestured toward her and showed her a warm smile. Thus, the infant as well as the mother both play an important part in the management of the infant's looking and looking away: the management of cycles of engagement, partial disengagement, and reengagement.

CHAPTER 7

Maternal Loom and Repair in the Origins of Secure Infant Attachment

DRAWINGS: MATERNAL LOOM AND REPAIR

This sequence depicts a mother and infant at four months where the infant was classified as secure attachment at one year (Beebe et al., 2010).

This sequence of drawings depicts 11 frames, over 19 seconds. In this pair, the mother begins with a loom, moving her head close in toward the infant's face. The infant's immediate response is to turn away. The mother reacts by moving back immediately. The infant gradually returns to look at his mother. The sequence ends with a mutually positive engagement, a repair.

Because this sequence begins with the mother already in a loom orientation, we provide one extra drawing to illustrate this mother in a mostly upright position, not looming, seen below. This frame is taken from another moment in the film, before the maternal loom and repair sequence begins.

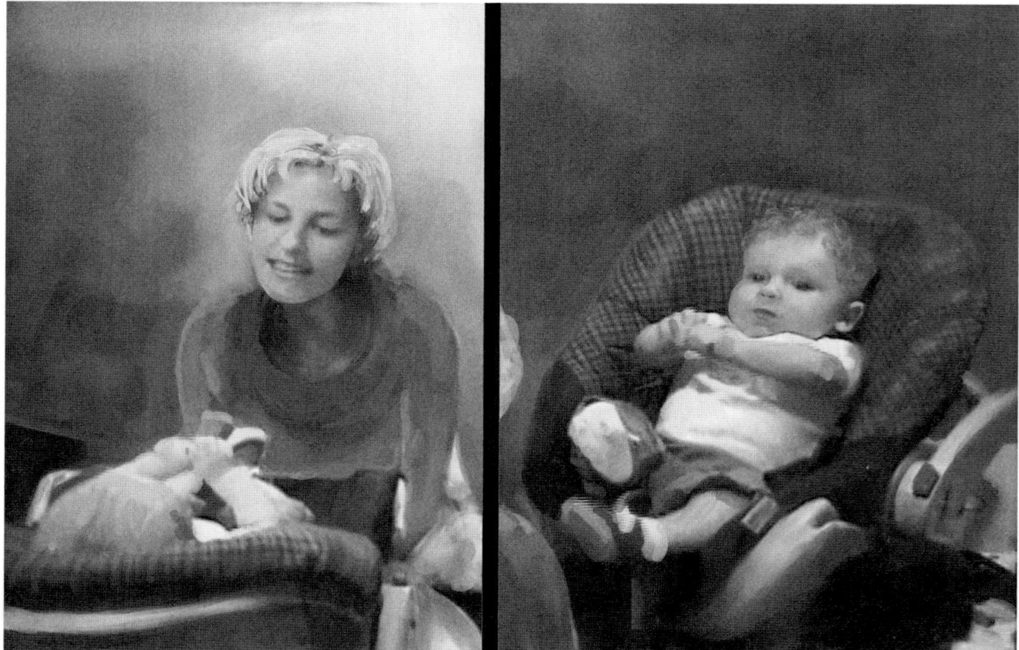

This frame shows the mother in a typical, mostly upright orientation position, before the loom sequence begins. In the view of the mother (left side of the frame), the infant is visible below the mother, as they interact face-to-face. In the view of the infant (right side of the frame), notice that the mother's hair is just slightly visible at the left edge. This also helps us see that mother and infant are seated face-to-face.

7.1 MINUTE:SECOND 02:05–02:07A

Storyline: As mother looms in, the infant brings his hands up and averts his head.

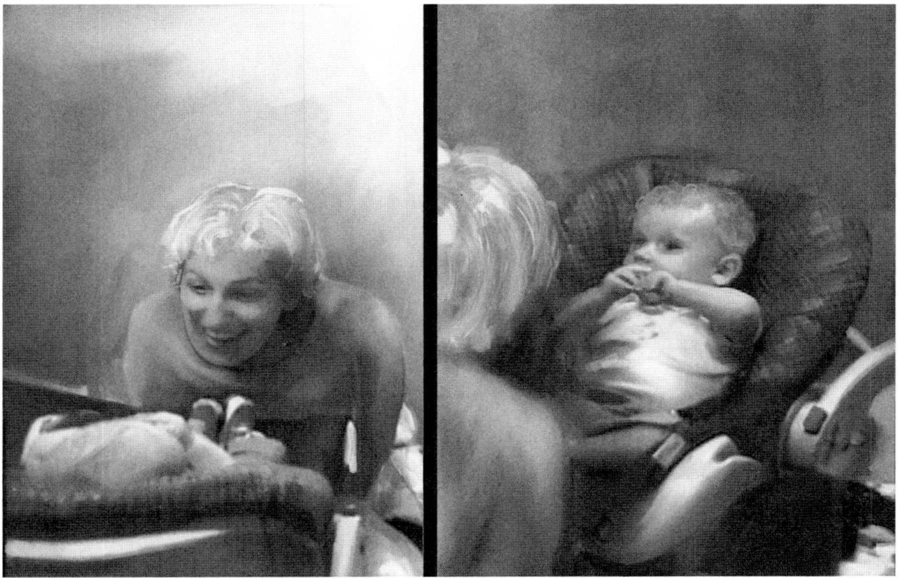

Frame 1. Minute:Second 02:05
The mother looms in closely toward her infant and smiles widely, with her mouth partially open and eyebrows raised. The infant has both hands clasped together and raises his arms to his mouth, looking at his mother.

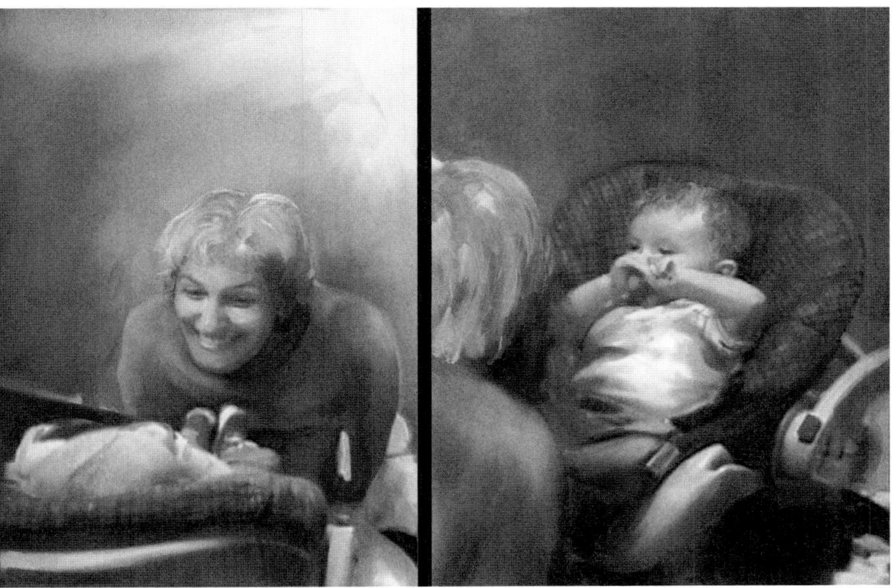

Frame 2. Minute:Second 02:06a
From Frame 1 to 2, a fraction of a second later, the mother still smiles widely. She begins to slightly close her mouth and continues her loom. The infant raises his hands further up toward his eyes. He peers out over his clasped hands.

Frame 3. Minute:Second 02:06b
From Frame 2 to 3, within the same second, the mother begins to move back slightly, sensing that she is too close. She continues to smile, but slightly less intensely. The infant covers his eyes with raised arms and moves his head 90 degrees to the right. His hands remain clasped.

Frame 4. Minute:Second 02:07a
From Frame 3 to 4, a fraction of a second later, the mother continues to move her head slightly back as her eyebrows lower. The infant remains averted at 90 degrees; his hands remain clasped, covering his eyes, and his right hand moves up just slightly. He parts his lips.

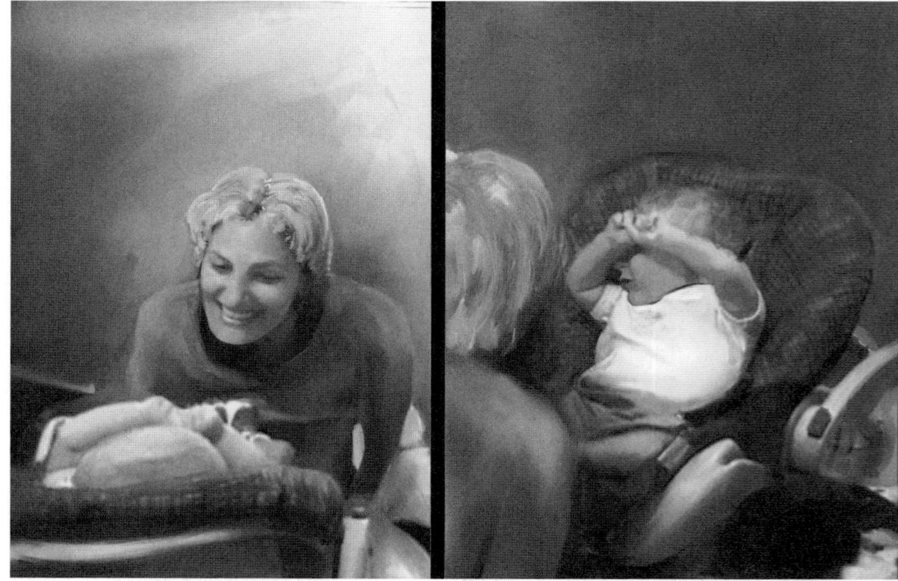

7.2 MINUTE:SECOND 02:07B–02:09

Storyline: Mother senses infant's discomfort and sobers, moving back; infant returns to vis-à-vis, letting his hands down and looking.

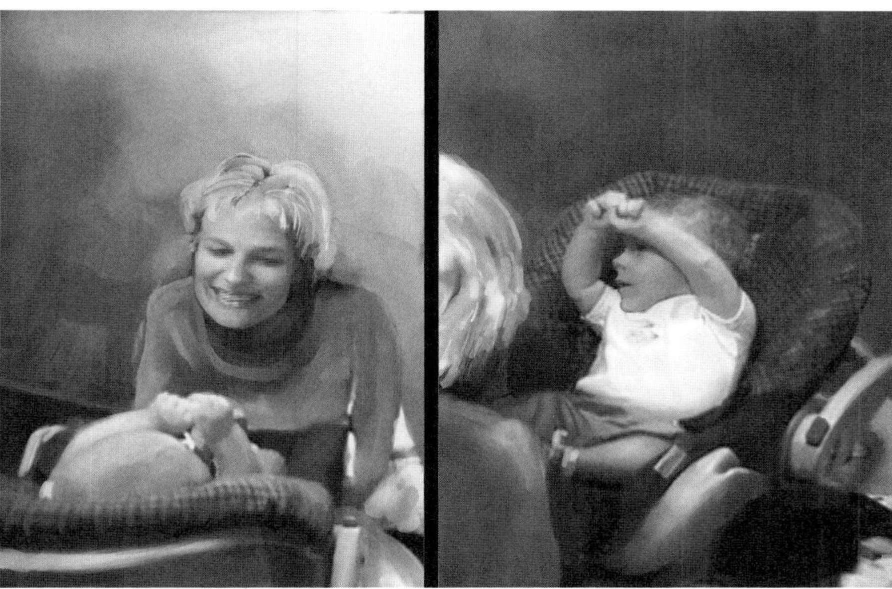

Frame 5. Minute:Second 02:07b
From Frame 4 to 5, within the same second, the mother continues to move back, and her smile is fading. The infant raises his arms and peeks out; his hands remain clasped.

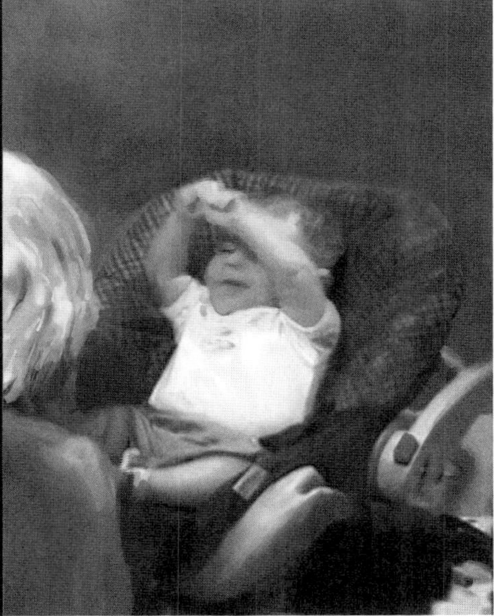

Frame 6. Minute:Second 02:08
From Frame 5 to 6, within the same second, the mother moves her head and body further back. Her face has a hint of positive affect. The infant reorients and looks at his mother from under his arms, which are raised above his head. He has a tentative look.

Frame 7. Minute:Second 02:09
From Frame 6 to 7, one second later, the mother continues to move her head slightly further back. Her face is soft with a hint of mouth widening (but not a smile). The infant lowers his hands and looks directly at his mother. His eyes are wide open. He seems wary. His hands are clasped at his chest.

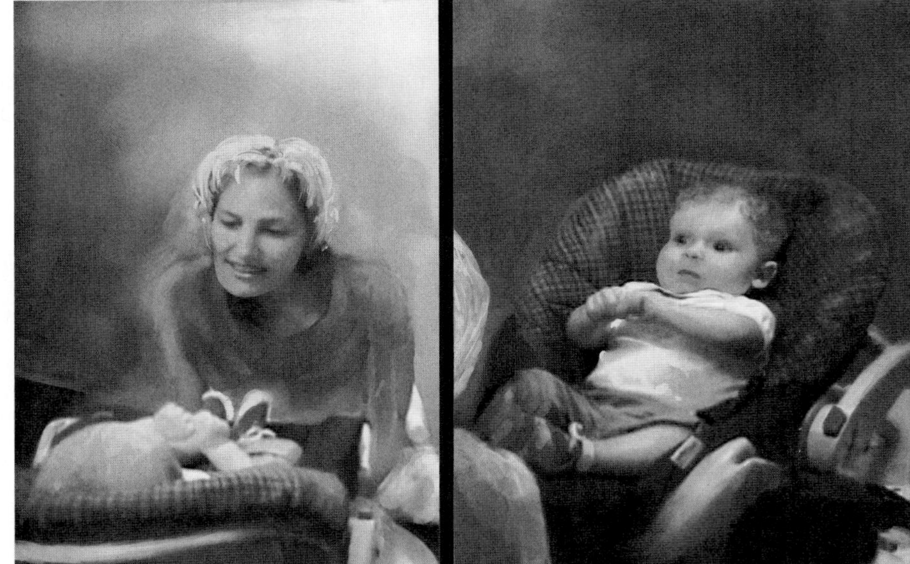

7.3 MINUTE:SECOND 02:21–02:25

Storyline: Mother stabilizes her posture fully upright; the infant is fully engaged. They play at matching expressions, ending with mutual smiles. The loom is repaired.

Frame 8. Minute:Second 02:21
From Frame 8 to 9, 11 seconds later, we reenter the sequence. The mother has moved back upright, and she is smiling. The infant is looking at his mother, kicking his feet and moving his arms excitedly.

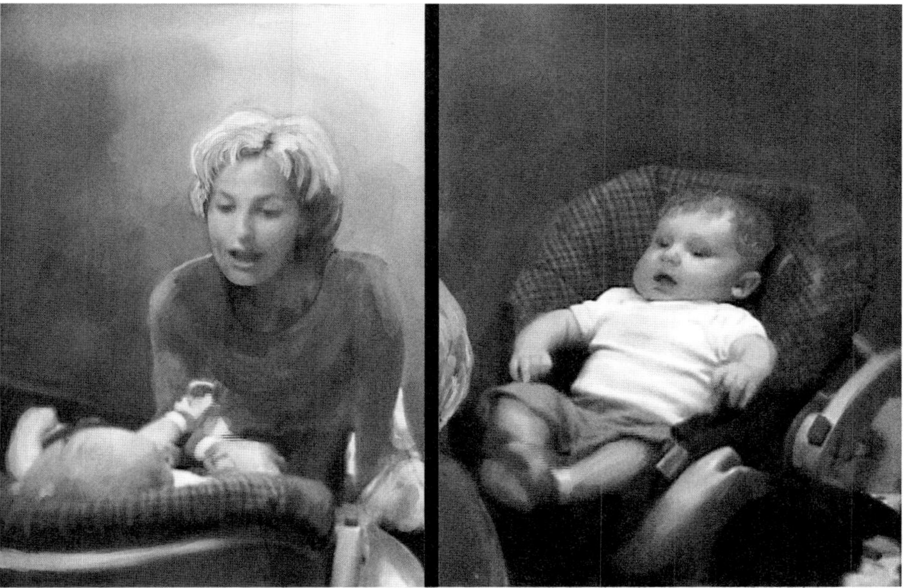

Frame 9. Minute:Second 02:22
From Frame 8 to 9, one second later, the mother and infant look at each other and simultaneously open their mouths, in similar partial surprise expressions with raised eyebrows. The infant's open mouth conveys some excitement. He moves his hands and arms excitedly.

Frame 10.
Minute:Second 02:23
From Frame 9 to 10, one second later, the mother and infant simultaneously close their mouths, matching their states. Both wait.

Frame 11.
Minute:Second 02:25
From Frame 10 to 11, two seconds later, the mother and infant now simultaneously smile happily at each other. The infant excitedly raises his right arm. The disruption has been repaired.

COMMENTARY ON MATERNAL LOOM AND REPAIR

Maternal orientation positions of sitting upright, moving forward, and especially looming in close to the infant's face, are powerful aspects of the mother's stimulation during a face-to-face encounter with her infant. Infants respond to maternal orientation changes with their own head orientation movements of approach or withdrawal, looking and looking away, and movements of their hands and feet. Maternal loom can be problematic. In response to maternal loom, infants often move their heads back and away, and sometimes pull their hands back and up, in a "don't touch me" gesture.

We chose the sequence "Maternal Loom and Repair in the Origins of Secure Attachment" because it illustrates one mother's sensitive awareness of the effect of her looming movement on her infant, and her immediate, intuitive pulling back to repair her orientational intrusion (Frames 3– 7). This infant withdraws from the maternal loom. But the secure loom sequence illustrates, in addition, the infant's flexibility to respond to the mother's pulling-back repair, and his gradual ability to regain a visually engaged, positive face-to-face encounter (Frames 8–11).

Illustrations of Expectancies

We now turn to the question of what the infant comes to expect from his or her interactive encounters. We attempt to translate the action-dialogue into language, as if the infant or mother could put the experience into words.

In the secure loom repair sequence of a dyad on the way to secure infant attachment, if the action-dialogue could be translated into language, we infer that the infant creates the following expectancies of their interaction: "You sense that I feel overwhelmed and invaded when you loom in so close. You know how I feel. When I turn away and pull my hands back, and especially if I hide my face, you know that I need you to move back. I can count on you to wait for a moment while I reregulate myself at my own pace. As I gradually come back to engage with you, you are right there, ready to join me bit by bit. Then I can anticipate that we will together find each other's faces again. And we will refind our smiles."

We infer that the mother comes to expect: "I am learning that my looming in close toward your face is hard for you. When I see you move away like that, pull your hands back, and hide your face, I know that I have moved in too far. I know how to help you. I can pull back, slow down, and wait for you to come back. Then I know that I can find you again. I can trust that gradually you will come back to me. We can find each other's faces again, and we can return to our smiles."

Relevant Research

Beebe et al. (2010) examined maternal loom behavior during four-month face-to-face interactions in mothers of infants who were classified as secure vs. insecure at one year. The research examined two and a half minutes of interaction for each dyad. Mother looming into the infant's face was a rare behavior.

At four months, mothers of infants who were classified as secure at one year loomed half as much (about 10 percent of the session) as mothers of infants who were classified as insecure (about 21 percent of the session). This difference was statistically significant.

Mothers were separated by levels of use of loom into *none*, "*moderate*" (1–29 seconds), and *high* use (30+ seconds). About half the mothers "never" loomed. Mothers of infants who were classified as secure mostly did not loom (about 62 percent of mothers), some mothers loomed moderately (about 26 percent of mothers), and a few were high loomers (about 12 percent). In contrast, about 42 percent of the mothers of infants who were classified as insecure attachment at one year were high loomers, over three times as many. This difference was statistically significant.

Occasional use of loom is natural, and mothers of infants who will be classified as secure may loom about 10 percent of the time. Perhaps mothers of secure infants are more aware of the potentially disruptive effects of loom, and perhaps these mothers can quickly move to repair a loom when they see their infants turning away. Our drawing sequence of maternal loom and repair illustrates such a mother–infant dyad.

In the illustration of "Maternal Loom and Repair in the Origins of Secure Attachment," what is at stake is a mutual capacity for managing a disruption and a repair that involved maternal loom. Both this mother and the infant mutually negotiate the repair. This mother is immediately aware, at a procedural, action-sequence level (although not necessarily consciously), of her spatial intrusion. Although the infant reacts to the mother's loom with extensive withdrawal behaviors, he is exquisitely sensitive to her immediate movements backward, which begin to repair her spatial intrusion. Bit by bit, he peeks out and comes back to her. Thus, the infant's ability to respond is critical to the repair process.

Introduction to Drawings Illustrating the Origins of Insecure-Avoidant and Insecure-Resistant Attachment

The next two sets of drawings present mother–infant interaction sequences at infant age four months, which illustrate the origins of insecure avoidant and resistant attachment patterns at one year.

Insecure attachment at one year is associated with less optimal peer relations and school performance (Sroufe, 1983). Insecure attachment is associated with ineffective methods of dealing with negative emotions, either maximizing and escalating negative emotions or minimizing negative emotions, with methods such as distancing, repression, and dissociation. These methods of emotion regulation generate risk for maladaptive modes of alleviating emotional discomfort (Cassidy, 1994; Dozier, Stovall-McClough, & Albus, 2008). Insecurity may reflect internal models in which the self is viewed as unable, perhaps unworthy, of getting attachment needs met from attachment figures (Bowlby, 1980; Lay, Waters, Posada, & Ridgeway, 1995).

Insecure adult attachment poses risk for romantic relationships (Feeney, Noller, & Callan, 1994; Holland & Roisman, 2010), less optimal parenting (Haltigan, Leerkes, Supple, & Calkins, 2014; van IJzendoorn, 1995; Ward & Carlson, 1995), and offspring insecure attachment (Kovan et al., 2009; Steele et al., 1996). Insecure women are less sensitive to infant distress, more likely to make negative attributions to infant cries, and are less accurate in identifying infant emotions (Haltigan et al, 2014; Leerkes & Siepak, 2006; Leerkes et al., 2014).

INSECURE-AVOIDANT INFANT ATTACHMENT

Whereas securely attached infants immediately seek contact with the parent during the reunion episodes of the strange situation at one year, insecure-avoidant infants actively avoid the parent (Cassidy, 1994). These infants are described as minimizing their response to fear by a shift of attention away from the parent toward the inanimate environment (Cassidy, 1994; Main & Hesse, 1990), which allows self-regulation and proximity, but at a price. These avoidantly attached infants do not become distressed during the separation, nor do they show pleasure at the reunion.

This neutral behavior by avoidantly attached infants is part of a strategy of minimizing negative emotions, and of minimizing the importance of the caregiver as a source of comfort (Cassidy, 1994; Main & Solomon, 1986). Infants develop this strategy as a result of rejection by their caregivers, especially at times of distress (Cassidy, 1994). Infant attempts to elicit care may risk further rebuff by the mother. As part of a strategy of minimizing the importance of the attachment relationship, these insecure-avoidant infants also tend to minimize other emotions, such as joy (Cassidy, 1994). Minimizing emotions reduces the infant's arousal level and fear (Bowlby, 1980; Cassidy, 1994). The infant's goal is to maintain the bond with his attachment figure on whom he depends for survival (Bowlby, 1980; Main, 1981). Being less aroused, less needy, less emotional, is a strategy that will more likely maintain this bond with a mother who is dismissive herself of attachment needs.

DISMISSING ADULT ATTACHMENT (PARALLEL TO INFANT AVOIDANT ATTACHMENT)

The adult parallel to infant avoidant attachment is termed dismissing attachment in the AAI. In the AAI, parents of insecure-avoidant infants have a style of emotion regulation similar to that of their infants. They tend to minimize the importance of attachment in their own lives (Main & Goldwyn, 1994) and to restrict negative emotions (Riem et al., 2012). Whereas secure adults show a spontaneous capacity to acknowledge distress in past attachment experiences, and show a flexible range of strategies for resolving negative emotions, dismissing adults tend to give an overly positive picture of their attachment history that lacks credibility (Steele & Steele, 2005, 2008). They tend to rely on avoidance, contempt, or turning away from any difficulties in their own histories (Gottman, Katz, & Hooven, 1996).

INFANT RESISTANT ATTACHMENT

Because of their own histories of not being able to trust attachments, mothers of resistantly attached infants feel more comfortable when the attachment system is activated, to be sure that their infants need them (Cassidy & Berlin, 1994). In the strange situation at 12 months, mothers of resistant infants often linger as they leave, activating the child's request that the mother stay, perhaps in an effort to be sure to be needed.

During the reunion episodes of the strange situation at one year, insecure-resistant infants become extremely distressed, seek the parent, but cannot calm down (Cassidy, 1994). Resistantly attached infants are unable to separate from the parent and to resume play after the separation. They show repeated expressions of anger, crying, and petulance. They seem inconsolable in spite of efforts by the parent to comfort them. These mothers are inconsistent in their response, generally nonnurturant, neglectful, and rejecting, but at times sensitive and caring. The parents may have been able to respond to their infant's distress minimally, or inconsistently.

Whereas insecure-avoidant infants minimize negative emotions, insecure-resistant infants heighten their emotional expression to increase their chances of a response. This strategy involves a heightening of the importance of the attachment relationship (Cassidy, 1994). Maximizing fearfulness and distress increases the likelihood that the mother will attend to the child. Relaxing and allowing oneself to be soothed may run the risk of losing contact with a possibly inconsistent or inattentive parent (Cassidy, 1994; Main & Hesse, 1990). While this maximizing strategy can be effective in gaining attention from the parent, it can also disturb the possibility of an intimate relationship with the parent, and it may interfere with other developmental tasks, such as exploration (Bowlby, 1973; Cassidy, 1994).

PREOCCUPIED ADULT ATTACHMENT (PARALLEL TO INFANT RESISTANT ATTACHMENT)

Parents of insecure-resistant infants tend to be classified as *preoccupied* (the adult attachment term that parallels infant resistant attachment), an attachment pattern that parallels that of their infants. Adults with a preoccupied classification are still very involved and preoccupied with their early attachment experiences. They tend to express heightened negative emotions and to emphasize the impact, often negative, of their attachment experiences (Riem et al., 2012). Preoccupied adults tend to escalate their negative emotions and an angry stance; or to retreat into quiet despair, a passive stance (Steele & Steele, 2008).

In the two sets of drawings that follow, we first illustrate the origins of infant resistant attachment in Chapter 8, and then the origins of infant avoidant attachment in Chapter 9.

CHAPTER 8

Chase and Dodge in the Origins of Insecure-Resistant Attachment

DRAWINGS: CHASE AND DODGE

This sequence depicts a mother and infant at four months in a chase and dodge sequence. This pattern was found to predict insecure-resistant attachment at one year (Beebe et al., 2010).

This sequence of drawings presents 36 frames, across 53 seconds. Mother and infant begin in mutual gaze with mildly positive expressions. But quickly the interaction takes on the quality of mother chasing and infant dodging. By the end, the infant shows a remarkable collapse of body tonus.

Following the interaction with the mother, this infant then played immediately with the stranger, a novel partner.

8.1 MINUTES:SECOND 01:10–01:18: 9 FRAMES ACROSS 9 SECONDS

Storyline: The infant and the mother begin in mutual gaze with mildly positive expressions. But as the mother looms, the infant turns away, and the mother then pulls the infant toward her (Frames 4–5). After the infant turns away again to a full 90-degree aversion, the mother picks him up (Frames 8–10).

Frame 1. Minute:Second 01:10
The mother leans in close toward her infant. She smiles. The infant is looking at his mother with a slightly positive interest expression. His head is slightly tipped to his left.

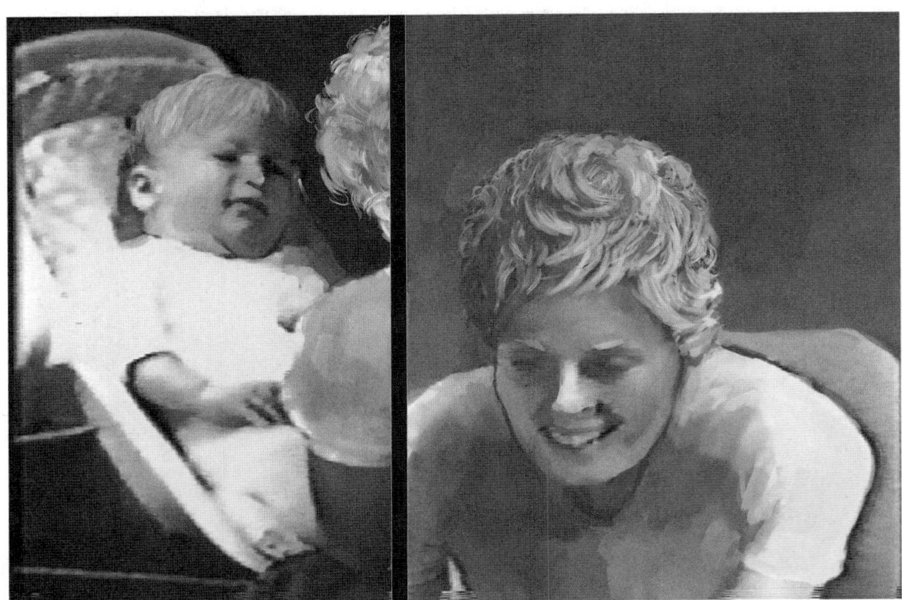

Frame 2. Minute:Second 01:11
From Frame 1 to 2, one second later, the mother looms in toward the infant's face, and she increases her smile. Her left hand reaches in and grabs the infant's right hand. As she looms in, the infant turns his head away to his left and looks away. His mouth has a compressed-lips expression.

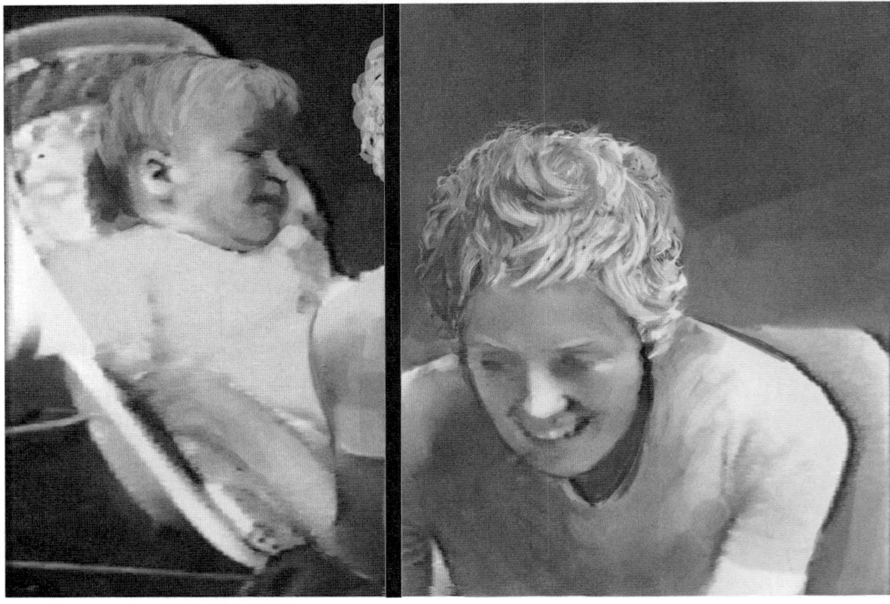

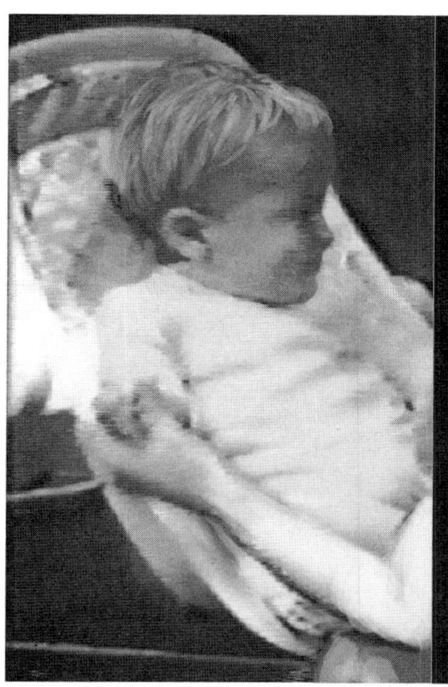

Frame 3. Minute:Second 01:12
From Frame 2 to 3, in the next second, the mother moves very slightly back, and her smile begins to dampen. With her left hand, she lifts the infant's right hand. The infant continues to look away, and his head moves slightly down and a bit further to his left.

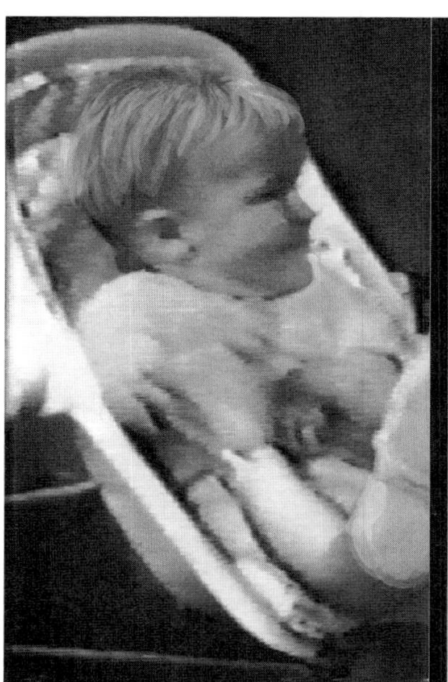

Frame 4. Minute:Second 01:13
From Frame 3 to 4, one second later, the mother brings her infant's hands together and pulls them to her left, attempting to pull him back toward the vis-a-vis. She continues her smile. The infant continues to look away toward his left, and his head has lifted slightly (because of the mother's pull).

Frame 5. Minute:Second 01:14
From Frame 4 to 5, in the next second, the mother looms in very close to her infant's face. She pulls both of her infant's hands further to her left. She seems to be intent on getting him back to a vis-à-vis position where he could look at her. Her smile is fading. The infant continues to look away to his left. His body is more upright, in response to his mother's pull.

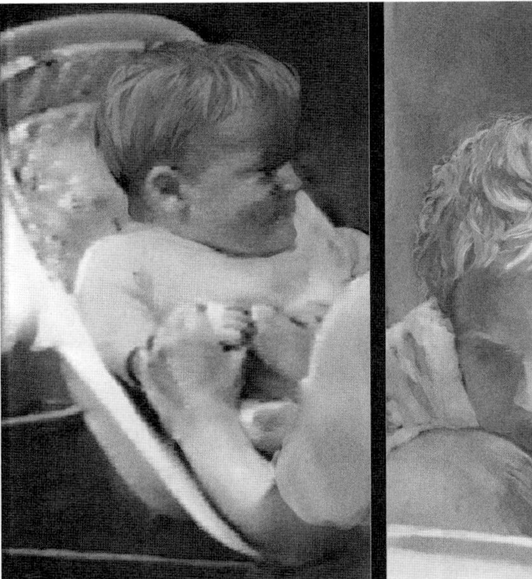

Frame 6. Minute:Second 01:15
Frame 5 to 6, one second later, the mother moves slightly back, although she is still looming in. She continues to hold her infant's hands, but her hands have moved outward and she is no longer pulling him. Her smile is slightly increasing. Even though the mother is starting to move back, the infant moves his head further away, almost 90 degrees to the left.

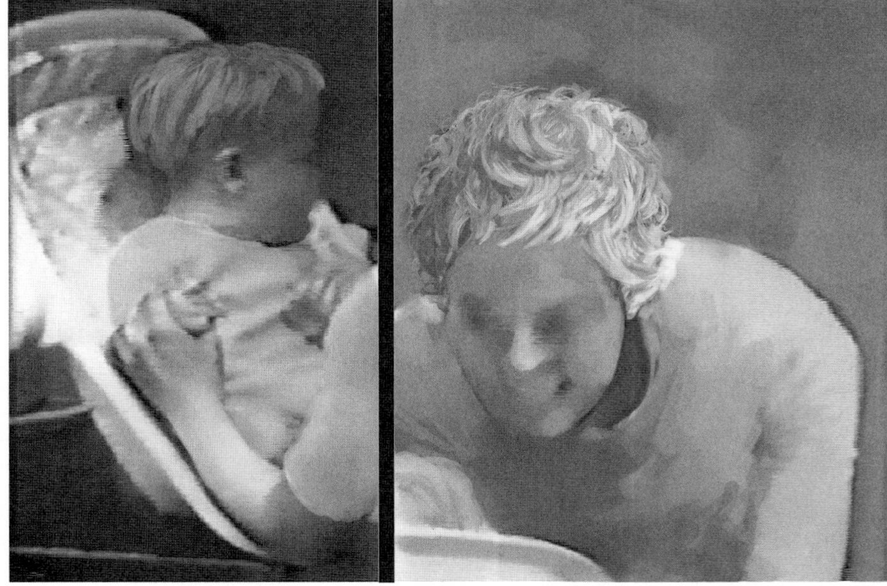

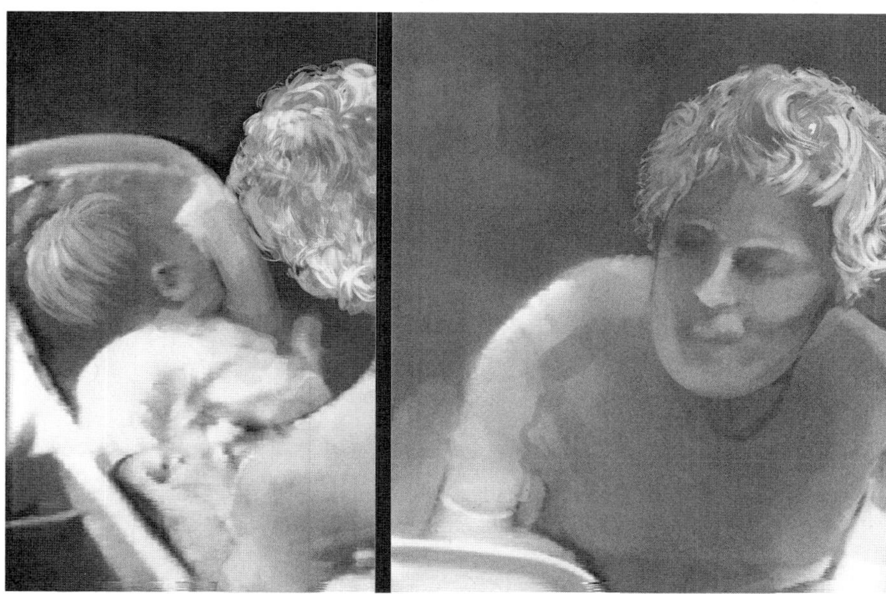

Frame 7. Minute:Second 01:16
From Frame 6 to 7, one second later, the infant turns his head 90 degrees away from his mother. The mother moves back and to her left. (Her hair is more visible in the infant's frame because of her movement to the left). Her smile is fading, but her mouth still slightly open. The mother's left hand moves toward the infant's body.

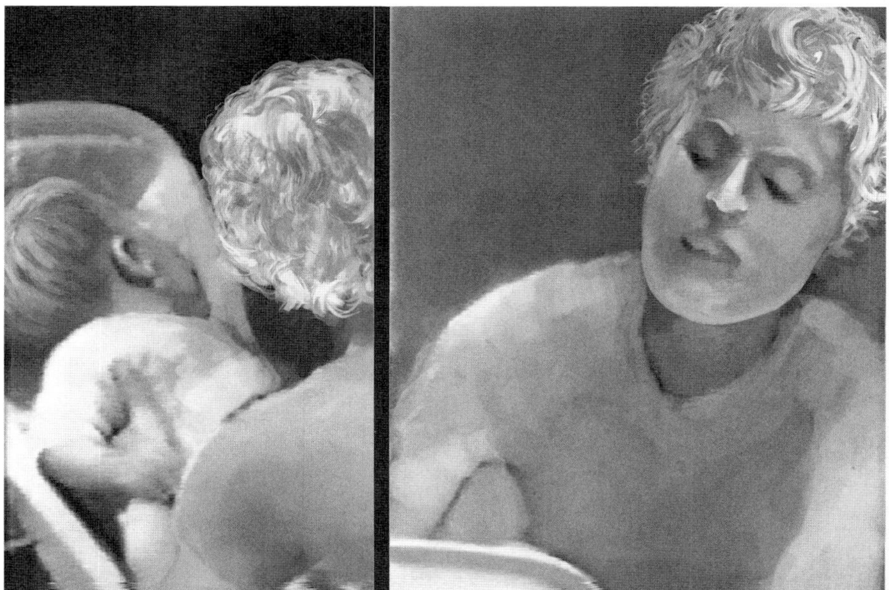

Frame 8. Minute:Second 01:17
From Frame 7 to 8, in the next second, the mother begins to lift her infant from under his arms. Her smile has completely faded. There is a hint of sadness. As she begins to lift him, the infant's head turns further to his left.

Frame 9. Minute:Second 01:18
From Frame 8 to 9, one second later, the mother continues to lift her infant. Her mouth is open, and her expression seems tentative.

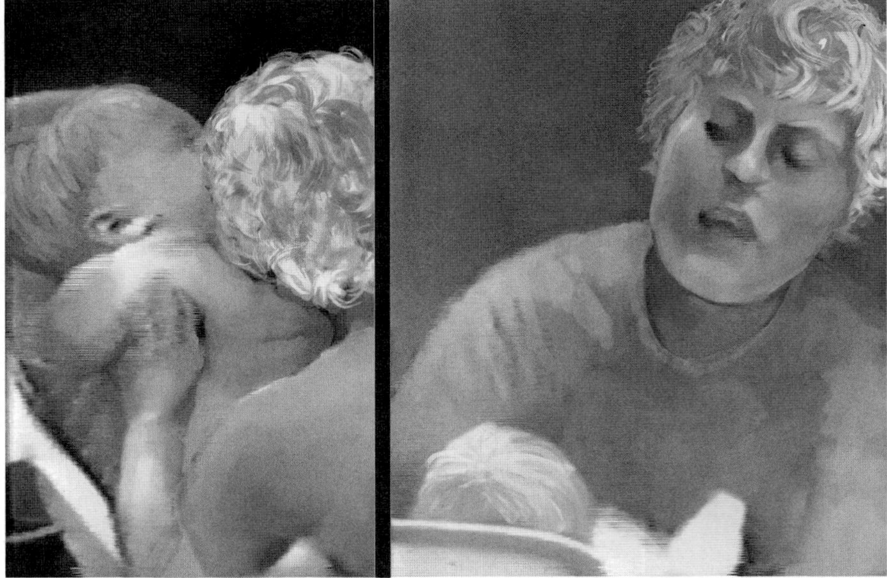

8.2 MINUTE:SECOND 01:19–01:42: 8 FRAMES OVER 24 SECONDS

Storyline: By the time the mother puts the infant down on her lap, he has turned away from her yet again. Then the mother stands him up, but he turns away more and more.

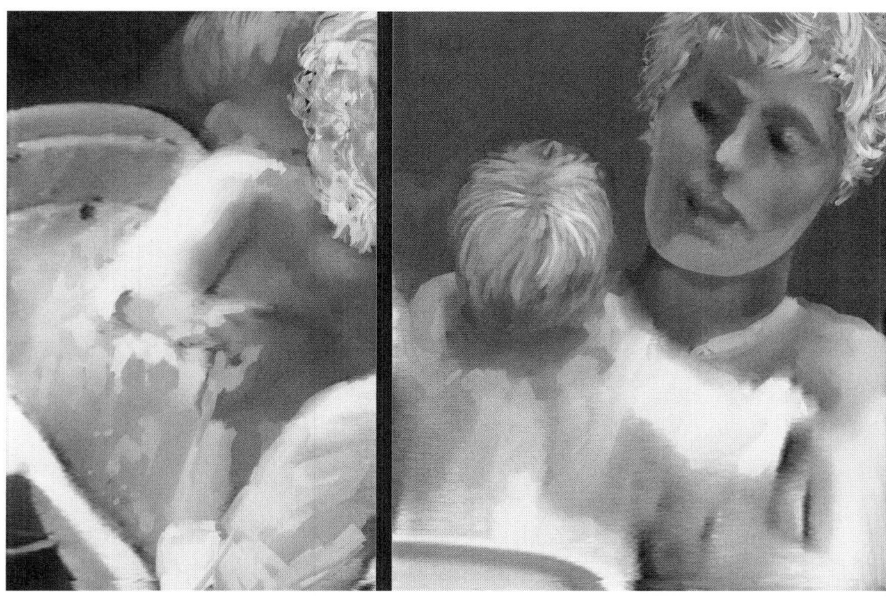

Frame 10. Minute:Second 01:19
From Frame 9 to 10, one second later, the mother continues lifting her infant. Her mouth is still slightly open. As she lifts her infant, the infant's head recenters toward the vis-à-vis. He does not seem to be looking at his mother.

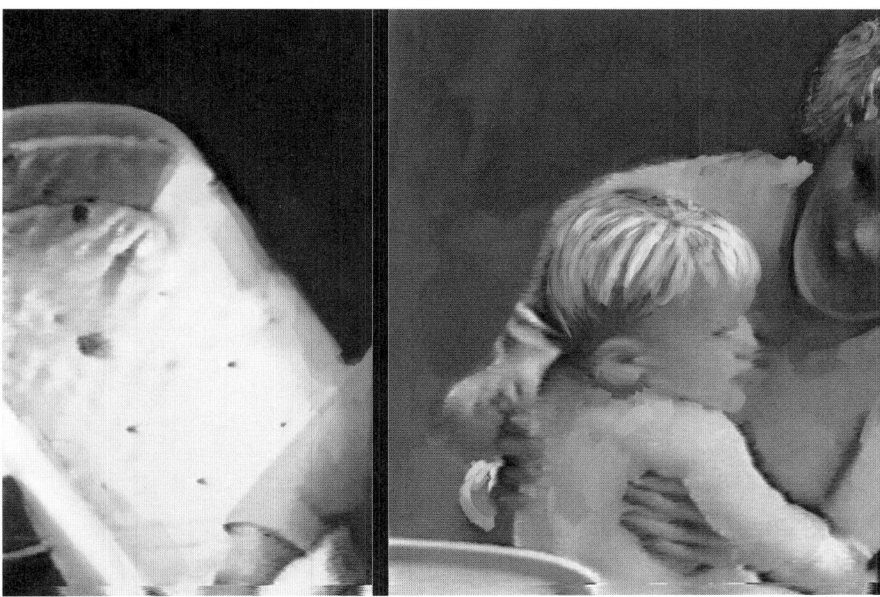

Frame 11. Minute:Second 01:20
From Frame 10 to 11, in the next second, as the mother puts her infant down on her lap, the infant has turned away toward his right and has looked away from her. The mother's head has tilted toward her left, following the direction of her infant's movement away.

TWENTY SECONDS LATER

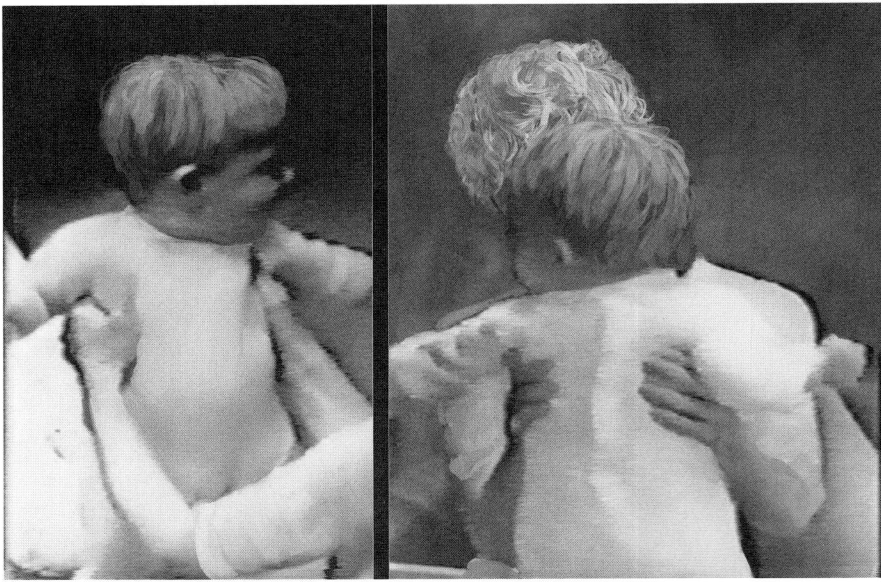

Frame 12. Minute:Second 01:40
In Frame 12, twenty seconds later, the mother picks the infant up and holds him close to her body. He is not looking, and his head is averted about 60 degrees.

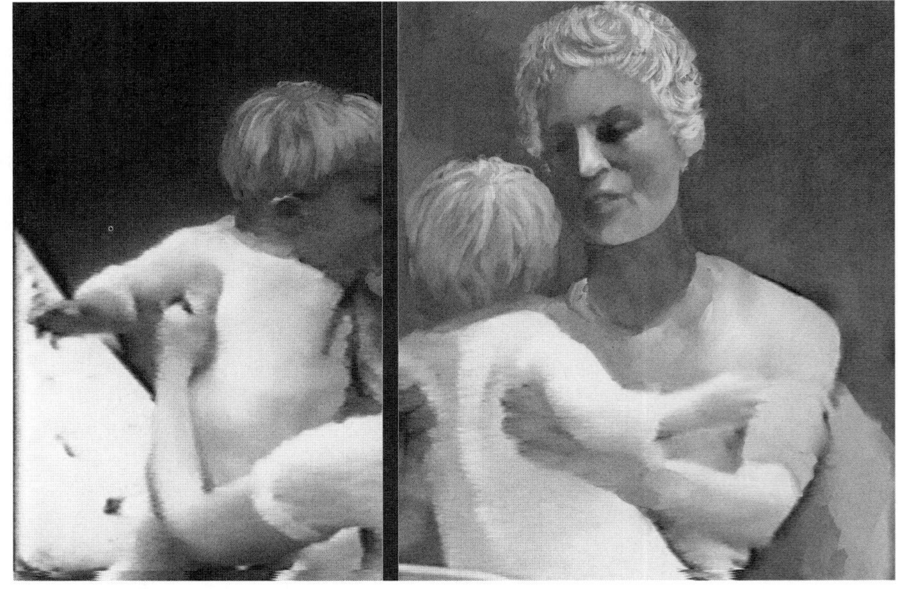

Frame 13. Minute:Second 01:41a
From Frame 12 to 13, less than one second later, the mother pushes the infant away from her body and to her right, simultaneously sobering, gritting her teeth, and moving her body upright. We see the infant's right arm flail out. He is still oriented away to his left, not looking at his mother.

Frame 14. Minute: Second 01:41b
From Frame 13 to 14, within a split second, the infant turns his head from his left side, through the midline with eyes shut, ending at 45 degrees from midline on his right side. Thus, he has gone through the midline vis-à-vis without looking at his mother. Simultaneously, the mother straightens her head with a sober look.

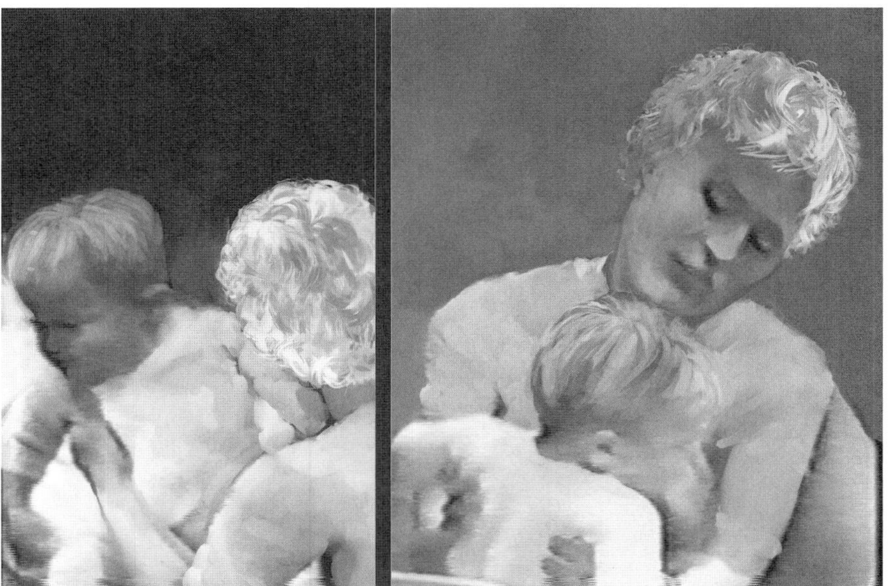

Frame 15. Minute:Second 01:41c
From Frame 14 to 15, still within the same second, the mother lowers the infant. As the infant moves his head to his right, the mother follows with her head in the same direction, tilted to her left. The mother has a sad expression.

Frame 16. Minute:Second 01:42a
From Frame 15 to 16, less than one second later, as the infant turns his head still further away, to 60 degrees from midline, the mother follows the direction of his movement, shifting her head down and forward, closer to him.

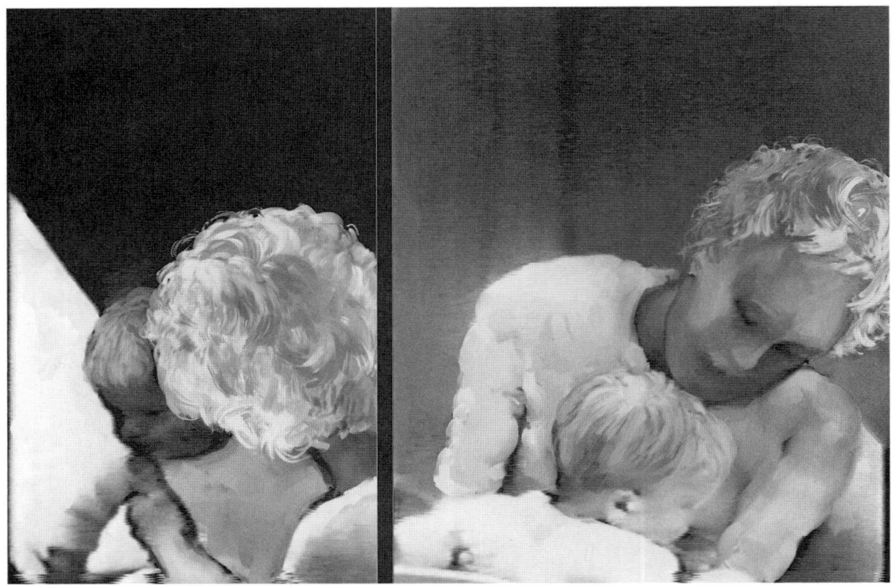

Frame 17. Minute:Second 01:42b
From Frame 16 to 17, within the same second, the infant begins to swing his head through the vis-à-vis to his left. The mother seems sad.

8.3 MINUTE:SECOND 01:43–01:47: 6 FRAMES ACROSS 5 SECONDS

Storyline: In this sequence, the mother begins with a disappointed look. Then she tries bouncing the infant on her lap. At first, he likes it, and they both smile (Frame 20). But when he suddenly turns away, the mother again becomes disappointed (Frame 22).

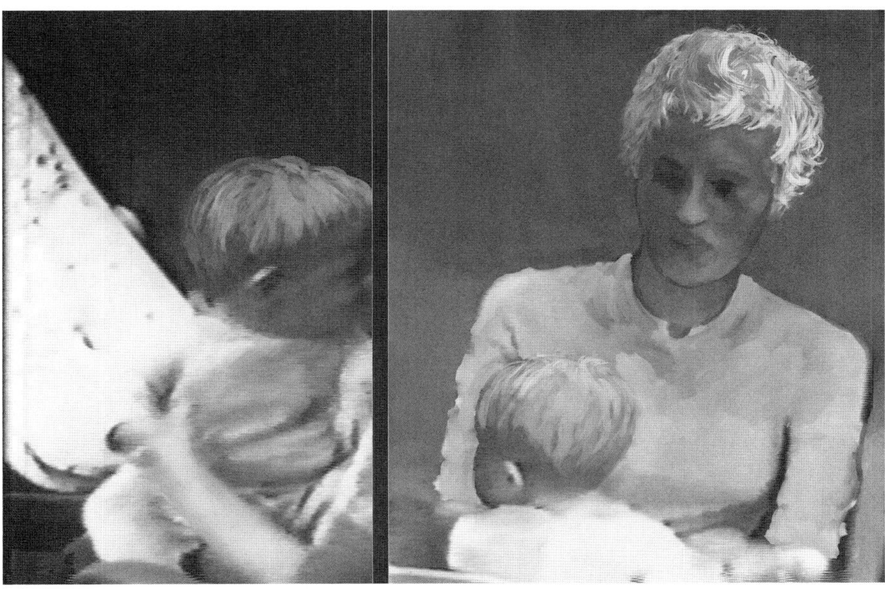

Frame 18. Minute:Second 01:43a
From Frame 17 to 18, less than one second later, the infant completes his head turn through the midline, moving his head out to his left. The mother has a disappointed expression.

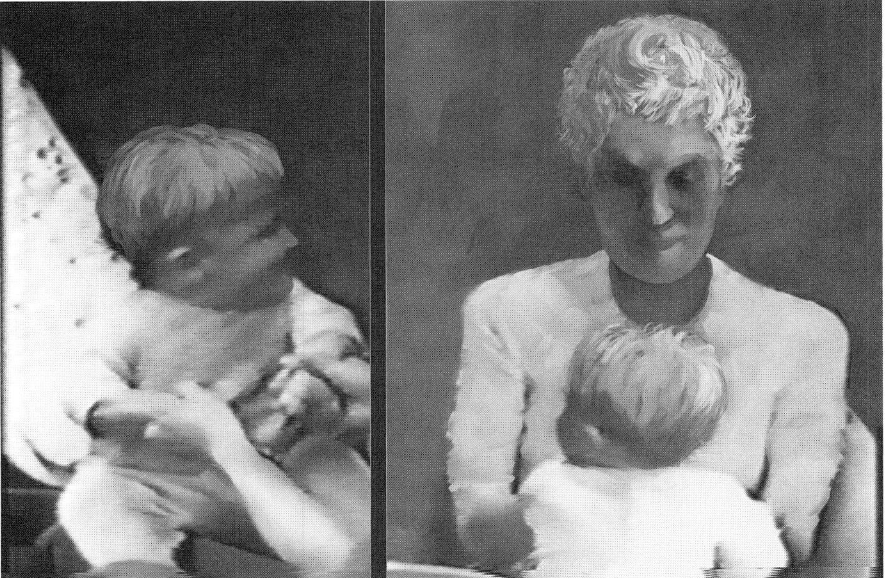

Frame 19. Minute:Second 01:43b
From Frame 18 to 19, within the same second, the mother sobers with a tight-lipped expression. She grabs the infant's hands and begins to bounce him.

Frame 20. Minute:Second 01:44
From Frame 19 to 20, within less than one second, the infant responds to the bouncing by orienting to his mother directly vis-à-vis, looking and smiling broadly. The mother joins with her own broad smile. It is a moment of mutual delight.

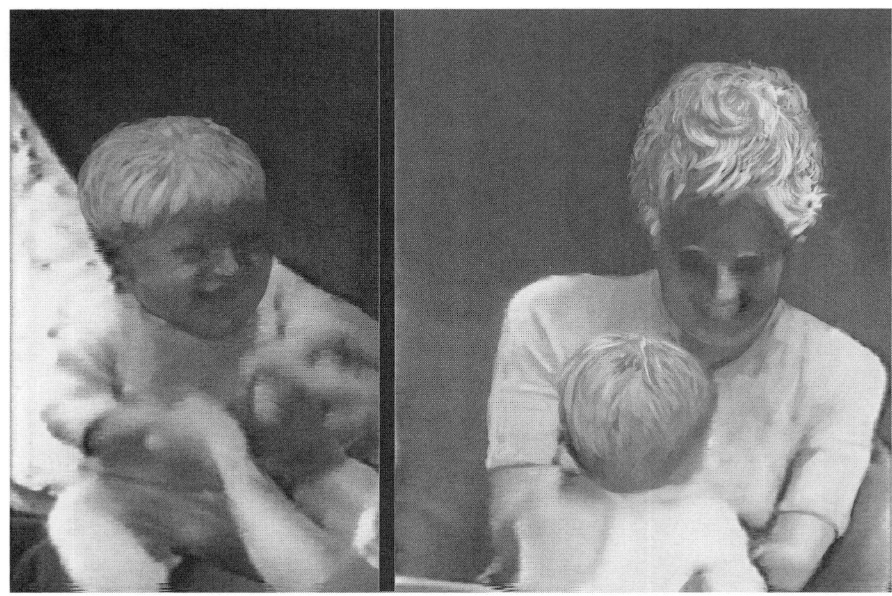

Frame 21. Minute:Second 01:45
From Frame 20 to 21, in the next second, the infant turns his head away slightly to his right, closes his eyes, and dampens his smile. The mother moves her head slightly back and upright, and she continues her broad smile.

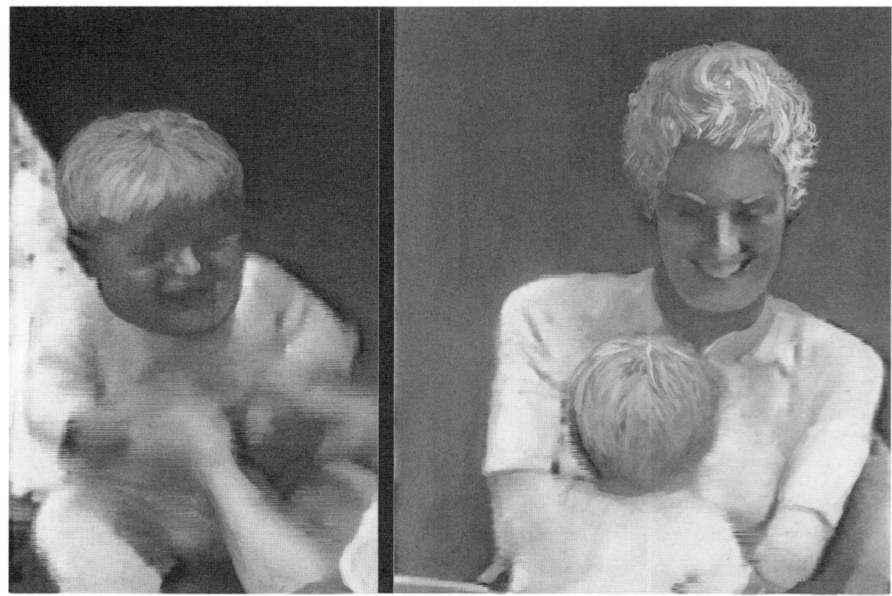

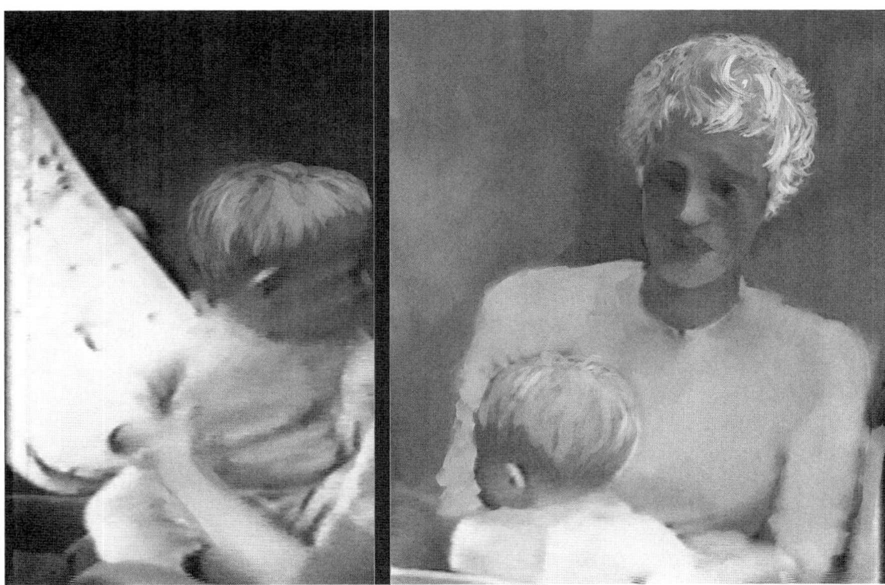

Frame 22. Minute:Second 01:46
From Frame 21 to 22, in the next second, as the infant suddenly turns away and looks away from his mother, her face becomes very sad. She seems very disappointed.

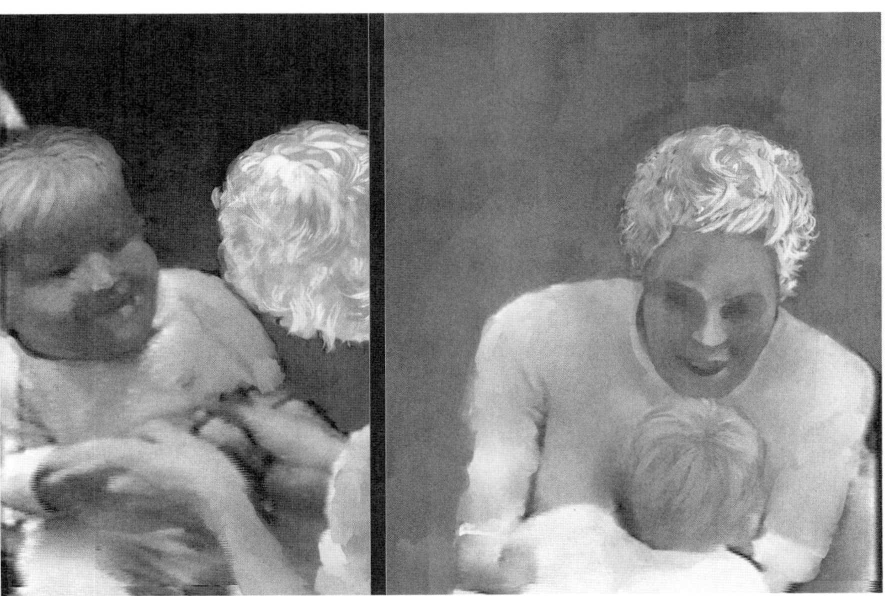

Frame 23. Minute:Second 01:47
From Frame 22 to 23, one second later, the mother looms in toward the infant's face with a mock surprise expression. As the mother pulls both of the infants' hands toward the center, the infant returns to vis-à-vis, looking at his mother, but he tilts his head back from her loom and slightly to his right. He has a tight, compressed-lips expression.

8.4 MINUTE:SECOND 01:50–01:56: 6 FRAMES ACROSS 7 SECONDS

Storyline: As the mother escalates her chasing, the infant escalates his dodging, and reciprocally, as the infant escalates his dodging, the mother escalates her chasing. The infant ends in a 90-degree head aversion (Frame 29).

Frame 24. Minute:Second 01:50a
From Frame 23 to 24, approximately two and a half seconds later, the mother's hands still tightly hold her infant's hands. The infant has moved his head down, and his body is leaning away from his mother, to his right. The mother's head is tilted down, and her body leans at the same angle as the infant leans. She has a slight smile.

Frame 25. Minute:Second 01:50b
From Frame 24 to 25, within the same second, the infant begins to reorient toward the vis-à-vis, but his head is still down. The mother still has a slight smile.

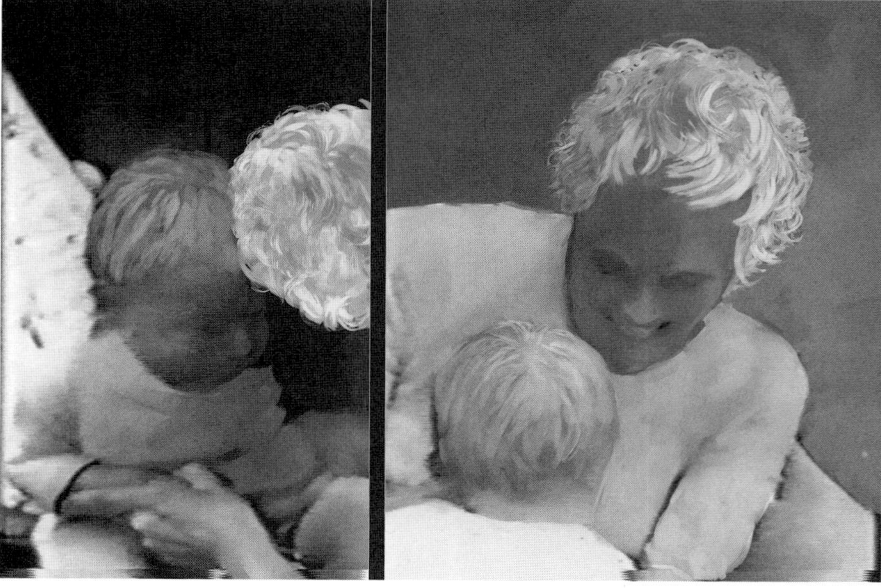

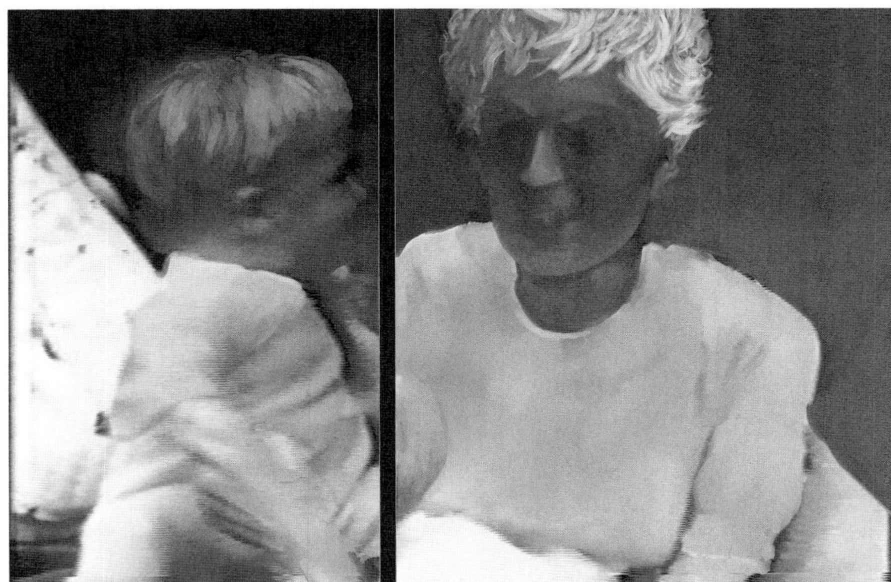

Frame 26. Minute:Second 01:51
From Frame 25 to 26, approximately one half second later, the infant has twisted his body all the way around, through the vis-à-vis without looking, ending up with his head oriented approximately 60 degrees away from his mother. The mother continues to have a slight smile.

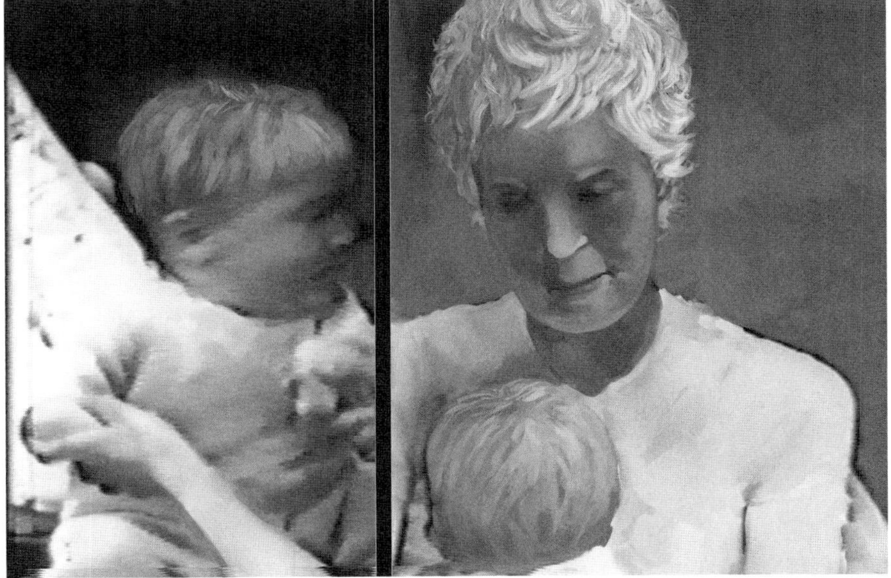

Frame 27. Minute:Second 01:52
From Frame 26 to 27, in the next second, with her right hand, the mother pulls the infant's left hand hard, toward the center vis-à-vis. She has a tight, compressed-lips expression. Although it is hard to see, the infant seems to have his eyes closed, and his lips also seem tight.

Frame 28. Minute:Second 01:54
From Frame 27 to 28, two seconds later, the mother now holds the infant's body with her hands under his armpits, as she begins to place him back into the infant seat. Her face seems curious. The infant's head is down. From the bottom of the mother's frame, we can see that the infant's head has a collapsed quality.

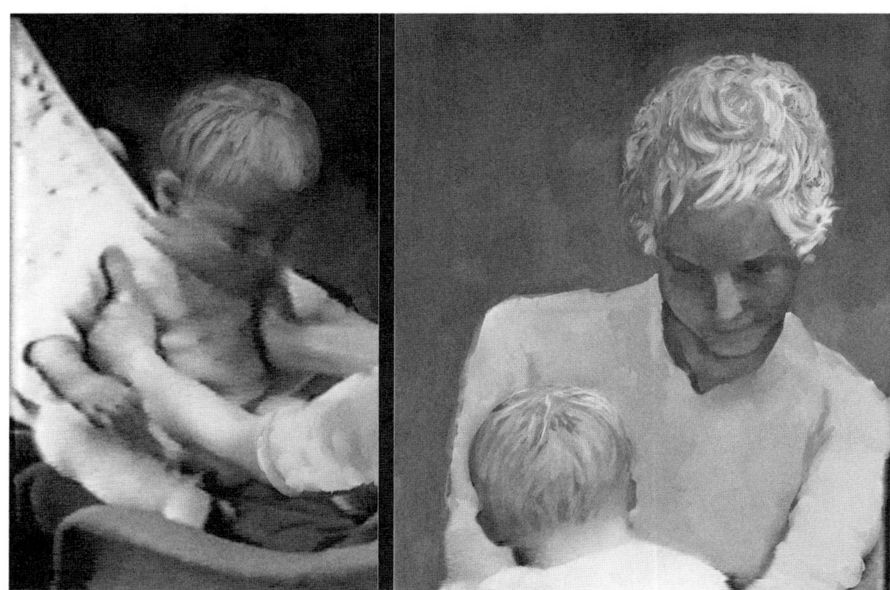

Frame 29. Minute:Second 01:56
From Frame 28 to 29, two seconds later, the mother has put the infant back in the infant seat. Her face has a slightly positive interest expression. The infant has turned his head all the way to his right, a 90-degree aversion.

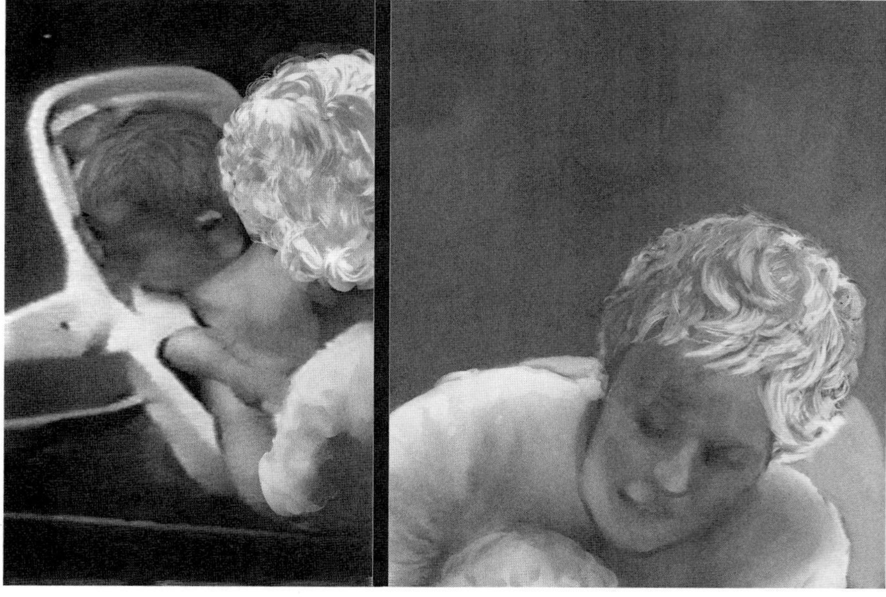

8.5 MINUTE:SECOND 01:58–02:03: 7 FRAMES ACROSS 6 SECONDS

Storyline: The infant collapses body tonus and goes limp. By the end, the mother becomes upset.

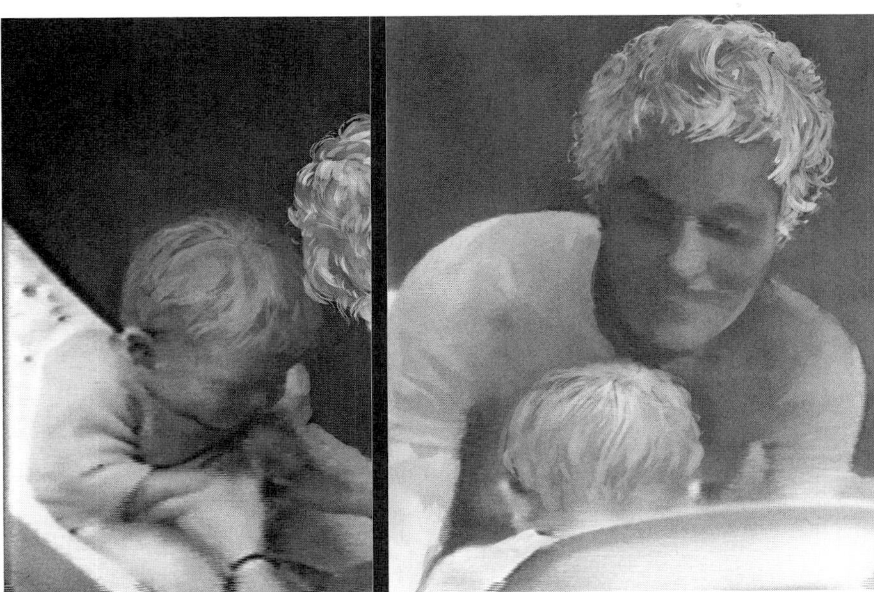

Frame 30. Minute:Second 01:58
From Frame 29 to 30, two seconds later, the infant's head and body have slumped over and down, losing tonus. The mother has a slight smile. Her face does not acknowledge the infant's withdrawal. Both mother's hands are holding her infant's hands.

Frame 31. Minute:Second 01:59
From Frame 30 to 31, in the next second, the mother has pulled his arms out. She continues her slight smile. The infant remains slumped over. This collapsed posture is a powerful way of saying, "no."

Frame 32. Minute:Second 02:00
From Frame 31 to 32, one second later, as the mother lets the infant's arms down, his head goes further down. He remains slumped over. The mother still has a slight smile. Her smile does not acknowledge her infant's profound withdrawal.

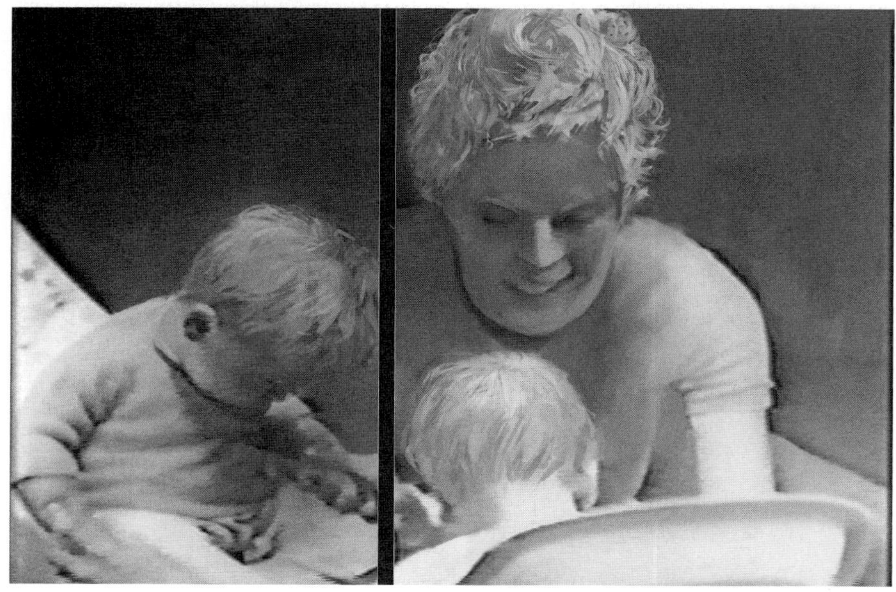

Frame 33. Minute:Second 02:01
From Frame 32 to 33, one second later, as the mother begins to move back, she moves the infant's hands toward the center, and the infant's body shifts slightly to his right. The infant has slumped over slightly further. Her face sobers. She seems to start to notice her infant's state.

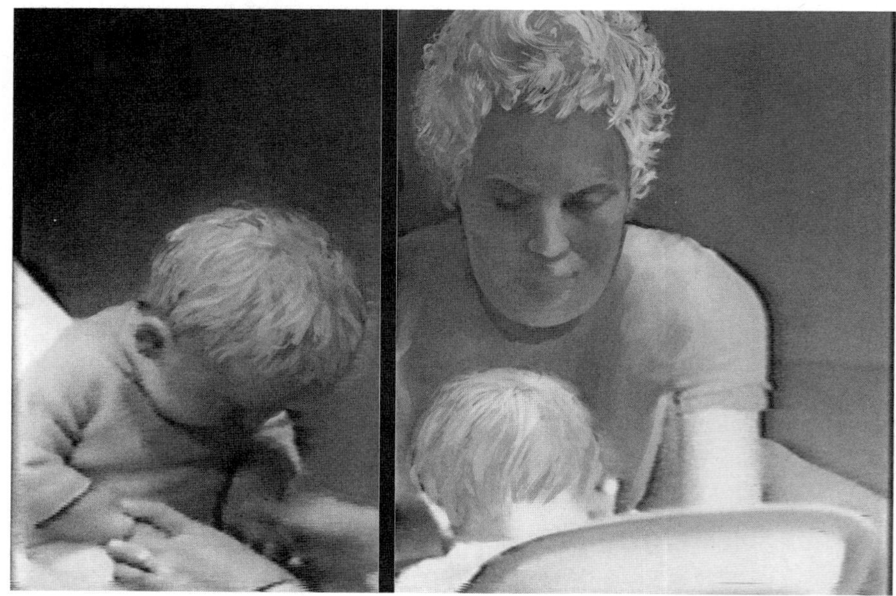

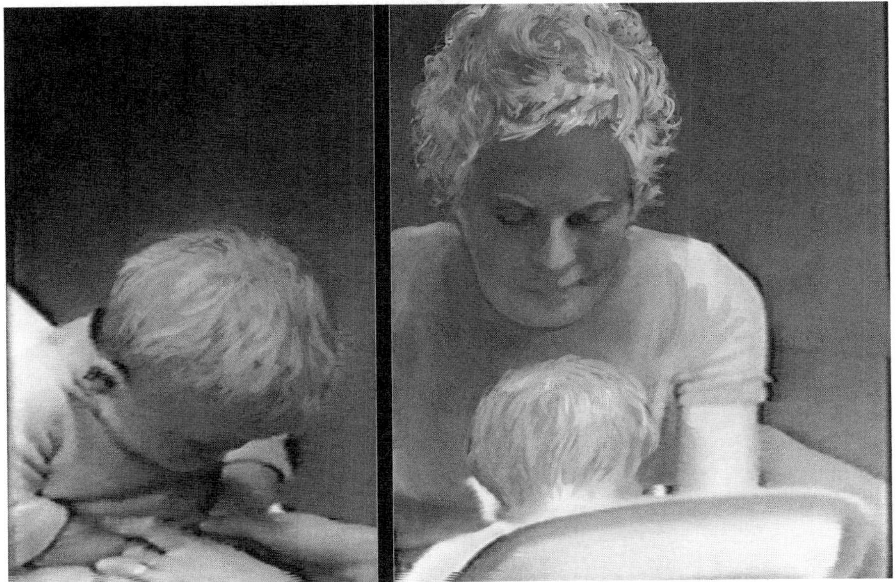

Frame 34. Minute:Second 02:02a
From Frame 33 to 34, less than a second later, the mother continues with her sobered face as she moves in further. Her hand slightly shifts on his hands. The infant collapses further down and his head hangs completely limp.

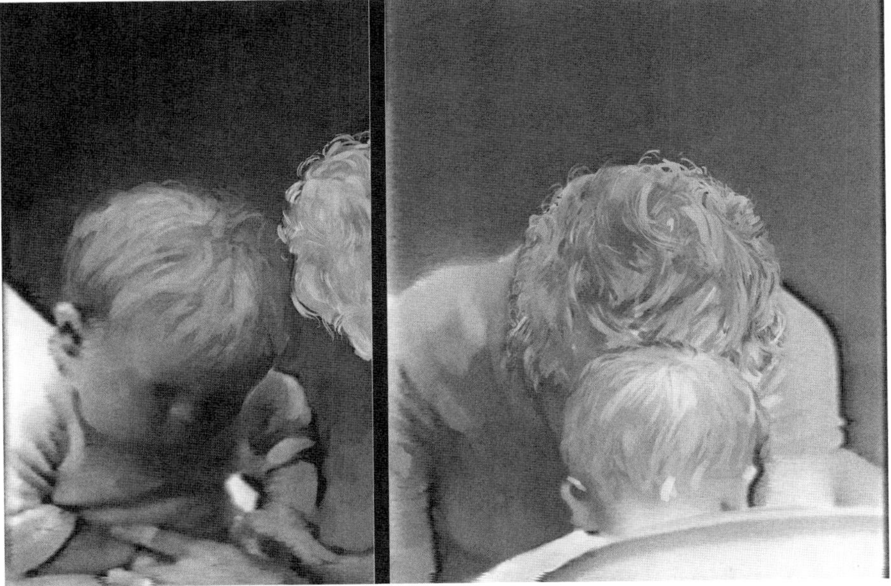

Frame 35. Minute:Second 02:02b
From Frame 34 to 35, within the same second, the mother suddenly looms in close to her infant's face. Simultaneously, the infant begins to move away to his right. We can see from this split-second head aversion that the infant has been monitoring his mother through peripheral vision in the previous frame. Her sudden loom activated him to shift from the limp head-hang into an active avoidance.

Frame 36. Minute:Second 02:03
From Frame 35 to 36, in less than a second, the infant quickly moves his head up, back, and away from his mother into a 90-degree aversion. The mother has a tight-lipped grimace. She is upset, possibly angry.

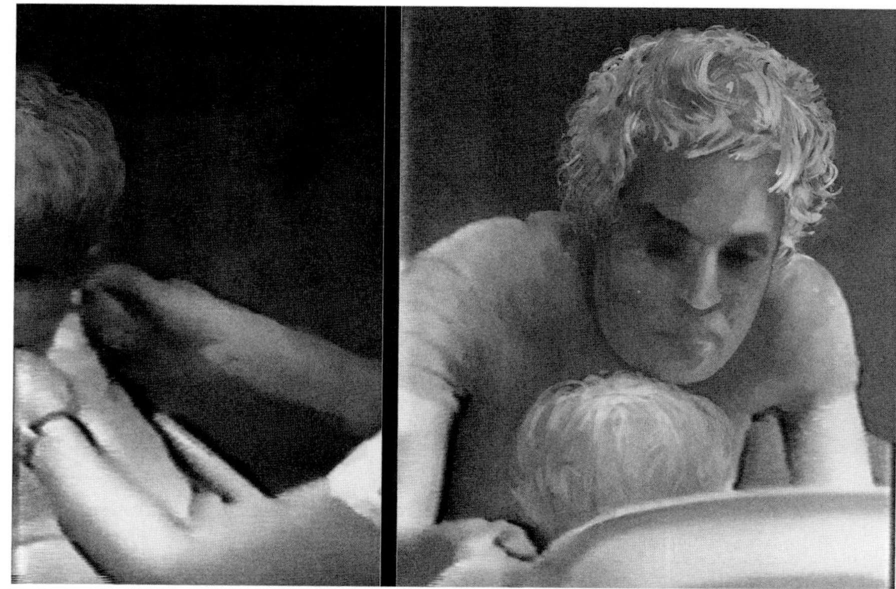

THE STRANGER–INFANT INTERACTION: DR. BEEBE AS STRANGER

Following the interaction with his mother, the infant played with the stranger, a novel partner. From minute:second 04:01 to 04: 07, a sequence of seven frames across seven seconds, the infant begins attentive but wary. He gradually becomes slightly more positive. By the end he gives the stranger a big smile, and they end with a mutually positive engagement.

8.6 MINUTE:SECOND 04:01–04:07

Storyline: The infant is attentive but seems wary. He gradually becomes slightly more positive. By the end, he gives the stranger a big smile, and they end with a mutually positive engagement.

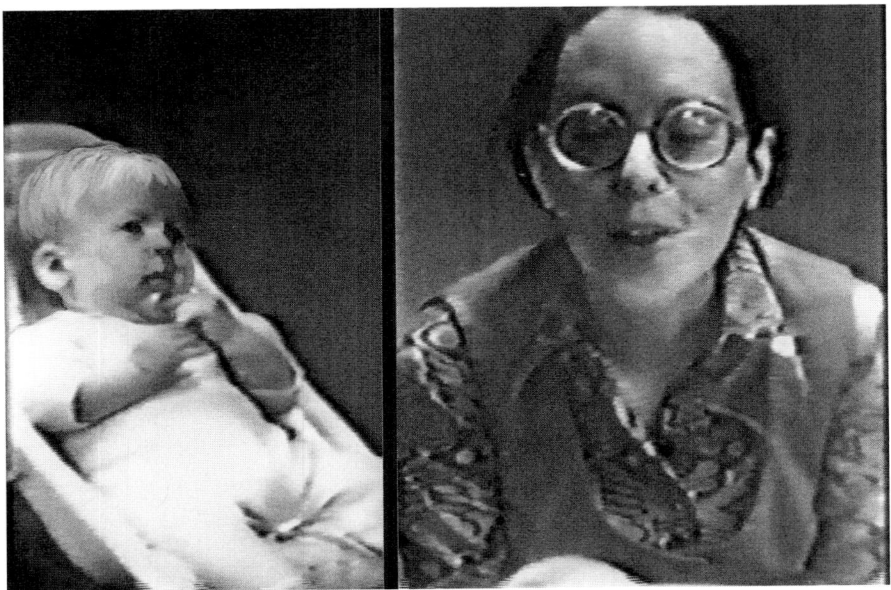

Frame 1. Minute:Second 04:01
In Frame 1, the infant and stranger begin with both looking at the other. The infant is attentive, but his expression is neutral, giving the impression of wariness. The stranger has a slightly widened mouth, a hint of a positive expression.

Frame 2. Minute:Second 04:02
From Frame 1 to 2, in the next second, the infant's face softens slightly, but he still has a neutral expression. The stranger slightly moves her head down, and she has the same slightly positive expression.

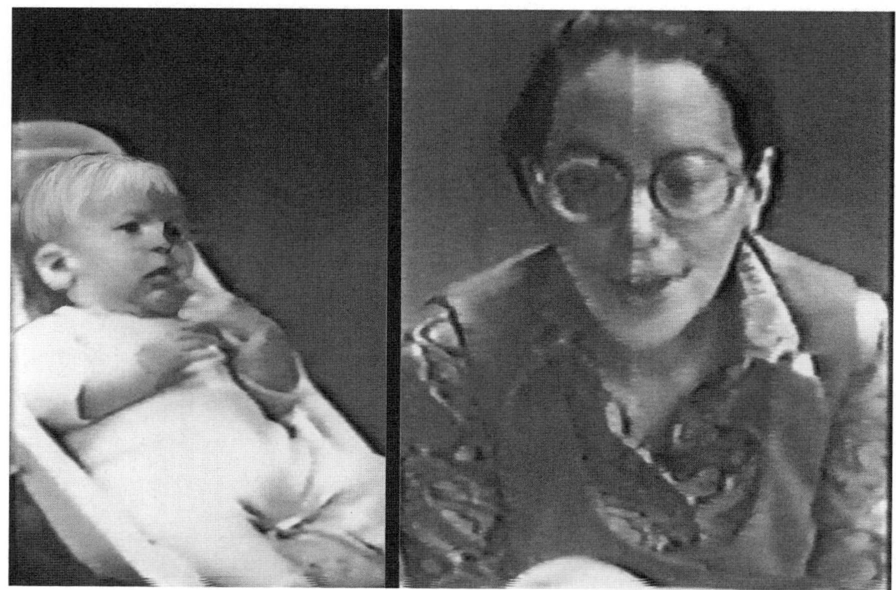

Frame 3. Minute:Second 04:03
From Frame 2 to 3, one second later, the infant still looks with the same expression, and the stranger moves her head down.

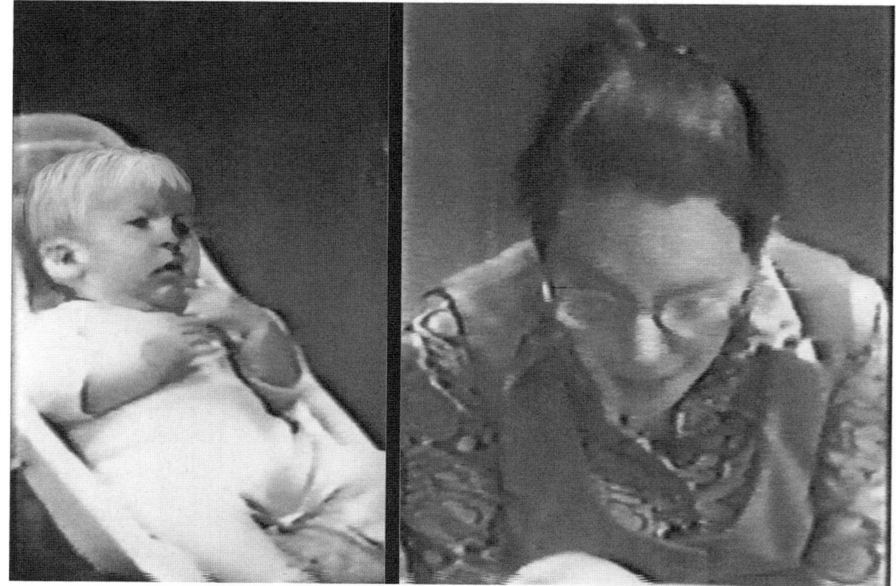

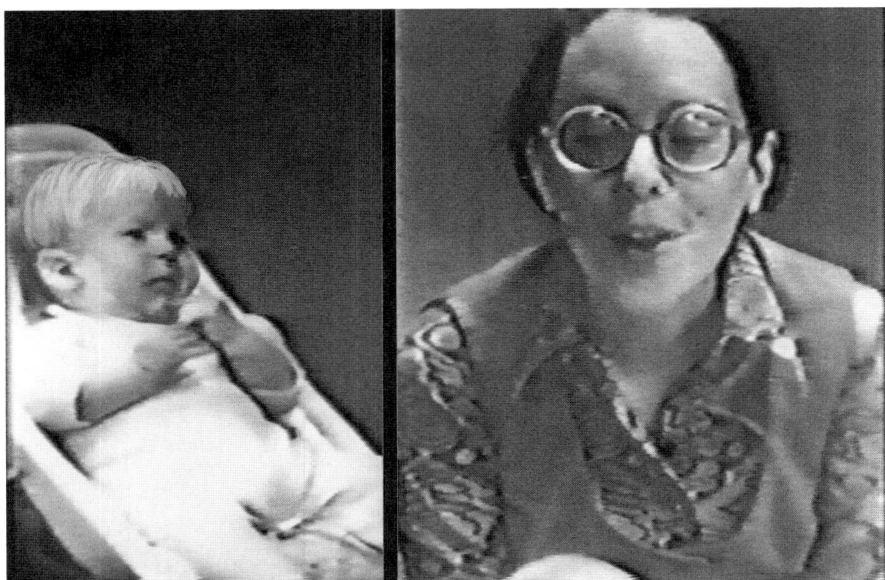

Frame 4. Minute:Second 04:04
From Frame 3 to 4, in the next second, the infant's face has a hint of an interest expression, with slight mouth widening. The stranger has the same expression as Frame 1.

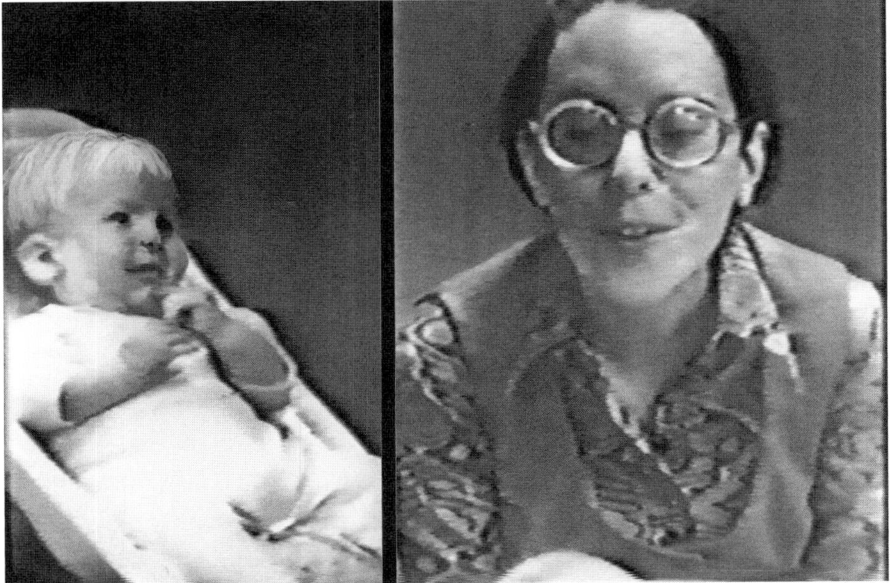

Frame 5. Minute:Second 04:05
From Frame 4 to 5, one second later, the infant begins to have more positive interest expression. The stranger has a hint of mouth widening, not yet a smile, with a slightly tense bottom lip.

Frame 6. Minute:Second 04:06
From Frame 5 to 6, in the next second, the infant begins to smile, and he puts his left finger in his mouth. The stranger slightly increases the widening of her mouth, which is not yet a smile.

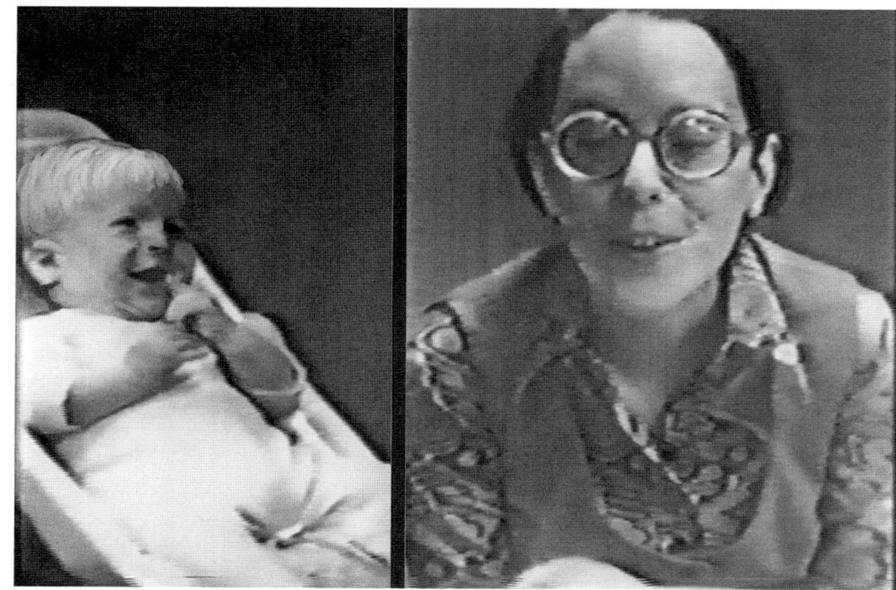

Frame 7. Minute:Second 04:07
From Frame 6 to 7, in the next second, the infant smiles fully. His finger remains in his mouth. The stranger now responds with a full, open smile. Both are delighted.

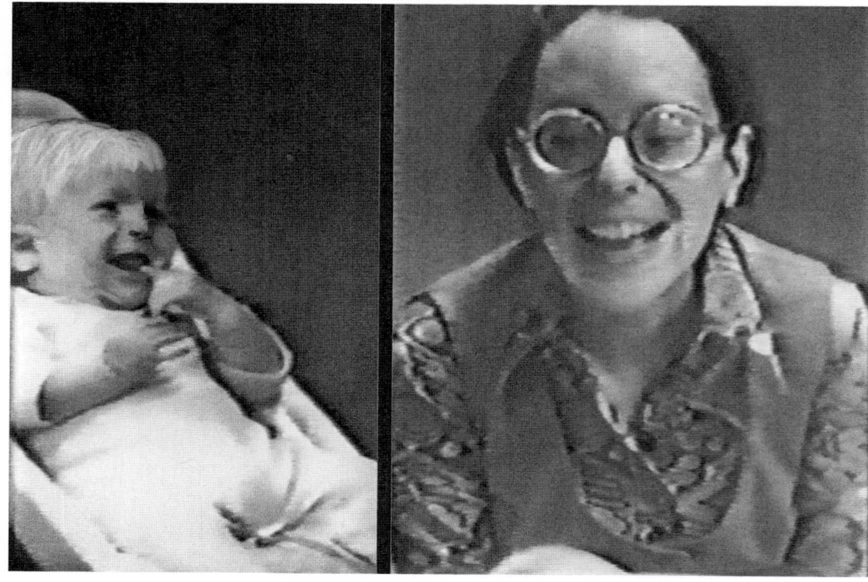

COMMENTARY ON CHASE AND DODGE

Every mother at times undershoots, or overshoots, an optimal level of stimulation (Stern, 1971). When the stimulation becomes intrusive, the infant has a virtuoso range of behaviors to use in coping with or defending against intrusion. We chose the chase and dodge sequence because it illustrates part of this range: maternal overstimulation and infant withdrawal. Portions of the following description are adapted from Beebe, Lachmann, & Jaffe (1997), Beebe et al. (2010), Beebe and Lachmann (1988, 2002), and Beebe and Stern (1977).

In this sequence of drawings of chase and dodge, this infant stays sensitive to each maternal movement from moment-to-moment, even though he moves primarily in the withdrawal direction. The interaction can be seen as a compromise between engagement and disengagement. In some sense, the infant is very engaged, highly responsive to every movement of the mother. The mother is also very engaged, continually attempting to make more contact with her infant, moving toward him and pursuing him. Nevertheless, the quality of the engagement is never one of sustained mutual visual regard with positive affect: Instead it has the quality of a chase and flight. Moreover, this pattern disturbs the infant's freedom to look away and his ability to calm down while looking away. Maternal pursuit each time the infant looks away does not give the infant the chance to reregulate his arousal.

This interaction illustrates infant coping or defensive activity that we characterize as vigilance and continuous responsivity in the withdrawal direction. To every maternal overture, the infant could duck, move back, turn away, pull away, or become limp and unresponsive. Through his virtuoso performance, this infant had near veto-power over his mother's efforts to engage him posturally and visually (Beebe & Lachmann, 2002; Beebe & Stern, 1977).

This interaction was hard for the mother. She often reacted to the infant's avoidance maneuvers with fleeting but marked signs of negative affect: sobering, grimacing, biting her lip, jutting out her jaw, and expressions of sadness. These moments are not visible in the video when played in real time. She did not understand that her chase movements were continuously influencing the infant to dodge. To stop this cycle, the mother would have had to pull back, wait, and trust that if she did not pursue, her infant would return to her after he calmed down. But this is often counterintuitive for a mother in the moment that she so intensely desires an engagement with her infant.

The interaction we illustrated in Chapter 6, a secure pattern of infant looking away, with a mother who was patiently able to wait while her infant looked away, would be the kind of adaptation recommended for this mother who is involved in the chase and dodge pattern. The pattern of interaction depicted in Chapter 7, "Maternal Loom and Repair in the Origins of Secure Attachment," illustrates one way that the chase and dodge interaction could have been repaired.

At the very end of the interaction, the infant collapses and goes limp (Frames 30–34). This is a remarkable sequence in which the infant gives up tonus. This limpness, like that of a rag doll, is not penetrable by the partner; the partner cannot make anything happen. From Frame 30 to 31 of this sequence, the mother raises the infant's hands out wide, and from Frame 31 to 32, she lets his hands down into his lap. But the infant does not respond. His head droops further into his chest, and he remains limp. From Frame 32 to 33, the mother moves his hands together to the center midline. Again, the infant does not respond, remaining limp, and the mother sobers in Frame 33, with a hint of sadness.

This is an extreme form of infant coping because it terminates the play encounter. On the one hand, it is a remarkable display of infant agency, an active refusal to be organized by the mother's ongoing behaviors, an "inhibition of responsivity" (Beebe & Stern, 1977). On the other hand, it shuts down for the moment the infant's capacity for social relatedness. Thus, it is an expensive form of coping, costing the infant his engagement with his mother.

But in the last two frames of this section (Frames 35–36), something else remarkable happens. As the mother looms close in toward the infant's face, the infant resumes his micromomentary responsivity and moves away from her. This demonstrates that he was carefully visually monitoring her while his body was limp. This moment illustrates infant peripheral visual monitoring. The infant remains capable of resuming his split-second responsivity if necessary.

The stranger–infant interaction proceeds immediately following the mother–infant interaction. At this age, infants are easily sociable with strangers. The novelty of the stranger may also engage the infant. In this sense, sometimes the stranger has an advantage over the mother.

With the stranger, the infant is at first a bit wary. But within about seven seconds, the infant shares a full open smile with the stranger (Frame 7). We included the stranger–infant interaction to show that this infant is fully capable of a sustained visual encounter with positive affect. But the infant's capacity to respond to the stranger emerged only when the stranger did not chase. In a second stranger–infant interaction, with a different stranger (not shown), when the stranger chased, again the infant dodged.

Illustrations of Expectancies

We now turn to the question of what the infant comes to expect from his or her interactive encounters. We attempt to translate the action-dialogue of the drawings into language, as if the infant or mother could put the experience into words.

As this pattern of chase and dodge repeats, over and over, in various ways, the infant's experience becomes organized by expectancies of misregulation without repair. The infant comes to expect the split-second mutual responsivity of mother chasing and infant dodging. If the action-dialogue could be put into words, each partner might come to expect, "As you move in, I move away; as I move away, you move in." The easy balance between moments of engagement and moments of disengagement is disturbed. For both partners, too much of the energy of the interaction is used to manage being away from, rather than being with, the partner.

Maternal chasing may generate an infant feeling of: "I don't feel free to look away; I can't get away when I need to settle down. When I stay close to you, I feel you are moving in on me: I feel overaroused and inundated. No matter where I move in relation to you, I cannot get comfortable. I can neither engage nor disengage" (Beebe et al., 2010; Beebe & Lachmann, 1988). The mother might experience something like: "When I want to connect with you, I become aware of how much I need to be responded to. I feel you move away from me as I show my wish to engage with you. I cannot find a comfortable place in relation to you. I feel anxious and rejected."

The chase and dodge interaction illustrates a mismatch between the level of stimulation that the infant might feel is comfortable, and the level of engagement that the mother desires. What is at stake is the dyad's capacity for a mutually satisfying engagement, with the possibility of periods in which both partners can sustain mutual gaze with positive affect.

Relevant Research

Beebe and Stern (1977) described split-second sequences of chase and dodge in which maternal chase movements predicted infant dodges, as the infant monitored the mother's every movement through peripheral vision; but infant dodges also predicted maternal chase behaviors, a reciprocal, bilateral interactive regulation. Through increasing head aversions, arching, or going limp, this infant had a remarkable veto power over the possibility of a sustained, mutual gaze encounter.

A microanalysis of this chase and dodge interaction (Beebe & Stern 1977) revealed the following statistically significant sequences:

(1) As the mother looms (head forward and down, leaning into the infant's face), the infant's head is likely to move back and away (a dodge);
(2) As the infant then dodges (head away, head moving through the vis-à-vis from one side to the other), the mother is likely to chase (to pull the infant's hand, to follow with her head or body in the direction of the infant's movement);
(3) As the mother then chases (pulls the infant's hand, tickles, follows by moving her head and body in the direction of the infant's movement), the infant again dodges (moves his head away, moves his head through the vis-à-vis from one side to the other, or moves his head or body back).

These sequences occurred with split-second responsivities, so that, even before one partner had completed a movement, which lasts on the average about one quarter to one third of a second (Beebe, 1982), the other partner had often already begun to respond. In this interaction, Beebe and Stern (1977) documented that the range of time from the onset of one partner's movement to the onset of the other partner's movement was one quarter of a second to three quarters of a second. These were semi-synchronized mutual adjustments.

Once the infant had moved his head quite far away, the mother tended to pick him up. But as she picked him up, the infant reflexively recentered his head without looking at her. As she put him down on her lap, his head had already moved away again. Thus, the very effort the mother made to reengage the infant in eye contact had already failed even before it was even completed, and he had already escaped her yet again.

Although this was an interaction of maternal overstimulation and infant withdrawal, its regulation was still bidirectional: The mother's movement in toward the infant's face influenced the infant to move away, and the infant's movements of head and body away from the mother influenced her to chase. We have called this interaction chase and dodge, but it could as well be called dodge and chase. The infant's withdrawal elicited the mother's intrusion, and the mother's intrusion elicited the infant's withdrawal. We infer that each partner comes to expect his own movement pattern in relation to that of the partner, and the partner's movement pattern in relation to his own.

Building on the chase and dodge pattern identified in Beebe and Stern (1977), Demetriades (2003), Kushnick (2002), and Beebe et al. (2010) coded 132 dyads for chase and dodge. Chase and dodge was defined as a minimum of two consecutive seconds in which the mother moves her head (from forward or loom positions) toward the infant's face, while the infant simultaneously in the same second, or in the following second, orients his head away from vis-à-vis. Kushnick (2002) found that chase and dodge interactions, and oscillations between loom and upright positions, were more likely in mothers with elevated dependency.

Beebe et al. (2010) found that chase and dodge interactions were twice as frequent in four-month dyads in which the infant would be classified as insecure-resistant attachment at twelve months, compared with those in which the infant would be classified as secure attachment at twelve months.

Because of their histories of not being able to trust attachments, mothers of infants on the way to resistant attachment feel more comfortable when the attachment system is activated, to be sure that their infants need them (Cassidy & Berlin, 1994). In the chase and dodge interaction at four months, mothers of future resistant infants may become upset when infants go away by dodging through looking away and orienting away. Perhaps these mothers then feel abandoned or unimportant. Clinically, we observed mothers of future resistant infants saying things like, "What are you looking at?" "Hey, look at me," or "Where are you going?"

Following Cassidy and Berlin (1994), the maternal chase behavior and tactile intrusion in mothers of future resistant infants are interpreted as ways of saying to the infant of "come here, don't go away, I need you" (Jude Cassidy, personal communication, October 18, 2006). We interpret mothers of future resistant infants as overly concerned with the infant's attention and emotional presence, and their intrusion behaviors as their wish for infants to stay with them.

Relevant Research on the Origins of Resistant Attachment

Using microanalysis, the research that is the basis for this book identified a number of new patterns of interaction at four months, which predicted resistant (vs. secure) attachment at one year (Beebe et al., 2010).

(1) Mothers of future resistant (vs. secure) infants were more likely to use progressively less affectionate and more active forms of touch over the course of the interaction.
(2) Mothers and infants were more likely to participate in chase and dodge when infants were on the way to resistant attachment.
(3) Mothers of infants on the way to resistant attachment showed less predictable spatial orientation patterns, a disturbance of the maternal spatial frame that mothers provide. Thus, as mothers moved from sitting upright, to leaning forward, to looming in, to chase, they were less predictable. This pattern indicates a form of unpredictable chase.

Together, these findings indicate that mothers of future resistant (vs. secure) infants showed a coherent constellation of progressively less positive touch, less self-predictable spatial orientation patterns, and a disturbance of the infant's freedom to look away by chasing with head and body in the direction of infant dodges (movements away from vis-à-vis). The constellation of less predictable orientation as mother reaches in to touch, and progressively less affectionate maternal touch, is likely to disturb the infant's development of a confident expectation that maternal touch will be affectionate and comforting.

Although mothers of resistant infants are generally described as remote and underinvolved (Cassidy & Berlin, 1994), these findings of maternal spatial and tactile intrusion are consistent with Cassidy and Berlin's (1994) description of studies, which document maternal interferences with infant autonomy, exploration, or ongoing activity.

(4) Infants on the way to resistant attachment lowered their emotional coordination with maternal touch, as if tuning it out. In this pattern, future resistant (vs. secure) infants were less likely to protest as maternal touch became more intrusive, and they were less likely to become positive as maternal touch became more affectionate. This finding indicates an active infant inhibition of responsivity to maternal touch, which is less affectionate; a refusal to be organized by maternal touch.

The infant's inhibition of a vocal protest in response to more intrusive maternal touch may lead to a disturbance in the infants' ability to communicate what they like or do not like. This is a form of learning to mask distress, which may ultimately lead to a confusion in sensing their own state in relation to maternal touch. Perhaps this pattern could lead to a dissociative loss of awareness of distress in relation to maternal touch, and to later somatization of distress (Mary Sue Moore, personal communication, July 2, 2007).

Infant inhibition of vocal protest in response to more intrusive maternal touch has a parallel in the strange situation at one year, in which resistant infants may be upset but passive, not doing anything to ameliorate their distress, or ineffective in getting comfort from mother (Cassidy & Berlin, 1994; Jude Cassidy, personal communication, October 18, 2006).

(5) Infants on the way to resistant attachment increased their facial-visual engagement coordination with maternal facial-visual engagement: an emotional vigilance. We suggest that this vigilance is an attempt to cope with maternal tactile/spatial intrusion.

These latter two findings (4) and (5) together indicate an infant discordance: Infant facial-visual engagement coordination is inhibited with maternal touch, but activated with maternal facial-visual engagement. In this remarkable discordance, the same behavioral constellation, infant engagement, is both inhibited to maternal touch and activated to maternal engagement.

In the touch domain, the infant's adaptation is a premature separation or autonomy; in the facial-visual domain, the infant's adaptation is a premature vigilance. These difficulties may set the stage for infant confusion regarding his response to his mother and for infant difficulties in sensing his own state.

In summary, the organization of intimate relating is at stake in these early interactions. Intimate relating entails the fundamental issue of how the infant comes to know, and be known by, another's mind, as well as how the infant comes to know his own mind. We construe mind from the point of view of the infant, that is, expectancies of procedurally organized action sequences. Based on the research in Beebe et al. (2010), we offer the following conclusions:

- Regarding feeling known by his mother, the future resistant infant may have difficulty feeling sensed and known by his mother during her spatial and tactile intrusion. Perhaps because of her need to feel needed, the mother does not seem to sense that her spatial/tactile intrusion may force her infant to withdraw emotionally from her touch.
- Regarding knowing his mother, perhaps the future resistant infant will have difficulty knowing his mother's mind as he has difficulty predicting what she will do next spatially: sit upright, lean forward, loom in, or chase.
- Regarding knowing himself, perhaps the future resistant infant will have difficulty knowing himself as he simultaneously inhibits his engagement coordination with mother's touch, and activates his emotional engagement coordination with mother's emotional engagement. The infant thus generates opposite expectancies of the ways he responds to mother with his emotional engagement, a complex, confusing, but nevertheless adaptive organization.

CHAPTER 9

Infant Look Away in the Origins of Insecure-Avoidant Attachment

DRAWINGS: INFANT LOOK AWAY/INSECURE PATTERN

This sequence depicts a mother and infant at four months where the infant was classified as insecure-avoidant attachment at one year (Beebe et al., 2010).

This sequence of drawings presents 13 frames, over 36 seconds. They begin with the infant looking away, and the mother trying to get his attention. The mother makes many attempts to get her infant to interact with her. However, when her infant does look at her, she interrupts the potential moment of mutual gaze in several different ways. The first time he looks at her, she looks directly at the camera instead of at him; the next time he looks, she fails to greet him; and the final time he looks in this sequence, she shows him a sad face. As he looks away, she leans in and continues to pursue him. However, they stay connected through touch. Often, it is the infant who reaches for the mother.

Following the interaction with the mother, this infant then played immediately with the stranger, a novel partner.

9.1 MINUTE:SECOND 27:09–27:17

Storyline: Mother encourages the infant to "look at mommy!" However, as he does look at that moment (Frame 3), she looks into the camera instead of at him.

Frame 1. Minute:Second 27:09
The infant is looking away, with his finger at the corner of his mouth. The mother leans in and reaches her hand in with a smile. She is trying to get his attention. (In the video, she says, "hi, hi!")

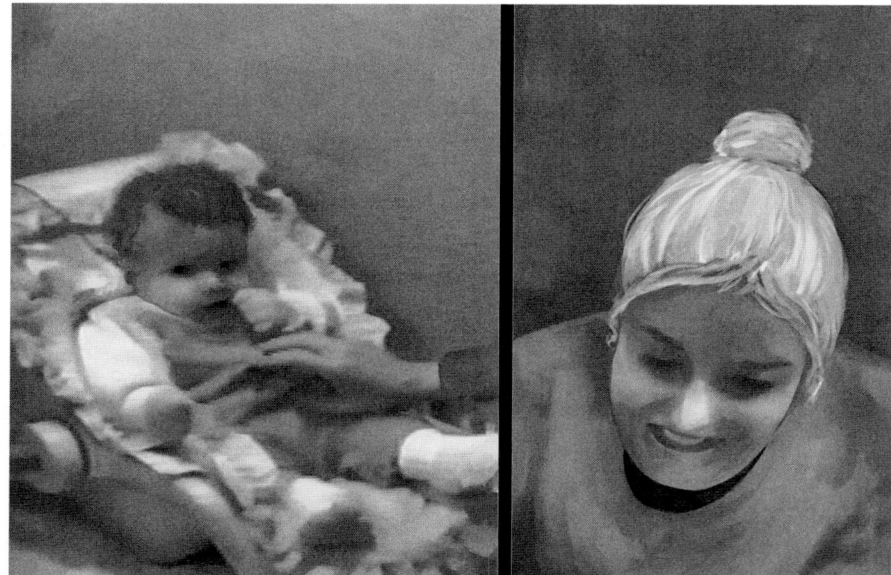

Frame 2. Minute:Second 27:14
From Frame 1 to 2, five seconds later, as the infant turns further away (approximately 30 degrees), the mother draws back with a slightly bigger smile. As the mother draws her hand slightly back and down, the infant reaches for her and gently fingers the top of her hand. The infant seems focused on something to his right, but the mother does not join his focus of attention.

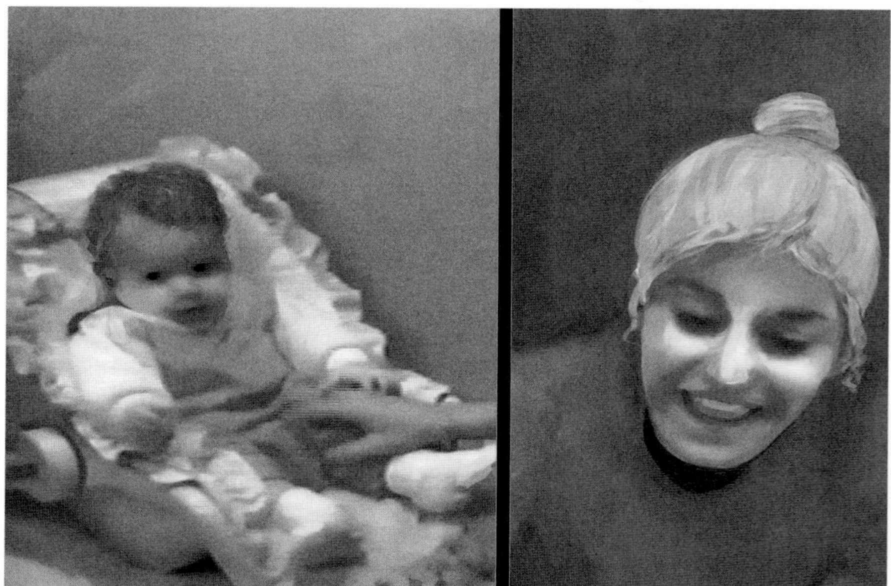

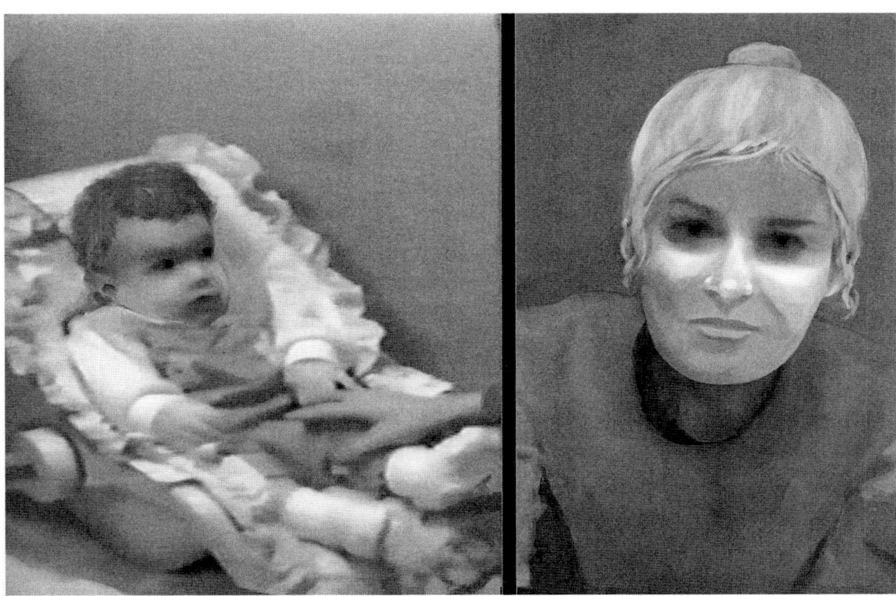

Frame 3. Minute:Second 27:17
From Frame 2 to 3, three seconds later, the infant reorients to his mother vis-à-vis. He looks directly at her, with a surprised expression (raised eyebrows). As he looks at her, she looks directly at the camera, and not at her infant. Her face seems to say, "Look what's happened." She has a sad, helpless pleading look, as if to say, "I don't know what to do." Their hands are still touching

9.2. MINUTE:SECOND 27:21–27:28

Storyline: After the mother looks at the camera (Frame 3), the infant turns away sharply (Frame 4); the mother alternates with bright smiles (Frames 4, 6) and sad faces (Frames 5, 7). The infant's gaze remains averted, but their hands remain connected.

Frame 4. Minute:Second 27:21a
From Frame 3 to 4, four seconds later, as the infant looks away with a strong 60-degree head aversion, the mother turns back to her infant. She looks at him with her head down. She smiles, but the smile seems slightly forced. She moves her hand, but their hands are still touching.

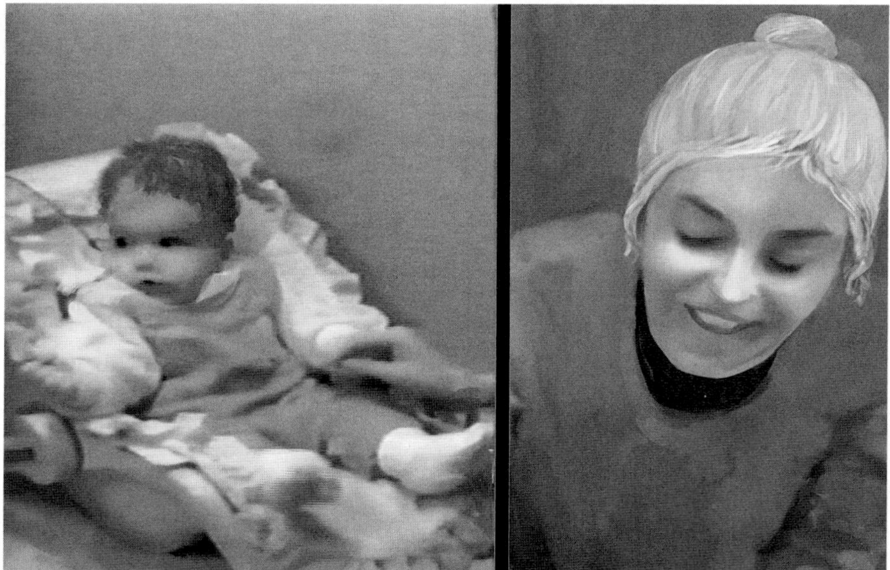

Frame 5. Minute:Second 27:21b
From Frame 4 to 5, within the same second, the infant reorients his head partially toward the mother (from 60 degrees to 30 degrees away). He closes his mouth; his eyes look vacant and distant. The mother looks very sad, and she grimaces. She shifts her hand slightly away from the infant, but he holds on to her finger.

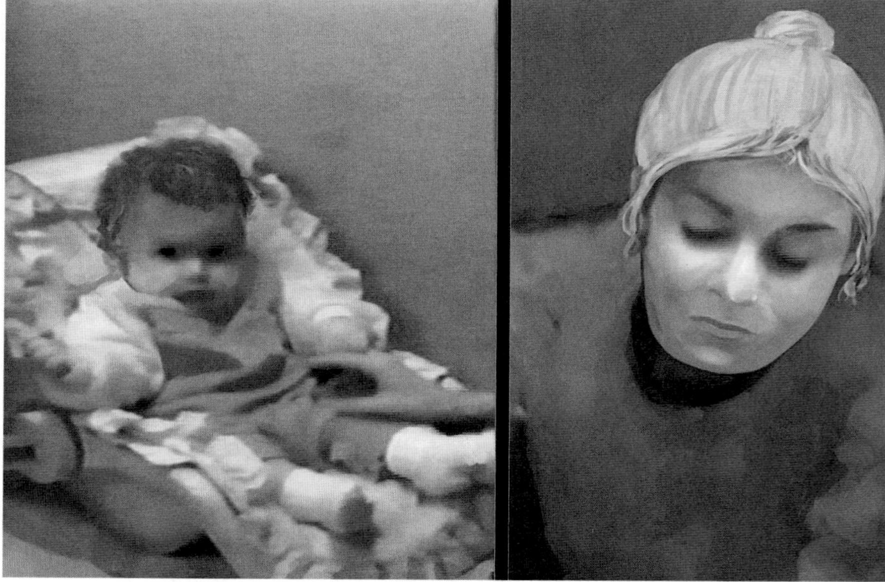

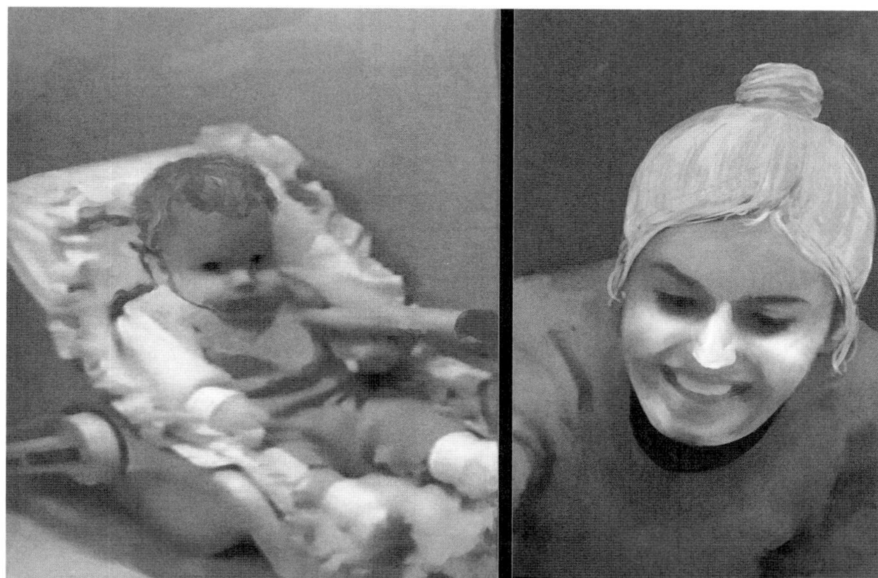

Frame 6. Minute:Second 27:23
From Frame 5 to 6, almost two seconds later, the mother looks directly at her infant with a full, vibrant smile and reaches in to touch his cheek. The infant's head orients closer to the mother (from 30 degrees to 15 degrees away). As the mother's hand moves to touch his face, the infant's hand continues to be in touch contact with her hand.

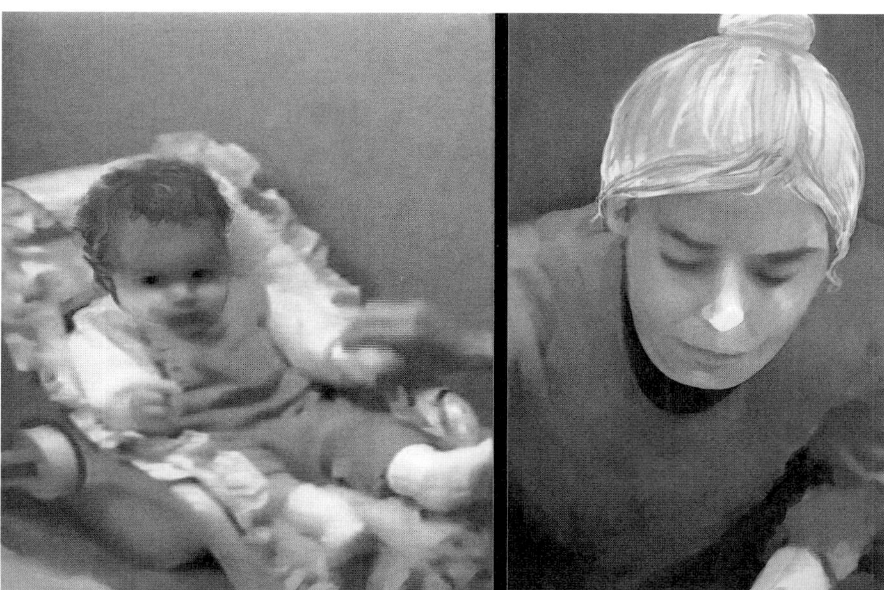

Frame 7. Minute:Second 27:28
From Frame 6 to 7, five seconds later, the infant moves his head slightly further away from his mother (from 15 degrees to 30 degrees away). The mother looks down with a sad face. The mother pulls her hand back, but she does not let go of his hand.

9.3 MINUTE:SECOND 27:29–27:34

Storyline: In this moment of mutual gaze (Frame 8), the mother's face is blank. When she does light up to greet him (Frame 9), the infant responds with an open-mouth positive interest face, his most positive, animated moment. In the next moment, the infant turns away, and mother's smile slightly lessens (Frame 10).

Frame 8. Minute:Second 27:29
From Frame 7 to 8, one second later, the infant orients vis-à-vis. He looks surprised; his eyebrows go up. This is their first moment of mutual gaze, but the mother does not greet her infant with a smile. She looks with a muted face and seems distant. Each is touching the other's hand.

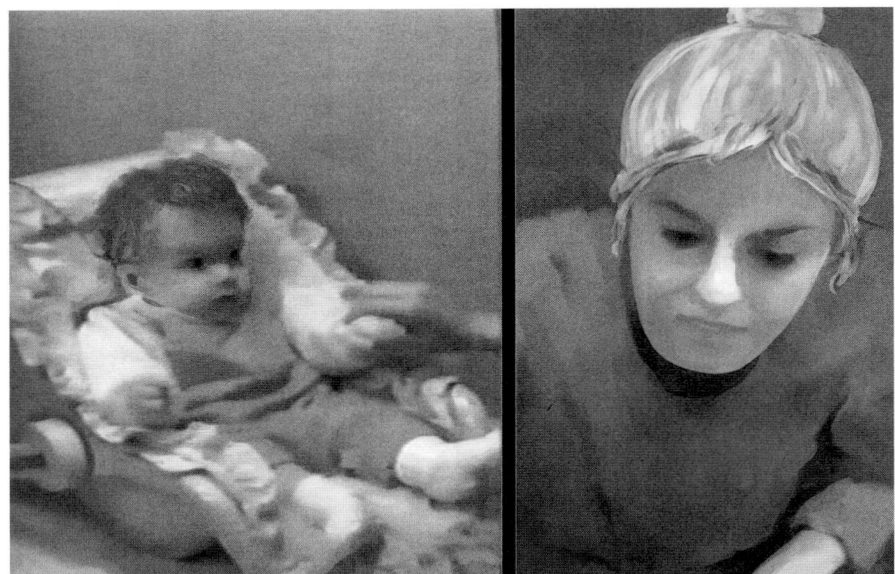

Frame 9. Minute:Second 27:31
From Frame 8 to 9, two seconds later, the mother lights up into a full greeting smile. She brings her left hand in, so now both her hands hold his hands. The infant continues looking, moving his head up. His mouth is open, with a positive interest expression. His raised eyebrows register that something surprising has just happened.

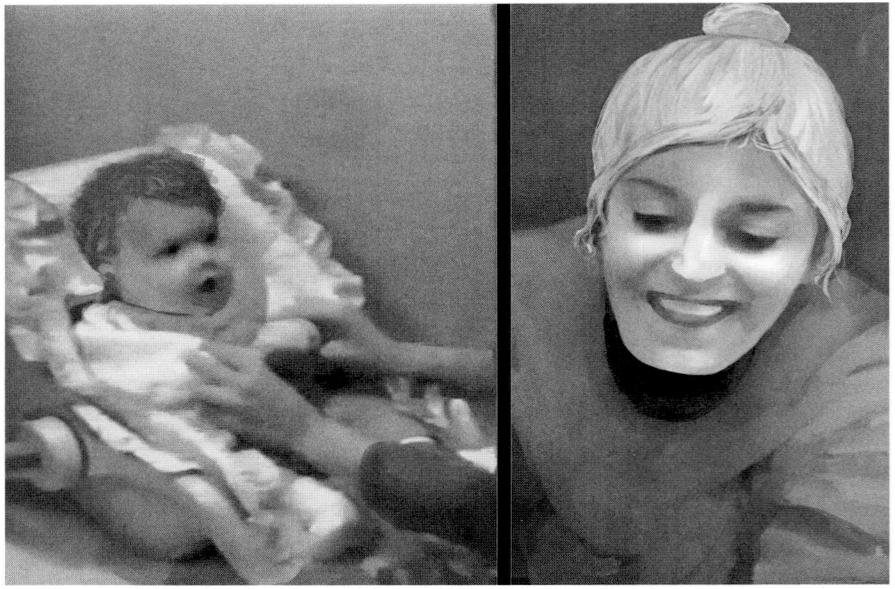

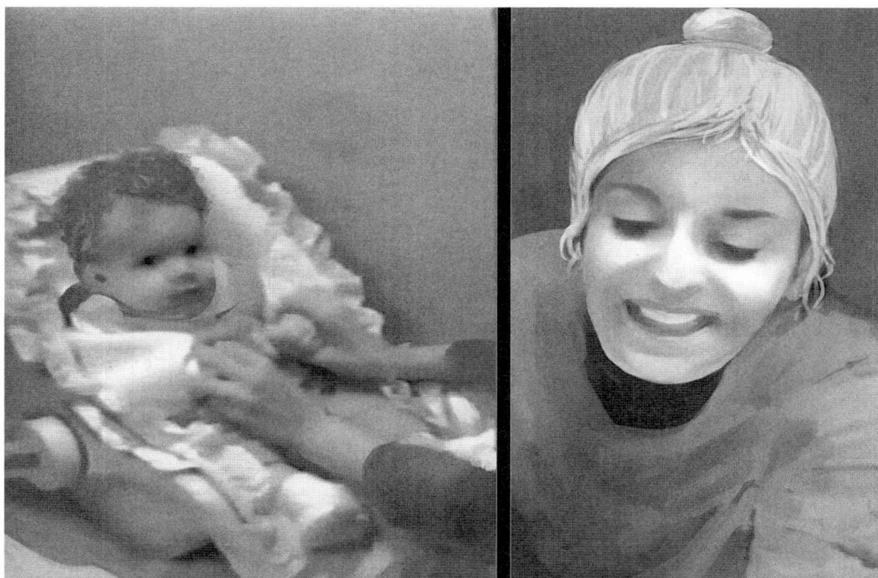

Frame 10. Minute:Second 27:34
From Frame 9 to 10, three seconds later, the infant looks away and turns away slightly, 15 degrees from vis-à-vis. His mouth closes. The mother's smile slightly dampens. She continues to touch him with both hands, and she moves in slightly.

9.4 MINUTE:SECOND 27:35–27:44

Storyline: The infant looks at mother. He seems surprised as his mother greets him with a sad face. As the infant averts, his mother pursues him, smiling, with her hands to his chest. But in the final frame (Frame 13), the infant lightly fingers the top of his mother's hands.

Frame 11. Minute:Second 27:35
From Frame 10 to 11, in the next second, the infant orients to his mother vis-à-vis and looks at her with surprise, his eyebrows up. The mother has become very sad, and she grimaces. Her head is down slightly. She continues to hold his hands with both of her hands.

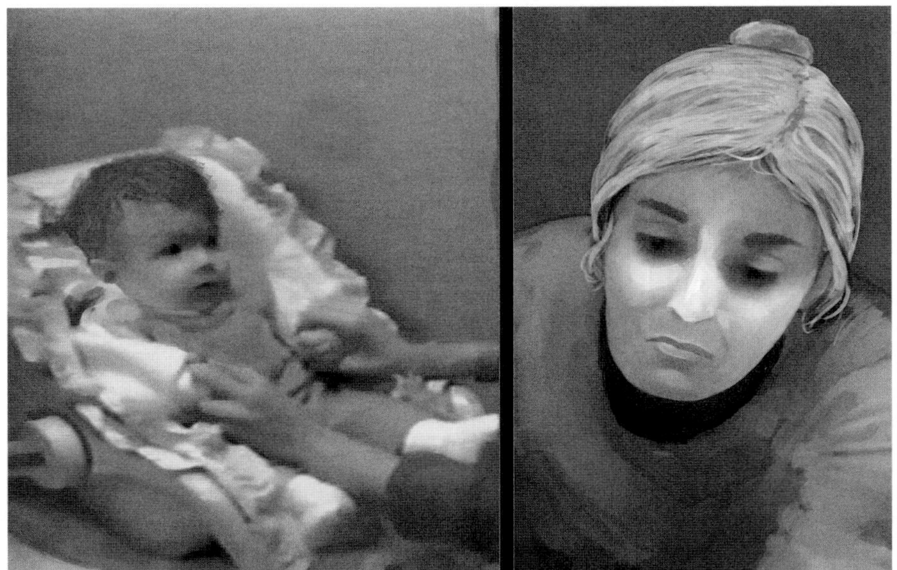

Frame 12. Minute:Second 27:41
From Frame 11 to 12, six seconds later, the infant looks away. He moves his head away 15 degrees and slightly down. He has an interest expression, with a slight mouth widening. The mother let go of his hands and moves her hands on to his chest, under his chin. She has a bright smile, and she is partially looming in. The infant's right hand reaches out for the bracelet on his mother's left hand; his left hand is lightly fingering her right hand.

Frame 13. Minute:Second 27:44
From Frame 12 to 13, three seconds later, the mother continues to touch the infant on his chest, under his chin. Her smile remains bright. The infant moves his head down, continuing to look away. He closes his mouth, with a neutral expression. Yet, at the same time, he shifts his hands to lightly finger his mother's hands.

THE STRANGER–INFANT INTERACTION: DR. BEEBE AS STRANGER

Following the interaction with the mother, seen above, this infant then played immediately with the stranger, a novel partner, in this case, Dr. Beebe. In this sequence of drawings of nine frames over seventeen seconds, the infant begins visually engaged, but with a sad face. He then looks down. After the stranger offers her hands to the infant, he begins to lightly finger the top of her hands, and then he looks back. In the final frames, he is less distressed. The stranger empathizes with the infant's distress. Her concern shows in her furrowed forehead. The infant seems to be able to manage his distress after he sees the stranger showing her understanding of his distress. He is particularly responsive to the stranger offering her hands.

9.5 MINUTE:SECOND 29:19–29:22

Storyline: The infant is distressed. The stranger first greets and then shows an empathic woe face with surprise. Then she becomes concerned.

Frame 1.
Minute:Second 29:19
The infant looks at the stranger with a frown. The stranger has an open face, with a partially open mouth. Her furrowed brow conveys concern.

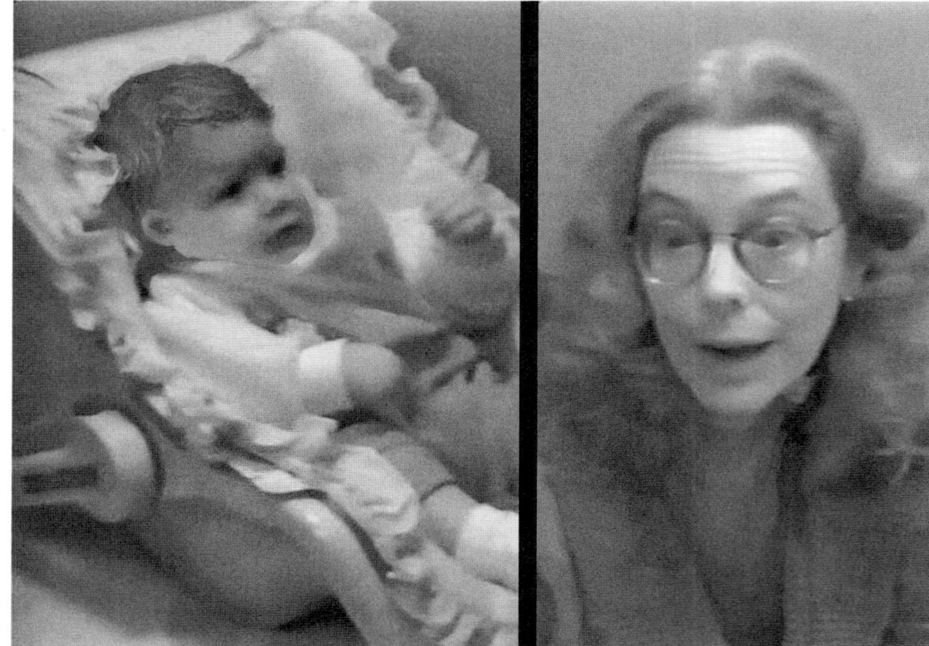

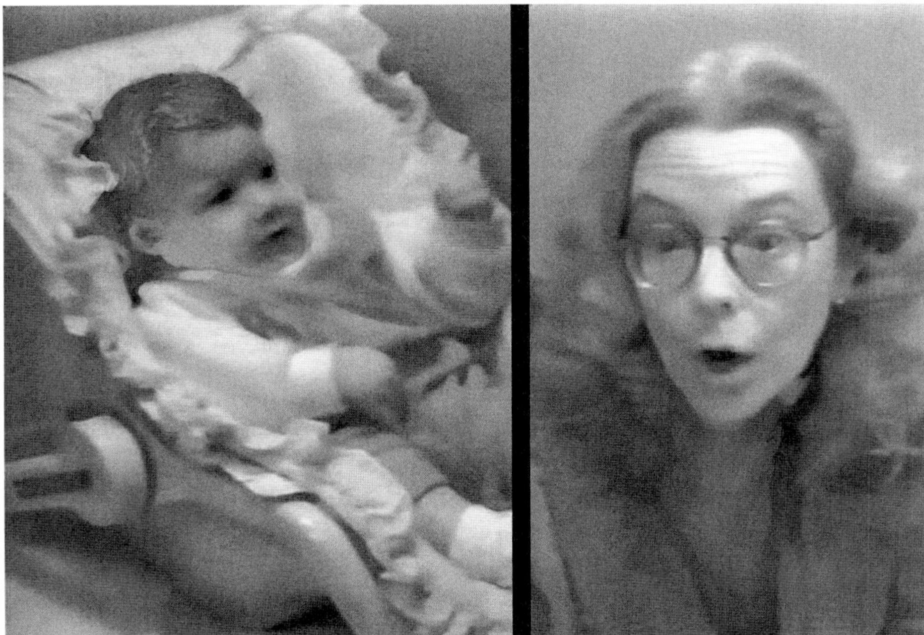

Frame 2.
Minute:Second 29:20
From Frame 1 to 2, in the next second, the infant continues to look. He has a sad face, and he looks as if he is about to cry. The stranger sympathizes with an empathic woe face. She also expresses surprise, with raised eyebrows, and concern, with a furrowed brow.

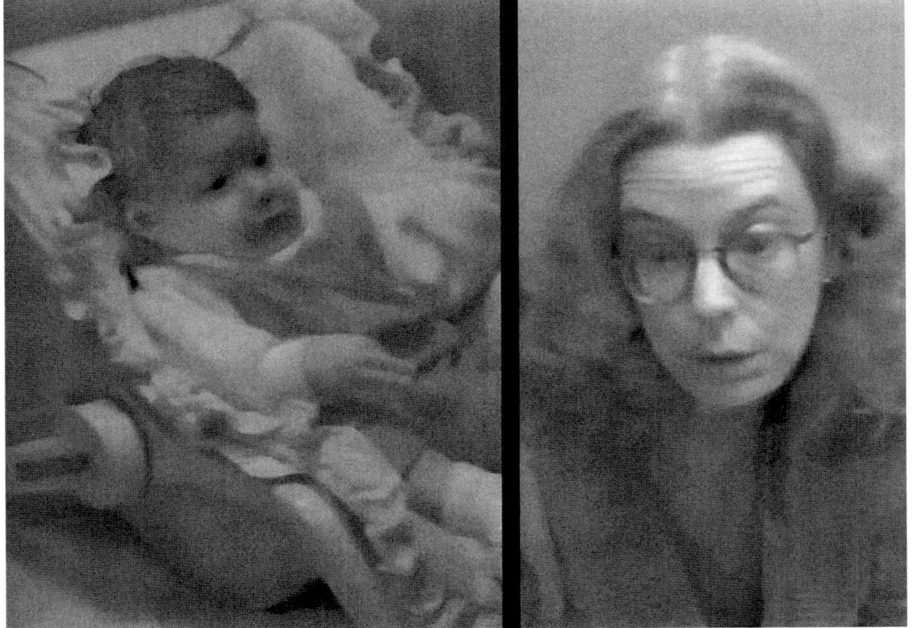

Frame 3.
Minute:Second 29:21
From Frame 2 to 3, in the next second, the infant continues to look, and he becomes slightly less upset. The stranger continues to show concern, with a furrowed brow, but with lower intensity. She moves her head slightly down.

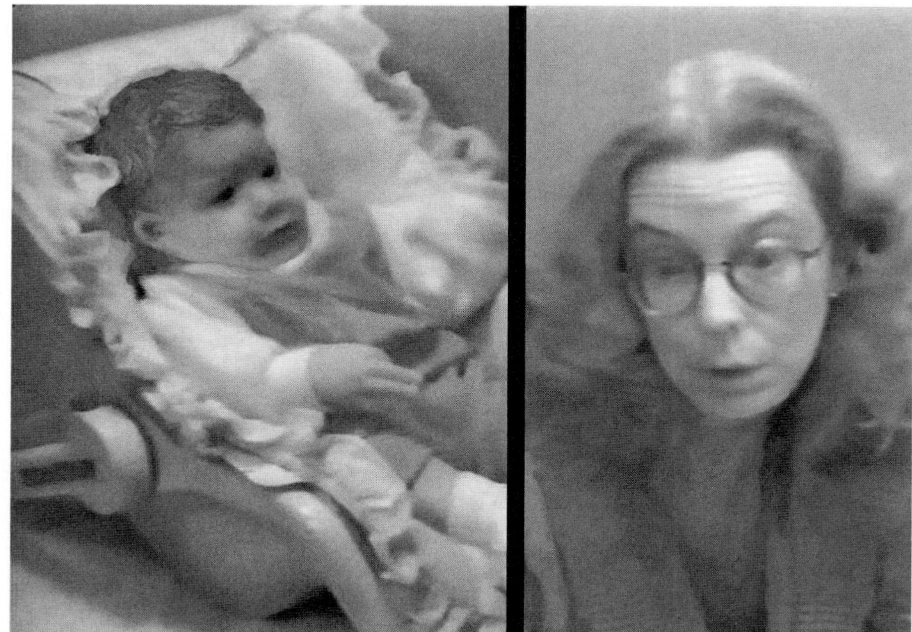

Frame 4.
Minute:Second 29:22
From Frame 3 to 4, one second later, the infant becomes more distressed, with a grimace. The stranger acknowledges his distress with a slight increase in the stranger's furrowed brow, and a slightly more open mouth.

9.6 MINUTE:SECOND 29:26–29:35

Storyline: Seven seconds later, the infant looks down; a slight frown remains until the last frame (Frame 9). The stranger offers her hand. The infant responds first by reaching for her hand, then looks directly at her and soothes by fingering her hand. By the last frame (Frame 9), the infant is calmly engaged.

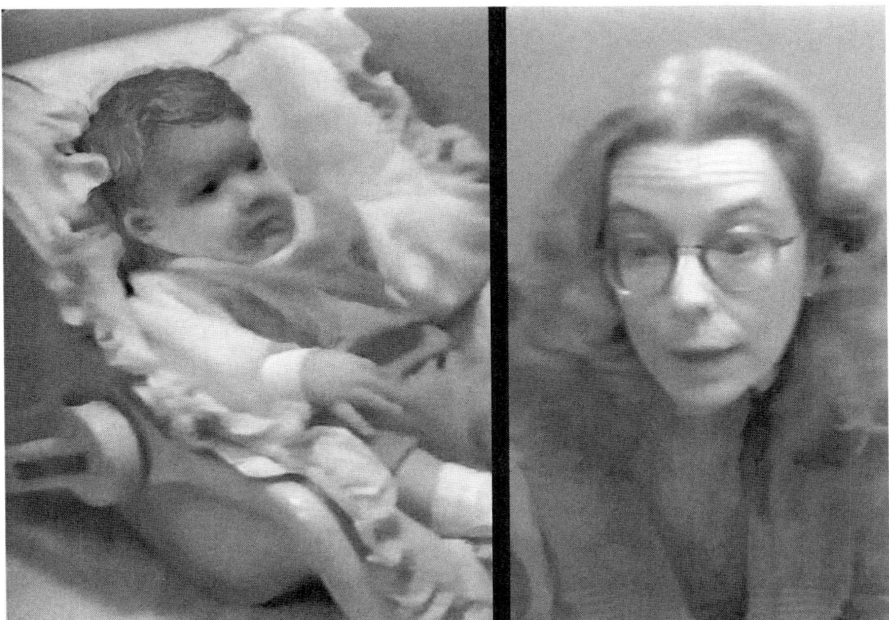

Frame 5. Minute:Second 29:29
From Frame 4 to 5, four seconds later, the infant looks down. His mouth is more relaxed. The stranger's face dampens somewhat, and she continues to show concern in her furrowed brow.

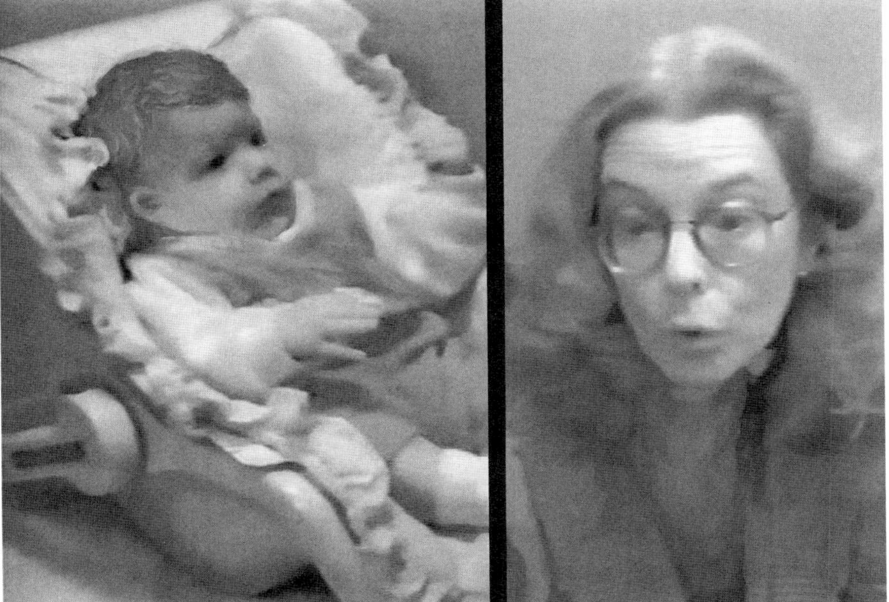

Frame 6. Minute:Second 29:31a
From Frame 5 to 6, two seconds later, the stranger offers her hand to the infant, and her brow still shows concern. Her mouth is closed and quiet, a neutral/interest expression. Although the infant is continuing to look down, his right hand lifts to make contact with the stranger's hand.

Frame 7. Minute:Second 29:31b
From Frame 6 to 7, within the same second, the stranger has leaned forward, and her hand is now resting on the infant's chest. Within a fraction of a second, the infant has responded by placing both of his hands on top of the stranger's hand. The infant's face is calmer with a tiny hint of distress still evident in his eyebrows. The stranger's face is also calmer, with a hint of her concern still visible in her brow.

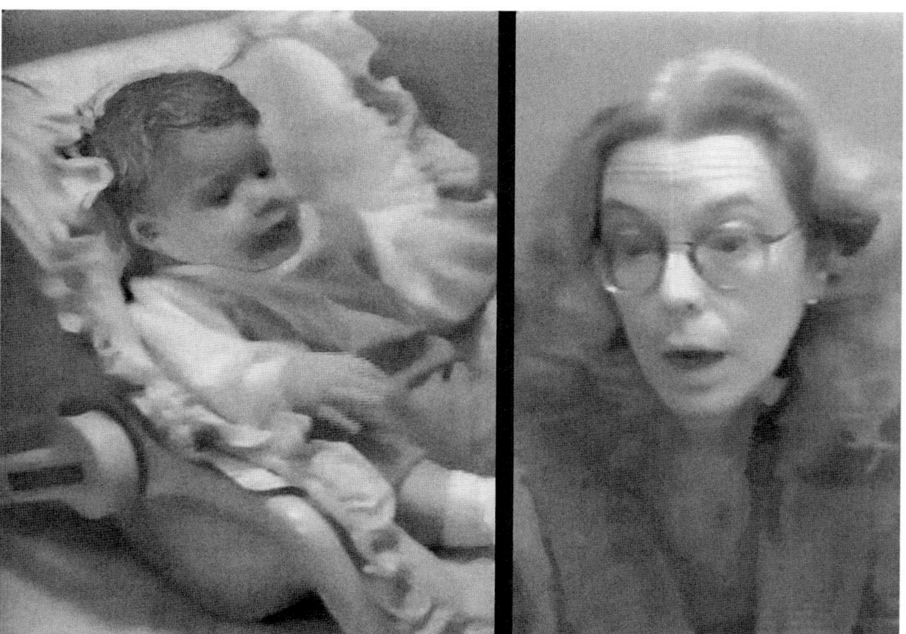

Frame 8. Minute:Second 29:32
From Frame 7 to 8, less than a second later, the infant looks up directly at the stranger with a positive interest face. He places his hands together on top of the stranger's hand. A tiny hint of distress continues to be evident in the infant's eyebrows. The stranger leans forward with a slightly open mouth, a softly open face. Her brow has relaxed with only a hint of concern remaining.

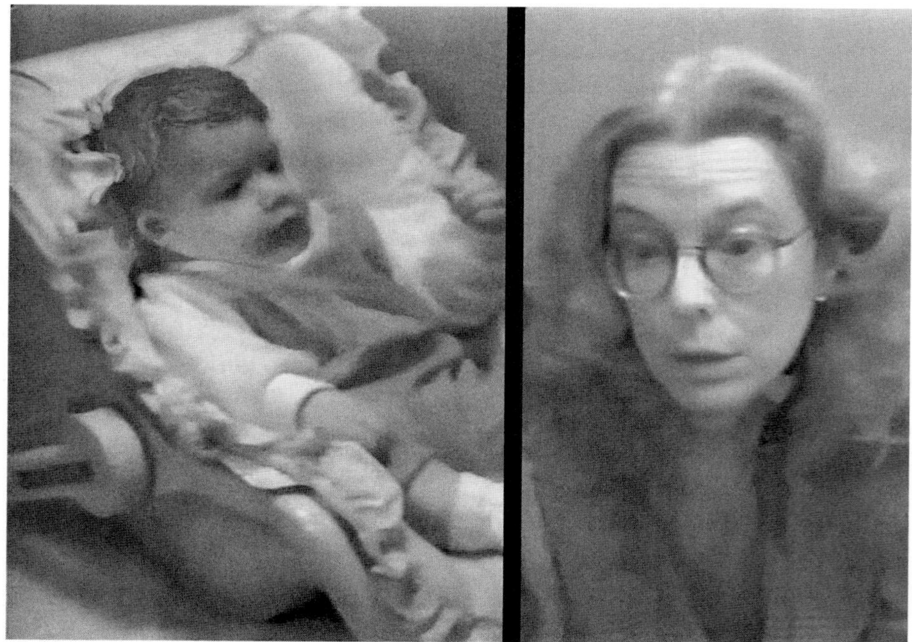

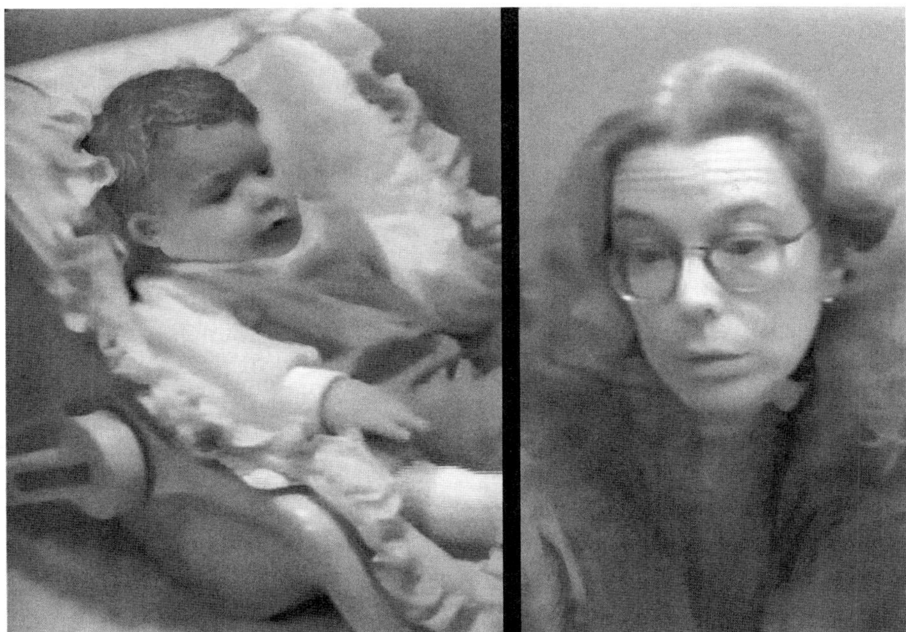

Frame 9. Minute:Second 29:35
From Frame 8 to 9, three seconds later, the infant remains looking. His brow finally relaxes with no hint of a frown. He seems relaxed and engaged. The infant's fingers continue to soothe on top of the stranger's hands. The stranger's mouth is slightly open. Her raised eyebrows and her furrowed brow again show concern, as if to say, "Are you really ok?"

COMMENTARY ON INFANT LOOK AWAY IN THE ORIGINS OF INSECURE ATTACHMENT

Mutual gaze is a critical foundation of the mother–infant face-to-face encounter. While mothers gaze at their infants fairly constantly, it is the infant who makes and breaks mutual gaze. By four months, infants actively look at the partner to initiate social engagement, and they look away from the partner to disengage and to manage level of stimulation and arousal. When infants look back after a moment of looking away, mothers tend to greet their infants by meeting the infant's gaze with their own, and by smiling or showing a mock surprise face.

We chose the sequence "Infant Look Away in the Origins of Insecure-Avoidant Attachment" because it illustrates a complex and fascinating difficulty in the regulation of mother and infant looking patterns. Portions of the following description are adapted from Beebe (2014), Beebe et al. (2010), Beebe and Stern (1977), Cohen and Beebe (2002), and Kushnick (2002).

You may want to compare the interaction we presented in Chapter 6, "Infant Look Away in the Origins of Secure Attachment" with this one in Chapter 9, "Infant Look Away in the Origins of Insecure-Avoidant Attachment." This way, you can clearly see the differences in the ways that mothers and infants may manage moments of infant looking away, in two dyads where the infant is on the way to secure attachment, compared with insecure-avoidant attachment.

In this sequence, the mother and infant do not find their way into any sustained moments of mutual gaze. Nor do they show a mutually positive engagement. This infant was classified as insecure-avoidant attachment at one year. But this dyad had another difficulty as well: The mother was also depressed when the infant was four months old. In the research study on which this book is based (Beebe et al., 2010), some mothers did endorse depression in self-report scales, but maternal depression was unrelated to attachment in these dyads. In some studies, however, maternal depression is associated with insecure attachment (Carter, Garrity-Rokous, Chazan-Cohen, Little, & Briggs-Gowan, 2001). Thus, the interaction of this dyad illustrates not only the origins of avoidant attachment but also a complex interplay with maternal depression when the infant was four months old.

Maternal depression carries its own risks for infant development (Beebe et al., 2008; Field, 1995; (Murray & Cooper, 1997; Tronick & Reck, 2009). Infants of depressed mothers are at risk for less positive affect and impaired social engagement (Campbell & Cohn, 1991; Field, 1995; Lyons-Ruth, Repacholi, McLeod, & Silva, 1991; Tronick, 1989; Zlochower & Cohn, 1996). Compared with controls, depressed mothers and their infants spend more time in negative states and match negative states more than positive (Cohn et al., 1990; Field, Healy, Goldstein, & Guthertz, 1990).

The video of this sequence run in real time shows that the infant is mostly looking away from the mother's face. Overall, the mother attempts to engage her infant with a high level of stimulation. She often uses hand movements toward the infant that are probably too intense for this infant.

But the microanalysis shown in the drawings reveals a more complex story. Whenever this infant does look at his mother's face, his mother interrupts the moment. The first time the infant looks at his mother's face, in that same split second, the mother looks at the camera with a sad face, perhaps as if to say, "I feel awkward and unsure of myself" (Frame 3). Her beseeching look seems to say, "What do I do now?" The infant has a surprised expression as his mother looks at the camera instead of him. Thus, in this moment, the mother does not acknowledge the infant's gaze at her and returns it. She looks at the camera instead of her infant. By the time she looks back at her infant, he is already looking away. We note that, through the mother's peripheral vision, she knows that the infant is looking at her at this moment. But her pull to look at the camera is stronger.

Looking directly at the camera is relatively unusual. It indicates that the mother is very aware of being filmed. When the mother and infant are filmed, they are alone in the filming chamber, but the filming team can see them from outside the filming chamber. This mother seemed to be indicating that she needed some kind of help, perhaps from Dr. Beebe, who was watching the interaction.

The second time the infant looks at his mother, she fails to greet him; her face is rather blank (Frame 8). But in the next moment she smiles. Even though she is late in greeting him, the infant then responds with an open-mouth interest face. This expression is not quite a smile, but it is the most positive face he shows in the interaction (Frame 9). The next time the infant looks, his mother responds with a sad partial-grimace face (Frame 11). This moment illustrates not only a striking absence of the usual positive greeting mothers give their infants, but also a highly unusual sad maternal greeting of the infant's gaze. And the infant immediately looks away. Meanwhile, even as the infant moves his head away and looks away, over and over he reaches for the mother's hands and lightly fingers them. But the mother is unable to respond to her infant's efforts to reach for her through touch. Almost every time he reaches for her hands, she moves her hands away.

As noted above, when infants look back after a moment of looking away, mothers tend to greet their infants by meeting the infant's gaze, and by smiling or showing a mock surprise face. This mother shows a steady absence of this mode of greeting the infant's gaze.

Critical aspects of this interaction were not visible when the film was run in real time. We were unable to see the many ways in which the mother disrupts the moment of her infant looking at her. We were unable to notice the many moments in which the infant continues to reach for his mother with his hands despite his looking away. And we did not notice that the mother continues to move her hands away when the infant is reaching for her hand, or fingering her hand. This information, which can only be derived from microanalysis, richly informs our understanding of the difficulty in the regulation of mother and infant looking patterns in this dyad.

Illustrations of Expectancies

We now turn to the question of what the infant comes to expect from his or her interactive encounters. We attempt to translate the action-dialogue into language, as if the infant or mother could put the experience into words.

In the insecure look away sequence of a dyad at four months on the way to insecure-avoidant infant attachment at one year, if the action-dialogue could be translated into language, we imagine that the infant creates the following expectancies of their interaction:

"I turn my head away when your hands become so intense, but I still reach for you. As I touch your hand, and finger your skin, you move your hand away. When I look at you, you look away; you aren't there for me. Sometimes when I look at you, you show me a surprised face; that surprises me. I don't know what to make of it. I feel like you don't know me."

We imagine that the mother may create the following expectancies of their interaction: "You don't look at me, and I don't understand why. I don't feel we are in sync. When I move toward you, you move your head a little bit away; why aren't you happy? Sometimes you make me feel like you don't love me."

Relevant Research

The research study that underlies this book examined 84 dyads and predicted secure vs. insecure infant attachment patterns at one year from an examination of the regulation of various patterns of interaction at four months (Beebe et al., 2010). Findings that are relevant to "Infant Look Away in the Origins of Insecure-Avoidant Attachment," discussed here, include looking and looking away, mother spatial orientation and infant head orientation, the dyadic pattern of chase and dodge, and maternal touch.

One analysis of the study (Beebe et al., 2010) compared dyads on the way to secure infant attachment with dyads on the way to insecure attachment (combining all types of insecure: avoidant, resistant, and disorganized). In that study, there were too few avoidant infants to analyze separately. Therefore, the discussion below presents findings relevant to all types of insecure attachment.

Mothers of four-month infants who were on the way to insecure attachment at one year showed less predictable rhythms of looking and looking away. Thus, these mothers were harder for infants to read, harder for infants to anticipate. If the action-dialogue could be translated into language, these infants might feel: "I do not know when you will look at me or for how long; I cannot count on your gaze." These mothers may themselves sense (out of awareness) a less steady ability to focus on their infants.

In the drawings discussed here, the mother's looking and looking away illustrates this less predictable pattern. She looks away at odd moments (see for example Frame 3). The infant may become confused about his mother's visual presence and availability.

Mothers of infants who were classified as insecure attachment at one year also showed less predictable patterns of spatial orientation as they moved moment-to-moment among the spatial orientation positions of sitting upright, leaning forward, and looming in. Thus, it was harder for their infants (as well as the mothers themselves) to anticipate maternal patterns of spatial orientation. In addition, these mothers showed more looming head movements.

Moreover, in these dyads where infants were classified as insecure attachment at one year, at four months, mothers and infants showed more moments of the pattern, "maternal chase—infant dodge." As we described in the previous chapter, this is a maternal approach—infant avoid pattern in which the mother moves her head and body toward the infant as the infant moves his head and body away from the mother. This pattern generates an expectancy of maternal intrusive head movements, both looming and chasing.

In the drawings of "Infant Look Away in the Origins of Insecure-Avoidant Attachment," the mother looms into the infant's face in the next to the last frame, and her infant moves his head away (Frame 12). This is an example of the chase and dodge pattern. The mother also puts her hands on the infant's chest at this moment, adding to the intensity. If we could translate the infant's experience into words, the maternal chasing may generate an infant feeling of, "I don't feel free to look away; I can't get away when I need to settle down."

These infants may come to sense the unpredictability of maternal looming, generating a fearful or unsettled feeling, such as, "You are coming too close to my face; I feel wary and a little trapped." Their mothers may come to sense (out of awareness) their own going after the infant, perhaps an urgent need for contact or acknowledgment, or a need to control the contact.

In those dyads where infants were classified as insecure attachment at one year, at four months, mothers had more intrusive touch. If the expectation could be translated into words, infants at four months who are on the way to insecure attachment may feel, "I don't like the way you touch me sometimes" (Frames 7 and 13).

In summary, the research showed that, in dyads where infants were classified as insecure attachment at one year, mothers were more likely to move in toward infants to touch intrusively, to loom, and to chase, and to become less predictable in spatial orientation (Beebe et al., 2010). This is a constellation of behaviors involving maternal intrusion into the infant's body, face-space, and freedom to look away. We propose that both infants and mothers come to expect this intrusive constellation as a central aspect of what it is like to be with each other.

So far, you have seen four patterns of drawings illustrating the origins of secure attachment, and two illustrating the origins of insecure attachment. In dyads where infants were on the way to secure attachment, the drawings illustrated many glorious moments as mother and infant crescendo to the heights of mutual gape smiles. We also saw many examples of common and relatively minor disruptions and rapid repairs in these dyads on the way to secure infant attachment. This repair process was mostly absent in the two insecure interactions we illustrated.

We now turn to four illustrations of dyads where infants were on the way to disorganized attachment. Here we see the most troubling sequences. There are many painful, agonizing moments in which infants are frantically distressed while mothers smile, show surprise faces, or look away; moments in which mothers display threat faces; and moments in which mothers become emotionally disconnected. When a mother or important caregiver does not recognize the infant's distress, the infant may generate experiences of not being sensed and known, which may disturb the fundamental integration of the person. These difficult maternal patterns of behavior are mostly out of the mother's awareness. Research has documented that mothers of disorganized attachment infants have unresolved experiences of loss and trauma. Thus, these difficult maternal patterns likely spring from the mother's own traumatic history. Research has found that disorganized attachment is transmitted across generations. The next section turns to a detailed discussion of disorganized attachment.

Introduction to Drawings Illustrating the Origins of Insecure-Disorganized Attachment

The four sets of drawings that we present next depict mother–infant interaction sequences at infant age four months, which illustrate the origins of a form of insecure infant attachment termed disorganized. Portions of the following descriptions are adapted from Beebe et al. (2010) and Beebe and Lachmann (2013).

Disorganized attachment at one year is of particular interest because it predicts many difficulties that the child will face at school age, adolescence, and young adulthood. These difficulties include various forms of psychopathology, such as dissociation (Carlson, 1998; Dutra, Bureau, Holmes, Lyubchik, & Lyons-Ruth, 2009; Lyons-Ruth & Jacobvitz, 2008; Ogawa, Sroufe, Weinfeld, Carlson, & Egeland, 1997; Sroufe et al., 2005a), self-injury, and conduct disorder (Lyons-Ruth, 2008; Lyons-Ruth, Bureau, Holmes, Easterbrooks, & Henninghausen, 2011; Shi et al., 2012).

These remarkable predictions from disorganized attachment at one year to difficulties in young adulthood do not mean, however, that development is set in stone in infancy. Instead, we view interactions in infancy as setting a transformational course in development (Sameroff, 1983). Development proceeds through a process of regular restructurings of the ways that a person relates to important attachment figures.

The field of longitudinal studies examining the course of development from infant attachment at one year to adult attachment and psychopathology outcomes is relatively new, in the past decade and a half. Although there have been striking predictions from infancy to adulthood (see van IJzendoorn, 1995 for a review), there have also been some failures of prediction (Groh et al., 2014; Lewis, Feiring, & Rosenthal, 2000). Moreover, although these studies show that early experience has a strong influence on development, at least through early adulthood, later experiences also play an important role. If the environment changes, the quality of a child's adaptation is likely to change (Sroufe, 1983, 2005). These studies use a transformational rather than linear model of development. Most take into account the role of changing life circumstances, such as the occurrence of trauma, in predicting development. Thus, transformations from secure to insecure are likely with trauma (Waters et al., 2000). Transformations from insecure to secure are also likely with special developmental advantages (Saunders, Jacobvitz, Zaccagnino, Beverung, & Hazen, 2011).

Nevertheless, infant experience has a special role. It sets a trajectory for the child's subsequent interactions with the environment, and it becomes the basis for various strategies for coping with stress, most prominently dissociation in young adulthood (Carlson & Sroufe, 1995; Sroufe et al., 1999). Dissociation involves disruptions in functions that are usually integrated, such as consciousness, memory, body awareness, and perception of the self and the environment. It may involve detachment from an overwhelming emotional experience (Lanius et al., 2010).

In the attachment assessment at one year, securely attached infants are easily comforted by contact with their caregivers upon reunion, quickly returning to play. Infants who are classified disorganized attachment show fearful, odd, and conflicted behaviors during the reunion. Disorganized infant attachment is often described as a breakdown of an organized strategy for dealing with the distress prompted by the separation. There is no resolution of the separation in the reunion episodes, and infants express fear, apprehension, and confusion (Main & Solomon, 1990). A core criterion for disorganized attachment is the infant's display of simultaneous or sequential approach and avoidance behaviors in relation to the mother, such as reaching for the mother while backing up. Infants may also show contradictory behavior, such as undirected, misdirected, or interrupted behavior; asymmetrical, mistimed, or anomalous behaviors; freezing, stilling, or slowed movements; or apprehension regarding the parent. Also very important, maternal behavior during the reunions of the attachment assessment has been found to be frightened and/or frightening (Hesse & Main, 2006; Jacobvitz, Hazen, & Riggs, 1997; Lyons-Ruth et al., 1999; Main & Hesse, 1990; Schuengel, Bakermans-Kranenburg & van IJzendoorn, 1999).

The four sets of drawings illustrating the four-month origins of disorganized infant attachment all convey very difficult moments that are painful to see. These infants tend to be very distressed, significantly more so than infants on the way to secure attachment (Beebe et al., 2010). You see many moments in which the mother cannot acknowledge her infant's distress and cannot coordinate with her infant's emotional ups and downs. When the infant is distressed, you see moments in which the mothers look away, or stonewall the infant with blank faces, or become happy and smile broadly. These are profoundly discordant and contradictory interactions, which predict disorganized attachment at one year (Beebe et al., 2010). We suggest that these experiences may disturb the integration of emotional experience in infancy (Beebe et al., 2010).

For most people, it is easier to empathize with the infant than with the mother. But it is essential that we understand and empathize with the mother as well. Thus before you look at these drawings, it is important to know more about the mothers themselves.

Mothers of infants who will be classified as disorganized attachment at one year bring their own difficult attachment histories. They are likely to suffer from unresolved loss, abuse, or trauma and to be in a continuing state of fear (Lyons-Ruth et al., 1999; Main & Hesse, 1990). In low-risk samples, the unresolved parental trauma most often concerns the death of a loved one (van IJzendoorn, 1995). However, a study Schuengel, Bakermans-Kranenburg, and van IJzendoorn (1999) showed that unresolved maternal loss predicted disorganized infant attachment among insecure mothers, but not among secure mothers. Maternal security of attachment was a protective factor against transmission of disorganized attachment to their infants.

The unresolved nature of these difficulties is like an open wound. When these mothers of disorganized infants are interviewed about their own attachment histories as children, they may become emotionally incoherent or dissociated; they may show lapses in their monitoring of reasoning or discourse. Their difficulties with their own distress are likely to disturb their ability to respond to distress in their infants.

We suggest that mothers of infants who are classified as disorganized attachment at one year cannot coordinate with infant emotional ups and downs, and cannot empathically acknowledge moments of infant distress, because they cannot bear to pay attention to their own emotional distress. Their own distress is likely triggered by the infant's distress. The mother's efforts to manage her own distress may then (out of awareness) become imperative, that is, take precedence over her infant's distress.

When individuals who are skilled at regulating their emotions are faced with another's distress, they are free to focus on the needs of the other; they do not become overly emotionally aroused as they vicariously experience the other's distress (Eisenberg & Fabes, 1992; Fabes, Eisenberg, & Miller, 1990; Peck, 2003). This picture might describe mothers of future secure infants. In contrast, less skilled individuals, or individuals who have experienced trauma, such as mothers of disorganized infants, may experience their own personal distress in response to another's distress, and then need to manage their own distress.

As we have already described, infant and mother attachment patterns tend to be correlated. A recent longitudinal study linking the parent's own infant attachment pattern with that of their infant helps us understand the intergenerational transmission of disorganized attachment patterns vividly from a prospective approach. Infants with disorganized attachment at one year were followed into adulthood. When they became parents and had infants of their own, their infants were also likely to be classified with disorganized attachment (Raby et al., 2015). This is new data supporting the notion of the intergenerational transmission of trauma. A mother with an infant classified with disorganized attachment is likely to have had a disorganized attachment history herself as an infant. Understanding this intergenerational transmission of trauma can help us not blame the mother.

In the four sets of drawings, we present below illustrating the origins of disorganized attachment, the mothers frequently have difficulty helping their infants with their distress. But all mothers at times have such difficulty. All mothers have moments of awkwardness, embarrassment, or irritation when their infants are distressed. It is important to remember that only when such moments are frequent and characteristic of the interaction is there a problem. Research has identified repetitive patterns in the origins of disorganized attachment that significantly differ from the patterns in the origins of secure attachment (Beebe et al., 2010).

RESEARCH FINDINGS

As we view each of the sets of drawings that follow, research specific to each interaction pattern is discussed. Here we give a brief general overview of our research findings on patterns of interaction at four months that differentiated infants who were classified secure, compared with disorganized, at one year (Beebe et al., 2010).

Four-month infants on the way to disorganized attachment at one year, compared with infants on the way to secure attachment, showed complex forms of emotional distress and dysregulation:

(1) They were more vocally distressed, and they showed more combined facial and vocal distress.
(2) They showed more *discrepant* facial and vocal affect, in which, in the same second, infants might be smiling but whimpering. This finding suggests infant affective conflict, confusion, and struggle. Discrepant affect may make it difficult for future disorganized infants eventually to know what they feel, and to tolerate and integrate conflicting feelings.
(3) Their own rhythms of facial-visual engagement were less predictable from moment-to-moment, an emotional destabilization.
(4) They were less likely to touch (touch one's own skin, object, or mother), particularly less likely to touch their own skin; and they were more likely to continue in states of not touching. These findings concerning touch compromise the infant's ability to self-soothe through touch, in the context of increased distress.

Mothers of four-month infants on the way to disorganized attachment, compared with mothers of infants on the way to secure attachment, showed the following patterns:

(1) Mothers were more likely to look away from the infant's face, and maternal patterns of looking and looking away from the infant's face were less predictable. These maternal looking patterns compromise the infant's ability to expect and rely on predictable maternal visual attention.
(2) Mothers were more likely to use looming head movements close into the infant's face, and their spatial orientation patterns of sitting upright, leaning forward, and looming in were less predictable. Both more looming, and the unpredictability of looming, are interpreted as potentially threatening.
(3) Mothers were more likely to show positive or surprise expressions while infants were distressed, interpreted as maternal emotional "denial" of infant distress. We view this maternal response as a way that mothers defend themselves against the threat of infant distress retriggering their own unresolved childhood distress.
(4) Mothers were less likely to follow their infants' positive and negative emotional ups and downs, interpreted as maternal emotional withdrawal from distressed infants.

(5) Mothers were more likely to overstabilize their faces, an overly predictable process, leading to momentarily closed-up faces, an emotional disconnection.
(6) The combination of maternal overly stable faces, but lowered facial and visual coordination with infant emotional ups and downs generated an imbalance. This imbalance tilts toward maternal preoccupation with managing her own face, becoming overly stabilized, unchanging, and thus likely emotionally disconnected. This is a self-regulation strategy that may help the mother feel more centered in herself. But it sacrifices her ability to respond to her infant, and thus it exacerbates her emotional disconnection from her distressed infant.
(7) Mothers were less likely to coordinate their own touch patterns with infant touch patterns. Lower maternal coordination with infant emotion and touch both compromise infant interactive efficacy in these domains. That is, infants are less able to expect to be able to influence mothers through their own emotion and touch behaviors.

EXPECTANCIES

We now turn to the question of what four-month infants on the way to disorganized attachment come to expect from their interactive encounters. The recurrent nature of the infant's experiences leads to the development of expectancies, procedural action-dialogue representations of self and others, that influence the infant's emotional experiences, as discussed in Chapter 3 (Beebe & Lachmann, 2002; Bowlby, 1973; Bretherton & Munholland, 1999; Main et al., 1985).

There are many forms of conflict and contradiction in our findings on the origins of disorganized attachment (Beebe et al., 2010). By conflict we mean that behavior is organized simultaneously in opposing directions. The most salient example is dyadic conflict: Infant behavior moving in the direction of increased distress, while maternal behavior moves in the direction of more positive affect, or surprise; or in the direction of shutting down by looking away or becoming blank and disconnected.

We argue that infants at four months who are on the way to disorganized attachment cannot develop an expectation of feeling sensed or known, particularly when distressed. Instead they come to expect emotional distress and emotional incoherence. They come to expect difficulty in obtaining comfort. They have difficulty predicting what will happen next. Their experiences of emotional recognition are profoundly derailed.

In the realm of attention, the future disorganized attachment infant may feel not seen; in the realm of emotion, the infant may feel not joined and stonewalled when distressed; in the realm of orientation, the infant may experience looming impingements; and in the realm of touch, unlike the future secure infant, the future disorganized infant cannot anticipate being touched more tenderly when he shows more aroused touch patterns. These infants at four months are often agitated and frantic, and at moments, these infants may feel alarmed or threatened.

The unresolvable dilemma of the disorganized attachment infant is that the very parent that he needs for comfort is the parent who alarms or frightens him. Thus, infants who are classified as disorganized may be alarmed or threatened by the parent (Hesse & Main, 2006; Main & Solomon, 1986). This generates a nonorganized or disrupted state (Siegel, 1999, 2012). They have no adaptive strategy available to them. As these interactions repeat, the infant experiences a powerful loss of efficacy and helplessness. He learns that, at such moments of intense distress, he will not be able to get help, and he will not be able to help himself. He learns that he will experience frantic moments of agitation with no anticipation of relief.

It is important to note that there are many ways in which maternal responsivity with infants is intact in mothers of future disorganized infants. These mothers do not have a general confusion, an overall failure of empathy, or a failure to register or read infant states. Instead, many of the difficulties of mothers of future disorganized infants are organized by moments of contradictory behavior patterns, triggered especially by their infants' distress.

We argue that mothers of future disorganized infants have unresolved fears about intimate relating, and fears of being retraumatized by infant distress, which are most likely out of awareness. Thus, at moments of infant distress, these mothers mobilize complex contradictory behaviors that derail their infants. The infant's distress may be so overarousing and terrifying to these mothers that, out of awareness, they repeat aspects of their own unresolved, traumatized childhood feelings of fear, anger, and helplessness through their modes of interacting with their infants. Or these mothers may protect themselves against reexperiencing their own childhood experiences by looking away or by becoming distant and emotionally disconnected.

In conclusion, we suggest that the interaction patterns identified by our research on the origins of disorganized attachment at four months define specific ways in which the infant's ability to know and be known by the mother's mind, as well as the infant's ability to know his own mind, may become disturbed (Beebe et al., 2010). In our view, the remarkable intrapersonal and dyadic contradictory communications and conflict are likely to disturb the coherence of the infant's experience. Thus, we propose that the four-month patterns documented in the origins of disorganized attachment are likely to set a trajectory in development, which disturbs the fundamental integration of the person.

CHAPTER 10

Infant Distress and Maternal Emotional Disconnection in the Origins of Insecure-Disorganized Infant Attachment

DRAWINGS: INFANT DISTRESS AND MATERNAL EMOTIONAL DISCONNECTION

This sequence depicts a mother and infant at four months where the infant was classified as insecure-disorganized attachment at one year (Beebe et al., 2010).

This sequence of drawings depicts ten frames, over eight seconds. As they begin, the infant is in severe distress, and the mother does not know what to do or how to help. As the infant begins to open her eyes, she is still profoundly distressed. The mother greets her infant with increasingly broad smiles, which are strikingly discrepant from the infant's distress. Eventually the infant's look of incomprehension and protest seems to wake the mother up to her infant's distress, but the mother seems helpless and becomes emotionally withdrawn.

Following the interaction with the mother, this infant then played immediately with the stranger, a novel partner.

10.1 MINUTE:SECOND 25:54–25:56A

Storyline: Across these three seconds, the infant becomes increasingly distressed; the mother becomes withdrawn, then frustrated. She seems helpless.

Frame 1. Minute:Second 25:54
The infant is very distressed. The infant's head is tilted down, her eyebrows are furrowed in a deep frown, her mouth is grimacing, and her eyes are tightly shut. The mother looks at her infant with her mouth partially open. She seems slightly surprised and uncomprehending. Her two hands hold her infant's torso (seen in the infant's frame). The mother is leaning in slightly, and her hair shows a bit in the infant's frame.

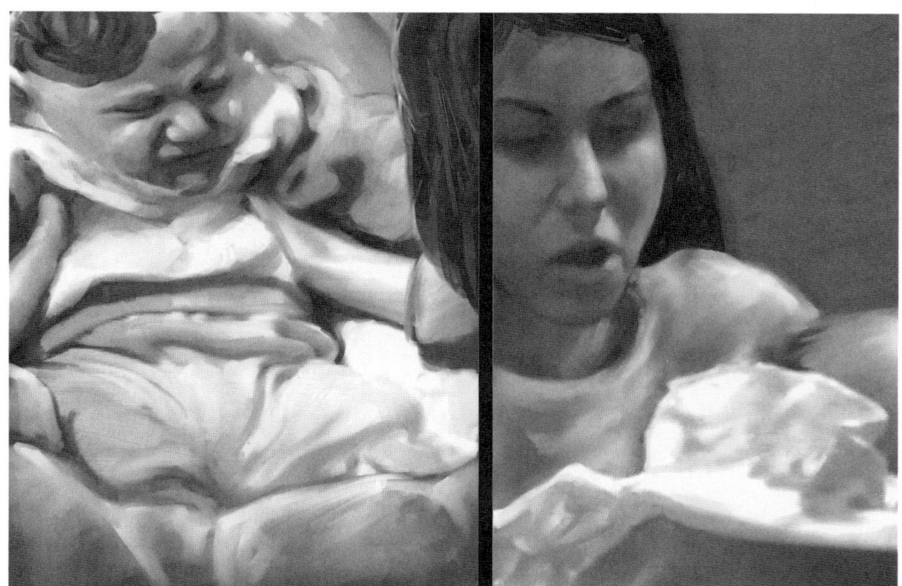

Frame 2. Minute:Second 25:55a
From Frame 1 to 2, approximately a half second later, the infant's distress increases to a pre-cry face as the infant lifts her head. The mother looks down, away from her infant, with a sad, withdrawn face. Her lips are compressed tightly, and her jaw is tight. She removes her hands, tilts her head to her left, and moves in slightly. Her hair shows more in the infant's frame. She seems far away and inside herself, disconnected.

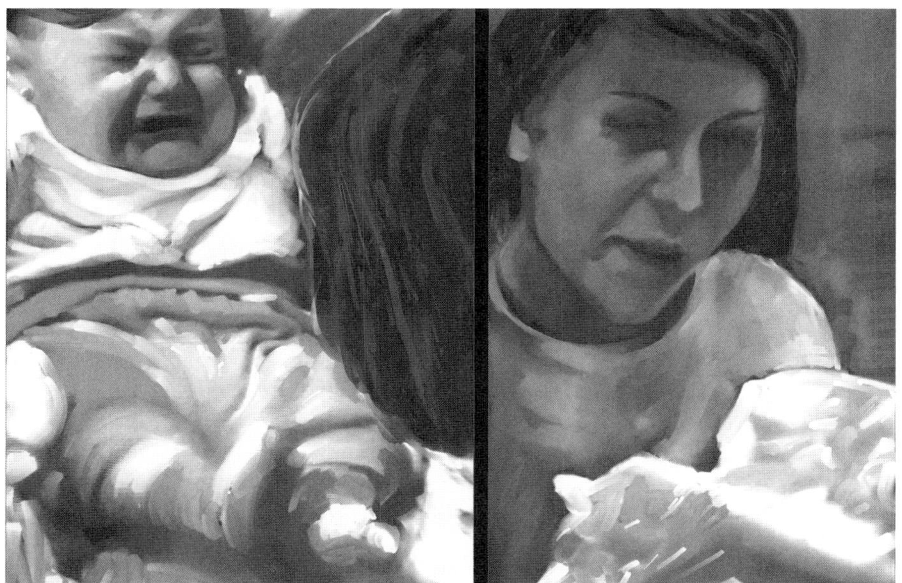

Frame 3. Minute:Second 25:55b
From Frame 2 to 3, within the same second, the infant's distress deepens into a full cry face with a more open mouth. The infant kicks her right foot up. The mother raises her head, looks at her infant, and moves her head further in. Her mouth is asymmetrical and tense, pulled to her right. She seems to be aware of her infant's distress, but she seems emotionally disconnected from it.

Frame 4. Minute:Second 25:56a
From Frame 3 to 4, a split-second later, the infant remains intensely distressed with a cry face. She lowers her chin. The mother has a discrepant look with a slight smile and a slight frown. She seems helpless and pleading. She seems uncertain of what to do. She reaches for her infant with her left hand.

10.2 MINUTE:SECOND 25:56B–25:58

Storyline: In the next three seconds, the infant begins to look, but remains distressed; the mother greets the infant with increasing smiles as if she does not see her infant's distress, until the final frame (Frame 8).

Frame 5. Minute:Second 25:56b
From Frame 4 to 5, within the same second, the infant remains intensely distressed with a cry face. The mother now smiles slightly, but with a helpless look. Her smile is discrepant from her infant's distress. Both of her hands touch the infant.

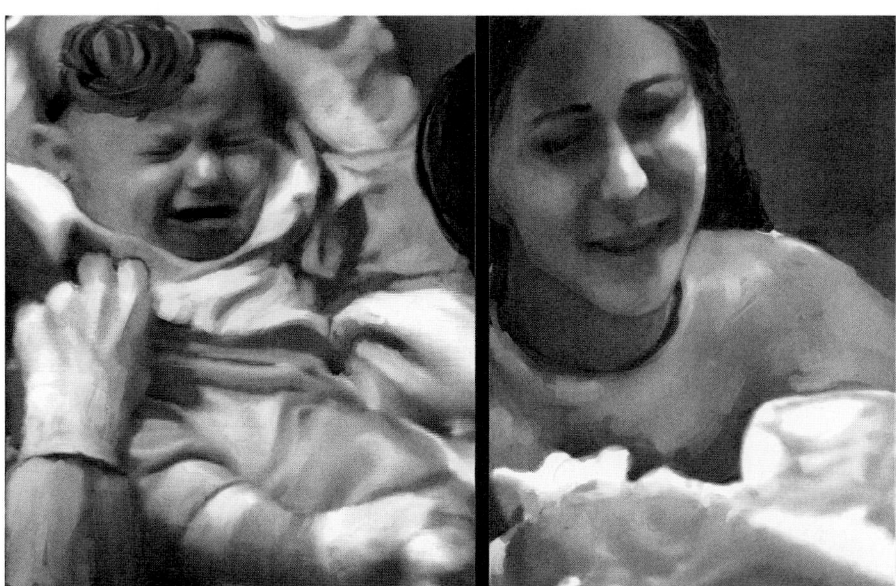

Frame 6. Minute:Second 25:57a
From Frame 5 to 6, a split-second later, the infant begins to open her eyes, still distressed with a cry face. The mother greets her with a bigger smile, but this smile is very discrepant from her infant's distress. The mother fingers her infant's clothing.

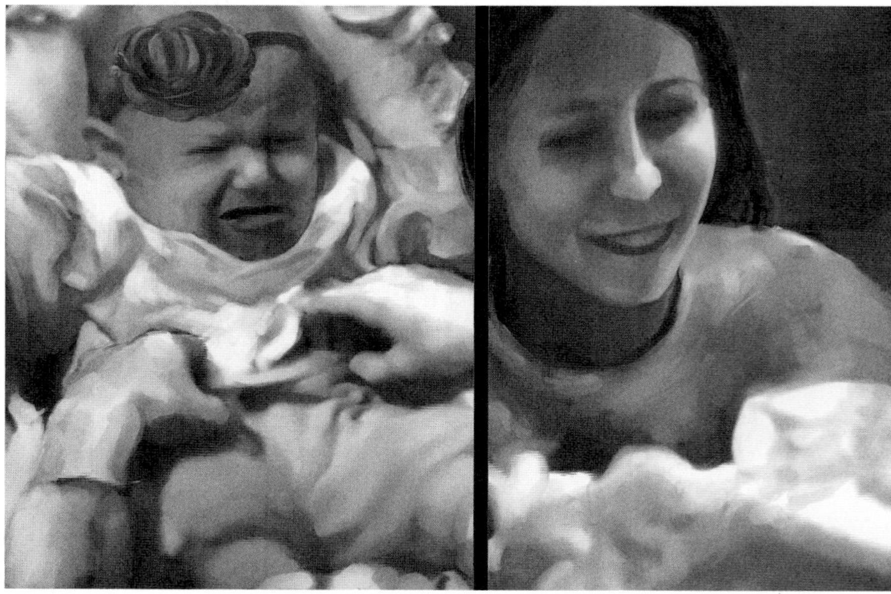

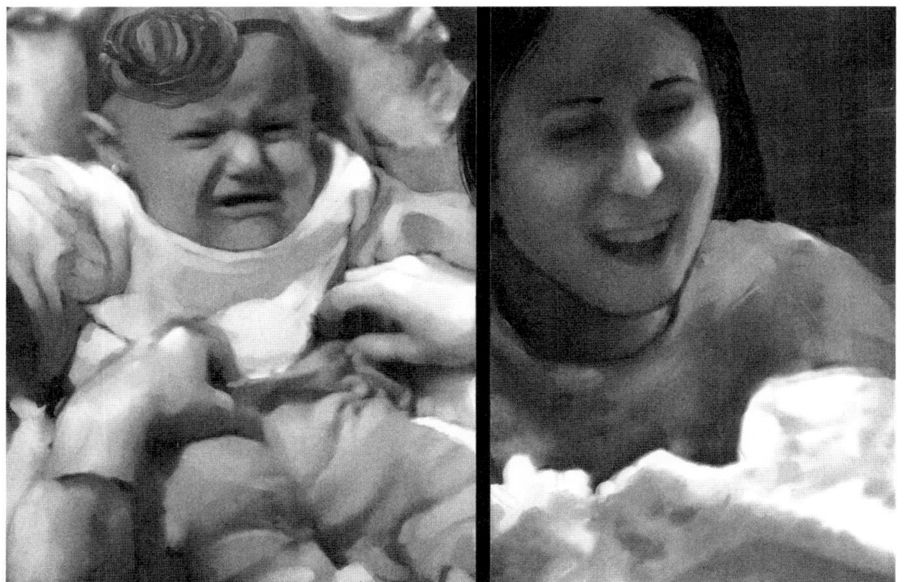

Frame 7. Minute:Second 25:57b
From Frame 6 to 7, within the same second, the infant opens her eyes fully, still very distressed. The mother greets the infant with a full, open smile. She gives her infant no recognition of her distress. Looking at the mother in isolation, we would have no idea that her infant is distressed to this degree. It is as if she is with a different infant than the one we see.

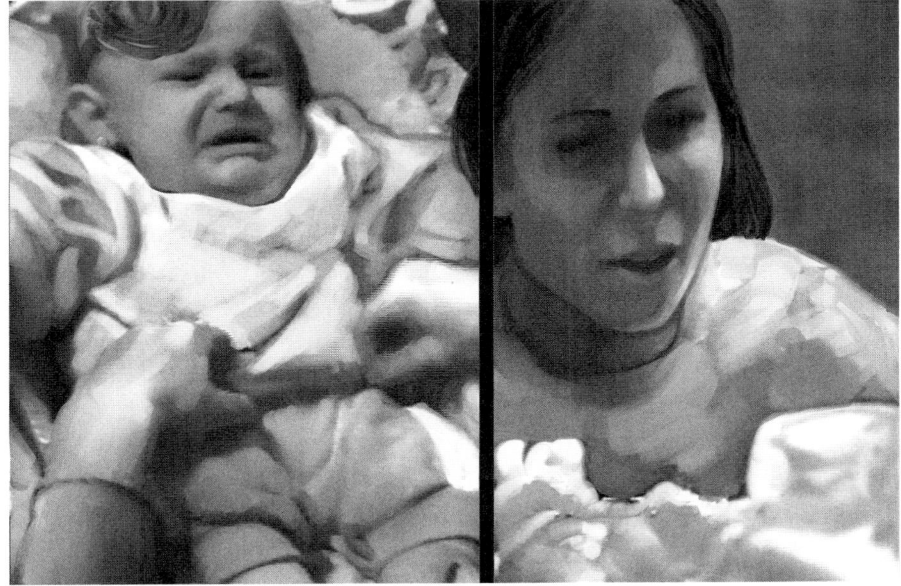

Frame 8. Minute:Second 25:58
From Frame 7 to 8, in the next second, the infant's distress increases. Her face has a strong grimace expression. She arches back, making eye contact, with a look of incomprehension and protest, perhaps aghast, as if to say: "What are you doing? Don't you see I'm upset? How can this be happening? Where are you? You are not with me." The mother sobers with a frustrated look, and her lips begin to purse with tension. She has an "uh-oh, what's happening?" look, as if lost or uncertain. The infant's look of incomprehension has "woken her up" to see her infant's distress.

10.3 MINUTE:SECOND 26:00–26:01

Storyline: In the final two seconds, the infant remains distressed, and the mother becomes emotionally absent.

Frame 9. Minute:Second 26:00
From Frame 8 to 9, two seconds later, the infant closes her eyes. Her distress slightly dampens. The mother reaches in to touch her infant's head. The mother seems concerned, intent, but helpless. The mother's slight asymmetrical downturned mouth on the right suggests irritation.

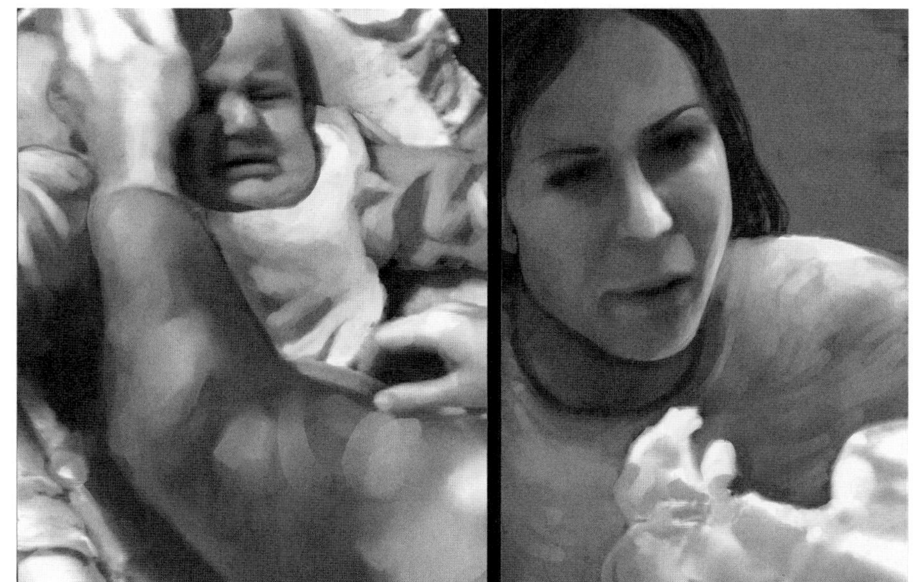

Frame 10. Minute:Second 26:01
From Frame 9 to 10, the infant slightly opens her eyes and continues to look distressed. The mother looks at her infant and pulls her hands back. She has a blank face, which does not convey sympathy for the infant's distress. The mother looks as if she does not know her infant. She seems emotionally absent. Again, their states are profoundly discrepant.

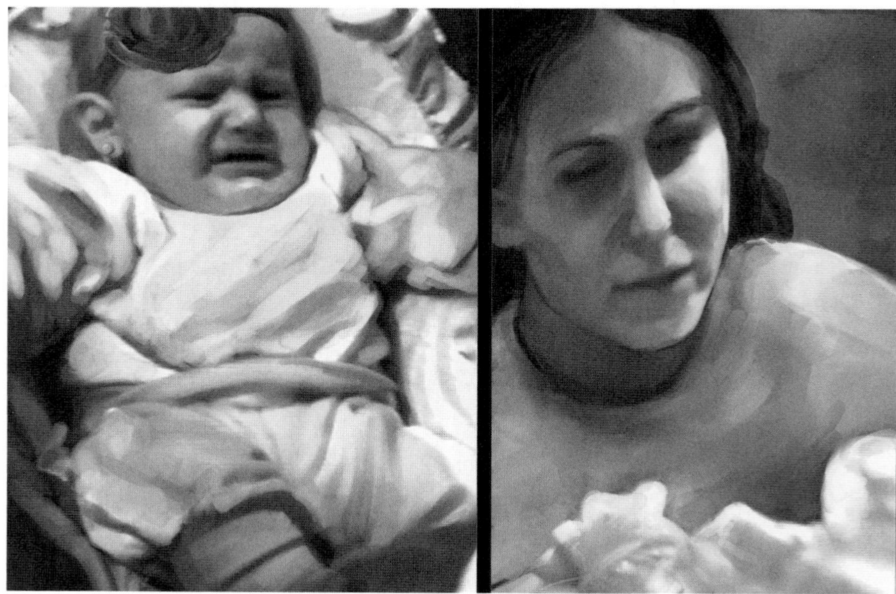

THE STRANGER–INFANT INTERACTION: INFANT EMOTIONAL WITHDRAWAL WITH THE STRANGER

Following the interaction with the mother, this infant then played immediately with the stranger, a novel partner. In this sequence of drawings of four frames over three seconds, the infant begins visually engaged, but she has a very sad expression. The stranger attempts to engage the infant in a positive way. But the infant does not respond, and then withdraws. The stranger then looks down.

We note that, in the following minutes of the interaction with the stranger (not shown), the infant continued to be dampened and mostly gazing away. The stranger was unable to engage this infant.

10.4 MINUTE:SECOND 27:32–27:34

Storyline: In these three seconds, the infant looks at the stranger briefly with a sad face, and then looks down. The stranger begins with an open, engaged face but then sobers as the infant looks down. By the final frame, the stranger joins the infant in looking down.

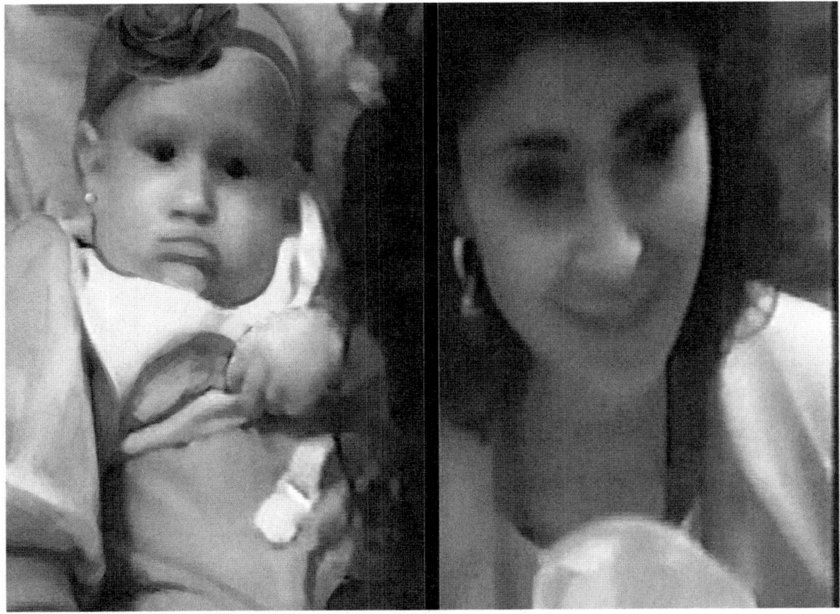

Frame 1. Minute:Second 27:32
Both the infant and the stranger look at each other. The infant pouts and stares with a sad face. The stranger looks engaged and has an inquisitive, slight smile.

Frame 2. Minute:Second 27:33a
From Frame 1 to 2, a half second later, the infant's face shifts to a more flat, blank stare. The stranger's eyebrows are raised as if to say: "Oh, what's happening?" Her smile slightly dampens.

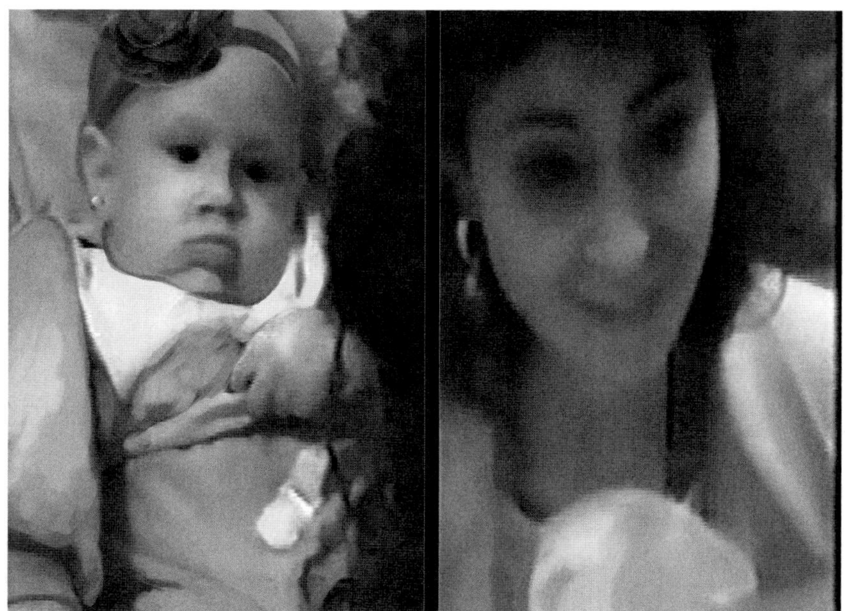

Frame 3. Minute:Second 27:33b
From Frame 2 to 3, within the same second, the infant looks down; her face takes on a neutral expression. The stranger continues to show an inquisitive look with raised eyebrows. But her smile continues to dampen slightly, and she looks concerned.

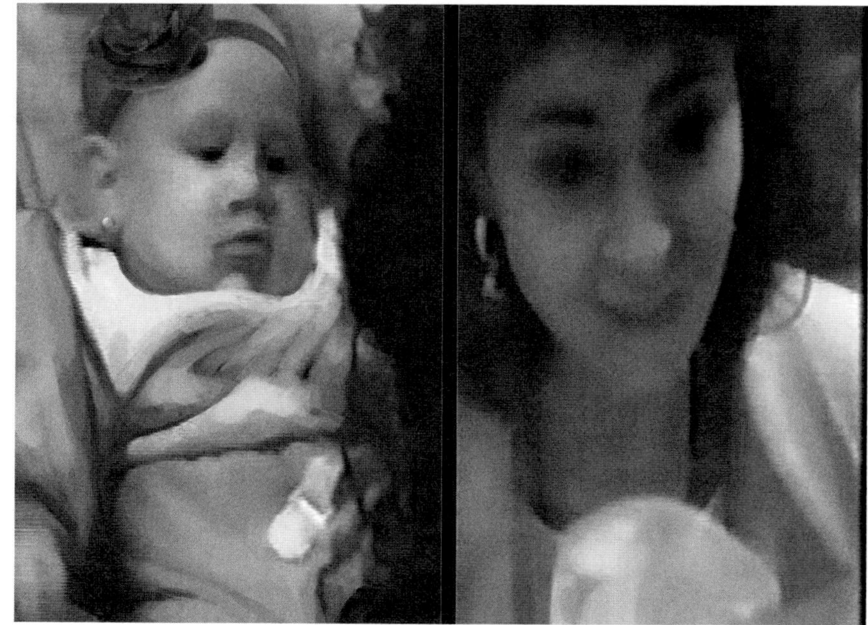

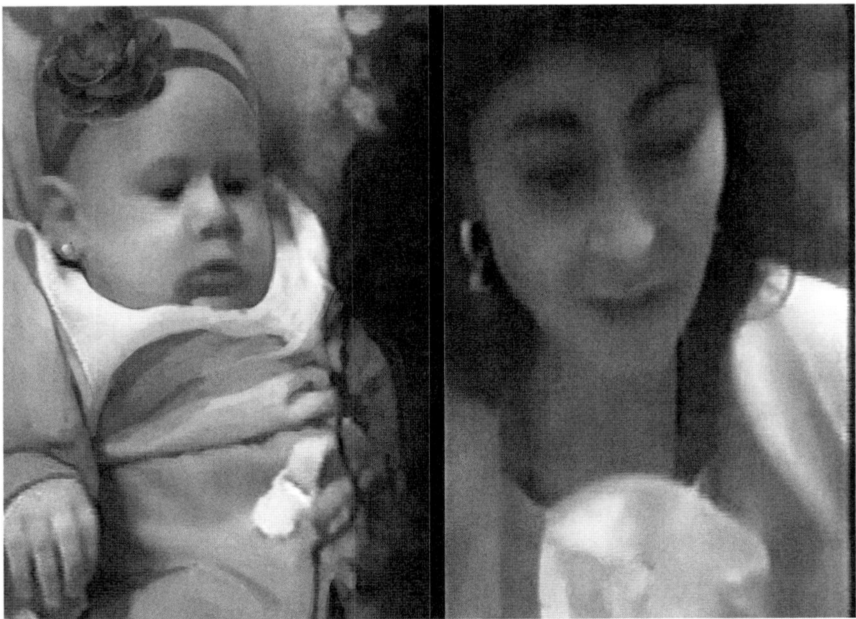

Frame 4. Minute:Second 27:34
From Frame 3 to 4, a half second later, the infant further withdraws into herself. Her head moves down. She seems emotionally absent. The stranger also looks down, beginning to sober. They seem to be in a matched state.

COMMENTARY ON INFANT DISTRESS AND MATERNAL EMOTIONAL DISCONNECTION

We chose this sequence on maternal disconnection from infant distress because it illustrates several patterns, which predicted insecure-disorganized attachment at one year in our research (Beebe et al., 2010). Portions of the following descriptions are adapted from Beebe and colleagues (2010, 2012).

Comment on Mother and Infant

As we enter this interaction, the infant is extremely distressed, and the mother seems unsure of what to do. By the second frame, the mother looks away from her distressed infant. This moment lasts only a fraction of a second. But we see in the mother's face that she has gone away deep inside herself. This moment illustrates our research finding that mothers of infants on the way to disorganized attachment look away from their infants more than mothers of infants on the way to secure attachment. But it does more; it hints at a place of sadness and emotional disconnection in this mother, visible only for a fraction of a second. This action is not visible in real time video.

As the infant's distress deepens, by Frame 5, three seconds into the interaction, the mother begins to smile. She smiles more and more broadly as her infant remains intensely distressed. Although this sequence lasts only two seconds, it reveals an extraordinary degree of mismatch. It is as if the infant that she is with is not the infant that we see. Perhaps the mother's increasing smiles are in response to her infant increasingly opening her eyes in these two seconds. But if so, she is attending to her infant looking at her, while blocking from awareness her infant's intense distress.

Suddenly the infant looks directly at the mother and arches back with a look of protest and incomprehension. This seems to jolt the mother into an awareness, to wake her up to her infant's intense distress. This moment reveals aspects of the infant's own social competence. The infant seems to understand that something is wrong. The infant makes a powerful effort to communicate protest to the mother.

But the mother does not seem to know how to respond. She does not become empathic. Her reach in to her infant's face in Frame 9 indicates concern. But she seems helpless. She looks as if she does not know her infant. She seems emotionally disconnected.

Mothers of infants on the way to disorganized attachment certainly perceive their infants' distress, reflected in comments such as, "Don't be that way," or "You don't want to be like that," or "No fussing, no fussing, you should be very happy." Research described in the previous section, "Introduction to the Drawings Illustrating the Origins of Insecure-Disorganized Attachment," showed that mothers of disorganized attachment infants are likely to have had a disorganized attachment themselves as infants. In this dyad, we infer that this mother is experiencing some kind of fear, lack of safety, or helplessness herself as her infant becomes so distressed.

We propose that maternal ongoing unresolved fears about intimate relating, particularly at moments of infant distress, trigger unresolved issues from the mother's own childhood. In the face of their infant's distress, these mothers may also have more general overwhelming and disorganizing negative emotions, such as fear, helplessness, anxiety, or anger. In this unintegrated emotional state, they feel helpless to alleviate the infant's distress, and yet they feel the pressure to do so (Miriam Steele, personal communication, July 18, 2015). These mothers then behave in complex and contradictory ways that derail the infant (Beebe et al., 2010; Karlen Lyons-Ruth, personal communication, October 17, 2008). These mothers often emotionally shut down or disconnect to protect themselves (Mary Sue Moore, personal communication, July 2, 2007).

Following the interaction with the mother, this infant played with the stranger, a novel partner. Following difficult interactions with their mothers, some infants at four months can reorganize and engage with the stranger, such as the infant in Chapter 8. The infant's ability to engage with the stranger is also dependent on the social skill of the stranger. In this interaction, the infant does not easily engage with the stranger. The infant begins visually engaged, but with a sad expression. The stranger attempts to engage the infant in a positive way. But the infant does not respond. The infant then withdraws into herself, looking down and moving her head down. She seems emotionally absent. The stranger then looks down.

Illustrations of Expectancies

We now turn to the question of what the infant comes to expect from his or her interactive encounters. We attempt to translate the action-dialogue into language, as if the infant or mother could put the experience into words.

We imagine that the infant may create the following expectancies of their interaction:

"I'm so upset. Don't you see how upset I am? What's wrong? Don't you understand? How can this be happening? Where are you? You are not with me. You look far away. You look like you don't know me. I feel so alone. You don't help me. This is how it is between us when I feel upset."

We imagine that the mother may create the following expectancies of their interaction:

"Why aren't you happy? You should be happy. I need you to be happy. When you are upset like that, I don't know what to do. It is too painful. I can't be controlled by you and your moods. I have to look away. I can't stand it. It's too much for me. I can't help you. This happens all the time. I can't count on you to be happy."

The infant's expectation of matching and being matched in the direction of affective change ordinarily lays the groundwork for feeling known or on the same wavelength (Beebe & Lachmann, 2002; Beebe et al., 2010). In these interactions, this infant expectation is disturbed. Mothers of infants on the way to disorganized (compared with secure) attachment are less likely to follow their infants up into more positive moments, and to follow their infants down into dampened or distressed moments. It is difficult for infants to feel that their mothers sense and acknowledge their distress. We infer that infants instead come to expect that they cannot count on their mothers to empathically share their distress.

Relevant Research

Infants at four months who are on the way to disorganized attachment at twelve months show more facial and vocal distress than infants on the way to secure attachment (Beebe et al., 2010). Most mothers intuitively empathize with their infants' distress states, sometimes only for a fraction of a second. Often they are not even aware of it. Mothers might show a sympathetic woe face. Or mothers may vocally join the infant's rhythm of whimpers or protest. We gave an example of a brief but striking moment of maternal empathic joining of her infant's distress in Chapter 5, Frame 6.

Disturbances of Maternal Facial Empathy

Unusual maternal responses to infant distress constitute difficulties in maternal facial empathy. Examples of these unusual maternal responses are maternal positive, surprise, or ignore expressions in response to infant expressions of anger, sadness, or pain (Malatesta et al., 1989). In this study, these unusual maternal responses to infant distress predicted a toddler affective style of attempting to dampen negative affect, through compressed lips, frowning, or sadness. Although we did not follow our infants past the age of one year, we conjecture that the disorganized attachment infants in our study may have developed a similar preoccupation with attempts to manage negative affect as toddlers.

Dyadic Affective Conflict: Maternal Smile/Surprise to Infant Distress

In our own research, mothers of infants on the way to disorganized attachment, compared with mothers of infants on the way to secure attachment, were more likely to show smiles or surprise faces during infant distress moments (Beebe et al., 2010). We construe this as the mother's emotional denial of infant distress. It may be a maternal effort to shift the infant's distress to a positive state, but without first acknowledging that the infant is in distress. Metaphorically, it is as if mothers are attempting to ride negative into positive, that is, to join the intensity of the infant's affect, but shift it from negative to positive. Thus, mothers of future disorganized infants oppose or counter infant distress, literally going in the opposite affective direction, generating dyadic affective conflict. Such moments were illustrated in this dyad especially in Frames 5–7.

Dyadic Conflict: Attention Dysregulation

A second form of dyadic conflict was documented in the research finding that, despite greater facial/vocal distress in future disorganized attachment infants, their mothers were more likely to look away from the infant's face, compared with mothers of future secure infants (Beebe et al., 2010). Such a moment was illustrated in this dyad in Frame 2. Maternal looking away may lead to infant feelings of being too visually separate from their mothers, of not being seen, and of being confused about mother's visual presence and availability. Moreover, these mothers of future disorganized attachment infants were less predictable in their patterns of looking at and away from the infant's face. Maternal excessive looking away, in a less predictable fashion, disturbs the visual frame of the face-to-face encounter: A background sense of structure that mothers usually provide. Thus, the infant's ability to rely on a predictable maternal pattern of visual attention is compromised.

In discussing the findings of our research on the origins of disorganized attachment (Beebe et al., 2010), we noted that extensive and unpredictable maternal looking away may reflect maternal discomfort with intimate engagement through mutual gaze (Karlen Lyons-Ruth, personal communication, January 12, 2007), or it may reflect moments of maternal dissociation (George Downing, personal communication, April 18, 2007). If the mother does look at her infant in distress, there may be a greater likelihood that similar levels of distress will be activated in her. Looking away may reflect a maternal attempt to downregulate arousal (Jude Cassidy, personal communication, October 23, 2006). Hodges and Wegner (1997) propose that individuals who become overwhelmed with the emotion of another can protect themselves from automatic forms of empathy with forms of exposure control, such as looking away (see also Peck, 2003).

Blocking Facial Mimicry Disturbs Emotional Understanding

Another way of protecting oneself from the emotion of the other is termed "blocking mimicry." As we noted in Chapter 3, during social interactions, usually out of awareness, people tend to roughly match or mimic the behavior of others, such as gestures, body postures, and facial expressions (Chartrand & Bargh, 1999; Dimberg et al., 2000; Kendon, 1970). Sometimes this matching process between two partners is so rapid that it is not visible. For example, facial matching (correspondences) may occur within one half a second (Beebe, 1982; Niedenthal et al., 2010). Thus, observing an action in the partner often elicits the performance of that action in the individual.

When an individual matches the behavior of the partner, it can be seen as an internal simulation of the perceived expression (gesture, posture) of the partner, which then facilitates an understanding of its meaning. Observing the partner's action, matching the partner's action, and understanding the partner's action all share the same neural substrates, including the brain's reward, motor, somatosensory, and affective systems (Niedenthal et al., 2010; Oberman et al., 2007). Compared with passive perception of a facial expression, matching the partner's expression is accompanied by greater activation in brain regions related to emotion processing.

Reciprocally, blocking this matching process impairs recognition of facial expressions (Oberman et al., 2007). Oberman et al. (2007) blocked the capacity for facial matching by asking the subjects to bite on a pen, which blocked the facial muscles associated with facial expression. Subjects were then asked to identify various emotional facial expressions. Those subjects who had been asked to bite on a pen were impaired in their verbal recognition of happy (but not sad) faces. Oberman and colleagues suggested that their findings were consistent with the proposal that people's ability to understand emotions in others involves simulating the other's emotional states. This study documents that the blocking led to an impairment in conscious verbalized recognition of emotions.

Hennelenlotter and colleagues (2008) used a different method to block facial matching, a Botox injection, which led to an impairment in nonconscious activation of emotions. In this experiment, the Botox injection produced a temporary paralysis of frown muscles, blocking facial matching of forehead expressions. Subjects were then shown sad and angry facial expressions while undergoing functional magnetic resonance imaging. For individuals with the reduced facial feedback from Botox, during imitation of angry (but not sad) expressions, the activation of the limbic system was reduced, compared with control individuals without the Botox injection. The authors concluded that peripheral feedback from facial muscles and skin during matching of facial expressions modulates the neural activity known to be involved in processing of emotional states. This is a potential physiological basis for the transfer of emotions during face-to-face social interactions. This study documents that Botox led to an impairment in the nonconscious bodily activation of emotion. Niedenthal et al. (2010) commented on this study, noting that by blocking the muscle pattern associated with anger, part of the embodied (nonconscious) meaning of the anger was lost, so that the emotion was experienced less intensely.

These studies help us understand why mothers of infants on the way to disorganized attachment may, out of awareness, dampen their own facial reactivity to their infants' facial expressions of distress, or at times even become facially blank, facially unresponsive. By doing so, mothers may experience their infants' emotional distress less intensely. They may even be less able to process the embodied (nonconscious) meanings of their infants' facial expressions of distress.

Trauma May Disrupt Maternal Brain Response to Infant Distress

Maternal unresolved trauma may also undermine the mother's optimal brain response to her infant's distress. First-time mothers underwent functional magnetic resonance imaging as they viewed happy-face and sad-face images of their own infants (Kim, Fonagy, Allen, & Strathearn, 2014). They also viewed happy-face and sad-face images of a matched unknown infant. Mothers with no trauma history, compared with mothers with trauma, demonstrated greater brain (amygdala) responses to the sad faces, compared with the happy faces, of their own infants. The amygdala is involved in processing information related to attachment (Davis & Whalen, 2001; Riem et al., 2012). It is part of the limbic system, and it is connected with other brain regions that are involved in processing emotional information (Riem et al., 2012). As one of its functions, it is involved in the detection of threat and the experience of fear and aversion.

Mothers with unresolved trauma in the AAI (coded with the Dynamic Maturational Model, Crittenden & Landini, 2011) displayed blunted amygdala responses to their own infants' sad, as compared with happy, faces. Mothers with and without a trauma history did not differ in their amygdala responses to the happy and sad faces of the unknown infants. The blunting of the amygdala response in mothers with unresolved trauma may be a neural indication of mothers' possible disengagement from infant distress. This neural process may be one link between maternal unresolved trauma and disruptions in maternal ability to respond optimally to infant distress (Kim et al., 2014). This study by Kim and colleagues is consistent with the studies by Oberman et al. (2007) and Hennelenlotter et al. (2008) described above. Kim and colleagues bring the research directly into traumatized mothers and their infants, and the mothers' difficulty in responding to their own infants' distress, as measured by amygdala activation.

Oberman and Hennelenlotter offer a behavioral means by which mothers may disturb their responses to their infants' distress, that is, by blocking behavioral matching of the infants' expressions of distress (by biting on a pen, or by a Botox injection). In the Hennelenlotter study, blocking behavioral matching was also associated with altered brain activation in response to emotional expressions. In this set of drawings (Chapter 10), we saw several examples of this mother's difficulties in responding to her infant's distress that fit the research of Kim, Oberman, and Hennelenlotter and colleagues, namely Frames 3, 4, and 10.

Although the studies by Hennelenlotter, Kim, and colleagues, above, document patterns of dampened amygdala activation, other research has shown activated patterns of amygdala activity in response to infant distress in individuals with an insecure attachment history. For example, in one study, when undergoing functional magnetic resonance imaging, adults with an insecure attachment history showed heightened amygdala activation when exposed to sounds of an infant crying, compared with individuals with a secure attachment history. In addition, insecure (compared with secure) individuals reported more irritation when exposed to sounds of an infant crying (Riem et al., 2012). Heightened amygdala activation is considered an index of hyperemotionality. It has been observed in depression, anxiety, intrusive mothers, and during exposure to infant crying (Atzil, Hendler, & Feldman, 2011; Rauch et al., 2000; Riem et al., 2012; Yang et al., 2010).

Other research has suggested that there may be two types of individuals, those who become more activated, or hyperaroused in the face of distressing stimuli; and those who become numb, or hypoaroused, a dissociative type. These two types were identified in individuals with Post Traumatic Stress Disorder (Lanius et al., 2010). Or there may also be a two-stage process in some vulnerable individuals, in which the first stage may be overarousal, associated with being emotionally overwhelmed; and the second stage may be a deactivation of arousal, a numbing, in an attempt to cope with and defend against feeling overwhelmed. As Lanius et al. (2010) note, both types of modulation are involved in a dynamic interplay.

All of these studies address disturbances in the adult's ability to acknowledge and empathize with the infant's distress. Such disturbances are a central feature of the origins of disorganized attachment. To have one's distress recognized and empathized with is a fundamental human need at all ages. The developmental trauma of nonrecognition is a central issue in psychoanalytic approaches to the treatment of adult psychopathology (Benjamin, 1995; Bromberg, 2011). But mothers of future disorganized infants also have profoundly confusing, disturbing experiences of their infants. They do not obtain from their infants the recognition they need, that is, the happy, smiling, welcoming infant.

CHAPTER 11

Maternal Difficulty Tolerating Infant Distress in the Origins of Insecure-Disorganized Infant Attachment

DRAWINGS: MATERNAL DIFFICULTY TOLERATING INFANT DISTRESS

This sequence depicts a mother and infant at four months where the infant was classified as insecure-disorganized attachment at one year (Beebe et al., 2010).

This sequence of drawings depicts nine frames, over seven seconds. As they begin, the infant has been fussing for a while. The mother has difficulty tolerating the infant's distress. Eventually, she displays a threatening face. However, at the end, she becomes sad, and the infant seems shut down.

11.1 MINUTE:SECOND 22:04–22:06A

Storyline: Across these three seconds, the infant is upset but increasingly orients to his mother. The mother leans in and then seems surprised.

Frame 1. Minute:Second 22:04
We begin with the infant whimpering (on the video). His eyes are closed, and he is partially turned away from his mother. He is upset with a frown. He is holding the diaper at his mouth with both hands. The mother is looking at her infant with a tense smile, clenching her teeth. She seems helpless, possibly annoyed or anxious.

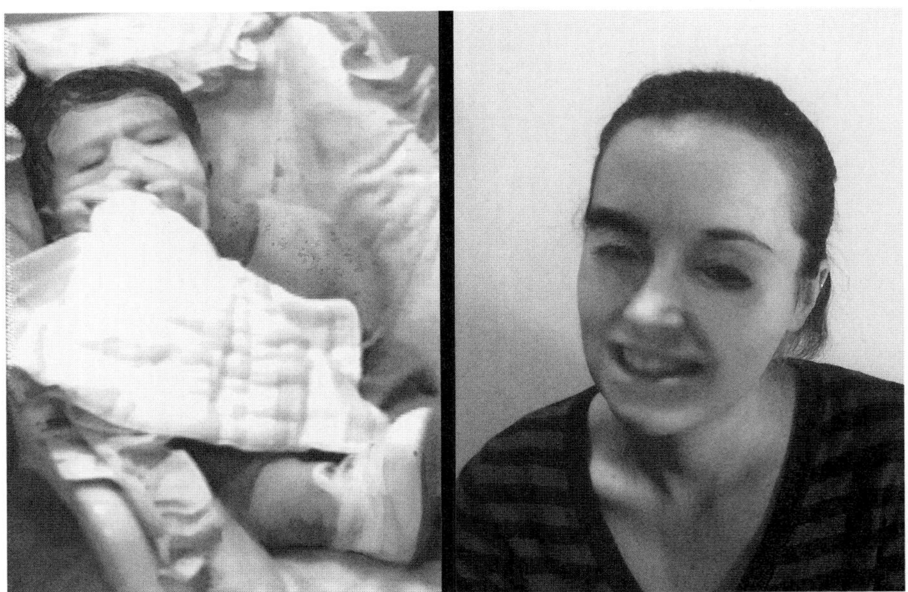

Frame 2. Minute:Second 22:05
From Frame 1 to 2, one second later, the mother begins to lean in, a partial loom (her hair begins to be visible in the infant's frame). She has a partially open mouth. The infant remains distressed. He has oriented slightly toward his mother, with his eyes still closed, still holding the diaper with both hands. He continues to whimper (in the video).

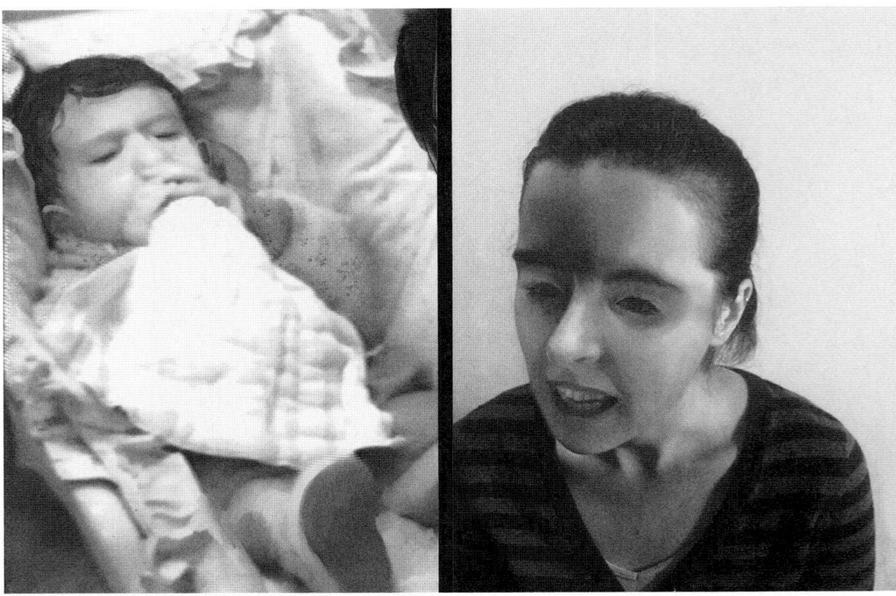

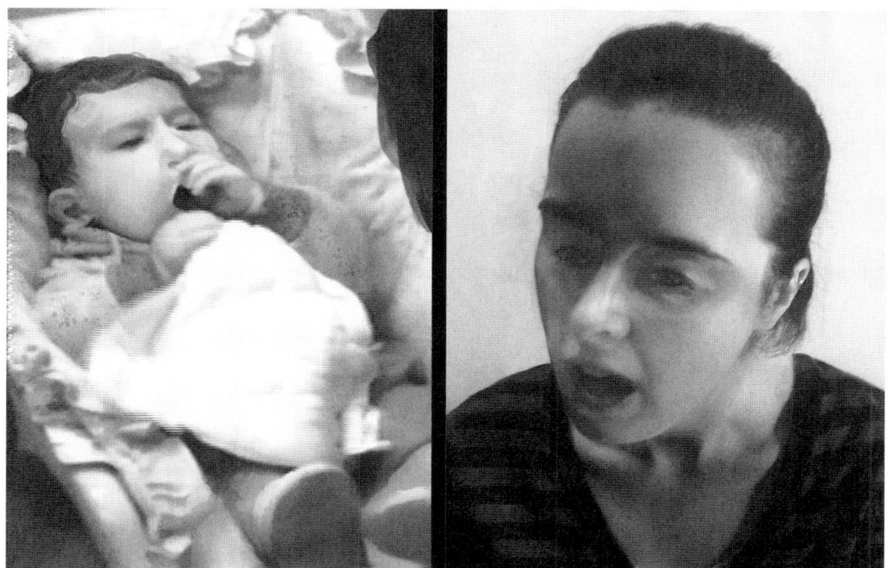

Frame 3. Minute:Second 22:06a

From Frame 2 to 3, a split second later, the infant has reoriented to his mother, fully vis-à-vis. He begins to look at his mother with his eyes half open, continuing to whimper (in the video). He has lowered the diaper with his right hand, while putting his left thumb in his mouth. The mother looks at her infant with a more open mouth, as if partially surprised, as she moves in closer. She might be feeling, "Oh, why is this happening? What am I going to do?"

11.2 MINUTE:SECOND 22:04–22:06A

Storyline: Across these two seconds, the infant remains upset. The mother clenches her teeth and then shows an angry bared-teeth bite face. We see the infant react with increased distress.

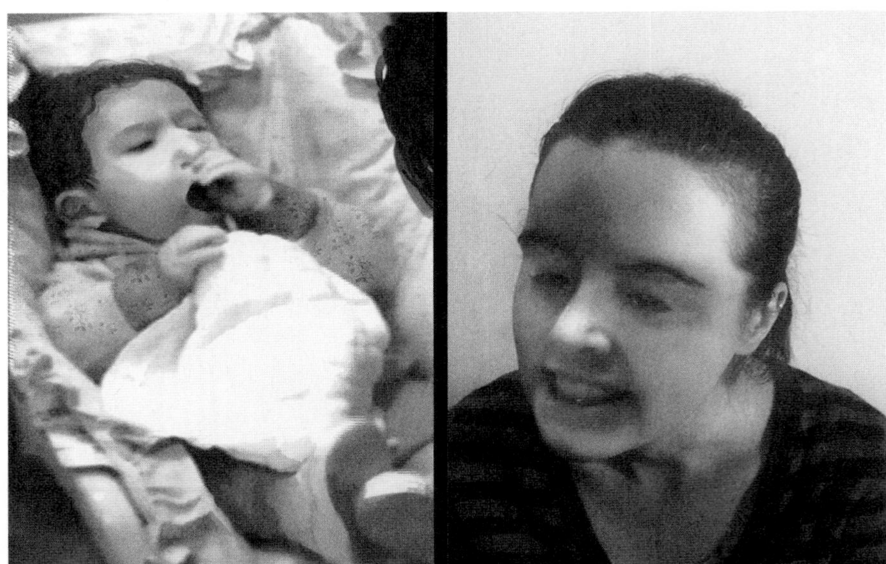

Frame 4. Minute:Second 22:06b
From Frame 3 to 4, again a split-second shift within the same second, the mother closes her mouth partially, clenches her jaw and grits her teeth. She seems angry. As the mother changes her expression, the infant moves his head slightly to his left, opens his mouth more, and moves his right hand slightly down on the diaper revealing a fully open mouth. Both his feet thrust abruptly forward. In addition to the infant's mouth opening, these infant hand and foot movements are other ways we know that the infant processes the change in the mother's expression.

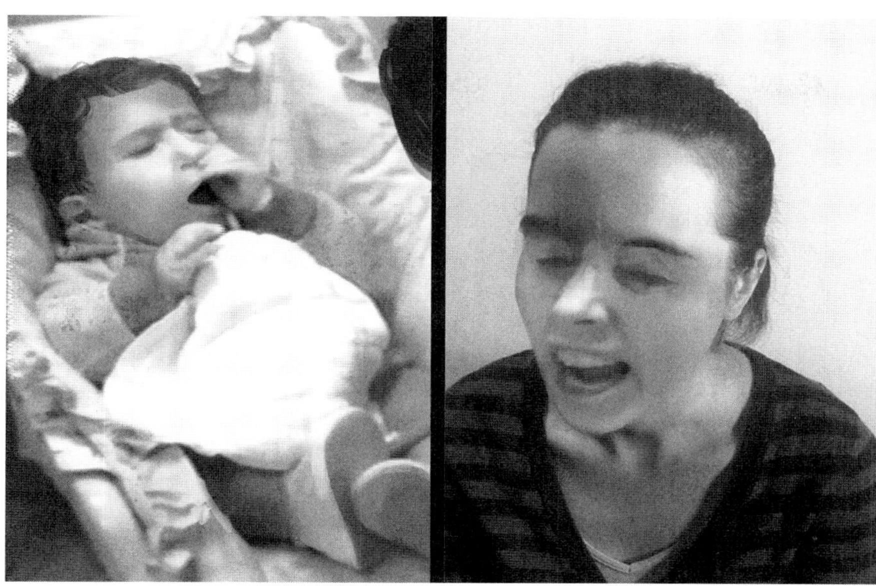

Frame 5. Minute:Second 22:06c
From Frame 4 to 5, again a split-second shift within the same second, the mother shifts into an angry, bared-teeth bite face. The infant's eyes are almost closed. Both mother and infant synchronize their slight head movements upward. The infant keeps his thumb in his mouth.

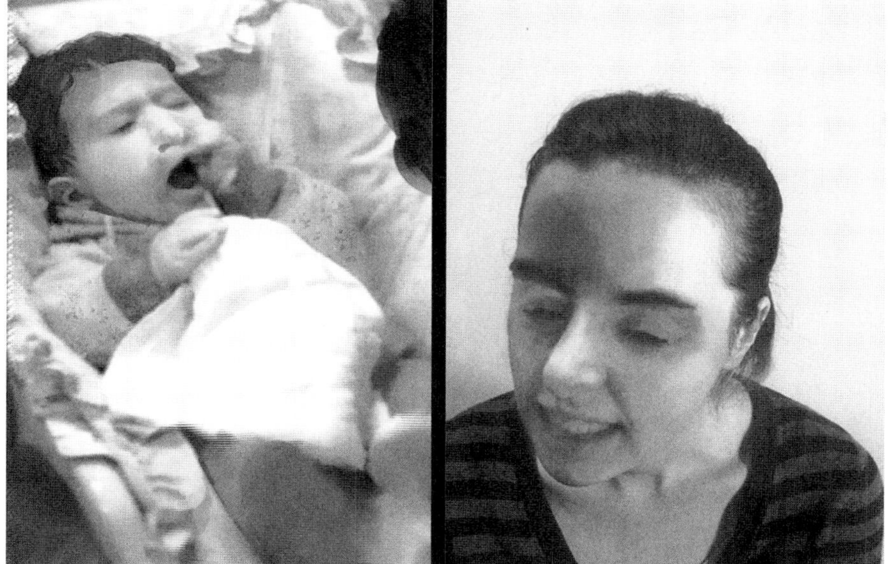

Frame 6. Minute:Second 22:07a
From Frame 5 to 6, in the first half of the next second, the mother closes her mouth partially and resumes the expression of Frame 4, with a clenched jaw. Her head lowers and moves in slightly. The infant opens his mouth more, and his distress deepens, visible in his brows, and his feet kick wildly. His head shifts slightly away from his mother, to his right.

11.3 MINUTE:SECOND 22:07–22:10

Storyline: As the infant begins to dampen down his intense distress, the mother shifts from a perplexed look to a sadness that seems detached and helpless. It is as if the threatening face never happened.

Frame 7. Minute:Second 22:07b
From Frame 6 to 7, within the same second, the mother's expression shifts dramatically. Her mouth has changed into a slightly open, more neutral pose. There is no longer anything threatening in her face. Instead she looks at her infant curiously as if she does not know him. She seems perplexed. It is as if the threatening face never happened. The infant remains extremely upset. His furrowed brow has deepened. He has let go of the diaper, and both of his hands move into his mouth, as his right foot kicks. His behavior seems to indicate that he still senses potential threat.

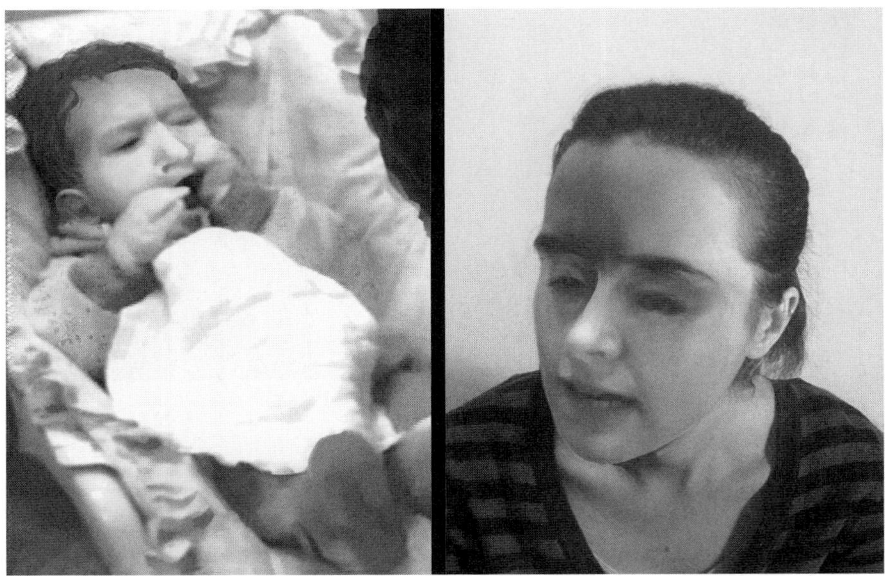

Frame 8. Minute:Second 22:09
From Frame 7 to 8, about one and a half seconds later, the mother's expression has softened. She has a slightly open mouth, the corners droop down, and her face has gone slack: a loss of facial tonus in the cheeks. There is a hint of sadness, perhaps helplessness. But she seems far away. Her head moves back slightly. Her eyebrows go up in a look of surprise, as if to say, "What is it, what is happening?" It is as if the threatening face she displayed two seconds ago never happened. However, the infant is still extremely distressed. He shows a cry face (with an angry protest vocalization in the video). His head moves away from his mother, slightly to his right, with his eyes closed. Both hands move down, and he takes his left thumb out of his mouth; his feet continue to flail.

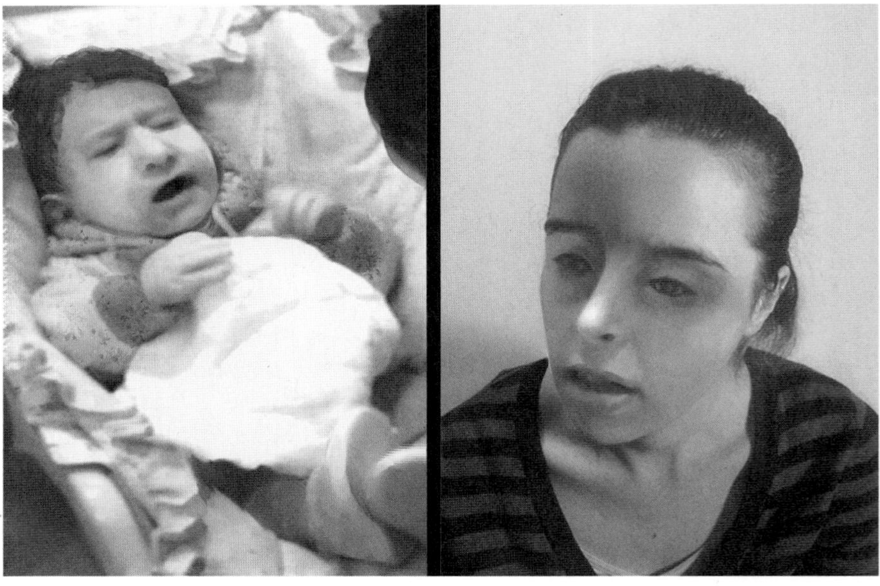

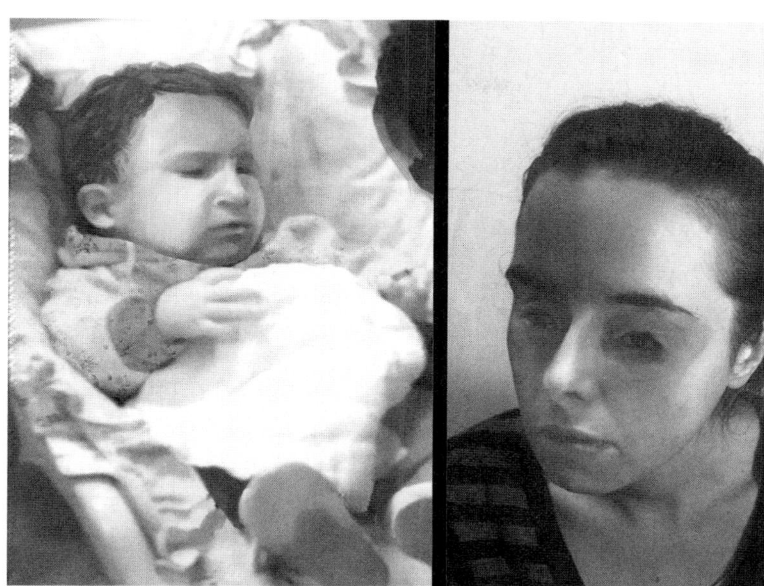

Frame 9. Minute:Second 22:10
From Frame 8 to 9, in the next second, the infant returns his head to the center vis-à-vis, and looks down, with his eyes almost closed. His eyebrow furrow has softened, and his forehead is calmer. But he looks sad. He continues to have a hint of a frown. His right hand rests lightly on the diaper. His right foot moves. He seems emotionally withdrawn and shut down. The mother closes her mouth, and the hint of sadness in the previous frame is now visible. There is a further loss of tonus in her cheeks and a further drooping of the corners of her mouth. She has a far-away, vacant look. She seems to know that something is wrong. But she also seems detached, absent. She may feel helpless. She may feel she needs to shut down.

COMMENTARY ON MATERNAL DIFFICULTY TOLERATING INFANT DISTRESS

We chose this sequence because it vividly illustrates maternal difficulty tolerating infant distress. Portions of the following descriptions are adapted from Beebe et al. (2010) and Beebe and Lachmann (2013).

Comment on Mother and Infant

Prior to the seven seconds, which are illustrated in these drawings, the infant has been fussing and whimpering. As we enter this sequence, in Frame 1 the infant is turned away from his mother, holding a diaper partially over his face, and he is upset. The mother has a tense smile with clenched teeth. In the next second, by Frame 4, as the infant continues to be upset, the mother clenches her jaw and grits her teeth. This clenched-jaw expression shifts into an angry, bared-teeth, bite face within the same second, Frame 5. This is a threatening face. The infant responds within a fraction of a second with deepening distress and by kicking his feet wildly.

But within the next second, Frame 7, the mother's expression shifts dramatically into an interest expression, with a curious look, as if she does not know her infant. The infant remains extremely upset. About one and a half seconds later, Frame 8, the mother's face droops with a hint of helplessness or sadness, and she seems far away. The sudden loss of facial tonus in the cheeks contributes to the far-away look. The infant is still very upset. In the next and final second, Frame 9, the mother's face shows sadness. She seems to know that something is wrong. Perhaps her sadness indicates regret. But she seems detached and emotionally disconnected. In this last frame, for the first time, the infant returns to the vis-à-vis, fully oriented toward his mother, but his eyes are almost closed. He is not as agitated, but he looks sad, withdrawn, and shut down. His mother cannot seem to help him.

During this sequence, the infant coordinated movements of his own body with the mother's movements, moment-by-moment. For example, examining the infant's movements from Frame 3 to Frame 4, as the mother shifts from an open-mouth face into a clenched jaw with gritted teeth, the infant moves his feet and his right hand, and he moves his head up slightly toward his mother, synchronized with the mother's jaw clenching movement. As the mother shifts from Frame 4 to Frame 5, into the bared-teeth bite-face expression, the infant's feet move, his right hand shifts, and the thumb of his left hand, which is in his mouth, moves upward as his mouth slightly closes. These tiny infant movements of coordination with the mother's movements indicate that the infant is processing her movements. The synchronized movements of coordination are hard to detect in the drawings, but it can be done by moving the eye back and forth from one drawing to the next to detect the changes. However, these movements of coordination are most easily detected by examining the original film frame-by-frame.

As we noted in the previous set of drawings (Chapter 10), mothers certainly perceive distress in their infants. We wonder whether this mother perceived her infant's distress as angry.

As we noted in the research described above in the "Introduction to the Drawings Illustrating the Origins of Insecure-Disorganized Attachment," mothers of disorganized attachment infants are likely to have had a disorganized attachment themselves as infants (Raby et al., 2015). We infer that this mother is experiencing some kind of heightened affect, such as fear, lack of safety, anger, or helplessness while her infant is distressed. She threatens her infant with her bared-teeth, bite face. But perhaps the infant's distress threatens her.

Perhaps her infant's distress triggered her own unresolved traumatic issues from her childhood. As in the previous set of drawings, we suggest that this mother becomes emotionally disconnected by the end of the sequence to protect herself. When she is in this state, she cannot comfort her infant.

Illustrations of Expectancies

We now turn to the question of what the infant comes to expect from his or her interactive encounters. We attempt to translate the action-dialogue into language, as if the infant or mother could put the experience into words.

We imagine that the infant may experience the interaction in the following ways:

"I'm upset. I'm trying to comfort myself with my diaper. You don't seem to understand. Where are you? What's wrong? Uh-oh, you are getting angry at me. Don't you see how upset I am? Oh no, now you are really angry! Don't you understand? I feel afraid of you when you have that face. Oh no! How can this be happening! I am terrified! Oh, now I see you're calming down. But you are still not there for me. You look far away. You look like you don't know me. I feel so alone. I feel so upset."

We imagine that the infant may create the following procedural, action-sequence expectancies of their interaction:

"When I am upset, I know I will feel so alone and frantic. I won't be able to get help from you when I need it. Instead you will be angry at me. It makes me feel so terrible. You will be mad or far away. You won't be with me. You won't comfort me. What can I do?"

We imagine that the mother may create the following procedural expectancies of their interaction, out of awareness:

"When you fuss like that, I don't like it. You sound angry. Just like my (mother/father). It's not nice! Why aren't you happy? You should be happy! I need you to be happy. When you get upset, it upsets me. It scares me. Stop it! When you look sad, I feel sad too. But it's too much for me. I can't help you. I can't count on you to be happy. Your upset threatens me."

This interaction again illustrates how difficult it is for infants on the way to disorganized attachment to feel that their mothers sense and acknowledge their distress. We infer that infants instead come to expect that they cannot count on their mothers to empathically share their distress.

This interaction also illustrates how difficult it is for mothers of disorganized attachment infants to find a way to respond to the infant's distress. It illustrates the concept that the mother's own unresolved distress, like an open wound, may be triggered by the infant's distress. This mother seems to have perceived her infant's distress as angry, and she became angry in return. However, this mother also expressed sadness at the end of the interaction. This sadness suggests that the mother was aware in some way that the infant was struggling, that she was able to notice the infant's distress.

Relevant Research

Disturbances in attachment may persist across generations (Fonagy et al., 1991; Kovan et al., 2009; Steele et al., 1996). For example, mothers with histories of attachment disorganization themselves, when they were children, are more likely to have infants who form a disorganized attachment (Raby et al., 2015). Thus, the mothers in our study (Beebe et al., 2010) who have infants at four months who are on the way to disorganized attachment are likely to have had a disorganized attachment history themselves.

In the attachment assessment at one year, research has shown that mothers of disorganized attachment infants are more likely to display frightened or frightening facial expressions, vocalizations, or gestures than mothers of secure infants (Hesse & Main, 2006). The frightening expression that we see on this mother's face is consistent with that literature.

Schechter and colleagues (2015) argue that routine displays of negative affect and helpless states in infants and young children can act as triggers of maternal posttraumatic stress disorder (PTSD). They studied traumatized mothers who had been involved in domestic violence. These mothers had themselves generally been involved in a persistently threatening environment. Maternal PTSD is associated with parenting stress and less sensitive maternal behavior. Mothers with PTSD tend to be less responsive to their children's social bids for attention (Cohen, Hien, & Batchelder, 2008; Schechter et al., 2010).

To investigate the proposal that routine displays of negative affect and helpless states in infants and young children can act as triggers of maternal PTSD in traumatized mothers, Schechter and colleagues used functional neuroimaging. The mothers had been involved in domestic violence. Mothers viewed videotapes of their own and unfamiliar toddlers during a stressful condition in which the child was upset while separated from the mother. This stressful condition was compared with a nonstressful play condition. The findings were consistent with the hypothesis that maternal dysregulation in response to seeing their young child's upset as a potential threat is mirrored in the brain activation patterns of the mothers. Examining mothers responding to seeing video clips of their children upset during separation (compared with the nonstressful play condition), two studies in different samples showed decreased neural activation of maternal brain regions that are important for emotion regulation and social cognition (i.e., the dorsal and ventral medial prefrontal cortex). The findings also showed increased neural activation of limbic regions that are associated with the maintenance of traumatic memory traces (anterior entorrhinal cortex and parahippocampal areas; Schechter et al., 2012; Schechter et al., 2015).

This research helps to explain why a mother of an infant on the way to disorganized attachment might show a threatening face. Based on the work of Raby et al. (2015), the mother likely has a disorganized attachment history of her own. Based on the work of Schechter and colleagues, the mother is likely to have been exposed in her childhood to fearful and threatening experiences. When her infant becomes upset, it is likely to trigger her own threatened, fearful, angry, and helpless states. We suggest that she is likely to feel threatened by her infant's distress. She may then threaten her infant in return. Moreover, based on Schechter and colleagues, her brain mirrors this state, with decreased emotion regulation, decreased social cognition, and increased activation of traumatic memory traces, when viewing her upset infant.

On a hopeful note, Raby et al. (2015) showed that when mothers who had a disorganized attachment history themselves were able to receive better social support, their infants were more likely to become securely attached. There are many forms of support available to mothers and infants (see for example Beebe et al., 2012; Cohen & Beebe, 2002; Downing, 2004; Lieberman, Ghosh Ippen, & Van Horn, 2006; Murphy et al., 2015; Powell, Cooper, Hoffman, & Marvin, 2013; Steele et al., 2014; Stern, 1995; Van den Boom, 1995).

CHAPTER 12

Infant Distress and Maternal Surprise, Anger, Disgust, and Emotional Disconnection in the Origins of Insecure-Disorganized Infant Attachment

DRAWINGS: INFANT DISTRESS AND MATERNAL SURPRISE, ANGER, DISGUST, AND EMOTIONAL DISCONNECTION

This sequence depicts a mother and infant at four months where the infant was classified as insecure-disorganized attachment at one year (Beebe et al., 2010).

This sequence of drawings presents 20 frames, over 48 seconds. As we begin, the infant is upset. The mother tries to engage her infant, but she seems unable to connect with her infant or empathize with her distress. The infant gradually shifts into looking fearful and then becomes extremely distressed. The mother's face shows expressions of mock surprise, anger, and finally disgust in response to the infant's distress. Intermittently, she touches her infant's hand. Eventually, the mother seems to withdraw emotionally from her infant.

12.1 MINUTE:SECOND 34:23–34:27

Storyline: The infant is upset. Her mother responds first with a worried face, then with a mock surprise face, as the infant becomes more distressed. Then, the mother smiles as her infant turns away and closes her eyes, covering her face (Frame 3).

Frame 1. Minute:Second 34:23
The mother and infant are both looking at each other's face. The infant is becoming distressed, frowning with her mouth partially open and her arms tensed. The mother has a slightly drooped mouth. She seems not to know how to respond to her infant's distress. She seems distant. The mother's right hand touches the infant's hand.

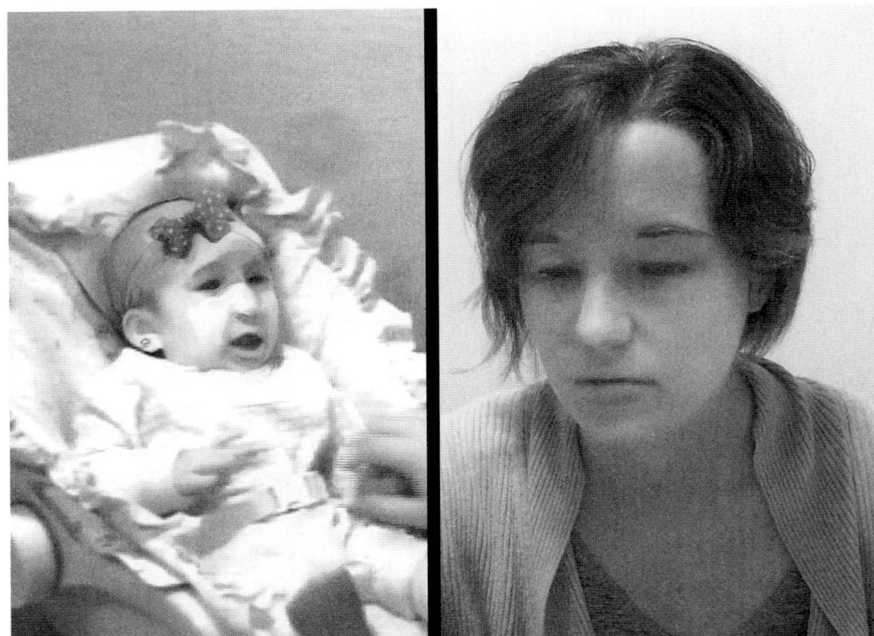

Frame 2. Minute:Second 34:24
From Frame 1 to 2, one second later, the infant's facial distress and frown increase. (From the video, we know the infant vocalizes with an angry protest.) The mother responds with a mock surprise face, with raised eyebrows, showing the whites of her eyes. This face does not seem to match the infant's distress. She keeps her hand on her infant's hand.

Frame 3. Minute:Second 34:27
From Frame 2 to 3, three seconds later, the infant has dramatically turned away, closed her eyes, and covered her face with her hand. It is as if the infant visually protects herself from viewing the mother's face that is so discrepant with the infant's own state. The mother has a big open-mouth smile that is completely at odds with the infant's distress. The infant's fingers and the mother's hand are still in contact.

Examining the video frame-by-frame to identify the exact sequence from Frame 2 to 3, first the mother displayed the mock surprise face (shown in Frame 2). Then, the infant began to turn away and cover her face (Frame 3). We infer that the infant found the mock surprise face too discrepant or too upsetting.

12.2. MINUTE:SECOND 34:29–34:30

Storyline: The infant continues to be distressed; the mother seems closed-up, then surprised.

Frame 4. Minute:Second 34:29
From Frame 3 to 4, two seconds later, the infant continues to close her eyes and cover her face, as if she is attempting to regulate or regroup. Following the large open-mouth smile in the previous frame that was so discrepant with the infant's state, the mother sobers, and her face darkens. Although we cannot see clearly, it seems that the infant's left hand is still in the same position as the previous frame, and likely still touching mother's hand.

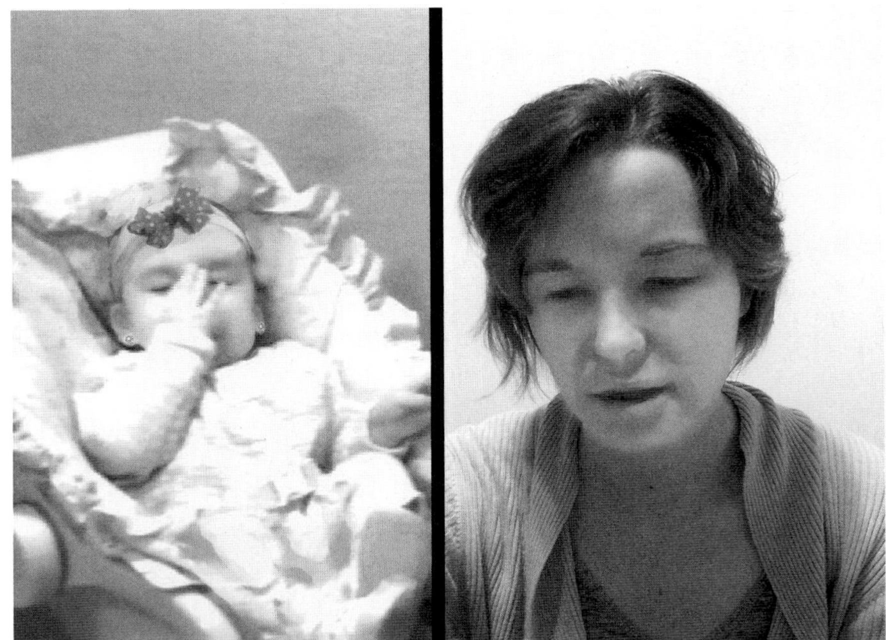

Frame 5. Minute:Second 34:30a
From Frame 4 to 5, a half a second later, the infant turns back to her mother and peeks out, while still covering her face with her right hand. The infant remains distressed, with a frown. The mother disconnects and seems emotionally absent. Her mouth sets, narrowed. Her eyes seem vacant, glazed, as if she is barely seeing her infant. She does not seem to register that the infant is peeking out. Nor does she respond to her infant's distress. Perhaps the mother feels discouraged. She seems to look at her infant from far away. The infant's left hand and the mother's hand are still in contact.

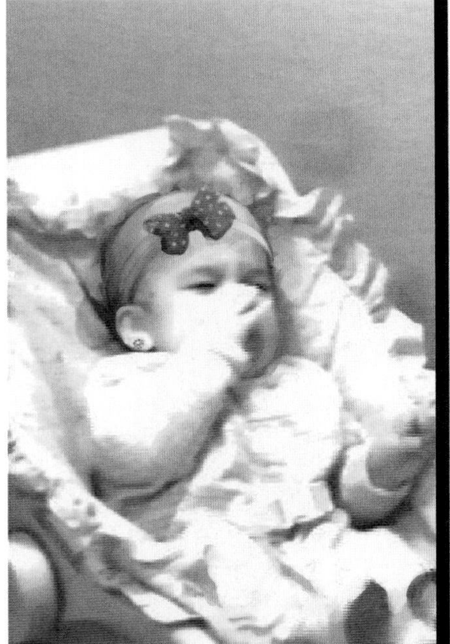

Frame 6. Minute:Second 34:30b

From Frame 5 to 6, within the same second, the infant looks directly at her mother with a cry face and a frown and puts her right hand down. The mother's mouth and eyes seem to carry different messages, a mixed signal. The mother has an open-mouth surprise expression with a questioning look as if to say: "Why are you upset?" This surprise expression is discrepant with the infant's distress. But the mother's eyes and eyebrows do not participate in the surprise expression. She moves toward the infant slightly. Although it is hard to see clearly, it looks like the infant has put her hand down and is no longer touching her mother's hand.

12.3 TEN SECONDS LATER: MINUTE:SECOND 34:41–34:43

Storyline: The mother puts her finger in her infant's mouth. The infant whimpers. The mother then displays a disgust face, which culminates in a full disgust display with bared teeth.

Frame 7. Minute:Second 34:41
At Frame 7, we reenter the film ten seconds later. The infant is distressed with a frown, looking at her mother. The mother has put her finger in the infant's mouth. The mother has a slight frown and an open mouth; she seems unsure, possibly worried.

(From the video, we can see the infant's feet kicking wildly as the mother puts her finger in the infant's mouth.)

Frame 8. Minute:Second 34:42a
From Frame 7 to 8, a half second later, the infant's distress continues. The infant's eyebrows rise with a frown, and her mouth is more open. The infant's left hand grasps the mother's pinkie. The mother's face shows disgust and possibly anger. She may be disappointed that the infant is not giving her a positive response, and instead is continuing to be distressed. The mother keeps her finger in her infant's mouth.

(On the video, the infant whimpers. Mother says, "Don't be that way." Her words are disapproving, her tone pleading.)

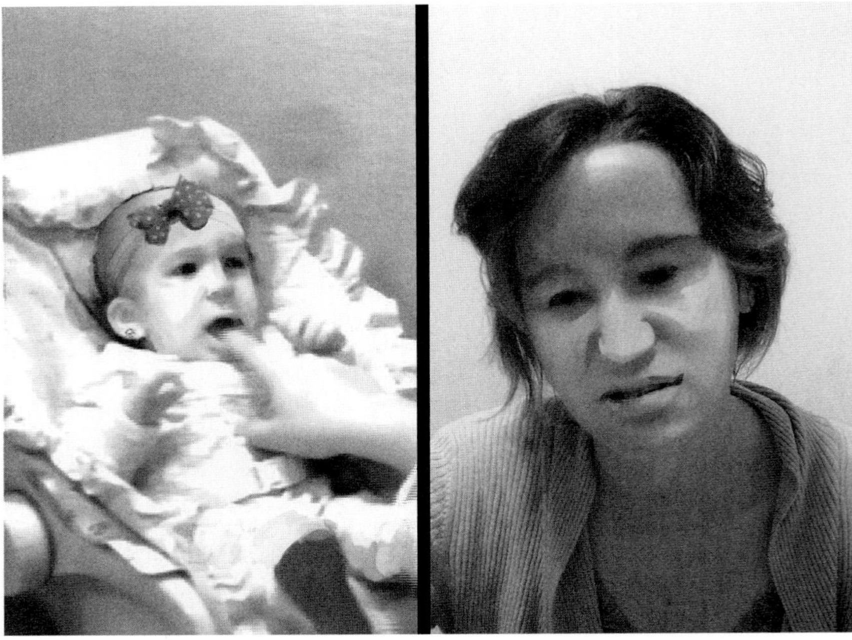

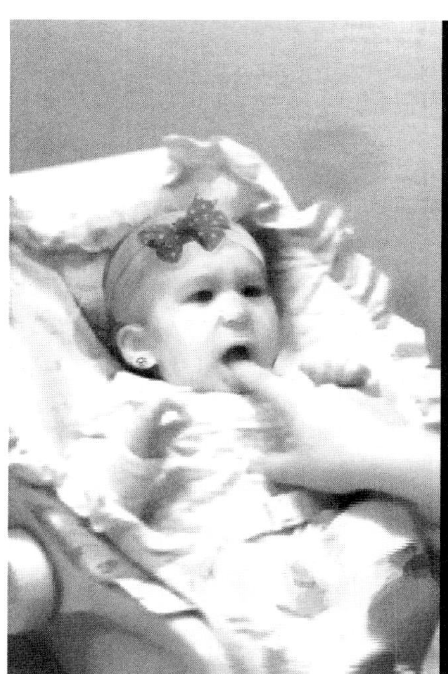
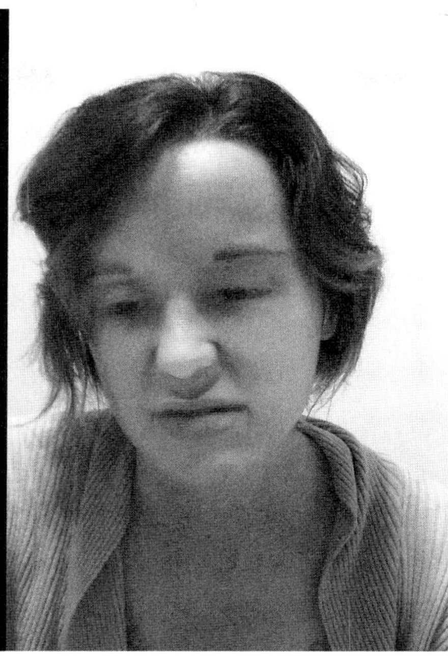

Frame 9. Minute:Second 34:42b
From Frame 8 to 9, a half second later, the infant continues to frown and to be distressed while she looks at her mother. The infant seems alarmed. She continues to hold onto the mother's pinkie. (On the video, the infant continues to whimper.) The mother has a deepening disgust face (seen in the nasolabial fold on the right side of her face). She seems dismayed and sad. She keeps her finger in her infant's mouth.

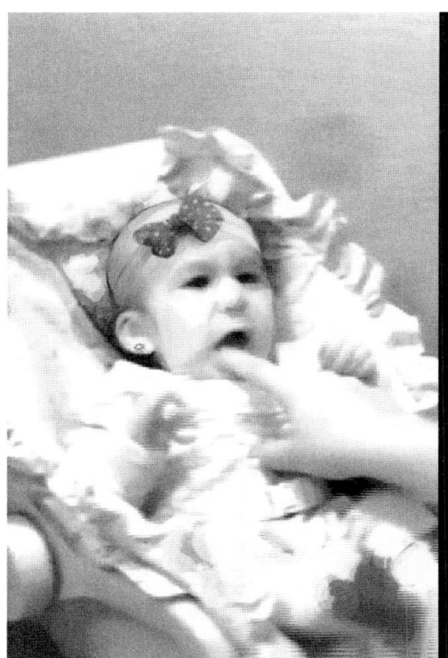
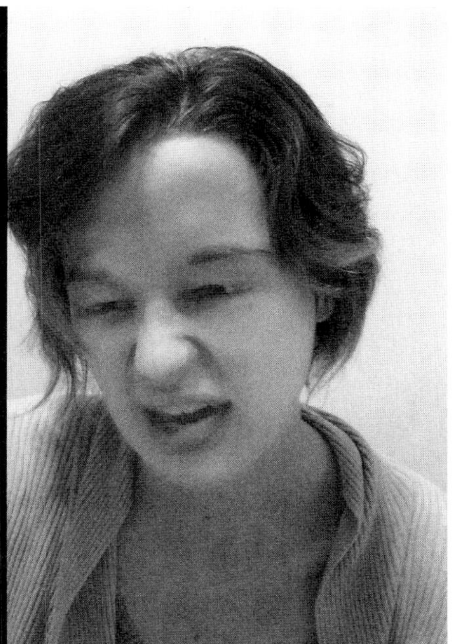

Frame 10. Minute:Second 34:42c
From Frame 9 to 10, still within the same second, the infant is still distressed as she continues to look at her mother. She shows a look of surprise with eyebrows raised. (In the video, she whimpers.) Her hands and feet flail. But she continues to hold onto her mother's pinkie. The mother shows a full-display disgust face and begins to bare her teeth, a potentially threatening face. She keeps her finger in her infant's mouth.

Frame 11. Minute:Second 34:43a
From Frame 10 to 11, a half second later, the mother continues to show a full-display disgust face. She opens her mouth further. The bared teeth display increases, and both the upper and lower teeth are bared. The infant moves her head back and almost closes her eyes. (In the video she continues to whimper.) She now lets go of her mother's pinkie. This frame shows a profound degree of discrepancy between the mother's expression and the infant's expression. The infant closes her eyes to the threat display.

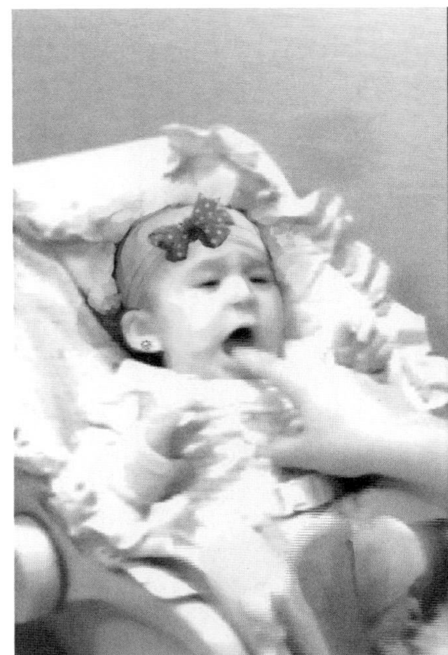
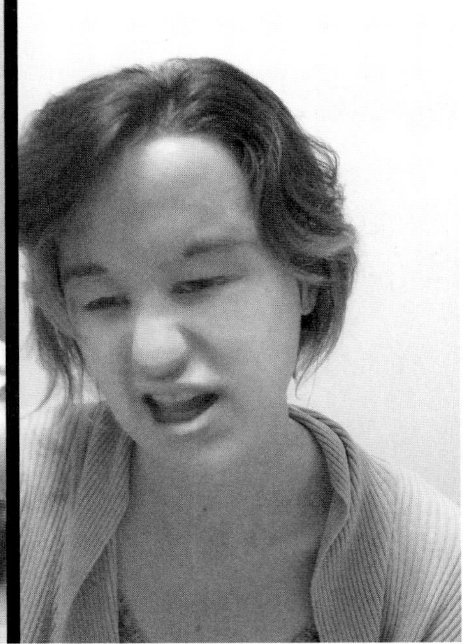

Frame 12. Minute:Second 34:43b
From Frame 11 to 12, within the same second, the infant opens her eyes, looks directly at her mother, and continues to be very upset. Her feet flail. The mother's disgust face begins to soften but is still discrepant with the infant's expression.

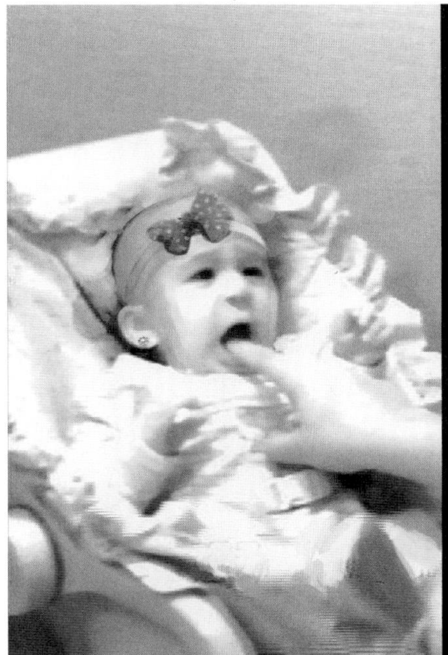
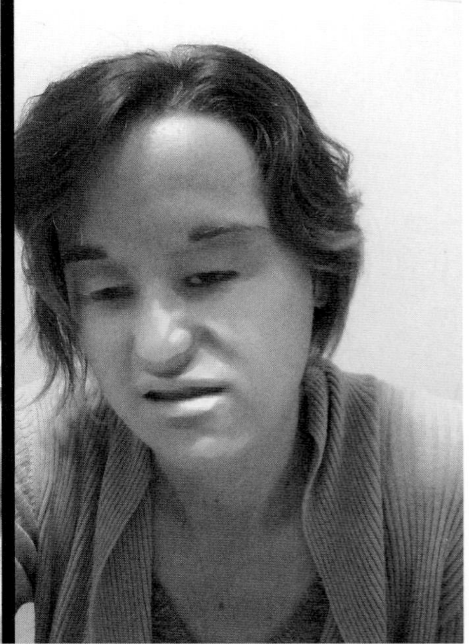

Frame 13. Minute:Second 34:43c
From Frame 12 to 13, within the same second, the infant continues to look intently at her mother, with a frown. Both the mother's mouth and the infant's mouth close; the mother starts to pull her finger out of her infant's mouth. The mother has a closed-up face. She seems distant, emotionally disconnected, possibly resigned. A hint of the disgust is still visible.

12.4 FOURTEEN SECONDS LATER: MINUTE:SECOND 34:57–35:10

Storyline: The infant becomes increasingly upset, lurches away from her mother. The mother has many rapidly changing reactions to her infant's distress: mock surprise, anger, looking away, surprise/shock, and partial sympathetic woe face. In the final Frame 20, the mother withdraws with a closed-up face as the infant breaks into a full cry.

Frame 14. Minute:Second 34:57
We enter 14 seconds later. Both mother and infant look at each other. The infant shows a surprised, fearful, pre-cry face with raised eyebrows and an intense frown. The infant seems alarmed, horrified. The mother has a mock surprise face with raised eyebrows, an expression very discrepant from her infant's distress. The mother keeps her hand on her infant.

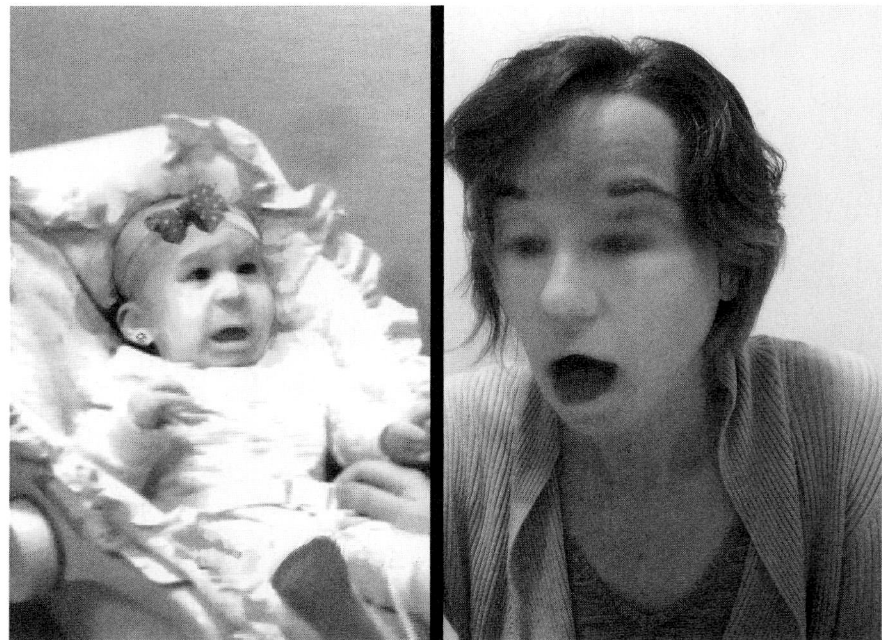

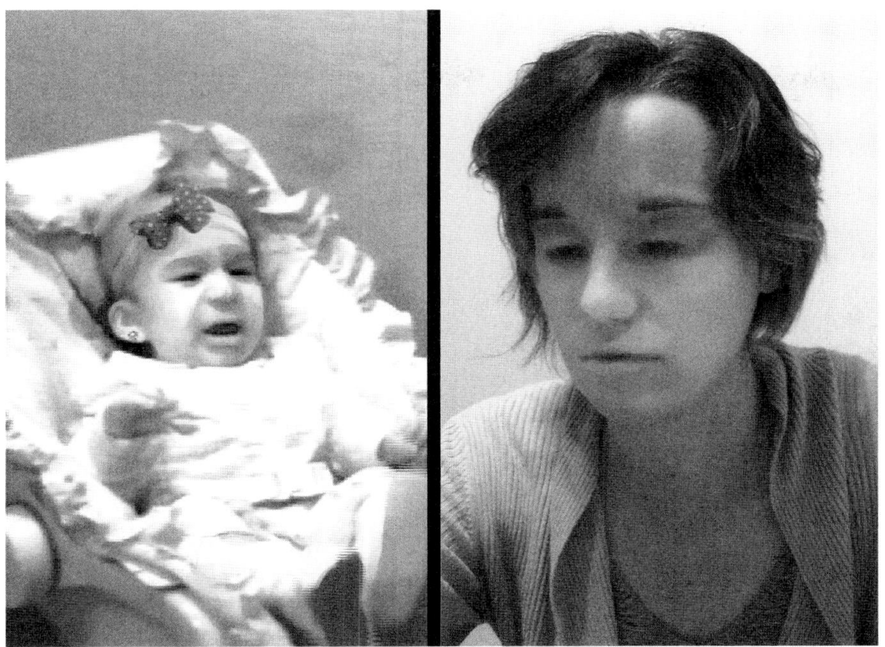

Frame 15. Minute:Second 34:58
From Frame 14 to 15, one second later, the infant continues to frown with a pre-cry face, but she looks down and narrows her eyes. The mother's lips purse in a slight pout. She seems resigned. She has withdrawn her hand.

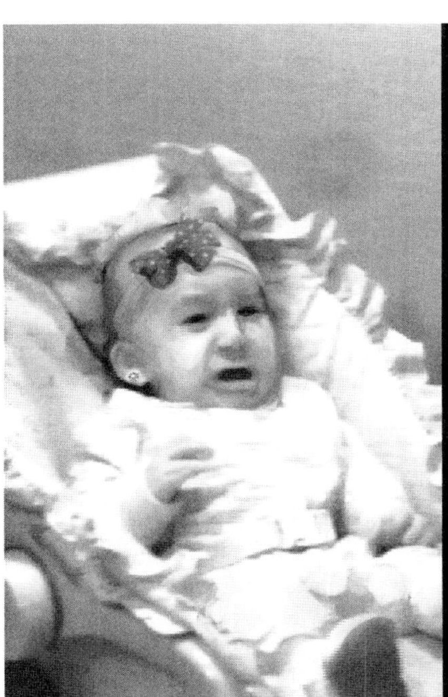

Frame 16. Minute:Second 35:02
Four seconds later, the infant is more upset, with a cry face. She looks toward at her mother, but without the same direct eye contact seen in Frame 14. Her right hand is moving in toward her body. She is very distressed. (In the video, her angry protest vocalization seems frantic.) The mother looks at her infant with a closed-up face. She seems emotionally withdrawn and disconnected. This is a profoundly discrepant moment. From the mother's face alone, we would have no idea that her infant is distressed to this degree.

Frame 17. Minute:Second 35:06
From Frame 16 to 17, four seconds later, the infant continues to be very distressed; she begins to lurch away from her mother. The infant seems less fearful and more angry. The mother looks down and away from her distressed infant. She seems helpless and emotionally disconnected.

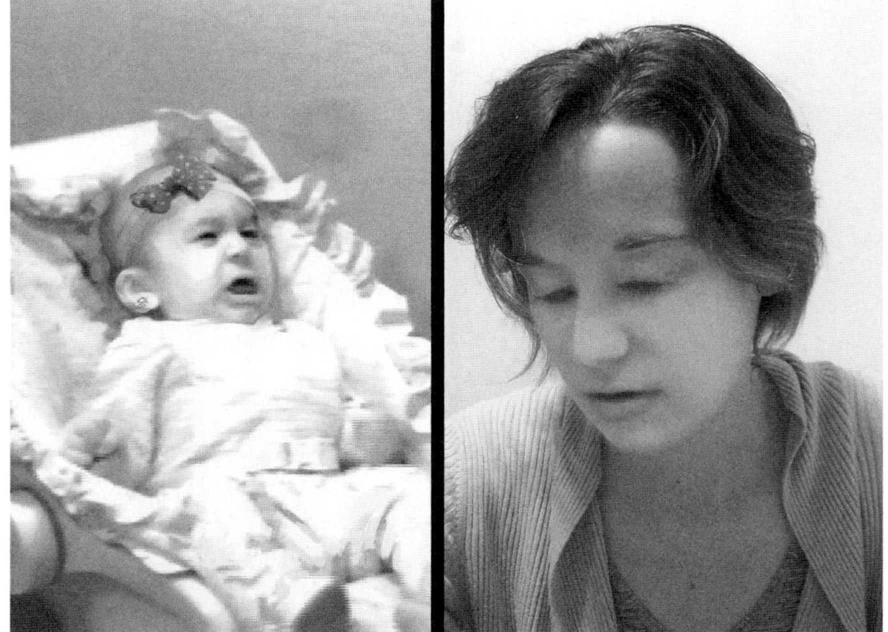

Frame 18. Minute:Second 35:07
From Frame 17 to 18, one second later, the infant remains frantic and sharply twists her body further away from her mother, looking away, with a cry face. This is an intense infant protest and aversion. (On the video, she protests angrily.) The mother is surprised, almost shocked. The mother's left hand is now visible between her infant's legs.

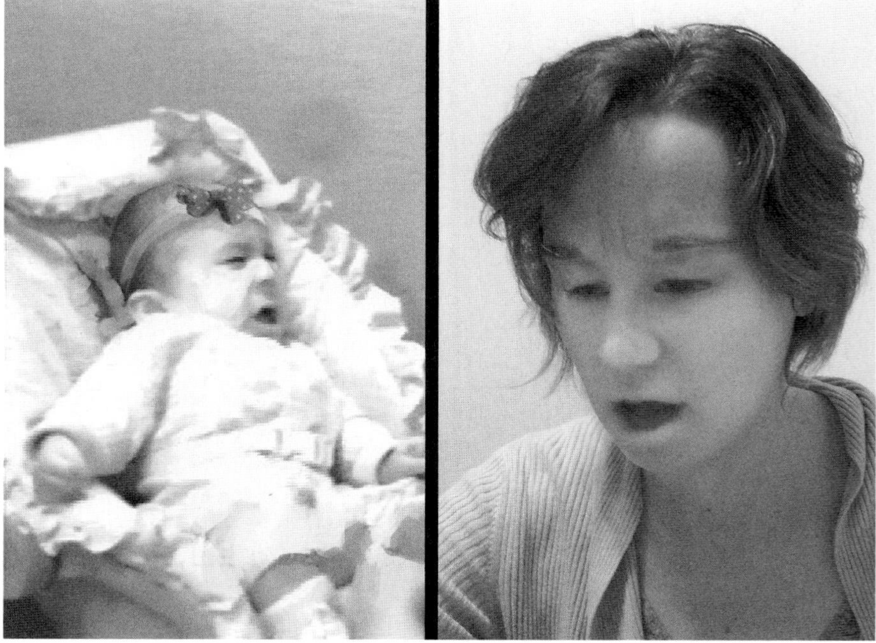

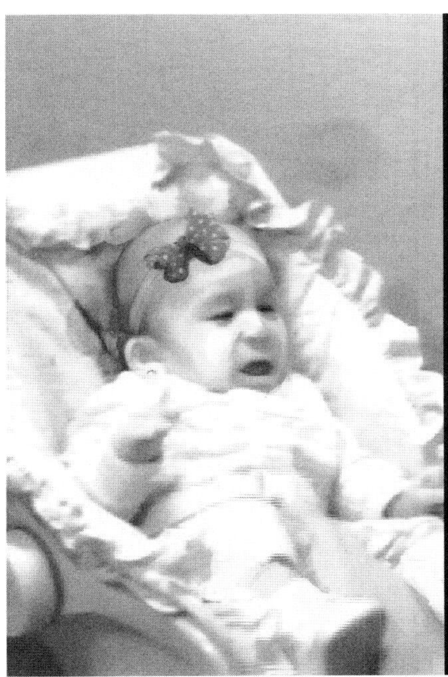

Frame 19. Minute:Second 35:08
From Frame 18 to 19, one second later, the infant shifts her body back toward her mother, but she is looking down and away from her mother, and she is still very upset. The mother seems more sympathetic with a partial woe face. Her left hand now touches the infant's right leg.

Frame 20. Minute:Second 35:10
From Frame 19 to 20, two seconds later, the infant becomes frantic and begins to cry angrily, kicking her right leg up. She closes her eyes, not looking at her mother, and she moves her hand to her mouth, perhaps to self-soothe. The mother has a closed-up, blank face. She seems emotionally disconnected, far away. She is not available to help the infant in her intense distress. This is another profoundly discrepant moment.

INFANT WARINESS WITH THE STRANGER

Following the interaction with the mother, seen above, this infant then played immediately with the stranger, a novel partner. In this sequence of drawings of four frames over four seconds, the infant is visually engaged but remains wary. The stranger works hard to engage the infant. The infant's face has a subtle hint of interest until the final frame. It is striking that the infant continues to make direct eye contact and to hold the stranger's hand across this sequence of four seconds. It is not unusual for infants to be wary at the beginning with a stranger. But this infant does not warm up across the entire two and a half-minute play interaction.

12.5 MINUTE:SECOND 32:17–32:20

Storyline: In these four seconds, the infant continues looking directly at the stranger while holding the stranger's hand. By the final frame, the stranger joins the infant in looking down.

Frame 1. Minute:Second 32:17
The infant looks directly at the stranger with an alert look. A very subtle widening of the right side of the infant's mouth is visible, a hint of an interest expression. The stranger leans in as she looks at the infant with raised eyebrows, an inquiring look, as if to say: "Can we engage?" The stranger's left hand holds the infant under the infant's right arm. The infant reaches her right arm out and holds the stranger's right hand.

Frame 2. Minute:Second 32:18
From Frame 1 to 2, in the next second, the infant continues to show a hint of interest. She continues to hold the stranger's hand. The stranger responds by pulling in her bottom lip slightly, as if to say, "Ohhhh."

Frame 3. Minute:Second 32:19
From Frame 2 to 3, in the next second, the infant does not change her body, gaze, or facial expression; she continues to hold the stranger's hand. She is wary, almost frozen. The stranger raises her eyebrows, as if to say: "Oh, what's happening? Are you ok?," and her expression shifts to a partial sympathetic woe face.

Frame 4. Minute:Second 32:20 From Frame 3 to 4, one second later, the infant's face loses its hint of positive interest. The infant has closed her face into a slightly more neutral, wary look. She continues to hold the stranger's hand. The stranger moves in slightly toward the infant (more of the stranger's hair is visible within the infant's frame); her eyebrows remain raised, and her face dampens, as if to say: "Oh, something is wrong."

COMMENTARY ON INFANT DISTRESS AND MATERNAL SURPRISE, ANGER, DISGUST, AND EMOTIONAL DISCONNECTION

We chose this sequence because it illustrates several patterns that predicted insecure-disorganized attachment at one year in our research (Beebe et al., 2010). Portions of the following descriptions are adapted from Beebe and colleagues (2010, 2012).

Comment on Mother and Infant

As we enter this sequence of drawings in Chapter 12, the infant is distressed. The mother initially shows a remote, neutral face that does not acknowledge her infant's distress (Frame 1). But immediately the mother shows a mock surprise expression, with raised eyebrows, showing the whites of her eyes (Frame 2). This expression is so discrepant from her infant's distress. Perhaps the mock surprise expression is the mother's attempt to ride negative into positive, that is, to ride the intensity of the infant's emotion, but shift the emotions from negative to positive. The mother's display of the whites of her eyes is potentially frightening for the infant (Hesse & Main, 2006). Thus, in this moment while the mother registers the infant's distress, she reacts with a discrepant, potentially frightening expression, rather than an empathic one.

The infant's distress then increases. As she turns away, closes her eyes, and partially covers her face, the mother smiles broadly, with her mouth wide open (Frame

3). Again we see a discrepancy between the infant's distress and the mother's big smile. Perhaps the infant closes her eyes and turns away to protect herself from viewing the mother's discrepant face. Again in this moment, the mother registers the infant's distress, but she reacts with laughter, rather than an empathic expression.

The mother then seems to disconnect from her infant, becoming remote, with a closed-up face (Frame 5). When the infant turns back to look at her mother, with a cry face, the mother seems quite surprised (Frame 6), as if she is confused by her infant's distress.

The most difficult portion of the interaction comes next. As the mother puts her finger in her infant's mouth (Frame 7), the infant whimpers. It seems that the infant's mouth hurts. From the video, we know that the mother says at that moment, "Don't be that way." The mother seems to be pleading with her infant not to be unhappy. But then the mother shows her infant an increasing disgust face, which culminates in an open-mouth, bared-teeth disgust face, overtly threatening (Frames 10 and 11). This is a dramatic moment in which the mother shows her own distress, which includes disgust and anger, at her infant's distress. Perhaps the mother feels, "You must stop this distress." She seems to have no idea that she has displayed a threatening face to her infant.

Fourteen seconds later, we reenter the sequence. As the infant now becomes increasingly upset, the mother shows a large open-mouth mock surprise face, and the infant seems horrified (Frame 14). But the mother then emotionally disconnects, with a pout, then a closed-up face, and then by looking away from her infant (Frames 15–17).

The infant now becomes increasingly even more upset. She vocalizes with an angry protest, shows a cry face, and seems angry. When the infant sharply lurches away from her mother, continuing to vocally protest, with a cry face, the mother again seems so surprised, almost shocked (Frame 18). At first the mother shows a hint of a sympathetic face (Frame 19). But then, the mother again emotionally disconnects, with a closed-up face, as her infant becomes frantic and cries (Frame 20). The mother is not emotionally available to help her infant. The mother's own emotional state seems shut down.

This mother is perceiving and responding to the infant's changes of behavior, noting every change. Thus, the difficulty is not a sheer absence of maternal responsiveness. There is a complex dance here, with each partner affecting the other, but it is an extremely uncomfortable and mismatched one.

We see here several repetitions of mother's smiles and/or mock surprise faces to her infant's distress, true surprise expressions, and moments of emotionally disconnecting. After she shows the threatening disgust face with bared teeth, the mother again emotionally disconnects. We see a mother struggling with her infant's distress. Both mother and infant seem to feel, for different reasons, that "This cannot be happening."

We conjecture that the mother's smiles or mock surprise faces to her infant's distress, or her moments of emotional disconnection, may be dissociative efforts to regulate herself. We infer that she becomes emotionally disconnected to protect herself from her own unresolved, unbearable distress, which is being triggered by the infant's distress. Perhaps her infant's distress triggered her own unresolved traumatic issues from her childhood. This mother likely has unresolved fears about intimate relating. The mother's complex self-protective behaviors, which are most likely completely out of her awareness, and which are so discrepant from the infant's distress, derail the infant.

Illustrations of Expectancies

We now turn to the question of what the infant and mother come to expect from their interactive encounters. We attempt to translate the action-dialogue into language, as if the infant or mother could put the experience into words.

We imagine that the infant may create the following procedural, action-sequence expectancies of their interaction:

"I know that when I feel upset, you won't be helping me. Sometimes when I feel upset, you are surprised. Sometimes you smile at me when I am distressed. I don't want to look at you when you do that. It makes me feel confused about what I feel and about what you feel. You do not recognize my distress or sympathize with me. Sometimes you look away from me when I am upset. That's awful too. Where are you? I feel so alone. But the worst is when I'm feeling distressed, and you are looking right at me, but you don't seem to really see me. Your face doesn't move, even when I get more and more upset. You stonewall me. Then I really don't know where you are. It's scary. You really don't get me. There's something wrong. You seem happy or surprised when I am upset. I don't understand you. I feel helpless to influence you. I feel frantic."

We imagine that the mother may create the following procedural expectancies of their interaction, out of awareness:

"Your distress makes me feel anxious and inadequate. Why don't you smile at me? What's wrong with you? I try to jolly you out of it, but it doesn't work. Stop it! I can't let myself be too affected by you; I'm not going to let myself be controlled by you or your moods. I just need you to smile and be happy. And I won't hear of anything else!"

Relevant Research

In our own research, mothers of infants on the way to disorganized (vs. secure) attachment were more likely to show smiles or surprise faces during infant distress moments (Beebe et al., 2010), a form of dyadic affective conflict. This pattern was prevalent in Chapter 10 above, and again is salient here, especially in Frames 2, 3, 6, and 14. We construe such moments as the mother's emotional denial of her infant's distress. It may be a maternal effort to shift the infant's distress to a positive state, but without first acknowledging that the infant is in distress. Thus, mothers of future disorganized infants oppose or counter their infants' distress, literally going in the opposite affective direction.

We infer that this maternal countering of infant distress confuses the infant, and makes it difficult for the infant to feel that her mother senses and acknowledges her distress. We infer that infants on the way to disorganized attachment in general come to expect that their mothers do not empathically share their distress. This finding evokes Winnicott's (1965) description of a maternal impingement. Instead of mirroring the infant's gesture, that is, joining the infant's distress, the mother substitutes her own gesture, such as a smile or mock surprise (personal communication, Lin Reicher, December 2, 2008).

In our research, we found that mothers of infants on the way to disorganized, compared with secure, attachment were more likely to display maternal smiles or surprise faces to infant facial and/or vocal distress (Beebe et al., 2010). Van Egeren, Baratt, and Roach (2001) analyzed maternal responses to infant vocal distress in a large sample of firstborn infants, without regard to attachment. They found that, when infants fussed, mothers were most likely to vocalize. They also found that, when infants fussed, maternal smile or social play was *suppressed,* that is, significantly unlikely.

Thus, our finding of maternal smile to infant vocal distress in mothers of infants on the way to disorganized attachment is highly atypical. It disturbs the infant's ability to come to expect that the mother will match the direction of the infant's affective change, which is one hallmark of interactions that predict secure infant attachment. In the secure pattern, mothers are not only likely to become positive as the infant becomes positive, but they are also likely to dampen and become empathic, with empathic faces and vocalizations, as the infant becomes distressed (Beebe et al., 2010).

Maternal Response to Infant Distress

Several studies have shown that maternal sensitive responsiveness (promptness and appropriateness of response to infant distress) predicts secure infant attachment and more optimal infant outcomes (see Ainsworth et al., 1978). For example, McElwain and Booth-LaForce (2006) found that greater maternal sensitivity to infant distress at six months predicted subsequent secure infant attachment at twelve to eighteen months. A very large study of 376 mother–child dyads by Leerkes and colleagues examined whether maternal sensitivity to bouts of infant distress and nondistress behavior predicted infant social-emotional adjustment. Maternal sensitivity to bouts of infant distress (but not nondistress) behavior at six months predicted fewer child behavioral problems and higher child social competence at two years and three years (Leerkes, Blankson, & O'Brien, 2009). This latter study points to the specific importance of maternal response to infant distress.

Leerkes and Crockenberg (2006) interviewed mothers regarding the ways that their own early experiences may affect how mothers feel about their infants' distress. Mothers whose emotional needs were not met in childhood were less confident in their ability to respond to their infants' distress, were less empathic, and experienced more negative emotions in response to their infant's distress.

Leerkes and colleagues also found that secure maternal attachment predicted higher maternal sensitivity to infant distress (Leerkes et al., 2014). Leerkes and Siepak (2006) showed that individuals with insecure attachment styles were more likely to make negative attributions when exposed to infant crying, attributions such as spoiled or difficult temperament; they were less accurate at identifying infant emotions, and were more likely to be amused or neutral in response to infant distress. Moreover, mothers who were more focused on their own needs when exposed to videotapes of infants crying were less sensitive to their infants' distress (Leerkes et al., 2014). Mothers who were more focused on their own needs were characterized by higher maternal negative emotionality, difficulties regulating their own emotions, and greater likelihood of reporting feeling anxious and angry in response to the infant cry videos. In these studies, Leerkes and colleagues identified aspects of the mother's own history and functioning that contribute to her difficulty in responding to her infant's distress.

Another study also sheds light on maternal responses to infant distress, comparing mothers who themselves had secure, compared with insecure, childhood histories of attachment, assessed with the AAI (coded with the Dynamic Maturational Model; Crittenden, 2004) before the birth of the mother's first child. On viewing photos of their own infants' smiling and crying faces during functional MRI scanning, mothers with secure (vs. insecure) attachment showed greater activation of reward regions of the brain (Strathearn, Fonagy, Amico, & Montague, 2009). Thus, secure maternal attachment was associated with more intense maternal reward activation to infant facial expressions, whether positive or negative. The authors suggest that, for securely attached mothers, infant facial emotions, whether positive or negative, may reinforce and motivate responsive maternal care.

Mothers with insecure, compared with secure, attachment histories had a different pattern of response to their infants' crying faces. Mothers with insecure attachment showed greater activation of a region associated with feelings of unfairness, pain, and disgust (the anterior insula). The authors suggested that this finding may indicate that these mothers were exerting cognitive control over their own negative affective response to their infants' crying faces. Comparing secure and insecure mothers in response to viewing their infants' crying faces, the pattern of activation of secure mothers was consistent with anticipation of gain, whereas the pattern of activation of insecure mothers was consistent with anticipation of loss (Strathearn et al., 2009).

This study by Strathearn and colleagues helps us understand the mother's disgust faces in response to her infant's distress in the mother and infant in Chapter 12. The infant's intense distress, such as a cry face, may activate feelings of unfairness, pain, and disgust in the mother when she herself has an insecure attachment history. The mother's experience of her crying infant may be one of loss—loss of love, loss of the expected smiling infant, loss of the infant she needs in order to feel like she is a good mother.

CHAPTER 13

Infant Distress and Maternal Sneer and Emotional Disconnection in the Origins of Insecure-Disorganized Infant Attachment

DRAWINGS: INFANT DISTRESS AND MATERNAL SNEER AND EMOTIONAL DISCONNECTION

This sequence depicts a mother and infant at four months where the infant was classified as insecure-disorganized attachment at one year (Beebe et al., 2010).

This sequence of drawings presents eleven frames, over eight seconds. The infant begins slightly distressed, and her distress continues to escalate across this sequence. The mother begins with a smile that is discrepant from the infant's distress. The mother then alternates between a sneer face and emotional disconnection, remaining out of reach. In the end, the infant slumps and disengages from her mother. The mother cannot recognize her infant's distress or comfort her.

Following the interaction with the mother, this infant then played immediately with the stranger, a novel partner.

13.1 MINUTE:SECOND 37:55–37:57A

Storyline: Across this three-second sequence, the infant is distressed, and the mother seems to be trying to engage her infant. But the mother's facial expressions do not match those of the infant.

Frame 1. Minute:Second 37:55
The mother looks at her infant with a smile and quizzical raised eyebrows. The infant looks at her mother with a wary, quizzical expression, and a slight frown. Although both are quizzical, the mother's smile seems mismatched with the infant's frown.

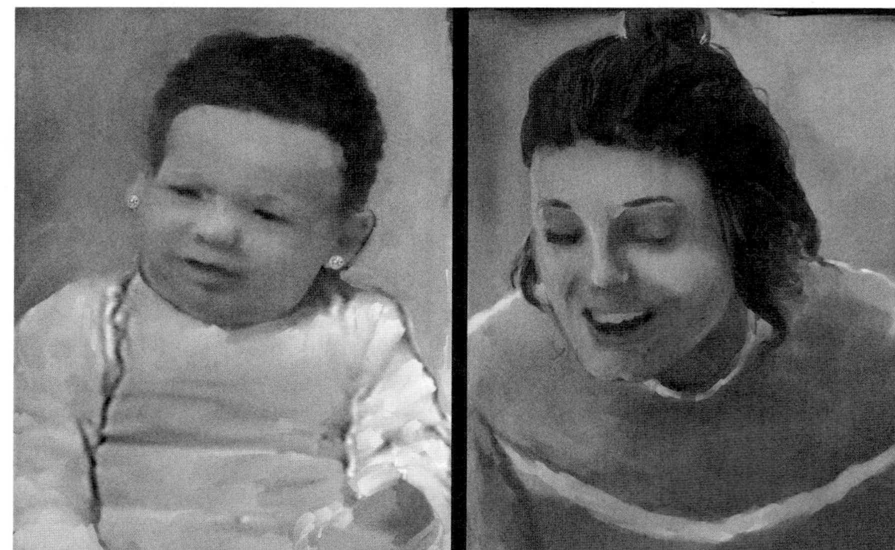

Frame 2. Minute:Second 37:56
From Frame 1 to 2, one second later, the infant's distress increases with more furrowed eyebrows. The mother sobers, with a tight closed mouth, while she continues to look at her infant. She reaches toward her infant's face.

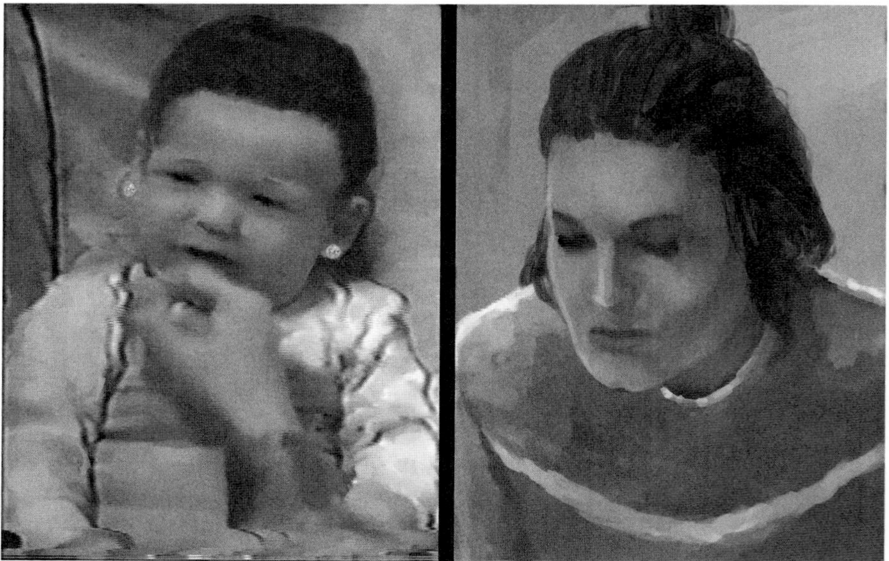

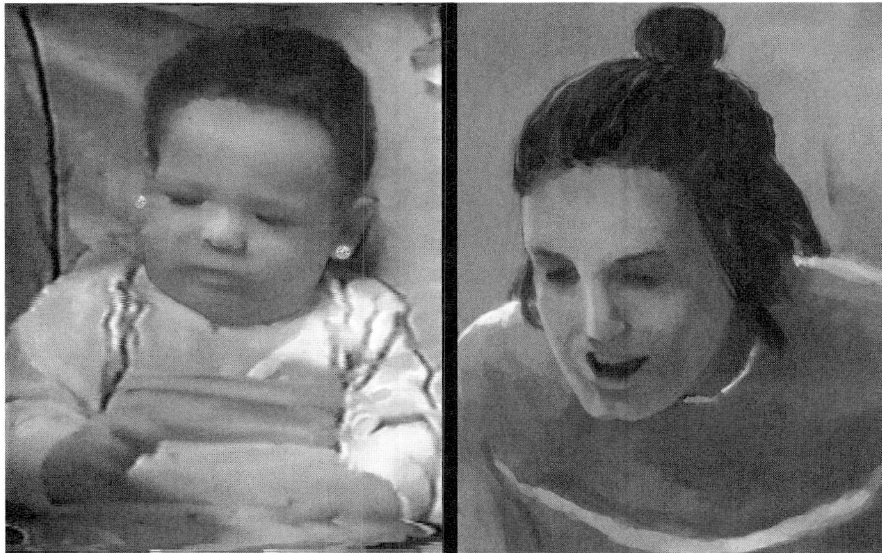

Frame 3. Minute:Second 37: 57a
From Frame 2 to 3, a half second later, the infant looks down and away from her mother, still frowning slightly. The mother opens her mouth with a hint of widening, a face that seems discrepant from the infant's state. Also, within this second, the mother has withdrawn her hand, and the infant begins to lift her own right hand.

13.2 MINUTE:SECOND 37:57A–37:59A

Storyline: Across this two-second sequence, the infant's distress builds to a high pitch. The mother looms in with a sneer expression and then seems to become detached.

Frame 4. Minute:Second 37:57b
From Frame 3 to 4, within the same second, the infant resumes looking at her mother, still with a slight frown, and her head is tilted down. The mother's slightly raised upper lip, showing a bit of teeth, seems annoyed or angry. She looms in slightly toward her infant's face.

(Note: The two cameras were slightly off in their spatial alignment at this moment in the filming. The mother's camera is higher than that of the infant here. This makes it seem as if the mother is looking down, but actually she is looking at her infant. Similarly, although the infant seems to be looking down, she is actually looking at her mother, although not with a direct full gaze.)

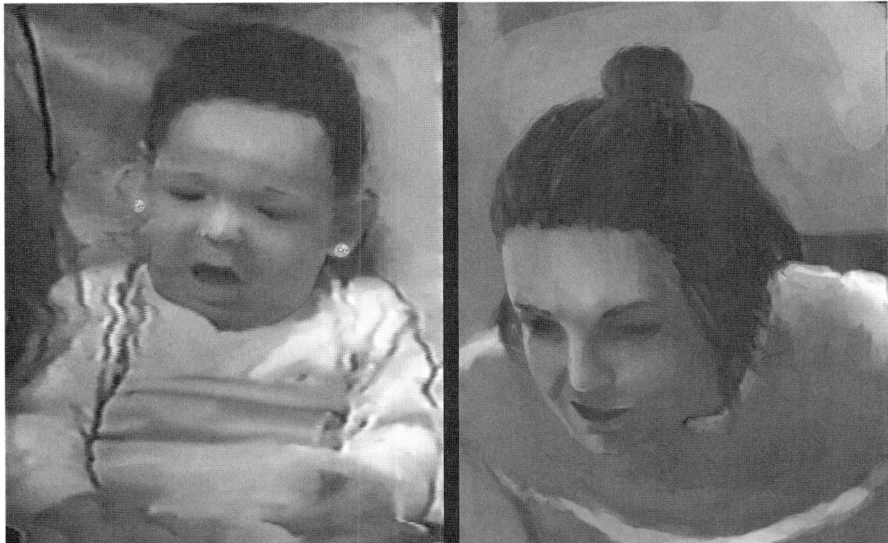

Frame 5. Minute:Second 37:58
From Frame 4 to 5, a half a second later, the mother looms in further. She has a sneer expression visible in the right corner of her mouth, which is lifted asymmetrically, showing a nasolabial fold. The infant opens her mouth with a pre-cry expression. The infant's eyes are cast down but are still open and monitoring the mother's expression. From the video, we know that she has an angry-protest vocalization as well. She seems alarmed.

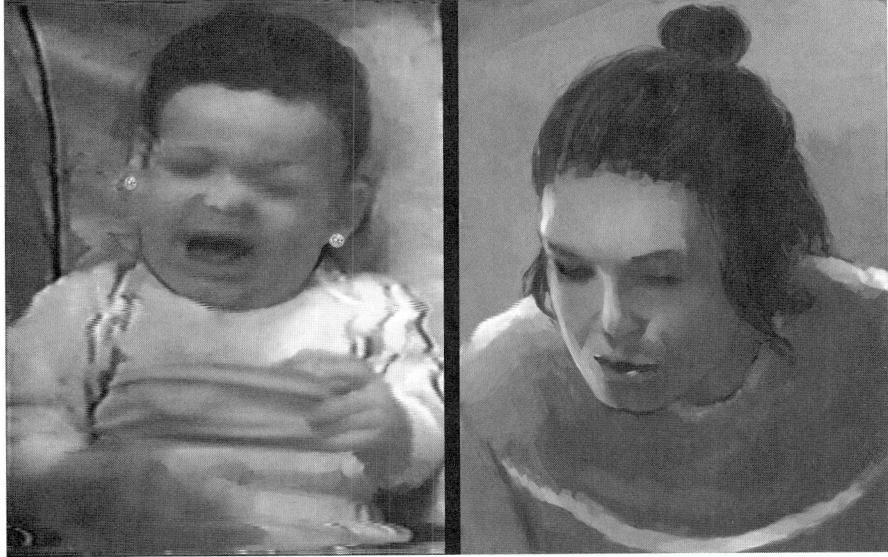

Frame 6. Minute:Second 37:59a
From Frame 5 to 6, a half second later, the infant's distress escalates into a full cry face, accompanied by an angry-protest vocalization (from the video). The infant moves her whole body back and begins to lift both hands up. The infant seems frantic. The mother's head moves back, and her face closes up with slightly pursed lips. The mother's sneer has diminished, and there is only a hint of it still visible. She seems emotionally distant from her infant.

13.3 MINUTE:SECOND 37:59A–38:02

Storyline: Across this four-second sequence, the mother begins by resuming her sneer expression, and the infant is frantic. The infant then looks at her mother, then again becomes frantic, and then turns away, slumped and distressed. The mother reacts to her infant but never becomes empathic.

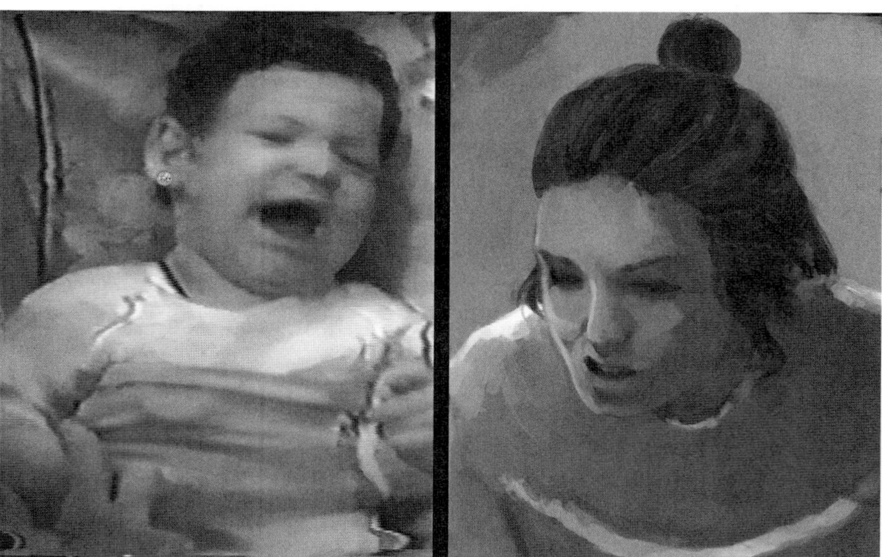

Frame 7. Minute: Second 37:59b
From Frame 6 to 7, within the same second, the mother's closed face shifts into a sneer expression, seen in the nasolabial fold in the right corner of her mouth. The infant's cry face escalates, accompanied by an angry-protest vocalization (from the video), and her head whips sharply 30 degrees to her left, away from her mother. She seems frantic.

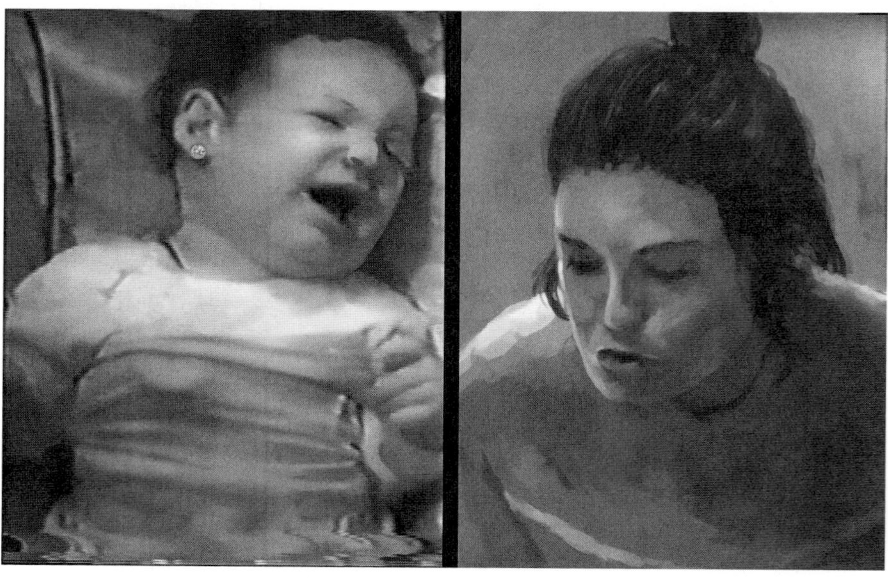

Frame 8. Minute:Second 37:59c
From Frame 7 to 8, still within the same second, the infant averts even further away from her mother, to a head orientation approximately 60 degrees away, continuing in her highly distressed state. The mother's face returns to an expression similar to that of Frame 6, a closed face with pursed lips. She does not acknowledge her infant's distress.

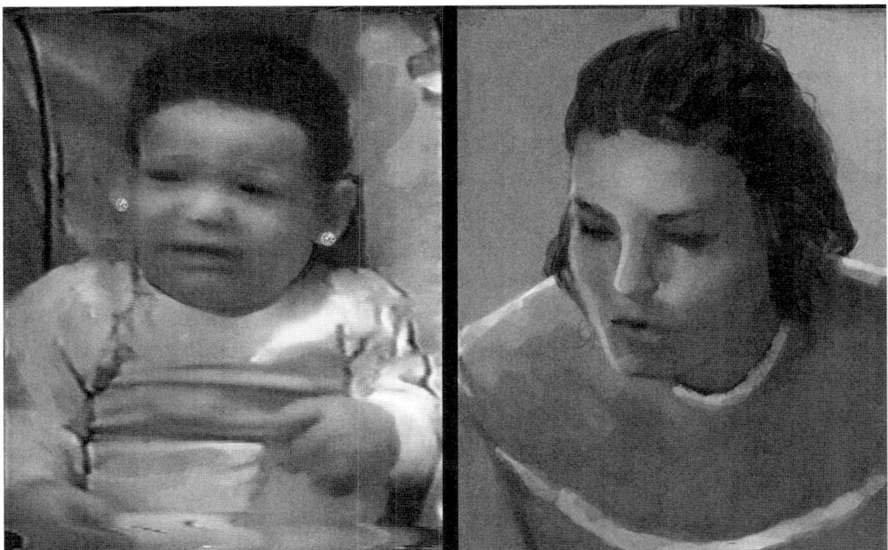

Frame 9. Minute:Second 38:00
From Frame 8 to 9, in the next second, the infant returns to look directly at her mother, with a fearful look, as if pleading. Her mother returns the look, but with a closed face, lips slightly pursed. She does not in any way recognize the infant's distress or acknowledge what has just happened. She seems emotionally disconnected from her infant.

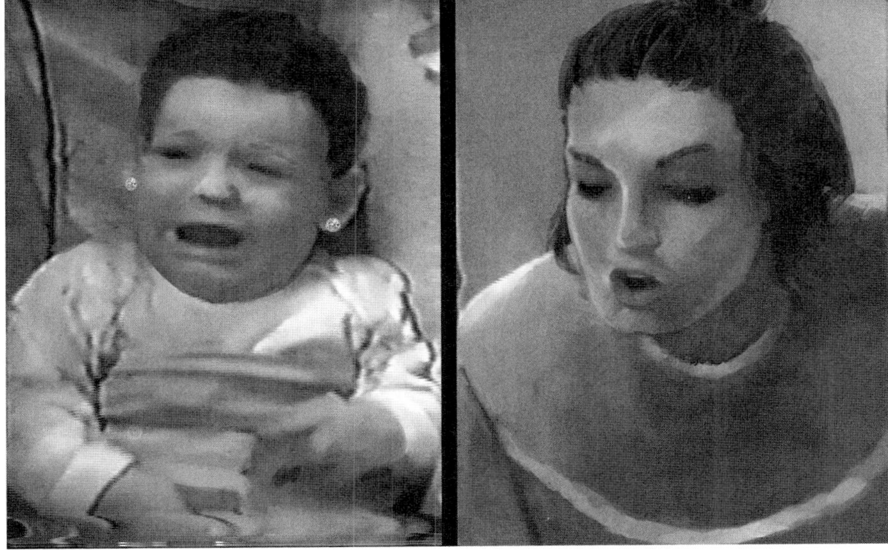

Frame 10. Minute:Second 38:01
From Frame 9 to 10, in the next second, the infant becomes frantic. She has an extremely distressed face with a frown, partial surprise expression, and a full cry face. She wails (from the video). Continuing to look directly at her mother, the infant's expression seems to say: "Don't you see me? You don't seem to recognize my distress or what is happening. How can you not see me?" The mother looks surprised, with eyebrows raised. She purses her lips, which are protruded out. She does not seem to acknowledge her infant's distress. She does not empathize. It is as if her threatening look never happened.

Frame 11. Minute:Second 38:02

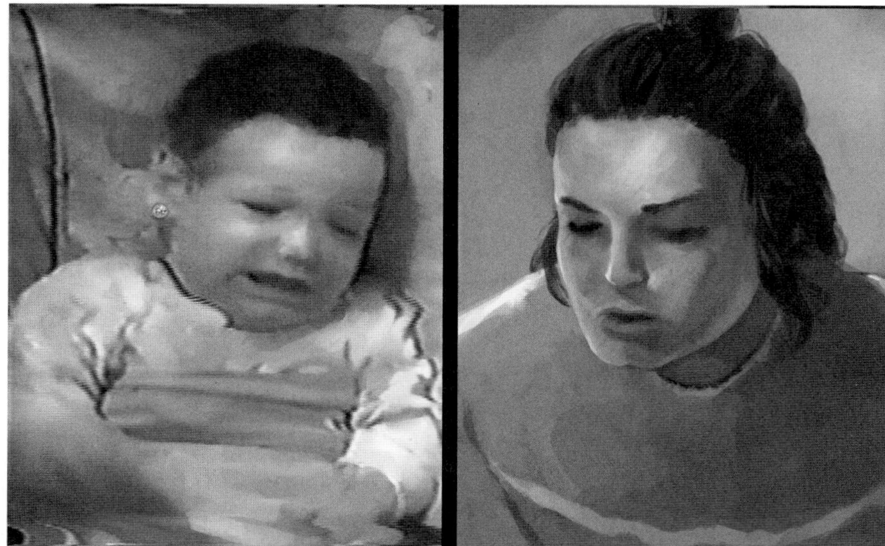

From Frame 10 to 11, in the next second, the infant turns and looks down and away. Her body slumps with a partial loss of tonus, and she drops her head down at an angle. Her distress has slightly dampened, but she is still very upset and protesting. The mother looks at her infant with surprise, showing raised eyebrows. The surprise is accompanied by a closed face with slightly pursed lips, similar to that seen in Frames 6 and 8. The mother's surprise suggests that she has no idea why her infant is upset. The mother seems dampened and emotionally disconnected. She does not show any recognition of the infant's distress.

INFANT EMOTIONAL RESILIENCE WITH THE STRANGER

Following the interaction with the mother, this infant then played immediately with the stranger, a novel partner. In this sequence of drawings of five frames over six seconds, the infant is dampened but nevertheless responsive and available for a low-key positive engagement. We see here a remarkable infant resilience with a new partner despite a difficult engagement with her mother.

13.4 MINUTE:SECOND 16:16–16:21

Storyline: The infant remains visually and emotionally engaged with the stranger. The infant shows subtle shifts in her degree of positive interest expressions. They end in a mutually positive moment.

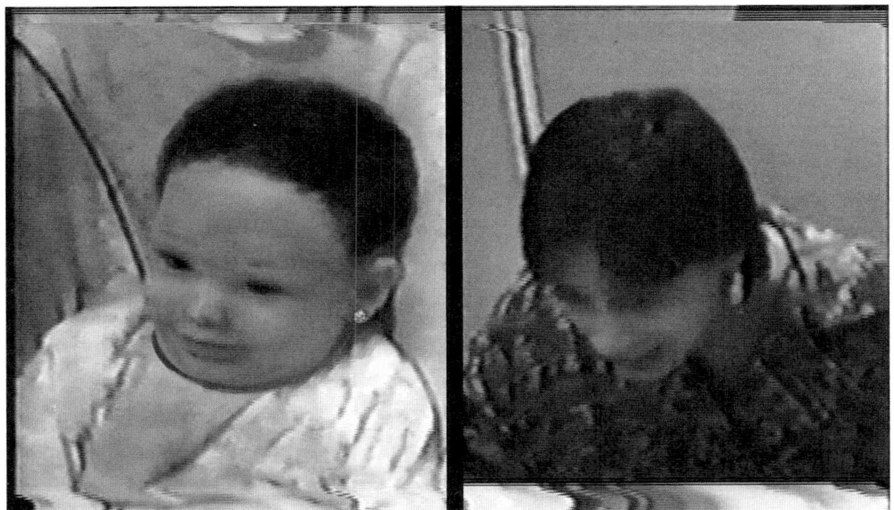

Frame 1. Minute:Second 16:16
In this first frame, both infant and stranger look at the other with a hint of positive expressiveness. The infant is interested, with a slight mouth widening. The stranger has an inquisitive look, as if seeking permission. Her head is slightly forward and down.

Frame 2. Minute:Second 16:17
From Frame 1 to 2, in the next second, the infant now has the beginning of a slight smile. The stranger is excited and smiles back with an open-mouth smile. She moves slightly back and raises her head, though still leaning forward.

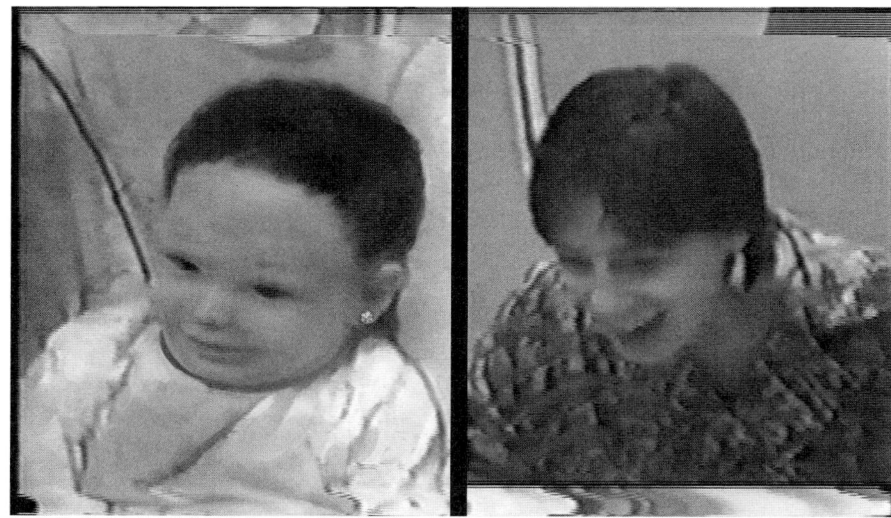

Frame 3. Minute:Second 16:19
From Frame 2 to 3, two seconds later, the infant continues looking, but her smile slightly dampens into an interest face. The stranger continues smiling. She raises her eyebrows with a quizzical look, as if to say, "What happened?" She seems to be aware that the infant has just dampened slightly.

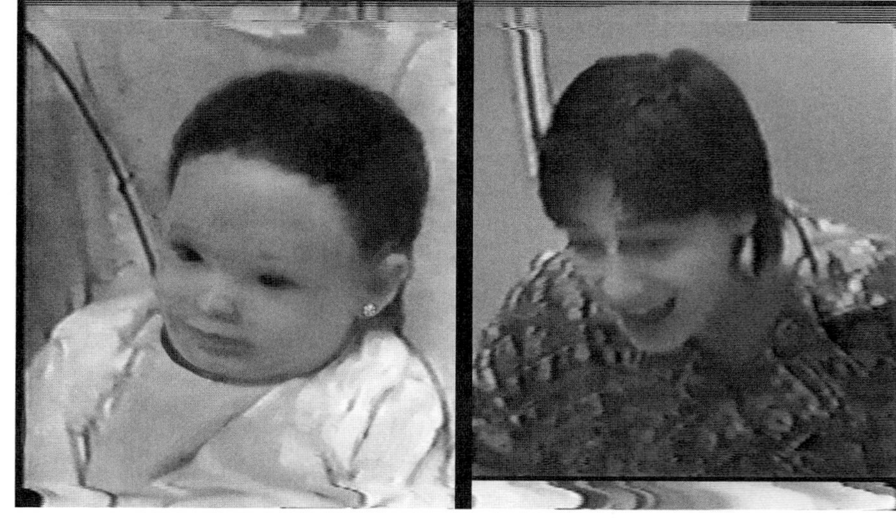

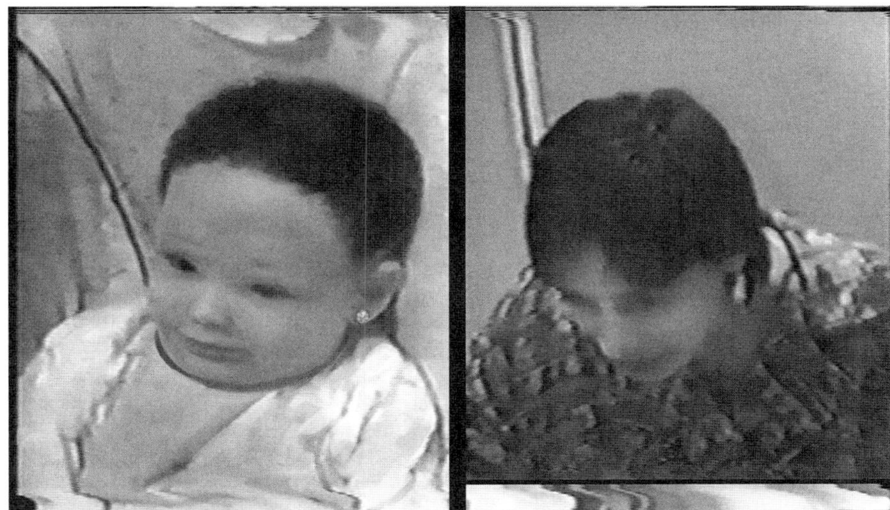

Frame 4. Minute:Second 16:20
From Frame 3 to 4, in the next second, the stranger leans in, with a dampened face, looking slightly concerned. The infant continues in an interest expression and raises her eyebrows.

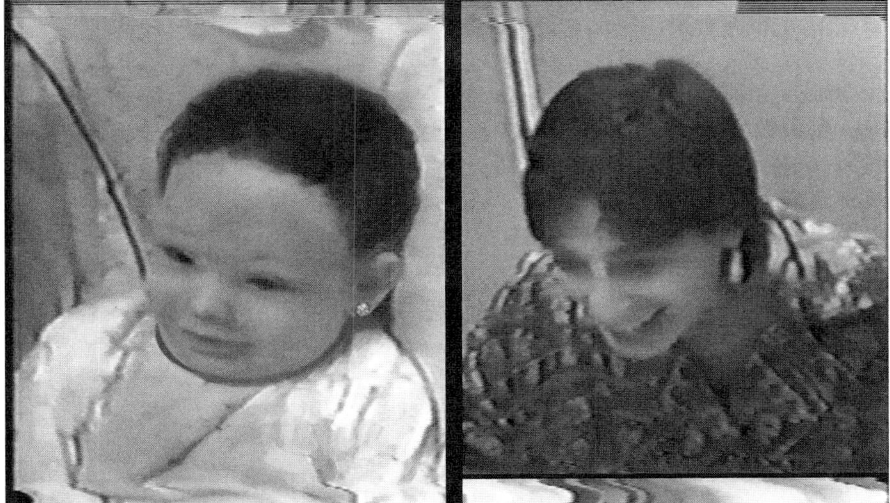

Frame 5. Minute:Second 16:21
From Frame 4 to 5, in the following second, the infant brightens a bit, with a slight hint of beginning to smile. The stranger reciprocates with a full smile and raises her head back slightly. It is a mutually positive moment.

COMMENTARY ON INFANT DISTRESS AND MATERNAL SNEER AND EMOTIONAL DISCONNECTION

We chose this sequence because it illustrates several patterns, which predicted insecure-disorganized attachment at one year in our research (Beebe et al., 2010). Portions of the following descriptions are adapted from Beebe and colleagues (2010, 2012). We also chose this mother–infant dyad because the stranger–infant interaction shows a remarkable infant resilience to reorganize her emotional state into a positively toned engagement with a novel partner.

Comment on Mother and Infant

As we enter this sequence, the infant is looking at her mother but seems hesitant, with a slight frown, and the mother is smiling. In the second frame, the mother reaches toward her infant's face, and the infant is slightly more distressed. The infant then looks down with a sober face (Frame 3); the mother's open, widened mouth with a hint of a smile seems slightly discrepant from the infant's state. However, to this point, nothing strikingly out of the ordinary has occurred.

In the next four frames (Frames 4 to 8), we see a remarkable and disturbing sequence. The infant's eyes are cast down but are still open and monitoring her mother's expressions during this sequence. A slight sign of the mother's beginning annoyance or possibly anger is visible in Frame 4, and the infant is now slightly distressed. But in Frame 5, the mother's sneer expression (with a nasolabial fold) emerges. This is a threatening face. The infant's pre-cry face and angry- protest vocalization seem to indicate that she is alarmed. In the next moment (Frame 6), the mother's sneer diminishes, with only a hint of it visible, but her face closes up with slightly pursed lips, and she seems emotionally distant, disconnected. But perhaps the pursed lips show us a hint of her pain. Here the infant's distress escalates into a full cry face, with an angry-protest vocalization, and she seems frantic. The mother shows no acknowledgment that her infant is frantic.

Now (Frame 7) the mother's sneer expression reemerges, and the infant lurches sharply away from her mother, while continuing the frantic cry face and angry-protest vocalization. This dramatic lurching away suggests that the infant senses threat. The infant's lurching away continues (Frame 8), as mother's expression shifts back to a closed face with pursed lips, which seems emotionally disconnected. There is no hint of emotional recognition of her infant's distress.

Then the infant looks back at her mother, as if to see what is happening (Frame 9). The mother returns the look, but with a closed face, lips slightly pursed. The infant then again becomes wildly upset, with a cry face and a wailing vocalization (Frame 10). Why does the infant become so upset at this moment? After all, her mother is not displaying a sneer face here. We conjecture that the infant becomes so upset because her mother shows no sign of recognition of her distress, no empathy with it; no indication that something just happened to scare her. It is as if the mother's threatening look never happened. The mother's state is too discrepant with the infant's state. We propose that maternal failure to indicate any recognition of the infant's intense distress is in itself fear-arousing for the infant.

By the last frame (Frame 11), the infant turns away and looks away from her mother. But we conjecture that this mother, out of awareness, is experiencing many emotions. The mother's tight-lipped purse might convey a hint of her own pain. We imagine that she is experiencing a lack of safety, helplessness, anger, or fear during this interaction. We imagine that she feels so disappointed that she cannot get her infant to smile. We imagine that this mother's emotional disconnection from her infant is the mother's way of protecting herself from intense emotions, which are fear-arousing for her, and which are triggered by her infant's distress. We see her moments of emotional disconnection as dissociative efforts to regulate herself, to protect herself from her own unresolved, unbearable distress, triggered by her infant.

Comment on Stranger and Infant

Remarkably, when this infant of Chapter 12 plays with the stranger, she shows moments of subtle positive responsiveness. The stranger is careful to stay close to the infant's emotional range, a low-key interest with just hints of positiveness. As we watch this infant play with the stranger, we hardly recognize her. She is so different with the stranger that she almost seems like a different infant. We call this "the resilience of the human spirit." It illustrates the capacity of a four-month infant to reorganize her emotional state into a positively toned engagement with an attuned novel partner.

Several of the stranger–infant interactions in this book illustrated the idea that, following a difficult interaction with the mother, some infants can repair and find a way to be more engaged with an attuned stranger. These stranger–infant interactions suggest that all infants potentially have the resilience to repair with an attuned partner at this age. At infant age four months, the infant's system is enormously flexible with the potential for a great range of interactive experience.

Illustrations of Expectancies

We now turn to the question of what the infant comes to expect from his or her interactive encounters. We attempt to translate the action-dialogue into language, as if the infant or mother could put the experience into words.

We imagine that the infant may experience the interaction in the following ways:

"I'm so upset. Don't you see me? You don't seem to recognize my distress or what is happening. How can you not see me? I feel so alone. You look far away. You look like you don't know me."

"I feel wary. You scare me. I don't know what you're going to do next. When you make those terrible faces, I feel afraid of you. I get so upset, I feel terrified. I feel frantic. "

We imagine that the infant may create the following procedural, action-sequence expectancies of their interaction:

"When I get upset, you get upset. You might get angry at me. You might threaten me with terrible, scary faces. And you won't even recognize that I'm upset. Maybe you won't even know you've done it. I know I will feel so alone and frantic. I won't be able to get any help from you. Instead you will be angry at me. It makes me feel so terrible. What can I do? I still need you. I still want you to love me."

We imagine that the mother may create the following procedural expectancies of their interaction, out of awareness:

"Why are you upset? It surprises me. Why aren't you happy? You should be happy! I need you to be happy. You disappoint me terribly. It's so hard to get you to smile. You make me feel you don't love me. It scares me. Stop it! It's too much for me. You always get this way. I won't have it! I need you to love me!"

This interaction again illustrates how difficult it is for infants on the way to disorganized attachment to feel that their mothers sense, recognize, acknowledge their distress. We infer that infants instead come to expect that they cannot count on their mothers to empathically share their distress.

This interaction also illustrates the possibility that the mother's own unresolved distress, like an open wound, may be triggered by the infant's distress. We assume that this mother was not consciously aware that she threatened her infant. We also imagine that she was not aware that she became emotionally disconnected from her wildly upset infant. We imagine that she feels profoundly wounded by her infant's response to her.

Relevant Research

The difficulties in this mother–infant pair in Chapter 13 are similar to those in Chapters 11 and 12. All three mothers display threat faces. In Chapter 11, the mother showed a bared-teeth bite face. In Chapter 12, the mother showed a disgust, which was then amplified by bared teeth. In the mother discussed here, in Chapter 13, the mother displayed sneer expressions, seen in the nasolabial fold in the right corner of her mouth. The infants in Chapters 11, 12, and 13 reacted to their mothers' threat faces with cry faces, angry-protest vocalizations, and turning away from their mothers. Often the infants closed their eyes for a fraction of a second at the peak of the mother's threat face display.

The similarities among these three dyads help us grasp the patterning of maternal threat faces and the infants' agonized responses. The differences in the kinds of maternal threat faces in these dyads, the angry, bared-teeth bite face, the disgust face with bared teeth, and the sneer expression, help us begin to appreciate the range of possible threat faces.

Baring teeth can be considered vestigial predatory behavior, a slight trace of an earlier human adaptation for survival (Hesse & Main, 2006; Jacobvitz, Leon, & Hazen, 2006). One-sided lip-raising, similar to the sneer expression we described, is a vestigial canine exposure, a threat gesture described by Darwin (1872), as noted by Hesse and Main (2006, p. 322). During the Ainsworth attachment paradigm conducted at infant age one year, observations of predatory forms of threat behavior, such as hissing, growling, and canine exposure, were found to be more frequent in parents whose infants were independently judged to be disorganized attachment (Abrams, Rifkin, & Hesse, 2006; Jacobvitz et al., 2006). Schuengel and colleagues found that frightening maternal behavior predicted disorganized infant attachment, and that mothers with unresolved loss and an insecure attachment had the highest likelihood of exhibiting frightening behavior (Schuengel et al., 1999).

An attentional bias toward facial expressions of fear, that is, a more prolonged engagement of attention to fearful facial expressions, in comparison to happy or neutral expressions, is typical of infants by six to seven months. However, a smaller attentional bias to fearful faces at seven months was found to be associated with insecure (vs. secure) attachment, and particularly with disorganized attachment, at fourteen months (Peltola, Forssman, Puura, van Ijzendoorn, & Leppanen, 2015). The stimulus used in this experiment is a fearful face: eyes completely wide open showing the whites of the eyes; eyebrows raised showing strong surprise; and the lips parted, slightly open, but relaxed. This finding suggests that infants on the way to disorganized attachment already have an altered sensitivity to fearful faces by seven months. The authors suggest that this fearful face is a threat-related cue. Whereas infants on the way to secure attachment pay more attention to fearful facial expressions, infants on the way to disorganized attachment pay less attention. The authors offer two possible explanations. One possibility is a blunted sensitivity, that is, dampened emotional arousal, to fearful faces in infants on the way to disorganized (vs. secure) attachment. An alternative explanation is that insecure attachment is associated with a tendency to divert attention away from fearful faces and, as emotion is aroused, to learn to suppress that emotional arousal (Dykas & Cassidy, 2011). Based on the observations of vigilant and intense negative reactivity to maternal threat faces in infants on the way to disorganized attachment in our own study, several of whom are illustrated here, we favor the interpretation that infants on the way to disorganized (vs. secure) attachment remain sensitive to fearful faces, but have learned to turn their attention away from these expressions.

Our examples of maternal threat behavior observed at infant age four months in face-to-face play are rapid and fleeting, sometimes lasting less than a second. Hesse and Main (2006) similarly noted that forms of parental threat observed at infant age one year in the Ainsworth attachment paradigm appeared suddenly, briefly, and without apparent context. Hesse and Main (2006) suggest that these fleeting threat behaviors are partially dissociated and are connected to the parent's own trauma or fear. Dissociation refers to a separation of mental processes, such as thoughts, emotions, and memories that are ordinarily integrated. In a dissociative state, the normally integrative functions of identity, memory, or consciousness are altered. In a dissociated moment, or a partially dissociated moment, the parent is not all there in the usual way that the infant expects (Hesse & Main, 2006). Hesse and Main (2006) noted that because the parent's experience is most likely linked to the parent's own traumatic past, the parent's frightening expressions are likely to be incomprehensible to the infant; thus the parent is simultaneously alarming and unavailable.

The research we cited by Kim and colleagues in the commentary in Chapter 10 is relevant here. Maternal unresolved trauma may blunt the mother's optimal brain response to her infant's distress (Kim et al., 2014). However, in the work by Riem et al. (2012), adults with an insecure (vs. secure) attachment history showed heightened amygdala activation, an index of hyperemotionality, when exposed to sounds of an infant crying. There may be two types of individuals, those who become hyperaroused in the face of distressing stimuli; and those who become numb, a dissociative type. Or there may also be a two-stage process, first overarousal, and then a numbing, in an attempt to cope with and defend against feeling overwhelmed (Lanius et al., 2010).

The research we cited by Schechter and colleagues in the commentary in Chapter 11 is also relevant here. Maternal dysregulation in response to seeing their young children as a potential threat was mirrored in the brains of traumatized mothers. Their brains showed decreased activation of brain regions important for emotion regulation and social cognition, and increased activation of regions that are associated with maintenance of traumatic memory traces (Schechter et al., 2012, 2015).

The research we cited by Strathearn et al. (2009) in the commentary in Chapter 12 is also relevant here. In viewing their infants' facial expressions, whether positive or negative, securely attached mothers showed more intense activation of reward centers in their brains than insecurely attached mothers. Infant facial emotions, both positive and negative, may thus motivate responsive maternal care (Strathearn et al., 2009). In viewing their infants' crying faces, mothers with insecure (vs. secure) attachment showed greater activation of a brain region associated with feelings of unfairness, pain, disgust, and anticipation of loss. Thus, the insecurely attached mother's experience of her crying infant may be one of loss—loss of love, loss of the expected smiling infant, loss of the infant she needs in order to feel like she is a good mother.

This research helps to explain why a mother of a child on the way to disorganized attachment might show a threatening face. The mother is likely to have been exposed in her childhood to fearful and threatening experiences. When her infant becomes upset, it is likely to trigger her own threatened, fearful, angry, and helpless states. She is likely to feel threatened by her infant's distress, and she may then threaten her infant in return. Moreover, the mother's brain mirrors this state.

When we first see the maternal threat faces in Chapters 11–13, they seem so extreme, almost unimaginable. But when we understand the role of the mother's unresolved trauma history, and the research showing altered brain activation patterns when viewing their distressed infants, it becomes understandable. The mother of an infant on the way to disorganized attachment may threaten her distressed infant because the infant's distress may threaten the mother.

Conclusion

This book offers a rare opportunity to see the complex details and rapidity of face-to-face communication between mothers and their four-month-old infants. These powerful interactions expand our views of the origins of intimate relating and attachment. Exploring mother–infant interactions through these drawings, detailed at the micro-level, increases our appreciation of the enormous range, subtlety, and emotional power of these early exchanges.

This book illustrates the power of largely *unmentalized* communications. They are not rooted in our usual language-based ways of knowing. Because of its rapidity and subtlety, much of face-to-face communication—between adults as well as between parents and infants—occurs outside of conscious awareness. Thus, much of our interpersonal understanding is prereflective. It is based on an action-sequence form of procedural knowledge, in which partners anticipate the other's behavior as well as their own. This anticipation enables each person to coordinate their own actions with the actions of the partner on a split-second basis. Emotional communication is also based on direct brain activation in response to the perception of emotions in others, which is also largely out of awareness.

When we watch mothers and infants interact in real time, usually their communication seems straightforward. But when we slow an interaction down and look at it second-by-second, we can train ourselves to see subtle and meaningful sequences that are not visible in real time. We see so much more than we ever imagined. The interaction sequences illustrated in this book help us to visualize the idea that so much emotional communication occurs in seconds and even split seconds.

We tried to put these preverbal, unmentalized, action-sequence dialogues into words. The advantage of doing so is that, through language, we can become aware of these patterns. It becomes more possible to think about them, to understand their importance, to teach expectant parents and clinicians about them, and where necessary, to create methods of clinical intervention.

Increasingly, we now know that the nature of communication in infancy sets the foundation for development through young adulthood. The power of these interactions depicted in the drawings helps us understand why infancy is such a formative period. As early as four months, parents and infants have already begun to co-create patterns, which set a trajectory for the infants' development. Thus, the ways that parents and infants communicate are critically important. The recurrent nature of the infants' experiences generates procedural expectancies of self and other. These expectancies continue to influence the infants' emotional experiences and lead toward secure or insecure infant attachment by one year. These infant patterns of attachment at one year in turn predict later patterns of development in childhood, adolescence, and adulthood. Nevertheless, we hasten to add that development is never set in stone; many important influences and transformations occur after infancy, and intervention can potentially change the path of development at any age.

To understand our research is to understand that, in face-to-face communication, we are always influencing each other, often on a split-second basis, and often out of awareness. This dyadic aspect of communication may be unsettling. The very idea of who we are, our identity, is always embedded in this continuous dyadic process. Moreover, this dyadic process is rooted in the patterns of our own early parent–infant interactions. To understand ourselves dyadically, in the context of our relationships, is to see ourselves as more porous and vulnerable to the state and behavior of the other than we might like to think we are.

Where do we go from here? Our students who are parent–infant clinicians tell us that parents often say that infants in the early months of life do not know anything and will not remember anything. Only when they are a little older, approaching one year, do infants pick up on what is happening. But when we show parents films of themselves interacting with their four-month-old infants, in slow motion or frame-by-frame, they say "Oh, I am so amazed! My baby notices every little thing. I never realized that!"

Our work, and that of our colleagues in infant research, calls for a dramatic shift in the way we, as adults, and as a culture, view infants. Already by four months, infants notice, remember, and come to expect every little thing. We hope that you join us in this book in appreciating the extraordinary social capacity of infants. We hope that our book enhances the ways that you see and hear parents and infants as they influence each other. Infants already tell us so much about how they feel. And we, out of awareness, are already communicating how we feel to our infants. Infants absorb these patterns of communication and use them as a foundation for who they will become. In conclusion, we hope that our book helps us understand infants better and helps infants understand us better!

References

Abrams, K., Rifkin, A., & Hesse, E. (2006). Examining the role of parental frightened/frightening subcategories in predicting disorganized attachment within a brief observational procedure. *Development and Psychopathology, 18,* 345–361.

Ainsworth, M. (1969). Object relations, dependency and attachment: A theoretical review of the infant–mother relationship. *Child Development, 40*(4), 969–1025.

Ainsworth, M., Bell, S., & Stayton, D. (1974). Individual differences in the development of some attachment behaviors. *Merrill-Palmer Quarterly of Behavior and Development, 18*(2), 123–143.

Ainsworth, M., Blehar, M., Waters, E., & Wall, S. (1978). *Patterns of attachment: A psychological study of the strange situation.* Hillsdale, NJ: Erlbaum.

Als, H. (1977). The newborn communicates. *Journal of Communication, 27*(2), 66–73.

Als, H., & Brazelton, T. (1981). A new model of assessing the behavioral organization in preterm and fullterm infants. *Journal of the American Academy of Child Psychiatry, 20,* 239–263.

Ambady, H., & Rosenthal, R. (1992). Thin slices of expressive behavior as predictors of interpersonal consequences: A meta-analysis. *Psychological Bulletin, 111*(2), 256–274.

Antonucci, T., & Levitt, M. (1984). Early prediction of attachment security: A multivariate approach. *Infant Behavior and Development, 7,* 1–18.

Atzil, S., Hendler, T., & Feldman, R. (2011). Specifying the neurobiological basis of human attachment: Brain, hormones, and behavior in synchronous and intrusive mothers. *Neuropsychopharmacology, 36,* 2603–2615.

Bates, J., Maslin, C., & Frankel, K. (1985). Attachment security, mother–child interaction, and temperament as predictors of behavior-problem ratings at three years. *Monographs of the Society for Research in Child Development, 50*(1–2, Serial No. 209), 167–193.

Beebe, B. (1973). Ontogeny of positive affect in the third and fourth months of the life of one infant. *Dissertation Abstracts International, 35*(2), 1014B.

Beebe, B. (1982). Micro-timing in mother–infant communication. In M. R. Key (Ed.), *Nonverbal communication today* (Vol. 33, pp. 169–195). New York, NY: Mouton.

Beebe, B. (1986). Mother–infant mutual influence and precursors of self and object representations. In J. Masling (Ed.), *Empirical studies of psychoanalytic theories* (Vol. 2, pp. 27–48). Hillsdale, NJ: The Analytic Press.

Beebe, B. (2000). Co-constructing mother–infant distress. *Psychoanalytic Inquiry, 20,* 421–440.

Beebe, B. (2003). Brief mother-infant treatment: Psychoanalytically informed video feedback. *Infant Mental Health Journal, 24*(1), 24–52.

Beebe, B. (2005). Mother–infant research informs mother–infant treatment. *Psychoanalytic Study of the Child, 60,* 7–46.

Beebe, B. (2014). My journey in infant research and psychoanalysis: Microanalysis, a social microscope. *Psychoanalytic Pyschology, 31*(1), 4–25.

Beebe, B., Bigelow, A., Messinger, M., Milne, D., Lee, S., & Buck, K. (2015). *Infant gaze affects mother–infant self- and interactive contingency.* New York: New York State Psychiatric Institute.

Beebe, B., Cohen, P., Sossin, M., & Markese, S. (Eds.). (2012). *Mothers, infants and young children of September 11, 2001: A primary prevention project.* New York, NY: Routledge.

Beebe, B., Igleheart, H., Steele, M., Steele, H., Lyons-Ruth, K., Feldstein, S., … Kala, J. (2015, March). *Infancy to adulthood: Vocal turn-taking in infancy, 12-month attachment, and adult attachment, depression, anxiety, dissociation.* Philadelphia, PA: Society for Research in Child Development.

Beebe, B., Jaffe, J., Chen, H., Buck, K., Cohen, P., Feldstein, S., & Andrews, H. (2008). Six-week postpartum depressive symptoms and 4-month mother–infant self- and interactive contingency. *Infant Mental Health Journal, 29*(5), 442–471.

Beebe, B., Jaffe, J., & Lachmann, F. (1992). A dyadic systems view of communication. In N. J. Skolnick & S. Warshaw (Eds.), *Relational perspectives in psychoanalysis* (pp. 61–81). Hillsdale, NJ: The Analytic Press.

Beebe, B., Jaffe, J., Markese, S., Buck, K., Chen, H., Cohen, P., … Feldstein, S. (2010). The origins of 12-month attachment: A microanalysis of 4-month mother–infant interaction. *Attachment & Human Development, 12*(1–2), 3–141.

Beebe, B., & Lachmann, F. (1988). The contribution of mother–infant mutual influence to the origins of self and object representations. *Psychoanalytic Psychology, 5*(4), 304–337.

Beebe, B., & Lachmann, F. (1994). Representation and internalization in infancy: Three principles of salience. *Psychoanalytic Psychology, 11*(2), 127–165.

Beebe, B., & Lachmann, F. (2002). *Infant research and adult treatment: Co-constructing interactions.* Hillsdale, NJ: The Analytic Press.

Beebe, B., & Lachmann, F. (2013). *The origins of attachment: Infant research and adult treatment.* New York, NY: Routledge.

Beebe, B., Lachmann, F., & Jaffe, J. (1997). Mother–infant interaction structures and presymbolic self and object representations. *Psychoanalytic Dialogues, 7*(2), 133–182.

Beebe, B., Margolis, A., Markese, S., Jaffe, J., Buck, K., Chen, H., … Reuben, J. (2009). *Mother–infant vs. stranger–infant: Depression and attachment* (Report to the International Psychoanalytic Association). New York: New York State Psychiatric Institute.

Beebe, B., Markese, S., Bahrick, L., Lachmann, F., Buck, K., Chen, H., … Jaffe, J. (2013). On knowing and being known in the 4-month origins of disorganized attachment: An emerging presymbolic theory of mind. In H. Terrace & J. Metcalfe (Eds.), *Agency and joint attention* (pp. 100–124). Oxford, England: Oxford University Press.

Beebe, B., & Steele, M. (2013). How does microanalysis of mother–infant communication inform maternal sensitivity and infant attachment? *Attachment & Human Development, 15*(5–6), 583–602.

Beebe, B., Steele, M., Jaffe, J., Buck, K., Chen, H., Cohen, P., … Feldstein, S. (2011). Maternal anxiety and 4-month mother–infant self- and interactive contingency. *Infant Mental Health Journal, 32*(2), 174–206.

Beebe, B., & Stern, D. (1977). Engagement-disengagement and early object experiences. In

N. Freedman & S. Grand (Eds.), *Communicative structures and psychic structures* (pp. 35–55). New York, NY: Plenum.

Beebe, B., Stern, D., & Jaffe, J. (1979). The kinesic rhythm of mother–infant interactions. In A. W. Siegman & S. Feldstein (Eds.), *Of speech and time: Temporal patterns in interpersonal contexts* (pp. 23–24). Hillsdale, NJ: Erlbaum.

Bell, R. (1968). A reinterpretation of the direction of effects in studies of socialization. *Psychological Review, 75,* 81–95.

Bell, S., & Ainsworth, M. (1972). Infant crying and maternal responsiveness. *Child Development, 43,* 1171–1190.

Belsky, J., Rovine, M., & Taylor, D. (1984). The Pennsylvania infant family development project III: The origins of individual differences in infant–mother attachment: Maternal and infant contributions. *Child Development, 55,* 718–728.

Benjamin, J. (1995). *Like subjects, love objects.* New Haven, CT: Yale University Press.

Bennett, S. (1971). Infant–caretaker interaction. *Journal of the American Academy of Child Psychiatry, 10*(2), 321–335.

Berlyne, D. (1966). Curiosity and exploration. *Science, 153,* 25–33.

Blehar, M., Lieberman, A., & Ainsworth, M. (1977). Early face-to-face interaction and its relation to later infant-mother attachment. *Child Development, 48,* 182–194.

Bowlby, J. (1958). The nature of the child's tie to his mother. *Journal of Psychoanalysis, 39,* 350–373.

Bowlby, J. (1969). *Attachment and loss, Vol. I.* New York, NY: Basic Books.

Bowlby, J. (1973). *Attachment and loss, Vol. II: Separation.* New York, NY: Basic Books.

Bowlby, J. (1980). *Loss: Sadness & depression* (Vol. 3 of Attachment and Loss). New York, NY: Basic Books.

Brazelton, T. (1992, May). *Touch and the fetus.* Presented to Touch Research Institute, Miami, FL.

Brazelton, T. (1993). Neonatal behavioral assessment scale. *Clinics in Behavioral Medicine, 50.* London: Heinemann Medical Books.

Brazelton, T. (1994). Touchpoints: Opportunities for preventing problems in the parent–child relationship. *Acta Paediatrica, 394,* 35–39.

Brazelton, T., Koslowski, B., & Main, M. (1974). The origins of reciprocity. In M. Lewis & L. Rosenblum (Eds.), *The effect of the infant on its caregiver* (pp. 49–70, 137–154). New York, NY: Wiley-Interscience.

Bretherton, I. (2013). Revisiting Mary Ainsworth's conceptualization and assessments of maternal sensitivity insensitivity. *Attachment and Human Development, 15,* 460–484.

Bretherton, I., & Munholland, K. (1999). Internal working models in attachment: A construct revisited. In J. Cassidy & P. Shaver (Eds.), *Handbook of attachment: Theory, research and clinical application* (pp. 89–111). New York, NY: Guilford.

Bromberg, P. (2011). *The shadow of the tsunami and the growth of the relational mind.* London, England: Routledge.

Bucci, W. (1985). Dual coding: A cognitive model for psychoanalytic research. *Journal of the American Psychoanalytic Association, 33,* 571–607.

Bucci, W. (1997). *Psychoanalysis and cognitive science.* New York, NY: Guilford.

Campbell, S. B., & Cohn, J. F. (1991). Prevalence and correlates of postpartum depression in first-time mothers. *Journal of Abnormal Psychology, 100,* 594–599.

Carlson, E. (1998). A prospective longitudinal study of attachment disorganization/disorientation. *Child Development, 69*(4), 1107–1128.

Carlson, E., & Sroufe, L. (1995). The contribution of attachment theory to developmental psychopathology. In D. Cicchetti & D. Cohen (Eds.), *Developmental processes and psychopathology: Vol. 1. Theoretical perspectives and methodological approaches* (pp. 581–617). New York, NY: Cambridge University Press.

Carrere, S., & Gottman, M. (1999). Predicting divorce among newlyweds from the first three minutes of a marital conflict discussion. *Family Processes, 38*(3), 293–301.

Carter, A., Garrity-Rokous, F., Chazan-Cohen, R., Little, C., & Briggs-Gowan, M. (2001). Maternal depression and comorbidity: Predicting early parenting, attachment security, and toddler social-emotional problems and competencies. *Journal of the American Academy of Child and Adolescent Psychiatry, 40,* 18–26.

Cassidy, J. (1994). Emotion regulation: Influences of attachment relationships. *Monographs of the Society for Research in Child Development, 59*(2–3, Serial No. 240), 228–249.

Cassidy, J., & Berlin, L. (1994). The insecure/ambivalent pattern of attachment: Theory and research. *Child Development, 65,* 971–991.

Chance, M. (1962). An interpretation of some agonistic postures. *Symposium of the Zoological Society of London, 8,* 71–89.

Chance, M., & Larsen, R. (Eds.). (1996). *The social structure of attention.* New York, NY: Wiley.

Chartrand, T., & Bargh, A. (1999). The chameleon effect: The perception-behavior link and social interaction. *Journal of Personality and Social Psychology, 76,* 893–910.

Cohen, L., Hien, D., & Batchelder, S. (2008). The impact of cumulative maternal trauma and diagnosis on parenting behavior. *Child Maltreatment, 13,* 27–38.

Cohen, P., & Beebe, B. (2002). Video feedback with a depressed mother and her infant: A collaborative individual psychoanalytic and mother–infant treatment. *Journal of Infant, Child & Adolescent Psychotherapy, 2*(3), 1–55.

Cohn, J., & Beebe, B. (1990). Sampling interval affects timeseries regression estimates of mother–infant influence. *Infant Behavior and Development, 13,* 317.

Cohn, J., Campbell, S., Matias, R., & Hopkins, J. (1990). Face-to-face interactions of postpartum depressed and nondepressed mother–infant pairs at 2 months. *Developmental Psychology, 26,* 15–23.

Cohn, J., Campbell, S., & Ross, S. (1991). Infant response in the still-face paradigm at 6 months predicts avoidant and secure attachments at 12 months. *Development and Psychopathology, 26,* 15–23.

Cohn, J., & Elmore, M. (1988). Effect of contingent changes in mothers' affective expression on the organization of behavior in 3-month-old infants. *Infant Behavior and Development, 11,* 493–505.

Cohn, J., & Tronick, E. (1989). Infant–mother face-to-face interaction: Age and gender differences in coordination and miscoordination. *Child Development, 59,* 85–92.

Crittenden, P. (2004). *Patterns of attachment in adulthood: A dynamic-maturational approach to analyzing The Adult Attachment Interview* (Unpublished manuscript).

Crittenden, P., & Landini, A. (2011). *Assessing adult attachment: A dynamic-maturational approach to discourse analysis.* New York, NY: Norton.

Crockenberg, S. (1983). Early mother and infant antecedents of Bayley skill performance at 21 months. *Developmental Psychology, 19,* 727–730.

Darwin, C. (1872). *The origin of species by means of natural selection, or the preservation of favored races in the struggle for life* (6th ed.). London, England: Murray.

Davis, M., & Whalen, P. (2001). The amygdala: Vigilance and emotion. *Molecular Psychiatry, 6,* 13–34.

DeCasper, A., & Carstens, A. (1980). Contingencies of stimulation: Effects on learning and emotion in neonates. *Infant Behavior and Development, 4,* 19–36.

DeGangi, G., Di Pietro, J., Greenspan, S., & Porges, S. (1991). Psychophysiological characteristics of the regulatory disordered infant. *Infant Behavior and Development, 14,* 37–50.

Demetriades, H. (2003). *Maternal anxiety and maternal spatial proximity in 4-month mother–infant face-to-face interaction* (Unpublished doctoral dissertation). Long Island University, Brookville, NY.

De Wolff, M., & van IJzendoorn, M. (1997). Sensitivity and attachment: A meta-analysis on parental antecedents of infant attachment. *Child Development, 68,* 571–591.

Dimberg, U., Thunberg, M., & Elmehed, K. (2000). Unconscious facial reactions to emotional facial expressions. *American Psychological Society, 11,* 86–89.

Downing, G. (2004). Emotion, body, and parent–infant interaction. In J. Nadel & D. Muir (Eds.), *Emotional development: Recent research advances* (pp. 429–449). Oxford, England: Oxford University Press.

Dozier, M., Stovall-McClough, K., & Albus, K. (2008). Attachment and psychopathology in adulthood. In J. Cassidy & P. Shaver (Eds.), *Handbook of attachment: Theory, research and clinical application* (pp. 718–744). New York, NY: Guilford.

Dutra, L., Bureau, J., Holmes, B., Lyubchik, A., & Lyons-Ruth, K. (2009). Quality of early care and childhood trauma: A prospective study of developmental pathways to dissociation. *Journal of Nervous and Mental Disease, 197*(6), 383–390.

Dykas, M., & Cassidy, J. (2011). Attachment and the processing of social information across the life span: Theory and evidence. *Psychological Bulletin, 137,* 19–46.

Egeland, B., & Farber, E. (1984). Infant–mother attachment: Factors related to its development and changes over time. *Child Development, 55*(3), 753–771.

Eibl-Eibesfeldt, I. (1970). *Ethology: The biology of behavior.* New York, NY: Holt, Rinehart & Winston.

Eisenberg, N., & Fabes, R. (1992). Emotion, regulation, and the development of social competence. In M. Clark (Ed.), *Emotion and social behavior: Review of personality and social psychology* (pp. 119–150). Thousand Oaks, CA: Sage.

Ekman, P., & Friesen, W. (1969). The repertoire of nonverbal behavior: Categories, origins, usage, and coding. *Semiotica, 1*(1), 251–270.

Ekman, P., Levenson, R., & Friesen, W. (1983). Autonomic nervous system activity distinguishes among emotions. *Science, 221,* 1208–1210.

Emde, R., Birengen, Z., Clyman, R., & Oppenheim, D. (1991). The moral self of infancy: Affective core and procedural knowledge. *Developmental Review, 11,* 251–270.

Erickson, M., Sroufe, A., & Egeland, B. (1983). The relationship between quality of attachment and behavior problems in preschool in a high-risk sample. *Monographs of the Society for Research in Child Development, 50*(1–2, Serial No. 209), 147–166.

Fabes, R., Eisenberg, N., & Miller, P. (1990). Maternal correlates of children's vicarious emotional responsiveness. *Developmental Psychology, 26,* 639–648.

Fantz, R., Fagan, J., & Miranda, S. (1975). Early perceptual development as shown by visual discrimination, selectivity, and memory with varying stimulus and population parameters. In L. Cohen & P. Salapatek (Eds.), *Infant perception: From sensation to cognition: Vol 1. Basic visual processes* (pp. 249–346). New York, NY: Academic Press.

Feldman, R. (2007). Parent–infant synchrony and the construction of shared timing; physiological precursors, developmental outcomes and risk conditions. *Journal of Child Psychology and Psychiatry, 48*(3,4), 329–354.

Feeney, J., Noller, P., & Callan, V. (1994). Attachment style, communication and satisfaction in the early years of marriage. *Advances in Personal Relationships, 5,* 259–308.

Fernald, A. (1993). Approval and disapproval: Infant responsiveness to vocal affect in familiar and unfamiliar languages. *Child Development, 64*(3), 657–674.

Field, T. (1981). Infant gaze aversion and heart rate during face-to-face interactions. *Infant Behavior and Development, 4,* 307–315.

Field, T. (1995). Infants of depressed mothers. *Infant Behavior and Development, 18,* 1–13.

Field, T., Healy, B., Goldstien, S., & Guthertz, M. (1990). Behavior-state matching and synchrony in mother–infant interactions of nondepressed versus depressed dyads. *Developmental Psychology, 26,* 7–14.

Field, T., Healy, B., Goldstein, S., Perry, D., Bendell, D., Schanberg, S., … & Kuhn, C. (1988). Infants of depressed mothers show "depressed" behavior even with nondepressed adults. *Child Development, 59,* 1569–1579.

Fogel, A. (1992). Movement and communication in human infancy: The social dynamics of development. *Human Movement Science, 11,* 387–423.

Fogel, A. (1993). Two principles of communication: Coregulation and framing. In J. Nadel & L. Camaioni (Eds.), *New perspectives in early communicative development* (pp. 9–22). London, England: Routledge.

Fonagy, P., Gergely, G., Jurist, E., & Target, M. (2002). *Affect regulation, mentalization, and the development of self.* New York, NY: Other Press.

Fonagy, P., Steele, H., & Steele, M. (1991). Maternal representations of attachment during pregnancy predict the organization of infant–mother attachment at one year of age. *Child Development, 62*(5), 891–905.

Fraiberg, S. (1982). Pathological defenses in infancy. *Psychoanalytic Quarterly, 51,* 612–635.

Gergely, G., & Watson, J. (1997). The social biofeedback theory of parental affect-mirroring. *The International Journal of Psychoanalysis, 77,* 1181–1212.

Gianino, A., & Tronick, E. (1988). The mutual regulation model: The infant's self and interactive regulation coping and defense. In T. Field, P. McCabe, & N. Schneiderman (Eds.), *Stress and coping* (pp. 47–68). Hillsdale, NJ: Erlbaum.

Gottman, J., Katz, L., & Hooven, C. (1996). Parental meta-emotion philosophy and the emotional life of families: Theoretical models and preliminary data. *Journal of Family Psychology, 10,* 243–268.

Grigsby, J., & Hartlaub, G. (1994). Procedural learning and the development and stability of character. *Perceptual Motor Skills, 79,* 355–370.

Groh, A., Roisman, G., Booth⊠LaForce, C., Fraley, R., Owen, M., Cox, M., & Burchinal, M. (2014). IV. Stability of attachment security from infancy to late adolescence. *Monographs of the Society for Research in Child Development, 79*(3), 51–66.

Grossmann, K., Grossmann, K., Spangler, G., Suess, G., & Unzner, L. (1985). Maternal sensitivity and newborn orienting responses as related to quality of attachment in northern Germany. *Monographs of the Society for Research in Child Development, 50*(1–2, Serial No. 209), 233–256.

Grossmann, K., Grossmann, K., Winter, M., & Zimmerman, P. (2002). Attachment relationships and appraisal of partnership: From early experience of sensitive support to later relationship representation. In L. Pulkkinen & A. Caspi (Eds.), *Paths to successful development* (pp. 73–105). Cambridge, England: Cambridge University Press.

Haith, M., Hazan, C., & Goodman, G. (1988). Expectation and anticipation of dynamic visual events by 3.5-month-old babies. *Child Development, 59,* 467–479.

Haltigan, J., Leerkes, E., Supple, A., & Calkins, S. (2014). Infant negative affect and maternal interactive behavior during the still-face procedure: The moderating role of adult attachment states of mind. *Attachment & Human Development, 16*(2), 149–173.

Hay, D. (1997). Postpartum depression and cognitive development. In L. Murray & P. Cooper (Eds.), *Postpartum depression and child development* (pp. 85–110). New York, NY: Guilford.

Hennelenlotter, A., Dresel, C., Castrop, F., Ceballos-Baumann, A., Wohlschlager, A., & Haslinger, B. (2008). The link between facial feedback and neural activity within central circuitries of emotion—New insights from botulinum toxin-induced denervation of frown muscles. *Cerebral Cortex, 19*(3), 537–542.

Hesse, E. (2008). The Adult Attachment Interview: Protocol, method of analysis, and empirical studies. In J. Cassidy & P. R. Shaver (Eds.), *Handbook of attachment: Theory, research, and clinical applications* (2nd ed., pp. 552–598). New York, NY: Guilford.

Hesse, E., & Main, M. (2006). Frightened, threatening, and dissociative parental behavior in low-risk samples: Description, discussion, and interpretations. *Development and Psychopathology, 18,* 309–343.

Hodges, S., & Wegner, D. (1997). Automatic and controlled empathy. In W. Ickes (Ed.), *Empathic accuracy* (pp. 311–339). New York, NY: Guilford.

Holland, A., & Roisman, G. (2010). Adult attachment security and young adults' dating relationships over time: Self-reported, observational, and physiological evidence. *Developmental Psychology, 46*(2), 552–557.

Iacoboni, M. (2009). Imitation, empathy, and mirror neurons. *Annual Review of Psychology, 60,* 653–670.

Iacoboni, M., Molnar-Szakacs, I., Gallese, V., Buccino, G., Mazziotta, J., & Rizzolatti, G. (2005). Grasping the intentions of others with one's own mirror neuron system. *PLoS Biology, 3,* 529–535.

Isabella, R., & Belsky, J. (1991). Interactional synchrony and the origins of infant–mother attachment: A replication study. *Child Development, 62,* 373–384.

Jacobsen, T., Edelstein, W., & Hofmann, V. (1994). A longitudinal study of the relation between representations of attachment in childhood and cognitive functioning in childhood and adolescence. *Developmental Psychology, 30*(1), 112–124.

Jacobvitz, D., Hazen, N., & Riggs, S. (1997). *Disorganized mental processes in mothers: Frightening/frightened caregiving and disoriented, disorganized behavior in infancy.* Paper presented in the biennial meeting of the Society for Research in Child Development, Washington, D.C.

Jacobvitz, D., Leon, K., & Hazen, N. (2006). Does expectant mothers' unresolved trauma predict frightened/frightening maternal behavior? Risk and protective factors. *Development and Psychopathology, 18,* 363–380.

Jaffe, J., Beebe, B., Feldstein, S., Crown, C., & Jasnow, M. (2001). Rhythms of dialogue in infancy. *Monographs of the Society for Research in Child Development, 66*(2 Serial No. 265), 1–132.

Kaye, K., & Fogel, A. (1980). The temporal structure of face-to-face communication between mothers and infants. *Developmental Psychology, 16*(5), 454–464.

Kendon, A. (1970). Movement coordination in social interaction: Some examples described. *Acta Psychologica, 32,* 101–125.

Kessen, W., Haith, M., & Salapatek, P. (1970). Human infancy: A bibliography and guide. In P. Mussen (Ed.), *Carmichael's manual of child psychology* (pp. 287–445). New York, NY: Wiley.

Keysers, C., & Gazzola, V. (2006). Towards a unifying neural theory of social cognition. *Progress in Brain Research, 156,* 379–401.

Kim, S., Fonagy, P., Allen, J., & Strathearn, L. (2014). Mothers' unresolved trauma blunts amygdala response to infant distress. *Social Neuroscience, 9*(4), 352–363.

Kobak, R., & Sceery, A. (1988). Attachment in late adolescence: Working models, affect regulation, and representations of self and others. *Child Development, 8*(59), 135–146.

Kopp, C. (1989). Regulation of distress and negative emotions: A developmental view. *Developmental Psychology, 25*(3), 343–354.

Kopp, C. (2002). Commentary: The codevelopments of attention and emotion regulation. *Infancy, 3*(2), 199–208.

Korner, A., & Grobstein, R. (1976). Individual differences at birth. In E. Rexford, L. Sander, & T. Shapiro (Eds.), *Infant psychiatry* (pp. 69–78). New Haven, CT: Yale University Press.

Koulomzin, M., Beebe, B., Anderson, S., Jaffe, J., Feldstein, S., & Crown, C. (2002). Infant gaze, head, face, and self-touch at four months differentiate secure vs. avoidant attachment at one year: A microanalytic approach. *Attachment and Human Development, 4,* 3–24.

Kovan, N., Chung, A., & Sroufe, L. (2009). The intergenerational continuity of observed early parenting: A prospective, longitudinal study. *Developmental Psychology, 45,* 1205–1213.

Kronen, J. (1982). *Maternal facial mirroring at four months* (Unpublished doctoral dissertation). Yeshiva University, New York.

Kushnick, G. (2002). *Maternal spatial intrusion patterns in mother–infant face-to-face play: Maternal dependency, depression, and mother–infant chase and dodge* (Unpublished doctoral dissertation). Long Island University, Brookville, NY.

Langhorst, B., & Fogel, A. (1982). *Cross-validation of microanalytic approaches to face-to-face interaction.* International Conference on Infant Studies, Austin, TX.

Lanius, R., Vermetten, E., Loewenstein, R., Brand, B., Schmahl, C., Bremner, J., & Spiegel, D. (2010). Emotion modulation in PTSD: Clinical and neurobiological evidence for a dissociative subtype. *American Journal of Psychiatry, 167,* 640–647.

Lay, K., Waters, E., Posada, G., & Ridgeway, D. (1995). Attachment security, affect regulation, and defensive responses to mood induction. *Monographs of the Society for Research in Child Development, 60*(2–3), 179–196.

Leerkes, E., Blankson, A., & O'Brien, M. (2009). Differential effects of maternal sensitivity to infant distress and nondistress on social-emotional functioning. *Child Development, 80,* 762–775.

Leerkes, E., & Crockenberg, S. (2006). Antecedents of mothers' emotional and cognitive responses to infant distress: The role of family, mother, and infant characteristics. *Infant Mental Health Journal, 27*(4), 405–428.

Leerkes, E., & Siepak, K. (2006). Attachment linked predictors of women's emotional and cognitive responses to infant distress. *Attachment & Human Development, 8,* 11–32.

Leerkes, E., Supple, A., O'Brien, M., Calkins, S., Hatigan, J., & Wong, M. (2014). Antecedents of maternal sensitivity during distressing tasks: Integrating attachment, social information processing, and psychobiological perspectives. *Child Development, 86,* 1–18.

Lester, B., Hoffman, J., & Brazelton, T. (1985). The rhythmic structure of mother–infant interaction in term and preterm infants. *Child Development, 56,* 15–27.

Levenson, R., Ekman, P., & Friesen, W. (1990). Voluntary facial action generates emotion-specific autonomic nervous system activity. *Psychophysiology, 27,* 363–384.

Levenson, R., & Ruef, A. Physiological aspects of emotional knowledge and rapport. In W. Ickes (Ed.), *Empathic accuracy* (pp. 44–73). New York, NY: Guilford Press.

Lewis, M., & Brooks, J. (1975). Infants' social perception: A constructionist view. In L. Cohen & P. Salapatek (Eds.), *Infant perception: From sensation to cognition* (Vol. 2, pp. 101–148). New York, NY: Wiley-Interscience.

Lewis, M., & Feiring, C. (1989). Infant, mother, and mother–infant behavior and subsequent attachment. *Child Development, 60,* 831–837.

Lewis, M., Feiring, C., & Rosenthal, S. (2000). Attachment over time. *Child Development, 71,* 707–720.

Lewis, M., & Goldberg, S. (1969). Perceptual-cognitive development in infancy: A generalized expectancy model as a function of the mother–infant interaction. *Merrill-Palmer Quarterly, 15,* 81–100.

Lewis, M., & Rosenblum, L. (Eds.). (1974). *The effect of the infant on its caregiver* (pp. 49–76). New York, NY: Wiley-Interscience.

Leyendecker, B., Lamb, M., Fracasso, M., Scholmerich, A., & Larson, C. (1997). Playful interaction and the antecedents of attachment: A longitudinal study of Central American and Euro-American mothers and infants. *Merrill-Palmer Quarterly, 43*(1), 24–47.

Lieberman, A., Ghosh Ippen, C., & Van Horn, P. (2006). Child–parent psychotherapy: 6-month follow-up of a randomized controlled trial. *Journal of the American Academy of Child and Adolescent Psychiatry, 45*, 913–918.

Lyons-Ruth, K. (2008). Contributions of the mother–infant relationship to dissociative, borderline, and conduct symptoms in young adulthood. *Infant Mental Health Journal, 29*(3), 883–911.

Lyons-Ruth, K., Bronfman, E., & Parsons, E. (1999). Maternal disrupted affective communication, maternal frightened or frightening behavior, and disorganized infant attachment strategies. *Monographs of the Society for Research in Child Development, 64*(3), 67–96.

Lyons-Ruth, K., Bureau, J., Holmes, B., Easterbrooks, M., & Henninghausen, K. (2011). *Borderline features and suicidality/self-injury: Prospective and concurrent relationship correlates from infancy to young adulthood* (Unpublished manuscript).

Lyons-Ruth, K., & Jacobvitz, D. (2008). Disorganized attachment: Genetic factors, parenting contexts, and developmental transformation from infancy to adulthood. In J. Cassidy & P. Shaver (Eds.), *Handbook of attachment: Theory research and clinical applications* (2nd ed., pp. 666–697). New York, NY: Guilford.

Lyons-Ruth, K., Repacholi, B., McLeod, S., & Silva, E. (1991). Disorganized attachment behavior in infancy: Short-term stability, maternal and infant correlates, and risk-related subtypes. *Development and Psychopathology, 3,* 377–396.

Main, M. (1981). Avoidance in the service of attachment: A working paper. In K. Immelmann, G. Barlow, M. Main, & L. Petrinovich (Eds.), *Behavioral development. The Bielfield Interdisciplinary Project* (pp. 651–693). New York, NY: Cambridge University Press.

Main, M., & Goldwyn, R. *Adult attachment rating and classification system: Manual in draft* (Version 6.0). Unpublished manuscript, University of California at Berkeley.

Main, M., & Hesse, E. (1990). Parents' unresolved traumatic experiences are related to infant disorganized attachment status: Is frightened and/or frightening parental behavior the linking mechanism? In M. Greenberg, D. Cicchetti, & E. Cummings (Eds.), *Attachment in the preschool years: Theory, research, and intervention* (pp. 161–182). Chicago, IL: University of Chicago Press.

Main, M., Hesse, E., & Goldwyn, R. (2008). Studying differences in language usage in recounting attachment history: An introduction to the AAI. In H. Steele & M. Steele (Eds.), *Clinical applications of the Adult Attachment Interview* (pp. 31–68). New York, NY: Guilford.

Main, M., Hesse, E., & Kaplan, N. (2005). Predictability of attachment behavior and representational processes at 1, 6, and 19 years of age. In K. E. Grossman, K. Grossman, & E. Waters (Eds.), *Attachment from infancy to adulthood: The major longitudinal studies* (pp. 245–304). New York, NY: Guilford.

Main, M., Kaplan, N., & Cassidy, J. (1985). Security in infancy, childhood, and adulthood: A move to the level of representation. *Monographs of the Society for Research in Child Development, 54*(1–2, Serial No. 209), 60–106.

Main, M., & Solomon, J. (1986). Discovery of an insecure-disorganized/disoriented attachment pattern. In M. Yogman & T. B. Brazelton (Eds.), *Affective development in infancy* (pp. 95–125). Norwood, NJ: Ablex.

Main, M., & Solomon, J. (1990). Procedures for identifying infants as disorganized/disoriented during the Ainsworth Strange Situation. In M. T. Greenberg, D. Cicchetti, & E. M. Cummings (Eds.), *Attachment in the preschool years: Theory, research, and intervention* (pp. 121–160). Chicago, IL: University of Chicago Press.

Malatesta, C., Culver, C., Tesman, J., & Shepard, B. (1989).The development of emotion expression during the first two years of life. *Monographs of the Society for Research in Child Development, 54*(1–2, Serial No. 219).

Malatesta, C., & Haviland, J. (1983). Learning display rules: The socialization of emotion in infancy. *Child Development, 53,* 991–1003.

Martin, J. (1981). A longitudinal study of consequences in early mother–infant interaction: A microanalytic approach. *Monographs of the Society for Research in Child Development, 46*(3, Serial No. 190), 1–52.

McElwain, N., & Booth-LaForce, C. (2006). Maternal sensitivity to infant distress and non-distress as predictors of infant-mother attachment security. *Family Psychology, 20,* 247–255.

McGrew, W. (1972). *An ethological study of children's behavior.* New York, NY: Academic Press.

Meltzoff, A. (1990). Foundations for developing a concept of self: The role of imitation in relating self to other and the value of social mirroring, social modeling, and self practice in infancy. In D. Cicchetti & M. Beeghly (Eds.), *The self in transition: Infancy to childhood* (pp. 1–30). Norwood, NJ: Ablex.

Messinger, D. (2002). Positive and negative: Infant facial expressions and emotions. *Current Directions in Psychological Science, 11,* 1–6.

Messinger, D., Fogel, A., & Dickson, K. (2001). All smiles are positive, but some smiles are more positive than others. *Developmental Psychology, 37*(5), 642–653.

Mikaye, K., Chen, S., & Campos, J. (1985). Infant temperament, mother's mode of interaction, and attachment in Japan: An interim report. In I. Bretherton & E. Waters (Eds.), Growing points in attachment theory and research (pp. 276–297). *Monographs of the Society for Research in Child Development, 50*(1–2, Serial No. 209).

Monk, C. (2001). Stress and mood disorders during pregnancy: Implications for child development. *Psychiatric Quarterly, 72*(4), 347–357.

Moore, G., Cohn, J., & Campbell, S. (2001). Infant affective responses to mother's still face at 6 months differentially predict externalizing and internalizing behaviors at 18 months. *Developmental Psychology, 27*(5), 706–714.

Murphy, A., Steele, H., Bate, J., Nikitiades, A., Allman, B., Bonuck, K., ... Steele, M. (2015). Group attachment-based intervention: Trauma-informed care for families with adverse childhood experiences. *Journal of Family and Community Health, 38,* 268–279.

Murray, L., & Cooper, P. (1997). *Postpartum depression and child development.* New York, NY: Guilford.

Murray, L., & Trevarthen, C. (1985). Emotional regulations of interactions between two-month-olds and their mothers. In T. M. Field & N. A. Fox (Eds.), *Social perception in infants* (pp. 177–197). Norwood, NJ: Ablex.

Niedenthal, P., Mermillod, M., Maringer, M., & Hess, U. (2010). The Simulation of Smiles (SIMS) model: Embodied simulation and the meaning of facial expression. *Behavioral and Brain Sciences, 33,* 417–480.

Oberman, L., Winkielman, P., & Ramachandran, V. (2007). Face to face: Blocking facial mimicry can selectively impair recognition of emotional expressions. *Social Neuroscience, 2*(3–4), 167–178.

Ogawa, J., Sroufe, L., Weinfeld, N., Carlson, E., & Egeland, B. (1997). Development and the fragmented self: Longitudinal study of dissociative symptomatology in a nonclinical sample. *Development and Psychopathology, 9,* 855–879.

Oster, H. (1978). Facial expression and affect development. In M. Lewis & L. Rosenblum (Eds.), *The development affect.* New York, NY: Plenum Press.

Pally, R. (2000). *The mind-brain relationship.* London, England: Karnac Books.

Pally, R. (2002). The neurobiology of borderline personality disorder: The synergy of "nature and nurture." *Journal of Clinical Psychiatry, 8,* 133–142.

Papousek, H. (1992). Early ontogeny of vocal communication in parent–infant interaction. In H. Papousek, U. Juergens, & M. Papousek (Eds.), *Nonverbal vocal communication* (pp. 230–261). New York, NY: Cambridge University Press.

Papousek, H., & Papousek, M. (1979). Early ontogeny of human social interaction. In M. Von Cranach, K. Koppa, W. Lelenies, & P. Ploog (Eds.), *Human ethology: Claims and limits of a new discipline* (pp. 63–85). Cambridge, England: Cambridge University Press.

Peck, C. (2003). Measuring sensitivity moment-by-moment: A microanalytic look at the transmission of attachment. *Attachment and Human Development, 5,* 38–63.

Peery, J. (1980). Neonate-adult head movement. *Developmental Psychology, 16,* 245–250.

Peltola, M., Forssman, L., Puura, K., van IJzendoorn, M., & Leppanen, J. (2015). Attention to faces expressing negative emotion at 7 months predicts attachment security at 14 months. *Child Development, 86,* 1321–1332.

Porges, S. (2003). Social engagement and attachment: A phylogenetic perspective. *Annals of the New York Academy of Sciences 1008,* 31–47.

Porges, S. (2011). *The polyvagal theory: Neurophysiological foundations of emotions, attachment, communication, self-regulation.* New York, NY: Norton.

Powell, B., Cooper, G., Hoffman, K., & Marvin, B. (2013). *The circle of security intervention.* New York, NY: Guilford.

Raby, K., Steele, R., Carlson, E., & Sroufe, L. (2015). Continuities and changes in infant attachment patterns across two generations. *Attachment and Human Development, 17*(4), 1–15.

Rauch, S., Whalen, P., Shin, L., McInerney, S., Macklin, M., Lasko, N., ... Pitman, R. (2000). Exaggerated amygdala response to masked facial stimuli in posttraumatic stress disorder: A functional MRI study. *Biological Psychiatry, 47,* 769–776.

Riem, M., Bakermans-Kranenburg, M., van IJzendoorn, M., Out, D., & Rombouts, S. (2012). Attachment in the brain: adult attachment representations predict amygdala and behavioral responses to infant crying. *Attachment & Human Development, 14,* 533–551.

Rizzolatti, G., Fadiga, L., Fogassi, L., & Gallese, V. (1996). Premotor cortex and the recognition of motor actions. *Cognitive Brain Research, 3,* 131–141.

Roe, K., Roe, A., Drivas, A., & Bronstein, R. (1990). A curvilinear relationship between maternal vocal stimulation and 3 month olds' cognitive processing. *Infant Mental Health Journal, 2,* 175–189.

Rosenthal, R., Hall, J., DiMatteo, M., Rogers, P., & Archer, D. (1979). *Sensitivity to nonverbal communication: The PONS Test.* Baltimore, MD: Johns Hopkins University Press.

Saffran, J., Aslin, R., & Newport, E. (1996). Statistical learning by 8-month-old infants. *Science, 274,* 1926–1928.

Sameroff, A. (1983). Developmental systems: Contexts and evolution. In W. Kessen (Ed.), *Mussen's handbook of child psychology* (Vol. 1, pp. 237–294). New York, NY: Wiley.

Sander, L. (1977). The regulation of exchange in the infant–caretaker system and some aspects of the context-content relationship. In M. Lewis & L. Rosenblum (Eds.), *Interaction, conversation, and the development of language* (pp. 133–156). New York, NY: Wiley.

Sander, L. (1995). Identity and the experience of specificity in a process of recognition. *Psychoanalytic Dialogues, 5,* 579–593.

Saunders, R., Jacobvitz, D., Zaccagnino, M., Beverung, L., & Hazen, N. (2011). Pathways to earned-security: The role of alternative support figures. *Attachment & Human Development, 13*(4), 403–420.

Schechter, D., Moser, D., Paoloni-Giacobino, A., Stenz, L., Gex-Fabry, M., Aue, T., … Rusconi Serpa, S. (2015). Methylation of NR3C1 is related to maternal PTSD, parenting stress and maternal medial prefrontal cortical activity in response to child separation among mothers with histories of violence exposure. *Frontiers in Psychology, 6,* 690.

Schechter, D., Moser, D., Wang, Z., Marsh, R., Hao, X. J., … Peterson, B. (2012). An fMRI study of the brain responses of traumatized mothers to viewing their toddlers during separation and play. *Journal of Social, Cognitive and Affective Neuroscience, 7*(8), 969–979.

Schechter, D., Willheim, E., Hinojosa, C., Scholfield-Kleinman, K., Turner, J., Mccaw, J., … Myers, M. (2010). Subjective and objective measures of parent-child relationship dysfunction, child separation distress, and joint attention. *Psychiatry, 73,* 130–144.

Schuengel, C., Bakermans-Kranenburg, M., & van IJzendoorn, M. (1999). Frightening maternal behavior linking unresolved loss and disorganized infant attachment. *Journal of Consulting and Clinical Psychology, 67,* 54–63.

Shi, Z., Bureau, J., Easterbrooks, M., Zhao, X., & Lyons-Ruth, K. (2012). Childhood maltreatment and prospectively observed quality of early care as predictors of antisocial personality disorder. *Infant Mental Health Journal, 33,* 1–14.

Siegel, D. (1999). *The developing mind.* New York, NY: Guilford.

Siegel, D. (2012). *Pocket guide to interpersonal neurobiology.* New York, NY: Norton.

Slade, A., Dermer, M., Gerber, J., Gibson, L., Graf, F., Siegel, N., & Tobias, K. (1995, March). *Prenatal representation, dyadic interaction and quality of attachment.* Paper presented at the meeting of the Society for Research in Child Development, Indianapolis, IN.

Sroufe, L. (1983). Infant–caregiver attachment and patterns of adaptation in the pre-school: The roots of maladaptation and competence. In M. Permutter (Ed.), *Minnesota Symposia on Child Psychology* (pp. 41–79). Hillsdale, NJ: Erlbaum.

Sroufe, L. A. (2005). Attachment and development: A prospective, longitudinal study from birth to adulthood. *Attachment & Human Development, 7,* 349–367.

Sroufe, L., Carlson, E., Levy, A., & Egeland, B. (1999). Implications of attachment theory for developmental psychopathology. *Development and Psychopathology, 11,* 1–13.

Sroufe, L., Egeland, B., Carlson, E., & Collins, W. (2005a). *The development of the person: The Minnesota study of risk and adaptation from birth to adulthood.* New York, NY: Guilford.

Sroufe, L., Egeland, B., Carlson, E., & Collins, W. (2005b). Placing early attachment experiences in developmental context. In K. E. Grossmann, K. Grossmann, & E. Waters (Eds.), *The power of longitudinal attachment research: From infancy and childhood to adulthood* (pp. 48–70). New York, NY: Guilford.

Sroufe, L., & Fleeson, J. (1986). Attachment and the construction of relationships. In W. Hartup & Z. Rubin (Eds.), *Relationships and development* (pp. 51–71). Hillsdale, NJ: Erlbaum.

Stayton, D., Ainsworth, M., & Main, M. (1973). Individual differences in infant responses to brief everyday separations as related to other infant and maternal behaviors. *Developmental Psychology, 9,* 213–225.

Stechler, G., & Carpenter, G. (1967). A viewpoint on early affective development. In J. Hellmuth (Ed.), *The exceptional infant* (Vol. 1, pp. 163–190). Seattle, WA: Straub & Hellmuth.

Steele, H., & Steele, M. (2005). Understanding and resolving emotional conflict: The London parent–child project. In K. Grossmann, K. Grossmann, & E. Waters (Eds.), *Attachment from infancy to adulthood: The major longitudinal studies* (pp. 137–164). New York, NY: Guilford.

Steele, H., & Steele, M. (2008). Ten clinical uses of the Adult Attachment Interview. In H. Steele & M. Steele (Eds.), *Clinical applications of the Adult Attachment Interview* (p. 3–30). New York, NY: Guilford.

Steele, H., Steele, M., & Fonagy, P. (1996). Associations among attachment classifications of mothers, father, and their infants. *Child Development, 67*(2), 541–555.

Steele, M., Steele, H., Bate, J., Knafo, H., Kinsey, M., Bonuck, K., … Murphy, A. (2014). Looking from the outside in: The use of video in attachment-based interventions. *Attachment & Human Development, 16,* 402–415.

Stepakoff, S., Beebe, B., & Jaffe, J. (2000). *Mother–infant tactile communication at four months: Infant, gender, maternal ethnicity, and maternal depression.* International conference on infant studies, Brighton, England.

Stern, D. (1971). A microanalysis of the mother–infant interaction. *Journal of the American Academy of Child and Adolescent Psychiatry, 10,* 501–507.

Stern, D. (1974). Goal and structure of mother–infant play. *Journal of the American Academy of Child and Adolescent Psychiatry, 13,* 402–421.

Stern, D. (1977). *The first relationship: Infant and mother.* Cambridge, Mass: Harvard University Press.

Stern, D. (1985). *The interpersonal world of the infant: A view from psychoanalysis and developmental psychology.* New York, NY: Basic Books.

Stern, D. (1995). *The motherhood constellation.* New York, NY: Basic Books.

Stern, D., Hofer, L., Haft, W., & Dore, J. (1985). Affect attunement: The sharing of feeling states between mother and infant by means of intermodal fluency. In T. J. Field & N. A. Fox (Eds.), *Social perception in early infancy* (pp. 249–268). Norwood, NJ: Ablex.

Stone, L., Smith, H., & Murphy, L. (Eds.). (1973). *The competent infant: Research and commentary.* New York, NY: Basic Books

Strathearn, L., Fonagy, P., Amico, J., & Montague, P. (2009). Adult attachment predicts maternal brain and oxytocin response to infant cues. *Neuropsychopharmacology, 34,* 2655–2666.

Squire, L., & Cohen, N. (1984). Human memory and amnesia. In G. Lynch, M. McGaugh, & N. Weinberger (Eds.), *Neurobiology of learning memory* (pp. 3–64). New York, NY: Guilford.

Tarabulsy, G., Tessier, R., & Kappas, A. (1996). Contingency detection and the contingent organization of behavior interactions: Implications for socioemotional development in infancy. *Psychological Bulletin, 120,* 25–41.

Thomas, E., & Martin, J. (1976). Analyses of parent–infant interaction. *Psychological Review, 83*(2), 141–155.

Tobias, K. (1995). *The relation between maternal attachment and patterns of mother–infant interaction at four months* (Doctoral dissertation). The City University of New York.

Trevarthen, C. (1977). Descriptive analyses of infant communicative behavior. In H. R. Schaffer (Ed.), *Studies in mother–infant interaction* (pp. 227–270). London, England: Academic Press.

Trevarthen, C. (1979). Communication and cooperation in early infancy: A description of primary intersubjectivity. In M. Bullowa (Ed.), *Before speech: The beginnings of human communication* (pp. 321–347). London, England: Cambridge University Press.

Trevarthen, C. (1998). The concept and foundations of infant intersubjectivity. In S. Braten (Ed.), *Intersubjective communication and emotion in early ontogeny* (pp. 15–26). Cambridge, England: Cambridge University Press.

Tronick, E. (1989). Emotions and emotional communication in infants. *American Psychologist, 44*(2), 112–119.

Tronick, E. (2007). *The neurobehavioral and social emotional development of infants and young children.* New York, NY: Norton.

Tronick, E., & Reck, C. (2009). Infants of depressed mothers. *Harvard Review of Psychiatry, 17,* 147–156.

Van den Boom, D. (1995). Do first-year intervention effects endure: Follow-up during toddlerhood of a sample of Dutch irritable infants. *Child Development, 66,* 1798–1816.

Van Egeren, L., Barratt, S., & Roach, M. (2001). Mother–infant responsiveness: Timing, mutual regulation, and interactional context. *Developmental Psychology, 37*(5), 684–697.

Van Hooff, J. (1967). The facial displays of the Catarrhine monkeys and apes. In D. Morris (Ed.), *Primate ethology* (pp. 7–68). London, England: Wiedenfeld and Nicolson.

van IJzendoorn, M. (1995). Adult attachment representations, parental responsiveness, and infant attachment: A meta-analysis on the predictive validity of the Adult Attachment Interview. *Psychological Bulletin, 117,* 387–403.

van IJzendoorn, M., Goldberg, S., Kroonenberg, P., & Frenkel, O. (1992). The relative effects of maternal and child problems on the quality of attachment: A meta-analysis of attachment in clinical samples. *Child Development, 63,* 840–858.

van IJzendoorn, M., Schuengel, C., & Bakermans-Kranenburg, M. (1999). Disorganized attachment in early childhood: Meta-analysis of precursors, concomitants and sequelae. *Development and Psychopathology, 11,* 225–250.

Vrticka, P. (2012). Interpersonal closeness and social reward processing. *The Journal of Neuroscience, 32*(37), 12649–12650.

Ward, M., & Carlson, E. (1995). Associations among adult attachment representations, maternal sensitivity, and infant–mother attachment in a sample of adolescent mothers. *Child Development, 66,* 69–79.

Waters, E., Merrick, S., Treboux, D., Crowell, J., & Albersheim, L. (2000). Attachment security in infancy and early adulthood: A twenty-year longitudinal study. *Child Development, 7,* 684–689.

Weinberg, K. (1991). *Sex differences in 6 month infants' behavior. Impact on maternal caregiving* (Unpublished doctoral dissertation). University of Massachusetts, Amherst.

Weinberg, K., & Tronick, E. (1998). The impact of maternal psychiatric illness on infant development. *Journal of Clinical Psychiatry, 59,* 53–61.

White, B., Castle, P., & Held, R. (1964). Observations of the development of visually-directed reaching. *Child Development, 35,* 349–364.

Winnicott, D. (1965). *The maturational processes and the facilitating environment.* New York, NY: International Universities Press.

Wolf, N., Gales, M., Shane, E., & Shane, M. (2001). The developmental trajectory from amodal perception to empathy and communication: The role of mirror neurons in this process. *Psychoanalytic Inquiry, 21,* 94–112.

Yang, T., Simmons, A., Matthews, S., Tapert, S., Frank, G., Max, J., … Paulus, M. (2010). Adolescents with major depression demonstrate increased amygdala activation. *Journal of the American Academy of Child and Adolescent Psychiatry, 49,* 42–51.

Zajonc, R. (1985). Emotion and facial efference: A theory reclaimed. *Science, 228,* 15–22.

Zelner, S. (1982). *The organization of vocalization and gaze in early mother–infant interactive regulation* (Unpublished doctoral dissertation). Yeshiva University, New York.

Zelner, S., Beebe, B., & Jaffe, J. (1982). *The organization of vocalization and gaze in early mother–infant interactive regulation.* International Conference Infant Studies, New York, NY.

Zlochower, A., & Cohn, J. (1996). Vocal timing in face-to-face interaction of clinically depressed and nondepressed mothers and their 4-month old infants. *Infant Behavior and Development, 19,* 371–374.

Index

About the Authors

Beatrice Beebe, PhD, is a Clinical Professor of Medical Psychology (in Psychiatry), College of Physicians & Surgeons, Columbia University; Department of Child and Adolescent Psychiatry, New York State Psychiatric Institute, where she directs a basic research lab on mother-infant communication. She is faculty at the Columbia Psychoanalytic Center, the Institute for the Psychoanalytic Study of Subjectivity, and the NYU Postdoctoral Program in Psychotherapy and Psychoanalysis; and honorary member, William Alanson White Institute and the American Psychoanalytic Association. She is co-author with Jaffe, Feldstein, Crown and Jasnow of *Rhythms of Dialogue in Infancy* (2001); author with Lachmann of *Infant Research and Adult Treatment: Co-Constructing Interactions* (2002); author with Knoblauch, Rustin and Sorter of *Forms of Intersubjectivity in Infant Research and Adult Treatment* (2005); author with Jaffe, Markese, et al. of *The Origins of 12-Month Attachment: A Microanalysis of 4-Month Mother-Infant Interaction* (2010); and author with Lachmann of *The Origins of Attachment: Infant Research and Adult Treatment* (2013). She directed with Phyllis Cohen a primary prevention project for mothers who were pregnant and widowed on 9/11, and she coauthored *Mothers, Infants and Young Children of September 11, 2001: A Primary Prevention Project* (Beebe, Cohen, Sossin, and Markese, Eds., 2012).

Phyllis Cohen, PhD, is a psychoanalyst and couple and family therapist in Brooklyn, New York. She is the Founder and Director of the New York Institute for Psychotherapy Training in Infancy, Childhood and Adolescence (NYIPT) where she teaches and supervises. With Dr. Beatrice Beebe she has co-directed a primary prevention project for women who were pregnant and widowed on 9/11/2001. She has published numerous professional papers and has coauthored *Mothers, Infants and Young Children of September 11, 2001: A Primary Prevention Project* (Beebe, Cohen, Sossin, and Markese, Eds., Routledge, 2012), and *Healing After Parent Loss in Childhood and Adolescence: Therapeutic Interventions and Theoretical Considerations*, (Cohen, Sossin, and Ruth, Eds., Rowman and Littlefield, 2014). She lectures and provides training at schools and community mental agencies in New York City.

Frank M. Lachmann, PhD, is a member of the Founding Faculty of the Institute for the Psychoanalytic Study of Subjectivity, New York; and a Clinical Assistant Professor, in the NYU Postdoctoral Program in Psychotherapy and Psychoanalysis. He is author or co-author of more than 150 journal publications, co-author of five books with Joe Lichtenberg and Jim Fosshage, most recently, *Enlivening the Self.* With Beatrice Beebe, he wrote *Infant Research and Adult Treatment and The Origins of Attachment.* He is sole author of *Transforming Aggression and Transforming Narcissism: Reflections on Empathy, Humor, and Expectations.* He is an Honorary Member of the Vienna Circle for Self Psychology, the William Alanson White Society, and the American Psychoanalytic Association.